LOGIC, LANGUAGE, AND MEANING

L. T. F. Gamut

Logic, Language, and Meaning

VOLUME I
Introduction to Logic

The University of Chicago Press
Chicago and London

The University of Chicago Press, Chicago 60637
The University of Chicago Press, Ltd., London
© 1991 by The University of Chicago
All rights reserved. Published 1991
Printed in the United States of America

11 10 09   9 8 7

First published as *Logica, Taal en Betekenis,* (2 vols.) by Uitgeverij Het
Spectrum, De Meern, The Netherlands. Vol. 1: *Inleiding in de logica,*
vol. 2: *Intensionele logica en logische grammatica,* both © 1982 by Het
Spectrum B. V.

Library of Congress Cataloging in Publication Data

Gamut, L. T. F.
     [Logica, taal en betekenis. English]
     Logic, language, and meaning / L. T. F. Gamut.
        p.   cm.
     Translation of: Logica, taal en betekenis.
     Includes bibliographical references.
     Contents: v. 1. Introduction to logic — v. 2. Intensional logic and logi-
cal grammar.
     ISBN 0-226-28084-5 (v. 1). — ISBN 0-226-28085-3 (v. 1, pbk.). —
ISBN 0-226-28086-1 (v. 2) — ISBN 0-226-28088-8 (v. 2, pbk.)
     1. Logic.   2. Semantics (Philosophy)   3. Languages—Philosophy.
I. Title.
BC71.G33513   1991
160—dc20
                                                               90-10912
                                                               CIP

⊗ The paper used in this publication meets the minimum requirements of the
American National Standard for Information Sciences—Permanence of
Paper for Printed Library Materials, ANSI Z39.48-1992.

Contents

Chapter 7   Formal Syntax

Foreword

The Dutch not only have what must be the greatest number of linguists per capita in the world, they also have a very long and rich tradition of combining linguistics, logic, and philosophy of language. So it should not be a surprise that it is an interdisciplinary collaboration of Dutch scholars that has produced the first comprehensive introduction to logic, language, and meaning that includes on the one hand a very fine introduction to logic, starting from the beginning, and on the other hand brings up at every point connections to the study of meaning in natural language, and thus serves as an excellent introduction and logical background to many of the central concerns of semantics and the philosophy of language as well.

This book is pedagogically beautifully designed, with the central developments very carefully introduced and richly augmented with examples and exercises, and with a wealth of related optional material that can be included or omitted for different kinds of courses (or self-teaching) for which the book could very well be used: I could imagine tailoring very fine but slightly different courses from it for inclusion in a linguistics curriculum, a philosophy curriculum, a cognitive science curriculum, or an AI/computational linguistics program. It would be less suitable for a logic course within a mathematics department, since there is less emphasis on proofs and metamathematics than in a more mathematically oriented logic book. There is certainly no lack of rigor, however; I think the authors have done a superb job of combining pedagogical user-friendliness with the greatest attention to rigor where it matters.

One very noticeable difference from familiar introductory logic texts is the inclusion of accessible introductions to many nonstandard topics in logic, ranging from approaches to presupposition and many-valued logics to issues in the foundations of model theory, and a wide range of more advanced (but still very accessible) topics in volume 2. The book thereby gives the student an invaluable perspective on the field of logic as an active area of growth, development, and controversy, and not simply a repository of a single set of eternal axioms and theorems. Volume 2 provides an outstanding introduction to the interdisciplinary concerns of logic and semantics, including a good introduction to the basics of Montague grammar and model-theoretic semantics more generally.

I first became acquainted with this book in its Dutch version during a sabbatical leave in the Netherlands in 1982-83; it made me very glad to have learned Dutch, to be able to appreciate what a wonderful book it was, but at the same time sorry not to be able to use it immediately back home. I started lobbying then for it to be translated into English, and I'm delighted that this has become a reality. I hope English-speaking teachers and students will appreciate the book as much as I anticipate they will. The authors are top scholars and leaders in their fields, and I believe they have created a text that will give beginning students the best possible entry into the subject matter treated here.

BARBARA H. PARTEE

Preface

Logic, Language, and Meaning consists of two volumes which may be read independently of each other: volume 1, *An Introduction to Logic*, and volume 2, *Intensional Logic and Logical Grammar*. Together they comprise a survey of modern logic from the perspective of the analysis of natural language. They represent the combined efforts of two logicians, two philosophers, and one linguist. An attempt has been made to integrate the contributions of these different disciplines into a single consistent whole. This enterprise was inspired by a conviction shared by all of the authors, namely, that logic and language are inseparable, particularly when it comes to the analysis of meaning. Combined research into logic and language is a philosophical tradition which can be traced back as far as Aristotle. The advent of mathematical logic on the one hand and structuralist linguistics on the other were to give rise to a period of separate development, but as these disciplines have matured, their mutual relevance has again become apparent. A new interdisciplinary region has emerged around the borders of philosophy, logic, and linguistics, and *Logic, Language, and Meaning* is an introduction to this field. Thus volume 1 establishes a sound basis in classical propositional and predicate logic. Volume 2 extends this basis with a survey of a number of richer logical systems, such as intensional logic and the theory of types, and it demonstrates the application of these in a logical grammar.

Logic is introduced from a linguistic perspective in volume 1, although an attempt has been made to keep things interesting for readers who just want to learn logic (perhaps with the exception of those with a purely mathematical interest in the subject). Thus some subjects have been included which are not to be found in other introductory texts, such as many-valued logic, second-order logic, and the relation between logic and mathematical linguistics. Also, a first attempt is made at a logical pragmatics. Other and more traditional subjects, like the theory of definite descriptions and the role of research into the foundations of mathematics, have also been dealt with.

Volume 2 assumes a familiarity with propositional and predicate logic, but not necessarily a familiarity with volume 1. The first half of it is about different systems of intensional logic and the theory of types. The interaction between the origins of these systems in logic and philosophy and the part they have to play in the development of intensional theories of meaning is a common thematic thread running through these chapters. In the course of the exposition, the careful reader will gradually obtain a familiarity with logic and philosophy which is adequate for a proper understanding of logical grammar. Montague grammar, the best-known form of logical grammar, is described in detail and put to work on a fragment of the English language. Following this, attention is paid to some more recent developments in logical grammar, such as the theory of generalized quantification and discourse representation theory.

One important objective of this book is to introduce readers to the tremendous diversity to be found in the field of formal logic. They will become acquainted with many different logics—that is, combinations of formal languages, semantic interpretations, and notions of logical consequence—each with its own field of application. It is often the case in science that one is only able to see which of one's theories will explain what, and how they might be modified or replaced when one gets down and examines the phenomena up close. In this field too, it is the precise, formal analysis of patterns and theories of reasoning which leads to the development of alternatives. Here formal precision and creativity go hand in hand.

It is the authors' hope that the reader will develop an active understanding of the matters presented, will come to see formal methods as flexible methods for answering semantic questions, and will eventually be in a position to apply them as such. To this end, many exercises have been included. These should help to make the two volumes suitable as texts for courses, the breadth and depth of which could be quite diverse. Solutions to the exercises have also been included, in order to facilitate individual study. A number of exercises are slightly more difficult and are marked by ◇. These exercises do not have to be mastered before proceeding with the text.

In order to underline their common vision, the authors of these two volumes have merged their identities into that of L. T. F. Gamut. Gamut works (or at least did work at the time of writing) at three different universities in the Netherlands: Johan van Benthem as a logician at the University of Groningen; Jeroen Groenendijk as a philosopher, Dick de Jongh as a logician, and Martin Stokhof as a philosopher at the University of Amsterdam; and Henk Verkuyl as a linguist at the University of Utrecht.

This work did not appear out of the blue. Parts of it had been in circulation as lecture notes for students. The exercises, in particular, derive from a pool built up through the years by the authors and their colleagues. The authors wish to express their thanks to all who have contributed in any way to this book. Special thanks are due to Piet Rodenburg, who helped write it in the early stages, to Michael Morreau for his translation of volume 1 and parts of volume 2, and to Babette Greiner for her translation of most of volume 2.

Summary of Volume 1

In chapter 1, logic is introduced as the theory of reasoning. Some systematic remarks are made concerning the connection between logic and meaning, and a short historical survey is given of the relationship between logic, philosophy, and linguistics. Furthermore, the role of formal languages and how they are put to use is discussed.

Chapter 2 treats propositional logic, stressing its semantic side. After the exposition of the usual truth table method, the interpretation of connectives as truth functions is given. In connection with this and also for later use, the concept of a function is introduced. Chapter 2 concludes with a section in which the syntax of propositional languages is developed in a way more akin to the syntax of natural language. The purpose of this section—which is not presupposed in later chapters—is to illustrate the flexibility of the apparatus of logic.

In chapter 3 predicate logic is treated. Here too, the semantic side is stressed. Much attention is paid to the translation of sentences from natural language to the languages of predicate logic. The interpretation of quantifiers is defined in two ways: by substitution and by assignment. Sets, relations, and functions are introduced thoroughly. Although in this book special attention is given to language and meaning, the introduction to classical propositional and predicate logic offered in chapters 2 and 3 has been set up in such a way as to be suitable for general purposes.

Because of this, chapter 4, in which the theory of inference is treated, contains not only a semantic but also a syntactic characterization of valid argument schemata. We have chosen natural deduction for this syntactic treatment of inference. Although at several places in volume 1 and volume 2 there are references to this chapter on natural deduction, knowledge of it is not really presupposed.

In chapter 5 several subjects are treated that to a greater or lesser extent transcend the boundaries of the classical propositional and predicate logic of chapters 2–4. Definite descriptions are a standard nonstandard subject which plays an important role in the philosophical literature. The flexible character of logic is illustrated in sections on restricted quantification, many-sorted predicate logic, and elimination of variables. The treatment of second-order logic is a step toward the logic of types, which is treated in volume 2. Unlike the subjects just mentioned, which presuppose predicate logic, the section on many-valued logic can be read right after chapter 2. An extensive treatment is given of the analysis of semantic presuppositions by means of many-valued logics.

Similarly, chapter 6 only presupposes knowledge of propositional logic. Some aspects of the meaning of the conjunctions of natural language are treated which do not seem to be covered by the connectives of propositional logic. A pragmatic explanation of these aspects of meaning is given along the lines of Grice's theory of conversational implicatures. Chapter 6 suggests how a logical pragmatics can be developed in which non-truth-conditional aspects of meaning can be described with the help of logical techniques.

Chapter 7 treats yet another subject which is common to logic and linguistics, viz., the mathematical background of formal syntax. It is treated here mainly in terms of the concept of automata which recognize and generate languages. In this way, obvious parallels between the syntax of a formal language and the syntax of natural language are discussed.

Bibliographical notes to the relevant literature, which do not pretend to be exhaustive, conclude this volume.

1   Introduction

1.1 Arguments, Valid Arguments, and Argument Schemata

Logic, one might say, is the science of reasoning. Reasoning is something which has various applications, and important among these traditionally is *argumentation*. The trains of reasoning studied in logic are still called *arguments*, or *argument schemata*, and it is the business of logic to find out what it is that makes a *valid* argument (or a *valid inference*) valid.

For our purposes, it is convenient to see an argument as a sequence of sentences, with the *premises* at the beginning and the *conclusion* at the end of the argument. An argument can contain a number of smaller steps, subarguments, whose conclusions serve as the premises of the main argument. But we can ignore this complication and similar complications without missing anything essential (see §4.1).

By a valid argument we mean an argument whose premises and conclusion are such that the truth of the former involves that of the latter: *if* the premises of a valid argument are all true, *then* its conclusion must also be true. Note that this says nothing about whether the premises are in fact true. The validity of an argument is independent of whether or not its premises and conclusion are true. The conclusion of a valid argument is said to be a *logical consequence* of its premises.

Here are a few simple examples of valid arguments:

(1)   John will come to the party, or Mary will come to the party.
John will not come to the party.
_____
Mary will come to the party.

(2)   John will come to the party, or Mary will come to the party.
If John has not found a baby sitter, he will not come to the party.
John has not found a baby sitter.
_____
Mary will come to the party.

(3)   All airplanes can crash.
All DC-10s are airplanes.
_____
All DC-10s can crash.

(4)   John is a teacher.
       John is friendly.
       _____

       Not all teachers are unfriendly.

(5)   All fish are mammals.
       Moby Dick is a fish.
       _____

       Moby Dick is a mammal.

All of these examples are valid: anyone who accepts that their premises are true will also have to accept that their conclusions are true. Take (1) for instance. Anyone can see that (1) is a valid argument without even being able to ascertain the truth or falsity of its premises. Apparently one does not even need to know who Mary and John are, let alone anything about their behavior with respect to parties, in order to say that this argument is valid. In order to say, that is, that *if* the premises are all true, *then* so must its conclusion be. Once again, the validity of an argument has nothing to do with whether or not the premises happen to be true. That the premises of a valid argument can even be plainly false is apparent from example (5). Obviously both premises of this argument are false, but that does not stop the argument as a whole from being valid. For if one were to accept that the premises were true, then one would also have to accept the conclusion. You cannot think of any situation in which the premises are all true without it automatically being a situation in which the conclusion is true too.

Not only is the factual truth of the premises not necessary for an argument to be valid, it is not sufficient either. This is clear from the following example:

(6)   All horses are mammals.
       All horses are vertebrates.
       _____

       All mammals are vertebrates.

Both the premises and the conclusion of (6) are in fact true, but that does not make (6) valid. Accepting the truth of its premises does not involve accepting that of the conclusion, since it is easy to imagine situations in which all of the former are true, while the latter, as the result of a somewhat different mammalian evolution, is false.

But if it is not the truth or falsity of the premises and the conclusion of an argument which determine its validity, what is it then? Let us return to example (1). We have pointed out that we do not even have to know who John is in order to say that the argument is valid. The validity of the argument actually has nothing to do with John personally, as can be seen if we exchange him for someone else, say Peter. If we write *Peter* instead of *John*, the argument remains valid:

(7)   Peter will come to the party, or Mary will come to the party.
        Peter will not come to the party.
        _____
        Mary will come to the party.

The name *John* is not the only expression which can be exchanged for another while retaining the validity of the argument:

(8)   Peter will come to the meeting, or Mary will come to the meeting.
        Peter will not come to the meeting.
        _____
        Mary will come to the meeting.

If we try out all of the alternatives, it turns out that *or* and *not* are the only expressions which cannot be exchanged for others. Thus (9) and (10), for example, are not valid arguments:

(9)   John will come to the party, or Mary will come to the party.
        John will come to the party.
        _____
        Mary will come to the party.

(10)   John will come to the party if Mary will come to the party.
        John will not come to the party.
        _____
        Mary will come to the party.

From this it is apparent that the validity of (1) depends only on the fact that one of the premises consists of two sentences linked together by the conjunction *or,* that the other premise is a denial of the first sentence in that premise, and that the conclusion is the second sentence. And (1) is not the only argument whose validity depends on this fact. The same applies to (7) and (8), for example. We say that (1), (7), and (8) have a particular *form* in common, and that it is this form which is responsible for their validity. This common form may be represented schematically like this:

(11)   A or B
        Not A
        _____
        B

These schematic representations of arguments are called *argument schemata.* The letters *A* and *B* stand for arbitrary sentences. Filling in actual sentences for them, we obtain an actual argument. Any such substitution into schema (11) results in a valid argument, which is why (11) is said to be a *valid argument schema.*

The 'form' we said could be represented by (11) is more than just a syntactic construction. The first premise is not just two sentences linked by a conjunction, for it is also important what conjunction we are dealing with. A different argument schema is obtained if the conjunction *or* in (11) is replaced by another conjunction, say, *if:*

(12)   A if B
        Not A
        ___
        B

This schema is not valid. One of the substitutions for *A* and *B* is, for example, (10), and that is not a valid argument. That expressions other than the conjunctions can lead to arguments being valid becomes apparent if we examine example (5) in more depth. Considerations similar to those for (1) lead to the following argument schema for (5):

(13)   All P are Q
        a is P
        ___
        a is Q

In this schema the letters *P* and *Q* stand for expressions which refer to properties, and *a* stands for an expression which refers to an individual or an entity, that is, to a material or an abstract object. It will be clear that every substitution for *a, P,* and *Q* results in a valid argument; (5) is one example of these. The validity of this schema derives from, among other things, the meaning of the quantifying expression *all*. Other examples of quantifying expressions to be found in argument schemata are *some* and *no*.

Logic, as the science of reasoning, investigates the validity of arguments by investigating the validity of argument schemata. For argument schemata are abstractions which remove all those elements of concrete arguments which have no bearing on their validity. As we have seen, argument schemata can be formed from a variety of expressions and syntactic constructions. Usually they are not all considered together but are taken in groups. So, for example, we can concentrate on those argument schemata which can be formed solely from sentences, grammatical conjunctions, like *or* and *if . . . then,* and negation. Or we can single out arguments containing quantifying expressions. But before going into this any further, let us briefly consider the relationship between logic and meaning.

1.2 Logic and Meaning

As we have pointed out, the meanings of certain kinds of expressions play an essential part in determining the validity of schemata in which they appear. So to the extent that logic is concerned with the validity of argument schemata, it is also concerned with the meanings of expressions. Take the conjunction *or,* for example; its meaning is partly responsible for the validity of argument schema (11). In investigating the validity of schemata in which this conjunction plays a part, then, we are also investigating its meaning. And if we were to succeed in determining exactly which of these schemata are valid and which are not, which is the business of logic, we would to some extent have succeeded in determining what *or* means. And the same applies, of course, to all of the other expressions which can play a part in the validity of argument schemata, like the other conjunctions, negation, and quantifying expressions. But would we, having characterized all the valid argument schemata in which a given expression occurs, have succeeded in determining all of that expression's meaning? That is a matter which we shall return to in chapter 2 and chapter 6. In the meantime we will just say that at least a large and important part of the meaning of an expression can be determined in this manner. Knowing what the word *and* means obviously involves knowing that the conclusion *A* (and the conclusion *B*) may be drawn from the expression *A and B*.

An investigation into the validity of arguments involves an investigation into one particular relation between the meanings of sentences, the relation of *logical consequence*, and thus at the same time into the meanings of particular expressions. Earlier we said that valid arguments are those with conclusions which are logical consequences of their premises. So a characterization of valid arguments is a characterization of what sentences follow from what others. The relation of *logical consequence*, which as we shall see can be defined in terms of the even simpler semantic notion of *truth*, can therefore in turn be used to characterize other relationships between the meanings of sentences and other kinds of expressions.

It is the connection between logic and meaning that makes logic interesting from a linguistic standpoint. And the contribution which logic can make to linguistics is not limited to giving precise descriptions of the meanings of the grammatical conjunctions, negation, quantifying expressions, and so on. It should be noted that logic gives semantic interpretations of syntactic operations. By that we mean the following. When we investigate what arguments are valid on the basis of the meanings of the grammatical conjunctions and negation, we are not interested in the actual meanings of the sentences conjoined by those conjunctions. We do not consider actual arguments like (1) and (10), but argument schemata like (11) and (12). But when we consider them we still say at least something about the meanings of sentences, in that we must at some stage say what *kinds* of entities the meanings of sentences are and *how* the meanings of composite sentences depend on the meanings of their composite parts. The nature of the concept 'meaning of a sentence' must, in other words, be made more precise, and a semantic interpretation must be given to the syntactic operations by which some sentences may be obtained from others. So we do not go into the actual meanings of particular predicating expressions, but we do determine the nature of their meanings and give a semantic interpretation to the syntactic rules by means of which sentences may be obtained from predicating and quantifying expressions. Logic thus gives a precise content to the principle which states that the meaning of a composite expression must be built up from the meanings of its composite parts. This principle, which is generally attributed to Frege, is known as *the principle of the compositionality of meaning.*

Furthermore, the fields in which logic can be applied can be expanded in two different directions. On the one hand, logic can be used for arguments analyzing expressions other than conjunctions, negation, and quantifying expressions, for example, temporal constructions, modal expressions, and the like. More about these presently. And on the other hand, we can attempt to give a semantic analysis of sentences other than indicative ones. Logic has in the past been concerned mainly with reasoning, which has resulted in a restriction to *indicative sentences,* sentences which express some state of affairs and are either true or false. An argument is composed of indicative sentences. It does not contain any questions, for example. But it is nevertheless quite possible to apply semantic notions developed for indicative sentences in the investigation of *nonindicative* sentences as well. There are relations between the meanings of the latter too, and quite often these are close parallels to relations holding between indicative sentences. Compare, for example, the relation between (14a) and (b) with that between (15a) and (b), and the same for (16) and (17):

(14) a. John and Mary are walking down the street.
     b. John is walking down the street.

(15) a. Are John and Mary walking down the street?
     b. Is John walking down the street?

(16) a. Everyone loves everyone.
     b. Every man loves every woman.

(17) a. Who loves whom?
     b. Which man loves which woman?

It will not be possible to go into the semantic analysis of nonindicative sentences here, but the reader should keep in mind that the restriction to indicative sentences is merely a traditional one and is not in any way principled.

A great contribution from logic to linguistics is then to be expected in the field of semantics, and this contribution is the main theme of volume 2. We will tend to take a semantic approach to logical theories, placing less emphasis on the syntactic approach. And one extremely important part of modern logic, the field of metalogic, in which logical systems are themselves the subject of logical and mathematical investigation, will be almost ignored, although some important results will be discussed briefly in §4.4.

1.3 Logical Constants and Logical Systems

Whether logic is seen as the science of reasoning or the science of relationships between meanings, either way there is no such thing as a universal logic which characterizes *all* valid arguments or the relationships between the meanings of *all* expressions. In practice, different *logical systems* are developed, each with its own particular class of arguments. What class this is depends on the kinds of expressions found in the logical language the logical system uses.

The system of *propositional logic,* the subject of chapter 2, is, for example, concerned with argument forms which depend for their validity on the meanings of the expressions *and, or, if* (. . . *then), if and only if,* and the negation *not.* Everything else which affects the validity of arguments is left out. Thus argument schemata like (11) and (12) are a part of propositional logic, while schemata like (13) are not. The second important logical system which we will go into, the system of *predicate logic* discussed in chapter 3, is concerned not only with propositional argument schemata but also with argument schemata involving quantifying expressions, like *all* and *some.* These include argument schemata like (13).

So each logical system characterizes its own class of valid argument schemata; their validity is based on the meanings of certain expressions which that system uses. The expressions which play this part in a logical system are called its *logical constants,* since within that system their meaning is completely fixed.

One interesting question is this. What kinds of expressions can be treated as logical constants in a logical system? An important fact that may help us is that in logic we are interested in the *structure* of arguments, i.e., in argument schemata. Arguments must be valid only in virtue of their external forms and not in virtue of their content. So an expression must lend structural validity to argument schemata if it is to be treated as a logical constant. Purely descriptive terms such as *mammal, party,* or *airplane* are ruled out by this criterion. And expressions like *and, or, if* (. . . *then), if and only if,* the negation *not,* and the quantifying expressions *all* and *some* are clear examples of constructions which can lend structural validity to argument forms. That is indeed their only function in language. Their meaning is entirely determined by the part they play in argument, since they have no descriptive content. So the conjunctions *and, or, if* (. . . *then), if and only if,* and the negation *not* are taken as the logical constants of propositional logic; and these together with the quantifying expressions *all* and *some* form the logical constants of predicate logic.

Besides these logical systems, there are also others, each with its own set of logical constants. As we shall see, natural language conjunctions, negation, and quantifying expressions often form a part of these. Other logical systems have been created by adding more logical constants to those of propositional logic, which seem to be so fundamental that it would not make sense to develop a notion of validity without them.

It should be noted, however, that this is not the only way new logical systems can be developed. We can also consider the same set of logical constants under a new interpretation. This too results in a different class of valid argument schemata. So besides so-called classical propositional logic we have, among other alternatives, intuitionistic propositional logic (see §4.3.5), in which the same logical constants receive a slightly different interpretation. Strictly speaking, then, a logical system is characterized by its logical constants together with the interpretations placed on them.

Logical constants other than those mentioned so far are, for example, modal expressions like *possibly* and *necessarily,* which are treated in modal logic (see vol. 2), and temporal expressions and constructions like *it was the case that, it will be the case that, sometime, never,* and the tenses of verbs, which are treated in *tense logic* (also in vol. 2). All of these expressions and constructions play a structural part in lending validity to arguments. But unlike the logical constants of propositional and predicate logic, they also seem to have a certain descriptive content. Furthermore—and this is one of the main reasons why logical systems with these expressions as their logical constants have been developed in the first place—they are closely linked to traditional philosophical concepts like *necessity* and *time.* The same relevance to philosophical issues has also been the driving force behind the development of *epistemic logic,* in which notions like *belief* and *knowledge* form the logical core, and deontic logic, which is concerned with concepts like *permission* and *obligation.*

The set of possible logical constants is an open one. We could give some more examples of expressions and constructions for which logical systems have in fact been developed, but it turns out to be extremely difficult to specify the set of all expressions and constructions for which this would make sense. Logical systems featuring the above-mentioned constants make sense, but a logical system in which the validity of arguments is wholly based on the descriptive content of certain terms would not make sense. Any such system would not be a description of the structural factors which determine the validity or nonvalidity of argument schemata but a description of the real world, and that is not the task of logic. A sharp boundary cannot be drawn between purely descriptive terms and the rest, however, since there are expressions which remain uncertain in this respect. There is a clear parallel here with the problem of saying what linguistic theories of meaning should explain and what they may ignore. There seems to be a gradual transition from structural aspects of meaning, which fall within the range of linguistic theories, and descriptive content, which does not.

We must make the following comments about the applications of logic in linguistics. First, if we say that *logic* is being applied, then we really mean that some logical system is being applied. Second, and in spite of our previous comments about the connections between logic and meaning, one cannot expect logic to provide a complete ready-made theory of meaning in natural language. Linguistic inspiration sometimes plays a part in the development of logical theories, but in general the kinds of problems which give rise to logical theories are rather different from those which result in linguistic theories. But there seems to be a growing recognition that there are some essential links between the two fields, in spite of the partly historical, partly systematic differences mentioned above.

In our opinion, the contribution of logic to linguistics is twofold. First, logic contributes systems which give a precise description of a number of expressions which, because of their importance to reasoning, cannot be ignored in a linguistic theory of meaning. This description provides a characterization of the various sorts of meanings which different syntactic categories can carry and of the way the meaning of a complex expression can be built up from the meanings of its composite parts. Second, logic contributes methods and concepts useful for the analysis of expressions and constructions which have not traditionally been dealt with in logic as a theory of reasoning, but which must be accounted for by a linguistic theory of meaning. Both contributions will be illustrated in what is to come.

In §§1.4 and 1.5 we will further discuss the historical links between logic and linguistics. This should place this book within a broader context and help explain why the semantics of natural language is increasingly important to linguistics, philosophy, and logic.

1.4 Logic and Linguistics before the Twentieth Century

The science of logic was born more than two thousand years ago, when Aristotle assembled and arranged a number of philosophical insights about reasoning, thus originating his *syllogistic logic*. Syllogisms are particular kinds of inferences in which a conclusion is drawn from two premises, like (5), (6), and (18):

(18)   All children are selfish.
        Some people are not selfish.

        Some people are not children.

Aristotle's theory of syllogisms indicates which of these kinds of inferences are valid and which are not.

Only the following kinds of subject/predicate propositions may appear in syllogisms:

(19)   All A are B   (Universal Affirmative)
        All A are not-B   (Universal Negative)
        Some A are B   (Particular Affirmative)
        Some A are not-B   (Particular Negative)

A and *B* are called *terms*. They refer to concepts like 'children', 'selfish', 'people', and so on. Aristotle was himself well aware that language contains many other kinds of expressions, for example, *singular* expressions such as:

(20)   a is B   (Singular Affirmative)
       a is not-B   (Singular Negative)

But his logic only intended to describe scientific reasoning, and in Aristotle's opinion, singular statements did not belong in scientific reasoning.

Aristotle also mentioned other forms of inference, like the well-known *modus ponens:*

(21)   If he is drunk, then he is dangerous.
       He is drunk.
       ———————————
       He is dangerous.

Whereas the validity of syllogistic inferences like (18) is primarily dependent on the meanings of quantifying expressions like *all* and *some,* the validity of (21) is dependent on the conjunction *if* (. . . *then*).

The Stoics (±400–200 B.C.) were responsible for the systematic development of the latter kind of inference. Furthermore, they were also interested in various semantic questions, such as the nature of truth. They (in particular, Eubulides, fourth century B.C.) were the originators of the well-known 'liar's paradox'. Here it is in a modern version:

(22)   Sentence (22) in chapter 1 is false.

Is sentence (22) now true or false? If, on the one hand, (22) is true, then what it says is false: that is, (22) is false. But if, on the other hand, (22) is false, then what it says is true, so (22) is true. It appears that excessive worry about this dilemma even proved fatal to one Philites of Kos. In the twentieth century, the eminent Polish logician Alfred Tarski turned what was a historical curiosity into the cornerstone of his semantic theory. The paradox led him to a methodological distinction between language seen as an object of discussion, the *object language,* and language as the medium in which such discussion takes place, the *metalanguage.* Confusion between these two levels of language is what makes (22) paradoxical.

The point being made here is that some central problems in modern logic already existed in classical times; important among these were quantifying expressions, grammatical conjunctions and the inferences which these allow, and various problems concerning the nature of truth. It is important to note that Aristotle's syllogistic logic only dealt with *simple quantification,* that is, with propositions containing just a single quantifying expression.

Aristotle also occupies a special place in the history of linguistics as the originator of systematic linguistic thought. Both *analysis* (in which sentences are divided into words and word groups according to function) and *parsing* (in which individual words are categorized) can be traced back to ideas of Aristotle. The distinction drawn between subject and predicate in linguistic analysis is, for example, a close parallel of Aristotle's subject/predicate distinction, which we have mentioned. And at the same time indications can be found in his work that words should be divided into categories like proper nouns, names, etc. According to Peter Geach, even modern-day categorial grammar (see vol. 2) can be traced back to Aristotle. Simple sentences like

(23)   Socrates is flying.

are parsed as noun-predicate (in Greek: onoma-rhèma). Does this mean that more complicated sentences like

(24)   Every man is flying.

should be parsed in the same manner, as (*Every man*)-*is flying?* No, writes Aristotle in *De Interpretatione*, for (23) and (24) exhibit different behavior under negation. The negation of (24) is:

(25)   Socrates is not flying.

whereas the negation of (24) is not (26) but (27):

(26)   Every man is not flying.

(27)   Not every man is flying.

Not is attached to *every man* to form *not every man* in (27), whereas a similar construction in the negation of (23) is out of the question: (*Not Socrates*)-*is flying* is clearly an incorrect analysis. Geach's conclusion is that Aristotle was aware of the differences (which exist, according to Geach) between *Socrates* and *every man*.

The first known grammatical traditions, those of Pergamum and of Alexandria, were strongly influenced by philosophy. Alexandria flew the Aristotelian flag, as is apparent from the conviction held by that school that language is a conventional system. And in the Pergamum school, a Stoic influence is apparent in the emphasis placed on what was seen as the essential irregularity of language. This emphasis was of course not conducive to the development of systematic theories of grammar, so not surprisingly, the first real grammar, that of Dionysius Thrax (±100 B.C.) was developed within the Alexandrian school.

Applying Aristotelian principles of classification, Dionysius arrived at a classification of language into the categories that we are still familiar with: nouns, verbs, participles, articles, pronouns, prepositions, adverbs, and conjunctions. His terminology, however, is according to some students derived from Stoic sources. It is interesting to consider what according to Dionysius are the objectives of studying grammar: accurate reading (aloud) of literary texts, explanation of literary figures and chosen subjects, an overview of grammatical regularities, and (most importantly) a better understanding of literature.

Returning to logic, in the Middle Ages we see, besides essentially classical theories about inference, quite highly developed theories of form and meaning. There was a considerable sensitivity to the great diversity of language, and explanations were sought for each different kind of expression. The well-known *supposition theory* can be seen as an attempt at a semantic analysis of the terms and their combinations found in language. As such, the supposition theory declined together with the rest of Scholasticism. Some distinctions drawn at the time, however, are still with us today. So, for example, the distinction between *suppositio formalis* and *suppositio materialis* is now known as the *use/mention* distinction. This distinction is apparent in the difference between sentences like (28) and (29):

(28)   Amsterdam is the capital city of the Netherlands.

(29)   Amsterdam has nine letters.

The Scholastics said that the term *Amsterdam* in (28) has *suppositio formalis*, that is, that it is *used* in order to refer to that Dutch city. But in (29) the term has *suppositio materialis*: it refers to the word *Amsterdam*; the term is *mentioned*. In this book we make a typographic distinction between use and mention, writing (29) as (30):

(30)   *Amsterdam* has nine letters.

The theory of the *distribution of terms*, which until recently was memorized by many generations of students, is another relic of the Middle Ages. In the universal affirmative sentence *All A are B*, the term *A* is 'distributed': the sentence says something about the whole concept *A*. The term *B*, on the other hand, is not distributed: the sentence does not necessarily say something about all *B*'s, but only about the *A*'s among them.

It should be noted that supposition theory was also supposed to deal with problems arising from sentences with more than one quantifier. As we have mentioned, such sentences were not included in Aristotle's theory of syllogisms. But as early as the thirteenth century, William of Shyreswood considered the validity of inferences like (31):

(31)   There is someone who is seen by (*suppositio determinata*)
        everyone
        ―――――――――――――――――――――――――――
        Everyone sees someone.   (*suppositio confusa tantum*)

Note that the inverse inference is not valid. It is surprising how Aristotle and some medieval philosophers were happy to make use of the (invalid) inverse of (31) when this suited their metaphysical purposes. So, for example, the conclusion that there is one cause which is the cause of all events was drawn from the premise that every event has a cause.

The Scholastics did not succeed in giving a satisfactory account of sentences with more than one quantifying expression. In fact, it wasn't until 1879 and the publication of Frege's *Begriffsschrift* that the problems of multiple quantification were definitively solved.

In the Middle Ages, linguistics was primarily searching for a rational basis for the rules of grammar. It was not enough for such rules to 'work' in the analysis of literary texts; what was important was how they are related to, or how they reflect, the nature of thought. The philosophical grammarians who considered language from this viewpoint are known as the Modists. Besides descriptive grammars for practical purposes, speculative grammars (*speculum* 'mirror') were developed. The ideal of a *universal grammar* gained popularity. After all, if human thought is the same everywhere, then the ideal grammar must be too. The different languages are, according to this view of grammar, all variations on and approximations to this one ideal theme.

That logic was thought indispensable for the grammarian is apparent from the following quote from Albertus Magnus (thirteenth century): "A (logically) unschooled grammarian is to a grammarian schooled in logic as an idiot to a wise man." And logic increasingly began to be occupied with the linguistic aspects of reasoning, as is apparent from William of Shyreswood's opinion that grammar teaches us to speak correctly, rhetoric teaches us to speak elegantly, and logic teaches us to speak the truth.

For the philosophical grammarians, logic was not so much a *scientia rationalis,* a science of concepts, as a *scientia sermocinalis,* a science of discourse concerned with terms. One of the fruits of this interest in terms and their semantics is the distinction between *categorematic* terms like *man* or *sick,* which refer to something, and *syncategorematic* terms like *every* or *no,* which are supposed not to have their own reference, but which are from a logical point of view essential to the meanings of sentences and the logical relations obtaining between them.

But as the Middle Ages progressed, the development of logic gradually seemed to grind to a halt. In 1789 Immanuel Kant wrote in the preface to the second edition of his *Critique of Pure Reason* that logic hadn't lost any ground since Aristotle, but that the subject hadn't gained any ground either, and that there was every indication that it would go no farther. But Kant was mistaken. As much as one hundred years before, working at the same time and in the same isolation as the Port-Royal school, the mathematician and philosopher Gottfried Wilhelm Leibniz (1646–1716) had proposed a program for logic and developed ideas which are still found in modern logical theories. He suggested that a *characteristica universalis* be developed, a universal language in which thought could be represented directly, without any of the ambiguities, vagueness, and figures of speech which are so characteristic of natural languages. Manipulation of the symbols of this universal language, the *ars combinatoria,* would then directly correspond to the operations we perform on our thoughts. Thus it would be possible to check the validity of chains of reasoning in this language by means of calculation, in the *calculus ratiocinator.* Differences of opinion, this optimistic philosopher thought, could then simply be resolved by means of computation: "Then, in the case of differences of opinion, no discussion between two philosophers will be any longer necessary, as (it is not) between two calculators. It will rather be enough for them to take pen in hand, set themselves to the abacus and (if it so pleases, at the invitation of a friend) say to one another: calculemus." Leibniz's vision was even more surprising in that according to him, all truths, even apparently accidental ones, were necessary, so that in principle all truths would be accessible to this method of calculation.

Leibniz's optimism proved somewhat excessive. He himself did not manage to realize much of this program for logic, and it is now the ideas behind it which are important. These have been extremely influential. The search for an ideal symbolic system for logic and the mathematization of the concept of the validity of chains of reasoning are essential characteristics of modern logic. But it was not until the nineteenth century and the work of pioneers like Bernard Bolzano, George Boole, Charles Saunders Peirce, and above all, Gottlob Frege that progress began to be made in the directions Leibniz had indicated. Finally, in Frege's predicate logic, a symbolic language was developed which is much more powerful than Aristotelian syllogistic logic. And for considerable parts of this language, testing the logical validity of inferences did indeed turn out to be a matter of calculation. It can, however, be proved that there is no mechanical method for testing the logical validity of arbitrary inferences between sentences of the language: predicate logic is said to be *undecidable* (see §4.4). So Leibniz's program is provably unrealizable. But it has nevertheless always been a valuable source of inspiration for logical research.

Predicate logic, as developed by Frege, combines both Aristotelian syllogistic logic and Stoic ideas about logical connectives. It also solves the medieval problems with multiple quantification, and this not with any extreme technical sophistication but by means of a few quite simple ideas. Predicate logic will be treated at length in chapter 3. But here, in order to place it in a historical context, we shall anticipate a few of the more important characteristics of the system.

Frege adopts the basic Aristotelian idea of propositions in subject-predicate form:

(32)   a is P

Here the property P is predicated of an entity a. But besides this form, he also appreciates the importance of relational forms like:

(33) $a_1 R a_2$ (a_1 bears the relation R to a_2)

as in sentences like *John deceives Mary* or *Two is less than three*. Besides these binary relations, there are also ternary relations between three things, like *lies somewhere between* and *prefers* (as in *John prefers Maud to Mary*), quaternary relations, and so on. From a philosophical point of view this is quite an innovation. Relations had previously not been considered as fundamental as properties and had always been explained away. Even Leibniz went to excess in trying to reduce relational propositions to propositions in subject-predicate form. One example of this is that (34) is paraphrased as (35):

(34)   Titus is taller than Gaius.

(35)   Titus is tall to the extent that Gaius is short.

Frege removed the grammatical notion of subject from the central place it had previously occupied in logic. It gives way to the concept of a constituent, a term which refers to an entity. Any number of different constituents may appear in relational propositions, and none enjoys a privileged position above the others. There is no need to single out a unique subject. Frege's own example motivating this departure from traditional practice is still quite instructive. He notes that the sentence

(36)   The Greeks defeated the Persians at Plataea.

which would appear to be about the Greeks (as subject), is in fact synonymous with the passive construction:

(37)   The Persians were defeated by the Greeks at Plataea.

If subjects are to be singled out, the Persians would seem to be the subject of (37). The lesson to be drawn is that neither of the constituents *the Greeks* and *the Persians* is logically more important than the other. There may be differences between (36) and (37), but they do not belong to logic.

Frege takes *not* (for the negation of sentences), *if* (. . . *then*) (for material implication), *all* (for universal generalization), and *is* (for the relation of identity) as the key words in his logical theory. Other logical constants can, as we shall see later, be defined in terms of these four.

This whole arsenal of expressions was not unknown to earlier logicians. The big advance was that nothing more than them is required to handle phenomena like multiple quantification, provided—and this was Frege's fundamental insight—one makes sure that every sentence, no matter how complicated, can be seen as the result of a systematic construction process which adds logical words one by one. In this way, a sentence with two quantifying expressions, such as *Everyone sees someone,* can be seen as the result of a construction with just the following steps. First, a basic sentence of the form *Jack sees Jill* is existentially generalized to *Jack sees someone,* and then the sentence is universally generalized as *Everyone sees someone.* As long as all sentences are obtained in this manner, they can get a semantic interpretation simply by interpreting the basic sentences and then giving a semantic parallel to the syntactic construction steps. And for each step there is just one quantifying expression to be accounted for.

This insight of Frege is now called the *principle of the compositionality of meaning, or Frege's principle.* If the syntax is kept simple, it is possible to give a parallel semantics, and theories of inference can be based on inference steps which deal with logical notions one by one. As with many important discoveries, Frege's discovery has an overwhelming simplicity and obviousness about it which makes it difficult to imagine why everything seemed so difficult before his time.

Predicate logic, as developed by Frege in his *Begriffsschrift,* was intended as a description of the way language is used in mathematics. It has served as a part of the tools of that school of research into the foundations of mathematics known as logicism. Logicism aimed at the reduction of the fundamental concepts and principles of mathematics to purely logical concepts and principles. Although the logicist program is generally considered to have been a failure, like many such broad programs, it has proved to be a wealthy source of new insights. Since then there have been intimate ties between mathematics and logic. The developments in logic since Frege have been largely in the field of *metalogic,* in which predicate logic and other logical systems are explored by means of mathematical techniques. (In this book we will not be able to spend much time on these developments; but §4.4 summarizes a few of the most important results.)

Frege himself showed increasing interest in natural language, as is apparent in his later publications. He was particularly interested in the relationship between his formal language, which was intended as a notation for the logical forms of sentences (what determines their logical behavior in inference), and natural language. Other logicians, like Bertrand Russell, Ludwig Wittgenstein, Rudolf Carnap, and Hans Reichenbach were to inherit this interest of his. Frege draws an instructive comparison between the natural and formal languages, on the one hand, and the naked eye and the microscope, on the other. The microscope has a much better resolution and thus enables one to see much more, if precision is required. But it lacks the ease and diversity of application which are characteristic of the naked eye. In order to obtain some of this diversity, one would have to develop a whole range of formal languages which could be extended if necessary. This book presents just such a range of formal logical systems, all based on predicate logic. The chapters on intensional logic and the theory of types in volume 2 are of particular importance from the point of view of natural language.

1.5 The Twentieth Century

1.5.1 *Logical Form versus Grammatical Form*

Russell's well-known and influential thesis of misleading form was developed in the footsteps of Frege's solution to the age-old problems with relational propositions and multiple quantification. As we have seen, Frege's solution departs from the insight that every sentence, however complicated it may be, must be considered the result of a systematic, step-by-step construction process, in each step of which one semantically significant syntactic rule is applied. This resulted in friction between the logical form of a sentence and what was then seen as its grammatical form. It was this friction that was expressed by Russell at the beginning of the twentieth century in his thesis of misleading grammatical form. Russell states that the grammatical form of a sentence, which we might nowadays describe as its surface structure, is often misleading. The grammatical form of a sentence can differ from its 'underlying' logical form in such a way that it appears to allow inferences which are in fact not justified. One of the tasks of philosophical analysis is then to expose the misleading grammatical forms of natural language sentences for what they are and thus to reveal their true logical forms.

One textbook example of an attempt at such an exposure of natural language is to be found in Russell's own theory of definite descriptions, which he presented in his article "On Denoting" in 1905. There Russell takes a position against a philosophical argument known as *Plato's beard*. This argument attempts to show that in order to deny that something exists, one must first assume that it does exist. If someone says *Pegasus does not exist,* then in answer to the question *What does not exist?* he will have to reply *Pegasus.* This reply would appear to commit him to the existence of what the name refers to.

Such arguments have led some philosophers, among them A. Meinong, to posit an ontological category of nonexistent things in addition to the more familiar category of things which do exist. Others, like Russell, have sought the problem in the argument itself. According to him, the grammatical forms of the sentences in it deviate in a misleading manner from their logical forms. In the article mentioned above, Russell is primarily concerned with statements containing definite descriptions, like *the present king of France, the golden mountain,* and *the square circle.* His position is that in spite of their grammatical form, these expressions do not refer to an entity. They must rather be analyzed as complex expressions which, among other things, assert that such an entity does exist. A sentence like *The present king of France is bald* asserts, among other things, that there is an entity which has the property of being the present king of France. Unlike its grammatical form, the true logical form of the sentence *The king of France does not exist* does not contain any expression which refers to a nonexistent king of France. It is simply the negation of a proposition asserting that there is some such individual. Russell thus avoids the ontological complications sketched above by assuming that the superficial grammatical forms of certain kinds of expressions deviate from their logical form. (For a discussion of definite descriptions in predicate logic, see § 5.2.)

This thesis of Russell has exerted a considerable influence on the development of two main philosophical traditions concerned with language in the twentieth century: *logical positivism* and *analytic philosophy.*

Logical positivism is a philosophical movement which developed in the twenties and which derives from the much older and strongly antimetaphysical empiricist tradition. Logical positivism insists that knowledge can be obtained only by methods developed in science, thus denying that there are special philosophical ways of obtaining knowledge. This idea undermines all philosophical disciplines which, like metaphysics, are supposed to be based on philosophical methods for obtaining knowledge. According to logical positivists, it is the task of philosophy to clarify what is true knowledge and to prune away everything else.

Logical positivism wielded two main weapons in its assault on metaphysics: (i) the *criterion of verifiability,* and (ii) the *thesis of grammatical incorrectness.* Both intended to demonstrate that metaphysical statements are nonsense. The criterion of verifiability states roughly that a proposition is meaningful only if there is some way of verifying it empirically. In this form, it throws away many babies with the metaphysical bathwater, since there are plenty of respectable scientific propositions which cannot be verified either. It was repeatedly amended and reinterpreted and finally died a quiet death. The story of its decease is told in an article published by Carl Hempel in 1950: "Problems and Changes in the Empiricist Criterion of Meaning." The influence of Russell's thesis of misleading form is perhaps clearer in the second weapon in the arsenal of logical positivism. The thesis of grammatical incorrectness explained the meaninglessness of metaphysical propositions in terms of their grammatical incorrectness. It is clearly stated by Rudolf Carnap in a strongly polemical article published in 1932, entitled "The Elimination of Metaphysics through Logical Analysis of Language." There he distinguishes two ways that expressions can be grammatically incorrect: (i) they can contain syntactic mistakes, as in *Caesar is a* and (ii) they can contain category mistakes, as in the sentence *Caesar is a prime number.*

The first kind of mistake does not cause any mischief, since everyone can see that such expressions are grammatically incorrect and therefore do not express meaningful propositions. But with the second kind of mistake, things can get out of hand. At first sight, Carnap argues, *Caesar is a prime number* would seem to be a grammatically correct sentence which just happens to be false. In reality, Carnap contends, it is an example of a 'pseudoassertion'. And metaphysics provides us with many more examples.

Carnap illustrates this with examples taken from an article by the well-known metaphysician Heidegger. In his "Was ist Metaphysik" (1929), the German philosopher writes: "We shall only go into that which is, and besides that nothing. . . . But what is this nothing? Where is this nothing to be sought?" According to Carnap, in asking questions like *Where is this nothing to be sought* we are being misled by natural language. There is an analogy between *What is there outside? Snow* and *What is there outside? Nothing.* The analogy is only strengthened by the superficial similarity of sentences like *There is snow outside* and *There is nothing outside.* But logical analysis shows that the two sentences, in spite of their similar grammatical forms, have completely different logical forms. Natural language, states Carnap, is misleading because it is not sharply defined and because it is not systematic enough. The syntactic rules governing the formation of natural language sentences do not enable us to distinguish between assertions and pseudo-assertions. The rules allow the formation of both meaningful assertions, like *17 is a prime number,* and meaningless assertions, like *Caesar is a prime number.* For this reason, natural language was rejected by the logical positivists as a medium for meaningful philosophical and scientific debate. They saw as one of the most important assignments of philosophy the construction of artificial languages whose syntax would be rigorous enough to forbid the formation of pseudoassertions. Not surprisingly, they considered logic an ideal aid for this endeavor.

It is doubtful that whatever is wrong with a sentence like *Caesar is a prime number* can be accounted for in syntactic terms. Nowadays it would seem much more natural to account for it in semantic terms. Presumably it was the absence of an adequate semantics that led Carnap to try another way, for at the time a rigorous semantics was not available for either natural language or artificial logical languages (see the comments in § 5.3). A semantic account can be given in terms of so-called selection restrictions or so-called sortal correctness. Most properties can be attributed meaningfully only to certain kinds of objects. In *Caesar is a prime number,* a property of numbers is predicated of what is not a number but an altogether different kind of object, a person.

Carnap's criticism of natural language as unsuited for philosophical and scientific debate was adopted by logical positivism, and attempts were made to construct artificial languages which would do a better job. Analysis of natural language ground to a temporary halt. Or at least almost to a halt, for Hans Reichenbach devoted a not unimportant part of his book *Elements of Symbolic Logic,* which appeared in 1947, to the logical analysis of natural language. Some of his ideas on the semantics of tenses and adverbs, for example, are still of importance, but his syntactic analysis of natural language is from a linguistic point of view not invariably satisfactory.

1.5.2 *Ordinary Language Philosophy*

A second important twentieth-century philosophical school which was much influenced by Russell's misleading form thesis is that of *analytic philosophy.* Thus Wittgenstein wrote in his influential *Tractatus Logico-Philosophicus* (1921): "All philosophy is a 'critique of language'. . . . It was Russell who performed the service of showing that the apparent logical form of a proposition need not be its real one." (*Tractatus* 4.00.31). Wittgenstein too is of the opinion that the grammatical form of a sentence in natural language can differ from its real logical form. And if the two are not carefully distinguished from each other, all kinds of pseudoproblems can arise, and all kinds of pseudo-theories may be used to try to solve them. It was for this reason that Wittgenstein saw the task of philosophy as a therapeutic one: the aim of philosophical analysis was a logical clarification of our thoughts, which are often muddled when "language goes on holiday," as he said in his later *Philosophische Untersuchungen* (Philosophical investigations) (1953).

In 1931, one of the key figures in analytic philosophy in England, Gilbert Ryle, published an article called "Systematically Misleading Expressions." He states that philosophy must attempt to discover which linguistic forms are the source of the continuous production of mistaken viewpoints and nonsensical theories in philosophy. So Ryle too sees natural language as something which misleads thought. But there is one important difference between him and the logical positivists like Carnap. The positivists' reaction to what they saw as the shortcomings of natural language was to construct artificial languages which would do better. They were not very interested in sorting out exactly which expressions and constructions lead to philosophical confusion. But Ryle, and with him many other analytic philosophers, saw such an analysis of natural language as one of the main philosophical challenges. The article mentioned above can be seen as an early attempt to meet this challenge.

The interest in natural language led to changing ideas about natural language and the relation between linguistic analysis and philosophy. The effects of a rigorous analysis of natural language are not only therapeutic, they may even lead to a better understanding of the way certain concepts may be expressed and used in natural language. The critical analysis of language thus obtained a new task, that of conceptual analysis, and together with the task a new method. It was assumed that a given concept, say knowledge, can be studied by carefully considering, for example, how the noun *knowledge* and the verb *to know* may be used in natural language. Thus analytic philosophy came to regard natural language not only as a source of philosophical confusion but also as a source of valuable philosophical insights. This did not mean rejecting Russell's misleading form thesis, which was actually an important inspiration for analytic philosophy. But it did mean a reinterpretation of the thesis and a re-evaluation of its importance.

A good example is to be found in Strawson's analysis of definite descriptions in his article "On Referring" (1950), in which he develops an alternative to Russell's theory. Russell thought the underlying logical form of definite descriptions was quite different from their superficial grammatical form. In order to escape the conclusion that nonreferring definite descriptions refer to nonexistent entities, he proposed that the logical form of a definite description like *the present king of France* includes the proposition that the described object does in fact exist, so that a sentence containing a nonreferring definite description, like *the present king of France is bald,* may be pronounced false. Strawson, on the contrary, was of the opinion that the use of a definite description carries with it the *presupposition* that the entity referred to exists. According to him, sentences which contain a nonreferring description are neither true nor false and therefore do not really express an assertion. (In § 5.5 we will discuss this at length in connection with presuppositions and many-valued logic.) Strawson saw no reason to distinguish between the superficial grammatical forms of sentences and their underlying logical forms. This partial rehabilitation of natural language does not, however, mean a total rejection of Russell's thesis. Strawson thought that natural language does not have any exact logic, and that where the grammatical forms of sentences suggest that there might be such a logic, the grammatical forms become misleading.

The conviction that there is no exact logic of natural language, and that language therefore does not lend itself to an analysis in terms of precise logical notions and rules, is common to just about all analytic philosophers, even those that were the most interested in natural language, like the later Wittgenstein and above all J. L. Austin. The opinion that the analysis of natural language can provide philosophical insights is very clear in the work of Austin. His work is even referred to as *linguistic phenomenology*. In an article published in 1956, "A Plea for Excuses," Austin observes the following about natural language: "our common stock of words embodies all the distinctions men have found worth drawing, and the connexions they have found worth marking, in the lifetimes of many generations: these surely are likely to be more numerous, more sound, since they have stood up to the long test of the survival of the fittest, and more subtle, at least in all ordinary and reasonably practical matters, than any that you or I are likely to think up in our arm-chairs of an afternoon—the most favoured alternative method." In Austin's method, the dictionary is an important source of philosophically relevant information; philosophical analysis should be carried out with a dictionary close at hand. It is not that Austin thinks that philosophical problems can be solved just by consulting a good dictionary. Natural language provides not ready-made answers but valuable distinctions and connections between the concepts we are dealing with. Austin writes: "Certainly, then, ordinary language is *not* the last word: in principle it can everywhere be supplemented and improved upon and superseded. Only remember, it *is* the *first* word" (1956). There are echoes here, although fairly weak ones, of Russell's thesis of misleading form. Natural language can be inadequate and can be improved upon. Especially, in Austin's opinion, if we consider some problem which has been much brooded upon by philosophers in the past, for the language we have at our disposal for discussing such problems is riddled with the jargon of long-abandoned philosophical theories. In such cases, natural language can mislead and confuse.

1.5.3 *Linguistics and Philosophy*

How much influence have developments in linguistics in the twentieth century had on modern philosophy, and in particular on analytic philosophy, with all its concern for linguistic facts and observations? Until the development of transformational-generative grammar, almost none at all. Modern structural linguistics, from Saussure to Bloomfield, Harris, Bloch, and others, seems to have been ignored by analytic philosophy, and within logical positivism it wasn't much different. One exception is the article "Logical Syntax and Semantics" (1953) by Yehoshua Bar-Hillel, a student of Carnap. Bar-Hillel suggests that structural linguistics, which was primarily based on distributive methods, could be augmented by logical methods, in both the syntax and the semantics. The original idea that natural language is too unsystematic and vague to be given a rigorous treatment is here at least being undermined. Furthermore, this seems to have been the first-ever defence of the application to natural language of the kind of semantics developed in logic. The linguists were not at all impressed. Chomsky's reply to Bar-Hillel, in "Logical Syntax and Semantics: Their Linguistic Relevance" (1954), was that at a descriptive level, linguistics was in no need of logical methods and notions. Only in the theory of grammar formalisms would logical and mathematical concepts be welcome as a methodological aid. With the exception of this attempt at reconciliation by Bar-Hillel and the work by Reichenbach mentioned above, there was no significant mutual stimulation between linguistics on the one side and philosophy and logic on the other until well into the sixties. Chomsky's own work in mathematical linguistics, with its clear traces of mathematical logic, is no exception to this, in view of Chomsky's point that logical methods do not belong within *descriptive* linguistics.

The arrival and subsequent success of transformational-generative grammar brought about a drastic change in the separate development of linguistics and philosophy. Initially it was the views about natural language held in analytic and later in more logical circles that were to change as a result of the innovations in linguistics. But toward the end of the sixties, partly as a result of the increasingly important role of semantics in transformational-generative grammar, logical and philosophical insights began to influence linguistics. There are various aspects of transformational-generative grammar which concern philosophical views on language. Chomsky's hypothesis that the capacity to learn language is innate, for example, can be seen as contributing to the traditional philosophical debate between empiricism and rationalism. But for our purposes, the distinction made in linguistics between deep structure and surface structure is more important, for it would seem to lend an empirical interpretation to the philosophical distinction between the grammatical form of a sentence and its logical form. The link between these two distinctions became even stronger in the early sixties, when semantics began to occupy a permanent place in transformational-generative grammar. Katz and Postal (1964) argued that syntactic deep structure is the level at which semantic interpretation should take place. This idea led to speculation on the possibility of identifying the deep structure of a sentence with its logical form. Such an identification is problematic, but the idea appeared so attractive that at the end of the sixties and in the early seventies a new trend emerged in linguistics, *generative semantics,* which rejected a purely syntactically motivated notion of deep structure in favor of a semantic notion of deep structure, which was then to be identified with logical form. But the developments in transformational-generative grammar in the seventies and eighties have followed a different route. Once again, logical form is strictly distinguished from grammatical form by the introduction of a separate component, called logical form, into grammar as a complement to the levels of representation provided by the syntactic component. The logical form contains structures which are derived from the syntactic component in order to account for certain structural aspects of the meanings of sentences, without considering the meanings of words or the pragmatic aspects of language.

The developments in transformational-generative grammar initially caused a sort of 'crisis' at the foundations of analytic philosophy. For in analytic philosophy, and especially in 'linguistic phenomenology', philosophical problems were approached by means of detailed investigations into the ways in which expressions and formulations bearing on those problems are dealt with in natural language. The description and analysis of natural language thus belonged to the proper work of analytic philosophers. But all of a sudden generative grammar produced a large amount of descriptive material, and furthermore it presented this material in a systematic packaging. There were many observations on language, but even better there was a theory of the structure of language. It began to seem that linguists and philosophers were becoming each other's rivals, and some encouraged this idea. For example, Katz and Fodor, in their article "What's Wrong with the Philosophy of Language?" (1962), criticized analytic philosophy's lack of a theoretical framework in which its many useful observations and descriptions could be integrated. Generative grammar had such a framework, and they argued that analytic philosophers should continue their work within this framework. This criticism was later repeated by Katz in his book *The Philosophy of Language* (1966), in which he also lets loose generative grammar, and in particular the semantic component he himself gave it, on a number of traditional philosophical questions, for example, the nature of the distinction between *analytic* and *synthetic* propositions. But the idea that analytic philosophy is really a branch of empirical linguistics never caught on. First, philosophers did not believe they could solve philosophical problems just by turning to natural language; Austin put this succinctly when he said that language has the first, but not the last, word. And second, there was the general idea that the propositions of linguistics are essentially different from those of philosophy and concern different kinds of things. Linguistic propositions concern language, whether one or more specific natural languages or natural languages in general. They are, then, empirical. Philosophical propositions, on the other hand, are not empirical, since they are about concepts. The philosopher is only interested in clarifying concepts and in making them more precise. His propositions are not empirical. The philosopher may in the process of clarifying concepts be thankful for empirical material gathered by his colleagues in the linguistics department, but that does not by itself make him an empirical linguist. A defence of analytic philosophy which goes along these lines is to be found in Vendler's *Linguistics in Philosophy* (1967).

Logical positivism had had its day when transformational-generative grammar became popular, but many of its ideas are still present in philosophical disciplines such as the philosophy of science and logic. The scepticism in logical circles about the possibility of describing natural language with logical methods does not differ much from that in logical positivism. Tarski, for example, thought that applying the semantics he developed for logical languages to natural languages would be problematic. One of his reasons was that any such semantics assumes a precisely formulated syntax, and he thought it out of the question that such could be found for natural languages. The developments in generative grammar made it seem more likely that natural languages could be given a precisely formulated syntax, and they thus inspired a hope that logical methods for semantic analysis would indeed turn out to be applicable to natural languages. Davidson, who was interested in transferring Tarski's semantics to natural language, wrote: "Recent work by Chomsky and others is doing much to bring the complexities of natural language within the scope of serious semantic theory" (1967). Montague seemed to share this hope, as is apparent from the following excerpt from his article "Universal Grammar": "There is in my opinion no important difference between natural languages and the artificial languages of logicians; indeed, I consider it possible to comprehend the syntax and semantics of both kinds of languages within a single natural and mathematically precise theory. On this point I differ from a number of philosophers, but agree, I believe, with Chomsky and his associates" (1970). Where logical positivists thought we needed formal languages in order to avoid the pitfalls inherent in natural languages, Montague argues that there is no fundamental difference between the two, and that both kinds of language can be described in the same manner.

The developments in generative grammar have done a great deal to shape what logicians and philosophers make of natural language. But logical and philosophical insights have also been assimilated in linguistics. This is apparent from the increasing use of logical notation in the descriptive apparatus, now that semantics plays an increasingly important part in generative grammar. And other logical concepts, like *predicate, argument, proposition, lambda abstraction, scope ambiguity* in expressions with multiple quantification, and many others, have also been annexed by generative theory, although the versions to be found there are from the point of view of logic sometimes a little exotic. Yet another example is the concept of *presupposition,* which was already present in Frege's writings and was 'reinvented' by Strawson in the article mentioned above. The theory of speech acts, which was outlined by Austin in his book *How To Do Things With Words* (1962a) and was expanded by the philosopher Searle in his book *Speech Acts* (1969), initially had some effect on syntax (in Ross's performative hypothesis), but it later also formed the basis for a linguistic pragmatics.

The most important contribution we think logic can make to linguistics is in the application of formal semantics to the description of natural language. Montague's theory, known as *Montague grammar,* is perhaps the most general and extensive example of logical methods being used in descriptive linguistics. We shall discuss Montague grammar in volume 2. That logic is more than just a tool in such enterprises, and that linguistics is more than a passive victim, is well expressed by Davidson and Harman, the editors of *Semantics of Natural Language* (1972), a collection of seminal papers in the interdisciplinary field between philosophy, linguistics, and logic; they write in their introduction: "The purpose of this volume is . . . to encourage the active exchange of ideas among logicians, philosophers and linguists who are working on semantics for natural languages. We trust it will be agreed that there is more to this than the usual business of rubbing together two or more disciplines in the expectation of heat and the hope of light. In the present case, a common enterprise already exists; our aim is to make it a cooperative one."

1.6 Formal Languages

Before turning in chapter 2 to the exposition of the first logical system, that of propositional logic, we need to say something more about the notion of a formal language and its use in logical theorizing.

One characteristic of modern logic is that it isn't so much concerned with arguments that can be made in one or another natural language as with reasoning in *formal languages*. There are a number of reasons for this.

The first is that, as we pointed out above, logic is interested in argument schemata. And expressions which together form an argument schema are not expressions in a natural language but can be considered to be drawn from a formal language. Just as an argument is a string of natural language sentences, so can an argument schema be considered to be a string of sentences drawn from a formal language. Our investigations into argument schemata then amount to investigations into arguments in one or another formal language. Which formal language will depend on what we are interested in. In propositional logic, for example, we are interested in arguments whose validity is dependent on the conjunctions of natural language and negation. We therefore choose a formal language with the *connectives* as its logical constants, since these symbols are the formal counterparts of the conjunctions and negation in natural language. The letters p, q, r stand for the simplest sentences of this formal language, which can be built into complex sentences by means of the connectives. Thus a formal distinction is drawn between what primarily interests us, the connectives, and elements whose exact meaning does not matter, the simplest sentences. These expressions, which unlike the logical constants do not have fixed meanings, we call the *logical variables* of the language in question.

A second reason why natural languages are less than ideally suited to investigations into the validity of arguments is that they contain ambiguities. These ambiguities can make it impossible to decide whether a given argument is valid or not. Consider, for example, the following argument:

(38)   Old men and women take priority.

My mother is a woman

My mother takes priority.

The validity of (38) depends on the reading given to its first premise. Only, if *old* is taken to apply to *women* as well as to *men*, the argument is valid. In a suitable formal language, such ambiguities would be resolved by means of brackets or some similar device which adds more structure.

A third reason for using formal languages in investigations into the validity of arguments is that in such investigations, one must make general statements about all sentences, or at least about all sentences of some particular form. And the truth of such statements can only be proved if we have at our disposal an explicit characterization of all the sentences of the language in question. Impressive though the progress in modern linguistics has been, there is still no such characterization of a natural language available to us. But it is precisely by means of such a characterization that a formal language comes into existence, since a formal language is something which has to be defined. But if investigations into the validity of formal arguments are to throw any light on arguments cast in natural language, then there will have to be some correspondence between the formal and natural languages in question. Fragments of the natural language which are of importance for the sort of reasoning involved will have to be 'translatable' into the formal language. Such correspondences will be presupposed when we get around to explaining the various logical systems themselves. But in volume 2 we will go into the topic of translation extensively.

A formal language is characterized by its *vocabulary* and *syntax*. The vocabulary of a formal language is what determines the *basic expressions* it contains. These can be subdivided into three distinct kinds: the logical constants, the logical variables, and the *auxiliary signs*. This last contains things like brackets, which are needed to give the language structure. In the syntax of the language, a definition is given of the *composite expressions* of the language. The definition is given in a number of explicit rules which say how expressions may be combined with each other, thus creating other expressions. The principle of compositionality presides over the whole process: the meaning of a composite expression must be wholly determined by the meanings of its composite parts and of the syntactic rule by means of which it is formed.

In the course of investigations into the validity of arguments, we will of course often want to say things about the formal language in which the arguments are couched. We use a language in order to say these things; in this book the language used is English. In logic, a language which is spoken of is called an *object language,* and a language in which an object language is spoken of is called a *metalanguage.* One and the same object language can, of course, be discussed in different metalanguages: in the original Dutch version of this book, Dutch took the place of English as the metalanguage, though the object languages considered were just the same. Sometimes it is convenient to expand the metalanguage by adding symbols which make it easier to speak about the object language, for example, symbols which refer to arbitrary object language expressions. Not surprisingly, such symbols are named *metavariables.* And there are other symbols which we will use in the metalanguage of this book.

Now there is no reason why object language and metalanguage need to differ. A language like English is rich enough to be able to say things about itself. Indeed, the preceding sentence is a proof of that. The point is that the terms object language and metalanguage refer to the *functions* which a language may have in a particular context. The distinction between these two functions of languages is closely related to the distinction between *use* and *mention* made earlier on, which was illustrated by means of:

(39)   Amsterdam is the capital city of the Netherlands.

(40)   *Amsterdam* has nine letters.

In (39) the expression *Amsterdam* refers to a particular Dutch city (use). In (40) the same expression refers to a word (mention).

Surprisingly enough, it is never necessary to actually exhibit the symbols of a formal language. Just as we do not have to build the city of Amsterdam to say, as in (39), that it is the capital city of the Netherlands, we can say everything we need to say about an object language by means of names in the metalanguage for the symbols in the object language. For example, in our discussion of propositional logic, the expressions p, q, and r, etc., are names functioning in English to *refer* to expressions in the language of propositional logic. This enables us to keep clear of the sticky use/mention difficulties which might otherwise arise in the description of formal languages: symbols and formulas never refer to themselves; we only refer to them by means of their names.

2   Propositional Logic

2.1 Truth-Functional Connectives

Propositional logic is the simplest and the most basic logical system there is. As its logical constants it has *connectives* and *negation;* the former link two sentences together into one new, composite sentence, and the latter operates on just one sentence. The restriction to indicative sentences mentioned in §1.2, that is, to sentences which are either true or false, suggests a class of connectives it seems natural to begin with. In order to make clear what these are, we must first introduce the concept of *truth value.* We say that the truth value of a sentence is 1 if the sentence is true and 0 if the sentence is false. Here we are dealing only with sentences which are true or false, so their truth value is either 1 or 0. The principle of compositionality (§1.2, §1.4) requires that the meaning (and thus the truth value) of a composite sentence depends only on the meanings (truth values) of the sentences of which it is composed.

By way of illustration, consider the following sentences:

(1)   John has bumped his head and he is crying.

(2)   John is crying because he has bumped his head.

(3)   John is crying.

(4)   John has bumped his head.

Let us suppose that John has in fact bumped his head and that he is indeed crying. So (1) is true. Now note that instead of (3), *John is crying* (we assume that this is what is meant by *he is crying*) we might just as well have written any other true sentence, such as, for example, *it is raining* (if this in fact happens to be the case). Then the sentence *John has bumped his head and it is raining* would also be true. It is quite different for (2): if John has in fact bumped his head and is indeed crying then (2) may well be true, but it certainly does not need to be (maybe he is crying because Mary doesn't love him); and conversely, if (2) is true then *John is crying because it is raining* is false even if it is raining.

This difference in the behavior of *and* and *because* can be put as follows. Sentence (1) is true if both (3) and (4) are true, and false if either is false. The truth value of an *and* sentence depends only on the truth values of the two parts of which it is composed. But this does not apply to sentence (2), whose truth depends on more than just the truth of sentences (3) and (4) of which it is composed. Connectives which give rise to sentences whose truth value depends only on the truth values of the connected sentences are said to be *truth-functional*. So *and* is, and *because* is not, a truth-functional connective.

Since we here restrict the meaning of sentences to their truth values, compositionality requires that we consider only truth-functional connectives and the corresponding conjunctions from natural language. And given that we only consider such connectives, investigating the way the truth values of sentences depend on each other, and in particular investigating the validity of schemata of reasoning in which connectives figure, becomes very simple. In order to determine the truth value of a sentence *A*, we need only pay attention to the sentences of which *A* is ultimately composed. This narrowing down of the meaning of sentences may seem rather rigorous at first, but in practice the restriction has turned out to be quite productive.

2.2 Connectives and Truth Tables

As its logical constants, the vocabulary of a language for propositional logic includes *connectives*. And as logical variables there are symbols which stand for statements (that is, 'propositions'). These symbols are called *propositional letters*, or *propositional variables*. In general we shall designate them by the letters p, q, and r, where necessary with subscripts as in p_1, r_2, q_3, etc. It is usual to use different letters for different propositional symbols. The propositional letters and the composite expressions which are formed from them by means of the connectives are grouped together as *sentences* or *formulas*. We designate these by means of the letters ϕ and ψ, etc. For these metavariables, unlike the variables p, q, and r, there is no convention that different letters must designate different formulas.

Table 2.1 sums up the connectives that we shall encounter in the propositional languages in this chapter, each with an example of a sentence formed by means of it and the meaning of the sentence. The connectives $\wedge$, $\vee$, $\rightarrow$, and $\leftrightarrow$ are said to be two-place, and $\neg$ is said to be one-place; this corresponds to the number of sentences which the connective in question requires;

Table 2.1 Connectives and Their Meanings

Connective	Composite sentence with this connective	Meaning
$\neg$ *(negation symbol)*	$\neg p$ *(negation of p)*	*it is not the case that p*
$\wedge$ (conjunction symbol)	(p $\wedge$ q) (conjunction of p and q)	p and q
$\vee$ (disjunction symbol)	(p $\vee$ q) (disjunction of p and q)	p and/or q
$\rightarrow$ (implication symbol)	(p $\rightarrow$ q) ((material) implication of p and q)	if p, then q
$\leftrightarrow$ (equivalence symbol)	(p $\leftrightarrow$ q) ((material) equivalence of p and q)	p if and only if q

p is said to be the first member (or *conjunct*) of the conjunction (p ∧ q), and q is the second. The same applies to implications, disjunctions, and equivalences, though the first and second members of an implication are sometimes referred to as its *antecedent* and its *consequent*, respectively, while the two members of a disjunction are referred to as its *disjuncts*.

Our choice of connectives is in a certain sense arbitrary. Some are obviously important. We shall discuss all five separately and consider the extent to which the corresponding expressions from natural language can be regarded as truth-functional. We shall also discuss a few other possible connectives which have not been included in this list.

The syntactic rules of propositional languages allow us to link up, by means of connectives, not only propositional letters (which are also referred to as *atomic* formulas), but also composite formulas. The terminology is just the same: if ϕ and ψ are formulas, then $\neg\phi$ is said to be the negation of ϕ, $(\phi \wedge \psi)$ is the conjunction of ϕ and ψ, etc.; $\neg\phi$ refers naturally enough to the string of symbols obtained by prefixing the string ϕ with a $\neg$; $(\phi \wedge \psi)$ refers to the string of symbols consisting of a left bracket, followed by the string ϕ, followed by the connective $\wedge$, followed by the string ψ, and closing with a right bracket.

The brackets serve to remove any ambiguities. Otherwise a sentence like p ∨ q ∧ r could have either of two different meanings. It could be (a) the disjunction of p, on the one hand, and the conjunction of q and r on the other; or (b) the conjunction of the disjunction of p and q, on the one hand, and r on the other. That these have distinct meanings can easily be seen from examples like (5) and (6):

(5)   McX has been elected, or Wyman has been elected and a new era has begun.

(6)   McX has been elected or Wyman has been elected, and a new era has begun.

Example (5) corresponds to (p ∨ (q ∧ r)) and as a whole is a disjunction, while (6) corresponds to ((p ∨ q) ∧ r) and as a whole is a conjunction. We shall return to these more complex formulas in §2.3. Now we shall expand upon the different meanings of the various connectives.

What concerns us is the way in which the truth value of a composite sentence formed from one or two simpler sentences depends on the truth values of the constituent sentences and the connective used. For each connective, this is prescribed in a *truth table*. The discussion of sentence (1) shows that the truth table for the conjunction is as in (7):

(7) ϕ	ψ	$(\phi \wedge \psi)$
1	1	1
1	0	0
0	1	0
0	0	0

Beside each possible combination of the truth values of ϕ and ψ we see the resulting truth value of $(\phi \wedge \psi)$. On the face of it, it might seem that the logical behavior of $\wedge$ is wholly in accordance with that of *and* in natural language. The agreement, however, is not perfect. If someone truthfully states (8), then according to the truth table sentence (9) is also true.

(8)   Annie took off her socks and climbed into bed.

(9)   Annie climbed into bed and took off her socks.

But it is very likely that the person in question would not be inclined to accept this, since placing one sentence after the other suggests that this was also the order in which the described events happened. Similar complications arise with all the other connectives. In chapter 6 we shall discuss whether this kind of phenomenon can be explained in terms of *conditions for usage*.

The left column of (10) is a list of sentences which have the same truth conditions as the conjunction of the two sentences to their right.

(10)

Zandvoort and Haarlem lie west of Amsterdam.	Zandvoort lies west of Amsterdam.	Haarlem lies west of Amsterdam.
John and Peter are married to Anne, and Betty, respectively.	John is married to Anne.	Peter is married to Betty.
Both the Liberals and the Socialists favored the motion.	The Liberals favored the motion.	The Socialists favored the motion.
John is at home but he is asleep.	John is at home.	John is asleep.
John is at home but Peter is not.	John is at home.	Peter is not at home.
Although it was extremely cold, John did not stay indoors.	It was extremely cold.	John did not stay indoors.
Even though it was beautiful out of doors, John stayed indoors.	It was beautiful out of doors.	John stayed indoors.

So the sentences in the left column all express a logical conjunction, although from a strictly linguistic point of view we are not dealing with two sentences linked by placing an *and* between them. Apparently the connotations which *but, although,* and *though* have do not alter the truth conditions of the sentences in which the words occur. Note also that not every sentence in which the word *and* figures is a conjunction. Here is an example that is not:

(11)   John and Peter are friends.

It seems rather unnatural to regard this as a conjunction, say, of *John is friends with Peter* and *Peter is friends with John.* And sentence (12) does not mean the same as the conjunction (13):

(12)   Cheech and Chong are fun at parties.

(13)   Cheech is fun at parties and Chong is fun at parties.

Perhaps they are only fun when they're together.

Negation is also a relatively simple matter. The truth table consists of just two rows; see (14):

(14)

ϕ	$\neg\phi$
1	0
0	1

There are more ways to express the negation of a sentence than by means of *not* or *it is not the case that*. See, for example, (15):

(15)   Porcupines are unfriendly.   Porcupines are friendly.
       John is neither at home nor at   John is either at home or at
       school.   school.
       No one is at home.   Someone is at home.
       John is never at home.   John is sometimes at home.
       John is not home yet.   John is home already.
       John has never yet been at   John has on occasion been
       home.   at home.

For the disjunction we give the truth table in (16):

(16)

ϕ	ψ	$\phi \vee \psi$
1	1	1
1	0	1
0	1	1
0	0	0

This is the obvious truth table for *and/or*, and in natural language *or* generally means *and/or*. This usage is said to be *inclusive*. If *or* is used in such a way as to exclude the possibility that both disjuncts are true—this is also expressed by an *either . . . or . . .* construction—then the *or* is said to be *exclusive*. Sometimes a separate connective ∞ is introduced for the exclusive disjunction, the truth table for which is given in figure (17):

(17)

ϕ	ψ	$\phi \infty \psi$
1	1	0
1	0	1
0	1	1
0	0	0

In this book, *or* is understood to be inclusive unless stated otherwise, as is also usual in mathematics.

Actually it is not very easy to find a natural example of an exclusive *or*. A sentence like (18) will not do:

(18)   It is raining or it isn't raining.

In sentence (18) there would be no difference in the truth value whether the *or* were inclusive or not, since it cannot both rain and not rain. What we need is an example of the form *A or B* in which there is a real possibility that both *A* and *B* hold; this eventuality is excluded by the exclusive disjunction. In natural language, this is usually expressed by placing extra emphasis on the *or*, or by means of *either . . . or*. For example:

(19)   Either we are going to see a film tonight, or we are going to the beach this afternoon.

Another construction which can be used to express an exclusive disjunction is that with *unless*. Sentence (19) has the same truth conditions as (20):

(20)   We are going to see a film tonight, unless we are going to the beach this afternoon.

The truth table for (material) implication is given in figure (21):

(21)

ϕ	ψ	$\phi \rightarrow \psi$
1	1	1
1	0	0
0	1	1
0	0	1

In everyday language, *if* (. . . , *then*) can usually not be considered truth-functional. First, a sentence like

(22)   If John bumps his head, he cries.

usually means that at any given moment it is the case that John cries if he has just bumped his head. If (22) is interpreted as

(23)   If John has just bumped his head then he is now crying.

then it is clearly true if John has just bumped his head and is in fact crying, and it is false if he has just bumped his head and is at the moment not crying. But what if John has not just bumped his head? One certainly would not wish to say that the sentence must always be false in that case, but it also doesn't seem very attractive to say that it must always be true. Since we have agreed that indicative sentences are either true or false, let us choose the least unattractive alternative and say that material conditionals are true if their antecedent is untrue. What we then get is just (21).

That the implications which one encounters in mathematics are material can be illustrated as follows. Sentence (24) is taken to be true and can for the sake of clarity also be rendered as (25):

(24)   If a number is larger than 5, then it is larger than 3.

(25)   For all numbers x, if x > 5, then x > 3.

The truth of a universal statement such as (25) implies the truth of each of its instantiations, in this case, for example, (26):

(26)   If 6 > 5, then 6 > 3.
       If 4 > 5, then 4 > 3.
       If 2 > 5, then 2 > 3.

Now these three combinations correspond precisely to the three different combinations of truth values such that $\phi \to \psi$ is true: 6 > 5 and 6 > 3 are both true, 4 > 5 is false, and 4 > 3 is true, while 2 > 5 and 2 > 3 are both untrue. Assuming we want a truth table for material implication, the one we have chosen is apparently the only real choice we had. Similar points can be made with regard to sentence (22). If (22) is taken to mean that John always cries if he has just bumped his head, then one must, assuming one accepts that (22) is true, accept that at any given point t in time there are just three possibilities:

(i)   At time t John has (just) bumped his head and he is crying.
(ii)   At time t John has not (just) bumped his head and he is crying.
(iii)   At time t John has not (just) bumped his head and he is not crying.

The eventuality that John has (just) bumped his head and is not crying is ruled out by the truth of (22). From this it should be clear that material implication has at least some role to play in the analysis of implications occurring in natural language. Various other forms of implication have been investigated in logic, for example, in intensional logic (see vol. 2). A number of sentences which can be regarded as implications are to be found in (27):

(27)

→ *(implication)*	*p (antecedent)*	*q (consequent)*
John cries if he has bumped his head.	John has bumped his head.	John cries.
John is in a bad mood only if he has just gotten up.	John is in a bad mood.	John has just gotten up.
In order for the party to function better, it is necessary that more contact be made with the electorate.	The party functions better.	More contact is made with the electorate.
In order for the party to function better, it is sufficient that Smith be ousted.	Smith is ousted.	The party functions better.

The truth table for material equivalence is given in figure (28):

(28)

ϕ	ψ	$\phi \leftrightarrow \psi$
1	1	1
1	0	0
0	1	0
0	0	1

It can be seen that $\phi \leftrightarrow \psi$ is true if ϕ and ψ both have the same truth values, and false if their truth values differ. Another way of saying this is that $\phi \leftrightarrow \psi$ is true just in case ϕ materially implies ψ while ψ also materially implies ϕ. *If and only if* is a very rare conjunction in natural language. A much more common one, which arguably has the same truth table, is *provided:*

(29)   We are going to see a film tonight, provided the dishes have been done.

In mathematical contexts, $\Leftrightarrow$ and *iff* are commonly written for *if and only if.*

2.3 Formulas

Having come this far, we can now capture the concepts we introduced above in precise definitions.

A *language L for propositional logic* has its own reservoir of propositional letters. We shall not specify these; we shall just agree to refer to them by means of the metavariables p, q, and r, if necessary with subscripts appended. Then there are the brackets and connectives ($\neg$, $\wedge$, $\vee$, $\rightarrow$, $\leftrightarrow$) which are common to all languages for propositional logic. Together these form the vocabulary of L. In the syntax we define what is meant by the *well-formed expressions* (*formulas, sentences*) in L. The definition is the same for all propositional languages.

Definition 1

(i)   Propositional letters in the vocabulary of L are formulas in L.
(ii)   If ψ is a formula in L, then $\neg\psi$ is too.
(iii) If ϕ and ψ are formulas in L, then $(\phi \wedge \psi)$, $(\phi \vee \psi)$, $(\phi \rightarrow \psi)$, and $(\phi \leftrightarrow \psi)$ are too.
(iv)   Only that which can be generated by the clauses (i)–(iii) in a finite number of steps is a formula in L.

The first three clauses of the definition give a recipe for preparing formulas; (iv) adds that only that which has been prepared according to the recipe is a formula.

We illustrate the definition by examining a few examples of strings of symbols which this definition declares are well-formed, and a few examples of strings which cannot be considered well-formed. According to definition 1, p,

¬¬¬¬p, ((¬p ∧ q) ∧ r), and ((¬(p ∨ q) → ¬¬¬q) ↔ r) are examples of formulas, while pq, ¬(¬¬p), ∧ p¬q, and ¬((p → q ∨ r)) are not.

That p is a formula follows from clause (i), which states that all propositional letters of L are formulas of L. And ¬¬¬¬p is a formula on the basis of (i) and (ii): according to (i), p is a formula, and (ii) allows us to form a new formula from an existing one by prefixing the negation symbol, an operation which has been applied here four times in a row. In ((¬p ∧ q) ∧ r), clause (iii) has been applied twice: it forms a new formula from two existing ones by first introducing an opening, or left, bracket, then the first formula, followed by the conjunction sign and the second formula, and ending with a closing, or right, bracket. In forming ((¬p ∧ q) ∧ r), the operation has been applied first to ¬p and q, which results in (¬p ∧ q), and then to this result and r. Forming disjunctions, implications, and equivalences also involves the introduction of brackets. This is evident from the fourth example, ((¬(p ∨ q) → ¬¬¬q) ↔ r), in which the outermost brackets are the result of forming the equivalence of (¬(p ∨ q) → ¬¬¬q) and r; the innermost are introduced by the construction of the disjunction of p and q; the middle ones result from the introduction of the implication sign. Note that forming the negation does not involve the introduction of brackets. It is not necessary, since no confusion can arise as to what part of a formula a negation sign applies to: either it is prefixed to a propositional letter, or to a formula that begins with a negation sign, or it stands in front of a formula, in whose construction clause (iii) was the last to be applied. In that case the brackets introduced by (iii) make it unambiguously clear what the negation sign applies to.

That pq, i.e., the proposition letter p immediately followed by the proposition letter q, is not a formula is clear: the only way to have two propositional letters together make up a formula is by forming their conjunction, disjunction, implication, or equivalence. The string ¬(¬¬p) does not qualify, because brackets occur in it, but no conjunction, disjunction, implication, or equivalence sign, and these are the only ones that introduce brackets. Of course, ¬¬¬p *is* well-formed. In ∧ p¬q, the conjunction sign appears before the conjuncts, and not, as clause (iii) prescribes, between them. Also, the brackets are missing. In ¬((p → q ∨ r)), finally, the brackets are misplaced, the result being ambiguous between ¬(p → (q ∨ r)) and ¬((p → q) ∨ r).

Exercise 1

For each of the following expressions, determine whether it is a formula of propositional logic.

(i)   ¬(¬p ∨ q)

(ii)   p ∨ (q)

(iii)   ¬(q)

(iv) $(p_2 → (p_2 → (p_2 → p_2)))$

(v)   (p → ((p → q)))

(vi)   ((p → p) → (q → q))

(vii) $((p_{28} \rightarrow p_3) \rightarrow p_4)$
(viii) $(p \rightarrow (p \rightarrow q) \rightarrow q)$
(ix) $(p \vee (q \vee r))$
(x) $(p \vee q \vee r)$
(xi) $(\neg p \vee \neg \neg p)$
(xii) $(p \vee p)$

Leaving off the outer brackets of formulas makes them easier to read and does not carry any danger of ambiguity. So in most of what follows, we prefer to abbreviate $((\neg p \wedge q) \wedge r)$ as $(\neg p \wedge q) \wedge r$, $((\neg(p \vee q) \rightarrow \neg\neg\neg q) \leftrightarrow r)$ as $(\neg(p \vee q) \rightarrow \neg\neg\neg q) \leftrightarrow r$, $((p \wedge q) \wedge (q \wedge p))$ as $(p \wedge q) \wedge (q \wedge p)$, $(p \rightarrow q)$ as $p \rightarrow q$, and $(\neg p \rightarrow q)$ as $\neg p \rightarrow q$. Analogously, we shall write $\phi \wedge \psi$, $\phi \vee \psi$, $\phi \rightarrow \psi$, $\phi \leftrightarrow \psi$, $\phi \wedge (\phi \vee \chi)$, etc.

Definition 1 enables us to associate a unique *construction tree* with each formula. $(\neg(p \vee q) \rightarrow \neg\neg\neg q) \leftrightarrow r$, for example, must have been constructed according to the tree given in figure (30).

(30)

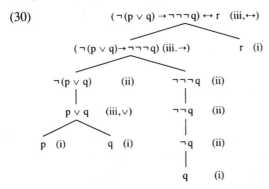

That each formula has a unique construction tree is due to the fact that, because of the brackets, logical formulas are unambiguous. Beside each *node* in the tree we see the number of the clause from definition 1 according to which the formula at that node is a formula. A formula obtained by applying clause (ii) is said to be a negation, and $\neg$ is said to be its *main sign;* similarly, the main sign of a formula obtained by clause (iii) is the connective thereby introduced (in the example, it is written next to the formula). The main sign of the formula at the top of the tree is, for example, $\leftrightarrow$, and the formula is an equivalence. Note that the formulas at the lowest nodes are all atomic.

A formula ϕ appearing in the construction tree of ψ is said to be a *subformula* of ψ. The subformulas of $\neg(p \vee q)$ are thus: p, q, p $\vee$ q, and $\neg(p \vee q)$, while the subformulas of $(\neg(p \vee q) \rightarrow \neg\neg\neg q) \leftrightarrow r$ are: p, q, r, $\neg q$, $\neg\neg q$, $\neg\neg\neg q$, p $\vee$ q, $\neg(p \vee q)$, $\neg(p \vee q) \rightarrow \neg\neg\neg q$, and $(\neg(p \vee q) \rightarrow \neg\neg\neg q) \leftrightarrow r$. Any subformula ϕ of ψ is a string of consecutive symbols occurring in the string of symbols ψ, which is itself a formula. And conversely, it can be shown that any string of consecutive symbols taken from ψ which is itself a formula is a subformula of ψ. The proof will be omitted here.

Exercise 2

(a) Draw the construction trees of $(p_1 \leftrightarrow p_2) \vee \neg p_2$ and $p_1 \leftrightarrow (p_2 \vee \neg p_2)$ and of $((p \vee q) \vee \neg r) \leftrightarrow (p \vee (q \vee \neg r))$. In each of the three cases give the subformulas of the formula under consideration.

(b) Give all formulas that can be made out of the following sequence of symbols by supplying brackets: $p \wedge \neg q \rightarrow r$. Also supply their construction trees.

(c) Classify each of the following sentences as an atomic formula, a negation, a conjunction, a disjunction, an implication, or an equivalence.

(i)	$p \rightarrow q$	(vi)	$(p \rightarrow q) \vee (q \rightarrow \neg\neg p)$
(ii)	$\neg p$	(vii)	p_4
(iii)	p	(viii)	$(p_1 \leftrightarrow p_2) \vee \neg p_2$
(iv)	$(p \wedge q) \wedge (q \wedge p)$	(ix)	$\neg(p_1 \wedge p_2) \wedge \neg p_2$
(v)	$\neg(p \rightarrow q)$	(x)	$(p \wedge (q \wedge r)) \vee p$

We now discuss the nature of the last clause of definition 1, which reads:

Only that which can be generated by the clauses (i)–(iii) in a finite number of steps is a formula in L.

A clause like this is sometimes called the *induction clause* of a definition. It plays a special and important role. If someone were to define a sheep as that which is the offspring of two sheep, we would not find this very satisfactory. It doesn't seem to say very much, since if you don't know what a sheep is, then you are not going to be much wiser from hearing the definition. The definition of a sheep as the offspring of two sheep is *circular*. Now it might seem that definition 1 is circular too: clause (ii), for example, states that a $\neg$ followed by a formula is a formula. But there is really no problem here, since the formula ϕ occurring after the $\neg$ is simpler than the formula $\neg\phi$, in the sense that it contains fewer connectives, or equivalently, that it can be generated by clauses (i)–(iii) in fewer steps. Given that this ϕ is a formula, it must be a formula according to one of the clauses (i)–(iii). This means that either ϕ is a propositional letter (and we know what these are), or else it is a composite formula built up of simpler formulas. So ultimately everything reduces to propositional letters.

In a definition such as definition 1, objects are said to have a given property (in this case that of being a formula) if they can be constructed from other, 'simpler' objects with that property, and ultimately from some group of objects which are simply said to have that property. Such definitions are said to be *inductive* or *recursive*.

The circular definition of a sheep as the offspring of two sheep can be turned into an inductive definition (i) by stipulating two ancestral sheep, let us call them Adam and Eve; and (ii) by ruling that precisely those things are sheep which are required to be sheep by (i) and the clause saying that the offspring of two sheep is a sheep. The construction tree of any given sheep, according to this inductive definition, would be a complete family tree going back to the first ancestral sheep Adam and Eve (though contrary to usual practice with family trees, Adam and Eve will appear at the bottom).

Most of what follows applies equally to all propositional languages, so instead of referring to the formulas of any particular propositional language, we shall refer to *the formulas of propositional logic*.

Because the concept of a formula is defined inductively, we have at our disposal a simple method by which we can prove that all formulas have some particular property which we may be interested in. It is this. In order to prove that all formulas have a property A, it is sufficient to show that:

(i)   The propositional letters all have property A;
(ii) if a formula ϕ has A, then $\neg\phi$ must too;
(iii) if ϕ and ψ have property A, then $(\phi \wedge \psi)$, $(\phi \vee \psi)$, $(\phi \rightarrow \psi)$, and $(\phi \leftrightarrow \psi)$ must too.

This is sufficient because of induction clause (iv), which ensures that every composite formula must be composed of some simpler formula(s) from which it inherits property A. A proof of this sort is called a *proof by induction on the complexity of the formula* (or a *proof by induction on the length of the formula*). As an example of a proof by induction on the complexity of a formula, we have the following simple, rigorous proof of the fact that all formulas of propositional logic have just as many right brackets as left brackets:

(i)   Propositional letters have no brackets at all.
(ii) If ϕ has the same number of right brackets as left brackets, then $\neg\phi$ must too, since no brackets have been added or taken away.
(iii) If ϕ and ψ each have as many right brackets as left brackets, then $(\phi \wedge \psi)$, $(\phi \vee \psi)$, $(\phi \rightarrow \psi)$, and $(\phi \leftrightarrow \psi)$ must too, since in all of these exactly one left and one right bracket have been added.

Quite generally, for every inductive definition there is a corresponding kind of proof by induction.

There are various points in this book where if complete mathematical rigor had been the aim, inductive proofs would have been given. Instead we choose merely to note that strictly speaking, a proof is required.

The fact that the concept of a formula has been strictly defined by definition 1 enables us to give strict inductive definitions of notions about formulas. For example, let us define the function $(\phi)^0$ from formulas to natural numbers by:

$(p)^0 = 0,$
$(\neg\phi)^0 = (\phi)^0$
$((\phi * \psi))^0 = (\phi)^0 + (\psi)^0 + 2$, for each two-place connective $*$.

Then, for each formula ϕ, $(\phi)^0$ gives the number of brackets in the formula ϕ.

Exercise 3 ◇

(a) The *operator depth* of a formula of propositional logic is the maximal length of a 'nest' of operators occurring in it. E.g., $((\neg p \wedge q) \wedge \neg r)$ has operator depth 3. Give a precise definition of this notion, using the inductive definition of formulas.

(b) Think of the construction trees of formulas. What concepts are defined by means of the following ('simultaneous') induction?

$$A(p) = 1 \qquad\qquad\qquad B(p) = 1$$
$$A(\neg\psi) = A(\psi) + 1 \qquad\qquad A(\neg) = \max(B(\psi), A(\psi) + 1)$$
$$A(\psi \circ \chi) = \max(A(\psi), (A\chi)) + 1 \qquad B(\psi \circ \chi) = \max(B(\psi), B(\chi),$$
$$\text{for the two-place connectives } \circ \qquad A(\psi) + A(\chi) + 1),$$

Exercise 4 ◇

(a) What notions are described by the following definition by induction on formulas?
$$p^* = 0 \qquad\qquad\qquad \text{for propositional letters p}$$
$$(\neg\phi)^* = \phi^*$$
$$(\phi \circ \psi)^* = \phi^* + \psi^* + 1 \qquad \text{for two-place connectives } \circ$$
$$p^+ = 1$$
$$(\neg\phi)^+ = \phi^+$$
$$(\phi \circ \psi)^+ = \phi^+ + \psi^+ \qquad\qquad \text{for two-place connectives } \circ$$

(b) Prove by induction that for all formulas ϕ, $\phi^+ = \phi^* + 1$.

Exercise 5

In this exercise, the reader is required to translate various English sentences into propositional logic. An example is given which shows the kind of thing that is expected. We want a translation of the sentence:

If I have lost if I cannot make a move, then I have lost.

This sentence might, for example, be said by a player in a game of chess or checkers, if he couldn't see any move to make and didn't know whether the situation amounted to his defeat.

Solution

Translation: $(\neg p \to q) \to q$
Key: p: I can make a move; q: I have lost.

Translate the following sentences into propositional logic. Preserve as much of the structure as possible and in each case give the key.

(1) This engine is not noisy, but it does use a lot of energy.
(2) It is not the case that Guy comes if Peter or Harry comes.
(3) It is not the case that Cain is guilty and Abel is not.
(4) This has not been written with a pen or a pencil.
(5) John is not only stupid but nasty too.
(6) Johnny wants both a train and a bicycle from Santa Claus, but he will get neither.
(7) Nobody laughed or applauded.

(8)   I am going to the beach or the movies on foot or by bike.
(9)   Charles and Elsa are brother and sister or nephew and niece.
(10) Charles goes to work by car, or by bike and train.
(11) God willing, peace will come.
(12) If it rains while the sun shines, a rainbow will appear.
(13) If the weather is bad or too many are sick, the party is not on.
(14) John is going to school, and if it is raining so is Peter.
(15) If it isn't summer, then it is damp and cold, if it is evening or night.
(16) If you do not help me if I need you, I will not help you if you need me.
(17) If you stay with me if I won't drink any more, then I will not drink any more.
(18) Charles comes if Elsa does and the other way around.
(19) John comes only if Peter does not come.
(20) John comes exactly if Peter does not come.
(21) John comes just when Peter stays home.
(22) We are going, unless it is raining.
(23) If John comes, then it is unfortunate if Peter and Jenny come.
(24) If father and mother both go, then I won't, but if only father goes, then I will go too.
(25) If Johnny is nice he will get a bicycle from Santa Claus, whether he wants one or not.
(26) You don't mean it, and if you do, I don't believe you.
(27) If John stays out, then it is mandatory that Peter or Nicholas participates.

2.4 Functions

Having given an exact treatment of the syntax of languages for propositional logic, we shall now move on to their semantics, which is how they are interpreted. The above has shown that what we have in mind when we speak of the interpretation of a propositional language is the attribution of truth values to its sentences. Such attributions are called *valuations*. But these valuations are functions, so first we shall say some more about functions.

A function, to put it quite generally, is an attribution of a unique *value* (or *image,* as it is sometimes called) to each entity of some specific kind (for a valuation, to each sentence of the language in question). These entities are called the *arguments* (or *originals*) of the function, and together they form its *domain.* The entities which figure as the possible values of a function are collectively called its *range.* If x is an argument of the function f then f(x) is the value which results when f is *applied* to x. The word *value* must not be taken to imply that we are dealing with a truth value or any other kind of number here, since any kind of thing may appear in the range of a function. The only requirement is that no argument may have more than a single value. A few examples of functions are given in table 2.2. The left column of the table is understood to contain names of functions, so that *date of birth of x,* for ex-

Table 2.2 Examples of Functions

Function	Domain	Range
Date of birth of x	People	Dates
Mother of x	People	Women
Head of state of x	Countries	People
Frame number of x	Bicycles	Numbers
Negation of x	Formulas of propositional logic	Formulas of propositional logic
Capital city of x	Countries	Cities
Sex of x	People	The two sexes (masculine, feminine)

ample, is a name of the function which accepts people as its arguments and attributes to them as their values their dates of birth. The value of *date of birth of x* for the argument Winston Churchill is, for example, 30 November 1874.

In order to make what we mean clearer, compare the following expressions similar to those in the table, which may *not* be considered names of functions: *eldest brother of x* (domain: people) may not be taken as a function, since not everyone has a brother, so it is not possible to attribute a value to every argument. *Parent of x* is not a function either, but not because some people lack parents; the problem is that everyone has, or at least has had, no less than two parents. So the values are not unique. Similarly, *direct object of x* (domain: English sentences) is not a function, because not every sentence has a direct object, and *verb of x* is not a function since some sentences have more than one verb.

In addition, there are also functions which require two domain elements in order to specify a value, or three elements or more. Some examples are given in table 2.3. Functions which require two arguments from the domain in order to specify a value are said to be *binary,* and to generalize, functions which require n arguments are said to be *n*-ary. An example of an expression which accepts two arguments but which nevertheless does not express a binary function is *quotient of x and y* (domain: numbers). We are not dealing with a function here because the value of this expression is undefined for any x if y is taken as 0.

Functions can be applied to their own values or to those of other functions provided these are of the right kind, that is, that they fall within the domain of the function in question. Examples of functions applied to each other are *date of birth of the mother of John, mother of the head of state of France, mother of the mother of the mother of Peter, sex of the mother of Charles* and *sum of the difference between 6 and 3 and the difference between 4 and 2:* $(6 - 3) + (4 - 2)$.

As we have said, each function has its own particular domain and range. If A is the domain of a function f and B is its range, then we write f: $A \rightarrow B$ and we say that f is a *function from A to B,* and that f *maps A into B.* There is one important asymmetry between the domain of a function and its range, and that is that while a function must carry each element of its domain to some element of its range, this is not necessarily true the other way around: not every element of the range of a function needs to appear as the value of the function when applied to some element of its domain. The range contains all *possible* values of a function, and restricting it to the values which do in fact appear as values of the function is often inefficient. In the examples given above, a larger range has been chosen than is strictly necessary: all women instead of just those that are mothers in the case of *mother of x*, all people instead of just heads of state in *head of state of x*, and roads instead of roads forming the shortest route between cities in the case of *the shortest route between x and y*. In the special case in which every element of the range B of a function f appears as the value of that function when it is applied to some element of its domain A, we say that f is a function of A *onto* B. Of the functions in table 2.2, only *sex of x* is a function onto its range, and in table 2.3 only the sum and difference functions are, since every number is the sum of two other numbers and also the difference of two others.

The order of the arguments of a function can make a difference: the difference between 1 and 3 is -2, whereas that between 3 and 1 is $+2$. A binary function for which the order of the arguments makes no difference is said to be *commutative*. The sum function is an example of a commutative function, since the sum of x and y is always equal to the sum of y and x. One and the same object may appear more than once as an argument: there is, for example, a number which is the sum of 2 and 2.

The value of a function f when applied to arguments $x_1, \ldots, x_n$ is generally written in *prefix notation* as $f(x_1, \ldots, x_n)$, though *infix* notation is more usual for some well-known binary functions, such as $x + y$ for the sum of x and y, and $x - y$ for their difference, instead of $+(x, y)$ and $-(x, y)$, respectively.

A binary function f is said to be *associative* if for all objects x, y, z in its domain $f(x, f(y, z)) = f(f(x, y), z)$, or, in infix notation, if $xf(yfz) = (xfy)fz$. Clearly this notion only makes sense if f's range is part of its domain, since otherwise it will not always be possible to apply it to xfy and z. In other words, f is associative if it doesn't make any difference whether f is applied first to the first two of three arguments, or first to the second two. The sum

Table 2.3 Examples of Binary and Ternary Functions

Function	Domain	Range
Sum of x and y	Numbers	Numbers
Difference between x and y	Numbers	Numbers
Shortest route between x and y	Cities	Roads
Time at which the last train from x via y to z departs.	Stations	Moments of time

and the product of two numbers are associative functions, since for all numbers x, y, and z we have: $(x + y) + z = x + (y + z)$ and $(x \times y) \times z = x \times (y \times z)$. The difference function is not associative: $(4 - 2) - 2 = 0$, but $4 - (2 - 2) = 4$. The associativity of a function f means that that we can write $x_1 fx_2 fx_3 \ldots x_{n-1} fx_n$ without having to insert any brackets, since the value of the expression is independent of where they are inserted. Thus, for example, we have: $(x_1 + x_2) + (x_3 + x_4) = x_1 + ((x_2 + x_3) + x_4)$. First one has $(x_1 + x_2) + (x_3 + x_4) = x_1 + (x_2 + (x_3 + x_4))$, since $(x + y) + z = x + (y + z)$ for any x, y, and z, so in particular for $x = x_1$, $y = x_2$, and $z = x_3 + x_4$. And $x_1 + (x_2 + (x_3 + x_4)) = x_1 + ((x_2 + x_3) + x_4)$, since $x_2 + (x_3 + x_4) = (x_2 + x_3) + x_4$.

2.5 The Semantics of Propositional Logic

The valuations we have spoken of can now, in the terms just introduced, be described as (unary) functions mapping formulas onto truth values. But not every function with formulas as its domain and truth values as its range will do as a valuation. A valuation must agree with the interpretations of the connectives which are given in their truth tables. A function which attributes the value 1 to both p and ¬p, for example, cannot be accepted as a valuation, since it does not agree with the interpretation of negation. The truth table for ¬ (see (14)) rules that for every valuation V and for all formulas ϕ:

(i) $V(\neg\phi) = 1$ iff $V(\phi) = 0$.

This is because the truth value 1 is written under $\neg\phi$ in the truth table just in case a 0 is written under ϕ. Since $\neg\phi$ can only have 1 or 0 as its truth value (the range of V contains only 1 and 0), we can express the same thing by:

(i′) $V(\neg\phi) = 0$ iff $V(\phi) = 1$.

That is, a 0 is written under $\neg\phi$ just in case a 1 is written under ϕ.

Similarly, according to the other truth tables we have:

(ii) $V(\phi \wedge \psi) = 1$ iff $V(\phi) = 1$ and $V(\psi) = 1$.
(iii) $V(\phi \vee \psi) = 1$ iff $V(\phi) = 1$ or $V(\psi) = 1$.
(iv) $V(\phi \rightarrow \psi) = 0$ iff $V(\phi) = 1$ and $V(\psi) = 0$.
(v) $V(\phi \leftrightarrow \psi) = 1$ iff $V(\phi) = V(\psi)$.

Recall that *or* is interpreted as *and/or*. Clause (iii) can be paraphrased as: $V(\phi \vee \psi) = 0$ iff $V(\phi) = 0$ and $V(\phi) = 0$; (iv) as: $V(\phi \rightarrow \psi) = 1$ iff $V(\phi) = 0$ or $V(\psi) = 1$ (*or* = *and/or*). And if, perhaps somewhat artificially, we treat the truth values 1 and 0 as ordinary numbers, we can also paraphrase (iv) as: $V(\phi \rightarrow \psi) = 1$ iff $V(\phi) \leq V(\psi)$ (since while $0 \leq 0$, $0 \leq 1$, and $1 \leq 1$, we do not have $1 \leq 0$).

A valuation V is wholly determined by the truth values which it attributes to the propositional letters. Once we know what it does with the propositions, we can calculate the V of any formula ϕ by means of ϕ's construction tree. If

$V(p) = 1$ and $V(q) = 1$, for example, then $V(\neg(\neg p \wedge \neg q))$ can be calculated as follows. We see that $V(\neg p) = 0$ and $V(\neg q) = 0$, so $V(\neg p \wedge \neg q) = 0$ and thus $V(\neg(\neg p \wedge \neg q)) = 1$. Now it should be clear that only the values which V attributes to the proposition letters actually appearing in ϕ can have any influence on $V(\phi)$. So in order to see how the truth value of ϕ varies with valuations, it suffices to draw up what is called a *composite truth table,* in which the truth values of all subformulas of ϕ are calculated for every possible distribution of truth values among the propositional letters appearing in ϕ. To continue with the same example, the composite truth table for the formula $\neg(\neg p \wedge \neg q)$ is given as (31):

(31)

	1	2	3	4	5	6
	p	q	$\neg p$	$\neg q$	$\neg p \wedge \neg q$	$\neg(\neg p \wedge \neg q)$
V_1	1	1	0	0	0	1
V_2	1	0	0	1	0	1
V_3	0	1	1	0	0	1
V_4	0	0	1	1	1	0

The four different distributions of truth values among p and q are given in columns 1 and 2. In columns 3 and 4, the corresponding truth values of $\neg p$ and $\neg q$ have been given; they are calculated in accordance with the truth table for negation. Then in column 5 we see the truth values of $\neg p \wedge \neg q$, calculated from columns 3 and 4 using the truth table for conjunction. And finally, in column 6 we see the truth values of $\neg(\neg p \wedge \neg q)$ corresponding to each of the four possible distributions of truth values among p and q, which are calculated from column 5 by means of the truth table for negation.

The number of rows in the composite truth table for a formula depends only on the number of different propositional letters occurring in that formula. Two different propositional letters give rise to four rows, and we can say quite generally that n propositional letters give rise to 2^n rows, since that is the number of different distributions of the two truth values among n propositions. Every valuation corresponds to just one row in a truth table. So if we restrict ourselves to the propositional letters p and q, there are just four possible valuations: the V_1, V_2, V_3, and V_4 given in (31). And these four are the only valuations which matter for formulas in which p and q are the only propositional letters, since as we have just seen, what V does with ϕ is wholly determined by what V does with the propositional letters actually appearing in ϕ. This means that we may add new columns to (31) for the evaluation of as many formulas as we wish composed from just the letters p and q together with connectives. That this is of some importance can be seen as follows.

Note that the composite formula $\neg(\neg p \wedge \neg q)$ is true whenever any one of the proposition letters p and q is true, and false if both p and q are false. This is just the inclusive disjunction of p and q. Now consider the composite truth table given in (32):

(32)

	1	2	3	4	5	6	7
	p	q	¬p	¬q	¬p ∧ ¬q	¬(¬p ∧ ¬q)	p ∨ q
V_1	1	1	0	0	0	1	1
V_2	1	0	0	1	0	1	1
V_3	0	1	1	0	0	1	1
V_4	0	0	1	1	1	0	0

What we have done is add a new column to the truth table mentioned above in which the truth value of p ∨ q is given for each distribution of truth values among p and q, this being calculated in accordance with the truth table for the disjunction. This shows clearly that the truth values of ¬(¬p ∧ ¬q) and p ∨ q are the same under each valuation, since

$$V_1(\neg(\neg p \wedge \neg q)) = V_1(p \vee q) = 1;$$
$$V_2(\neg(\neg p \wedge \neg q)) = V_2(p \vee q) = 1;$$
$$V_3(\neg(\neg p \wedge \neg q)) = V_3(p \vee q) = 1;$$
$$V_4(\neg(\neg p \wedge \neg q)) = V_4(p \vee q) = 0.$$

So for every valuation V we have: $V(\neg(\neg p \wedge \neg q)) = V(p \vee q)$. The formulas ¬(¬p ∧ ¬q) and p ∨ q are *(logically) equivalent*. To put it more explicitly, ϕ and ψ are said to be *(logically) equivalent* just in case for every valuation V we have: $V(\phi) = V(\psi)$. The qualification *logical* is to preclude any confusion with *material equivalence*.

In order to see how all formulas of the form ¬(¬ϕ ∧ ¬ψ) and ϕ ∨ ψ behave under all possible valuations, a composite truth table just like (32) can be drawn up by means of the truth tables for negation, conjunction, and disjunction. The result is given in (33):

(33)

ϕ	ψ	¬ϕ	¬ψ	¬ϕ ∧ ¬ψ	¬(¬ϕ ∧ ¬ψ)	ϕ ∨ ψ
1	1	0	0	0	1	1
1	0	0	1	0	1	1
0	1	1	0	0	1	1
0	0	1	1	1	0	0

In this truth table it can clearly be seen that the equivalence of formulas of the form ¬(¬ϕ ∧ ¬ψ) and ϕ ∨ ψ is quite general (for a general explication of relationships of this sort, see theorem 13 in §4.2.2).

Consider another example. All formulas of the forms ¬¬ϕ and ϕ are equivalent, as is apparent from (34):

(34)

ϕ	¬ϕ	¬¬ϕ
1	0	1
0	1	0

This equivalence is known as the *law of double negation*. And the last example we shall give is a truth table which demonstrates that (ϕ ∨ ψ) ∨ χ is equivalent to ϕ ∨ (ψ ∨ χ), and (ϕ ∧ ψ) ∧ χ to ϕ ∧ (ψ ∧ χ); see (35):

(35)

ϕ	ψ	χ	$\phi \vee \psi$	$(\phi \vee \psi) \vee \chi$	$\psi \vee \chi$	$\phi \vee (\psi \vee \chi)$	$\phi \wedge \psi$	$(\phi \wedge \psi) \wedge \chi$	$\psi \wedge \chi$	$\phi \wedge (\psi \wedge \chi)$
1	1	1	1	1	1	1	1	1	1	1
1	1	0	1	1	1	1	1	0	0	0
1	0	1	1	1	1	1	0	0	0	0
1	0	0	1	1	0	1	0	0	0	0
0	1	1	1	1	1	1	0	0	1	0
0	1	0	1	1	1	1	0	0	0	0
0	0	1	0	1	1	1	0	0	0	0
0	0	0	0	0	0	0	0	0	0	0

The latter two equivalences are known as the *associativity of* ∧ and the *associativity of* ∨, respectively, by analogy with the concept which was introduced in connection with functions and which bears the same name. (For a closer connection between these concepts, see §2.6.) Just as with functions, the associativity of ∨ and ∧ means that we can omit brackets in formulas, since their meaning is independent of where they are placed. This assumes, of course, that we are only interested in the truth values of the formulas. In general, then, we shall feel free to write $\phi \wedge \psi \wedge \chi$, $(\phi \to \psi) \wedge (\psi \to \chi) \wedge (\chi \to \phi)$ etc. $\phi \wedge \psi \wedge \chi$ is true just in case all of ϕ, ψ, and χ are true, while $\phi \vee \psi \vee \chi$ is true just in case any one of them is true.

Exercise 6

A large number of well-known equivalences are given in this exercise. In order to get the feel of the method, it is worthwhile to demonstrate that a few of them are equivalences by means of truth tables and further to try to understand why they must hold, given what the connectives mean. The reader may find this easier if the metavariables ϕ, ψ, and χ are replaced by sentences derived from natural language.

Prove that in each of the following, all the formulas are logically equivalent to each other (independently of which formulas are represented by ϕ, ψ, and χ):

(a) ϕ, $\neg\neg\phi$, $\phi \wedge \phi$, $\phi \vee \phi$, $\phi \wedge (\phi \vee \psi)$, $\phi \vee (\phi \wedge \psi)$
(b) $\neg\phi$, $\phi \to (\psi \wedge \neg\psi)$
(c) $\neg(\phi \vee \psi)$, $\neg\phi \wedge \neg\psi$ (*De Morgan's Law*)
(d) $\neg(\phi \wedge \psi)$, $\neg\phi \vee \neg\psi$ (*De Morgan's Law*)
(e) $\phi \vee \psi$, $\psi \vee \phi$, $\neg\phi \to \psi$, $\neg(\neg\phi \wedge \neg\psi)$, $(\phi \to \psi) \to \psi$
(f) $\phi \wedge \psi$, $\psi \wedge \phi$, $\neg(\phi \to \neg\psi)$, $\neg(\neg\phi \vee \neg\psi)$
(g) $\phi \to \psi$, $\neg\phi \vee \psi$, $\neg(\phi \wedge \neg\psi)$, $\neg\psi \to \neg\phi$
(h) $\phi \to \neg\psi$, $\psi \to \neg\phi$ (*law of contraposition*)
(i) $\phi \leftrightarrow \psi$, $(\phi \to \psi) \wedge (\psi \to \phi)$, $(\phi \wedge \psi) \vee (\neg\phi \wedge \neg\psi)$
(j) $(\phi \vee \psi) \wedge \neg(\phi \wedge \psi)$, $\neg(\phi \leftrightarrow \psi)$, $\neg\phi \leftrightarrow \psi$, (and $\phi \infty \psi$, though officially it is not a formula of propositional logic according to the definition)
(k) $\phi \wedge (\psi \vee \chi)$, $(\phi \wedge \psi) \vee (\phi \wedge \chi)$ (*distributive law*)
(l) $\phi \vee (\psi \wedge \chi)$, $(\phi \vee \psi) \wedge (\phi \vee \chi)$ (*distributive law*)
(m) $(\phi \vee \psi) \to \chi$, $(\phi \to \chi) \wedge (\psi \to \chi)$
(n) $\phi \to (\psi \wedge \chi)$, $(\phi \to \psi) \wedge (\phi \to \chi)$
(o) $\phi \to (\psi \to \chi)$, $(\phi \wedge \psi) \to \chi$

The equivalence of $\phi \vee \psi$ and $\psi \vee \phi$ and of $\phi \wedge \psi$ and $\psi \wedge \phi$ as mentioned under (e) and (f) in exercise 6 are known as the *commutativity* of ∨ and ∧, respectively. (For the connection with the commutativity of functions, see §2.6.) Both the equivalence mentioned under (h) and the equivalence of $\phi \to \psi$ and $\neg\psi \to \neg\phi$ given in (g) in exercise 6 are known as the *law of contraposition*.

Logically equivalent formulas always have the same truth values. This means that the formula χ' which results when one subformula ϕ of a formula

χ is replaced by an equivalent formula ψ must itself be equivalent to χ. This is because the truth value of χ' depends on that of ψ in just the same way as the truth value of χ depends on that of ϕ. For example, if ϕ and ψ are equivalent, then $\phi \rightarrow \theta$ and $\psi \rightarrow \theta$ are too. One result of this is that the brackets in $(\phi \wedge \psi) \wedge \chi$ can also be omitted where it appears as a subformula of some larger formula, so that we can write $(\phi \wedge \psi \wedge \chi) \rightarrow \theta$, for example, instead of $((\phi \wedge \psi) \wedge \chi) \rightarrow \theta$, and $\theta \rightarrow ((\phi \rightarrow \psi) \wedge (\psi \leftrightarrow \chi) \wedge (\chi \vee \psi))$ instead of $\theta \rightarrow (((\phi \rightarrow \psi) \wedge (\psi \leftrightarrow \chi)) \wedge (\chi \vee \psi))$. More generally, we have here a useful way of proving equivalences on the basis of other equivalences which are known to hold. As an example, we shall demonstrate that $\phi \rightarrow (\psi \rightarrow \chi)$ is equivalent to $\psi \rightarrow (\phi \rightarrow \chi)$. According to exercise 6(o), $\phi \rightarrow (\psi \rightarrow \chi)$ is equivalent to $(\phi \wedge \psi) \rightarrow \chi$. Now $\phi \wedge \psi$ is equivalent to $\psi \wedge \phi$ (commutativity of $\wedge$), so $(\phi \wedge \psi) \rightarrow \chi$ is equivalent to $(\psi \wedge \phi) \rightarrow \chi$. Applying 6(o) once more, this time with ψ, ϕ, and χ instead of ϕ, ψ, and χ, we see that $(\psi \wedge \phi) \rightarrow \chi$ is equivalent to $\psi \rightarrow (\phi \rightarrow \chi)$. If we now link all these equivalences, we see that $(\phi \wedge \psi) \rightarrow \chi$ is equivalent to $\psi \rightarrow (\phi \rightarrow \chi)$, which is just what we needed.

Exercise 7 ◇

Show on the basis of equivalences of exercise 6 that the following formulas are equivalent:

(a) $\phi \leftrightarrow \psi$ and $\psi \leftrightarrow \phi$ (commutativity of $\leftrightarrow$)

(b) $\phi \rightarrow \neg\phi$ and $\neg\phi$

(c) $\phi \wedge (\psi \wedge \chi)$ and $\chi \wedge (\psi \wedge \phi)$

(d) $\phi \rightarrow (\phi \rightarrow \psi)$ and $\phi \rightarrow \psi$

(e) $\phi \infty \psi$ and $\phi \leftrightarrow \neg\psi$

(f) $\phi \infty \neg\psi$, $\neg\phi \infty \psi$, and $\phi \leftrightarrow \psi$

In a sense two equivalent formulas ϕ and ψ have the same meaning. We say that ϕ and ψ have the same *logical meaning*. So the remark made above can be given the following concise reformulation: logical meaning is conserved under replacement of a subformula by another formula which has the same logical meaning.

It is worth dwelling on the equivalence of $\phi \infty \psi$ and $\phi \leftrightarrow \neg\psi$ for a moment (exercise 7e). What this means is that A *unless* B and A *provided not* B have the same logical meaning: in logical terms then, (36) means the same as (37) (= (20)):

(36) We are going to see a film tonight, provided we are not going to the beach this afternoon.

(37) We are going to see a film tonight, unless we are going to the beach this afternoon.

Analogous points can be made with reference to the equivalences given in exercise 7f: A *unless not* B and *not* A *unless* B have the same logical meaning as A *provided* B, which means, among other things, that (38), (39) and (40) (= (29)) all express the same logical meaning:

(38)   We are going to see a film tonight unless the dishes have not been done.

(39)   We are not going to see a film tonight unless the dishes have been done.

(40)   We are going to see a film tonight, provided the dishes have been done.

There are, of course, various reasons why one sentence may be preferred to another in any given context. What the equivalence of (38), (39), and (40) shows is that the reasons have nothing to do with the logical meaning of the sentences. The differences between these sentences are presumably to be explained in terms of their conditions of use, and it is there also that an explanation is to be sought for the peculiar nature of a sentence like:

(41)   We are not going to see a film tonight provided we go to the beach this afternoon.

That there is a connection between material and logical equivalence is apparent if we compare the truth tables of the logically equivalent formulas p and ¬¬p, and p ∧ q and q ∧ p, with those of the material equivalences p ↔ ¬¬p and (p ∧ q) ↔ (q ∧ p); see figures (42) and (43):

(42)

p	¬p	¬¬p	p ↔ ¬¬p
1	0	1	1
0	1	0	1

(43)

p	q	p ∧ q	q ∧ p	(p ∧ q) ↔ (q ∧ p)
1	1	1	1	1
1	0	0	0	1
0	1	0	0	1
0	0	0	0	1

In both cases we see that just one truth value occurs in the columns for the material equivalences, namely, 1. This is of course not entirely coincidental. It is precisely because under any valuation V, V(p) = V(¬¬p) and V(p ∧ q) = V(q ∧ p) that we always have V(p ↔ ¬¬p) = 1 and V((p ∧ q) ↔ (q ∧ p)) = 1. Now this insight can be formulated as a general theorem:

Theorem 1

φ and ψ are logically equivalent iff for every valuation V, V(φ ↔ ψ) = 1.

Proof: Generally speaking, a proof of a theorem of the form: A iff B is divided into (i) a proof that if A then B; and (ii) a proof that if B then A. The proof under (i) is headed by a ⇒: and usually proceeds by first assuming A and then showing that B inevitably follows. The proof under (ii) is headed by a ⇐: and usually proceeds by first assuming B and then showing that A inevitably follows. So the proof of our first theorem goes like this:

> ⇒: Suppose ϕ and ψ are logically equivalent. This means that for every valuation V for the propositional letters occurring in ϕ and ψ, $V(\phi) = V(\psi)$. Then condition (v) on valuations says that we must have $V(\phi \leftrightarrow \psi) = 1$.
>
> ⇐: Suppose that $V(\phi \leftrightarrow \psi) = 1$ for all valuations V. Then there can be no V such that $V(\phi) \neq V(\psi)$, since otherwise $V(\phi \leftrightarrow \psi) = 0$; so for every V it must hold that $V(\phi) = V(\psi)$, whence ϕ and ψ are logically equivalent. □

The box □ indicates that the proof has been completed.

In theorem 2 in ‡4.2.2 we shall see that formulas ϕ such that $V(\phi) = 1$ for every valuation V are of special interest. These formulas can be known to be true without any information concerning the truth of the parts of which they are composed. Such formulas ϕ are called *tautologies,* and that ϕ is a tautology is expressed by $\vDash\phi$. So theorem 1 can now be rewritten as follows:

$$\vDash\phi \leftrightarrow \psi \text{ iff } \phi \text{ and } \psi \text{ are logically equivalent.}$$

Now theorem 1 gives us an ample supply of tautologies all at once, for example: $((\phi \vee \psi) \vee \chi) \leftrightarrow (\phi \vee (\psi \vee \chi))$, $(\phi \vee \psi) \leftrightarrow \neg(\neg\phi \wedge \neg\psi)$, de Morgan's laws, etc. And given that $\vDash\phi \rightarrow \psi$ and $\vDash\psi \rightarrow \phi$ whenever $\vDash\phi \leftrightarrow \psi$, we have even more. (This last is because if for every V, $V(\phi) = V(\psi)$, then we can be sure that for every V, $V(\phi) \leqslant V(\psi)$ and $V(\psi) \leqslant V(\phi)$.) As examples of tautologies we now have all formulas of the form $(\phi \rightarrow \neg\psi) \rightarrow (\psi \rightarrow \neg\phi)$, and all those of the form $((\phi \vee \psi) \rightarrow \chi) \rightarrow ((\phi \rightarrow \chi) \wedge (\psi \rightarrow \chi))$. But there are many more, for example, all formulas of the form $\phi \rightarrow (\psi \rightarrow \phi)$, as is apparent from figure (44):

(44) ϕ	ψ	$\psi \rightarrow \phi$	$\phi \rightarrow (\psi \rightarrow \phi)$
1	1	1	1
1	0	1	1
0	1	0	1
0	0	1	1

Exercise 8

Show of the following formulas that they are tautologies (for each ϕ, ψ, and χ):

(i) $\phi \rightarrow \phi$ (this actually follows from the equivalence of ϕ to itself)
(ii) $(\phi \wedge \psi) \rightarrow \phi$
(iii) $\phi \rightarrow (\phi \vee \psi)$
(iv) $\neg\phi \rightarrow (\phi \rightarrow \psi)$ (*ex falso sequitur quodlibet*)
(v) $\phi \vee \neg\phi$ (*law of the excluded middle*)
(vi) $(\phi \rightarrow (\psi \rightarrow \chi)) \rightarrow ((\phi \rightarrow \psi) \rightarrow (\phi \rightarrow \chi))$

(vii) $(\phi \rightarrow \psi) \vee (\psi \rightarrow \phi)$
(viii) $((\phi \rightarrow \psi) \rightarrow \phi) \rightarrow \phi$ *(Peirce's law)*

Obviously all tautologies are equivalent to each other; if we always have $V(\phi) = 1$ and $V(\psi) = 1$, then we certainly always have $V(\phi) = V(\psi)$.

That a formula ϕ is not a tautology is expressed as $\nvDash \phi$. If $\nvDash \phi$, then there is a valuation V such that $V(\phi) = 0$. Any such V is called a *counterexample to* ϕ (*'s being a tautology*). In §4.2.1 we shall go into this terminology in more detail. As an example we take the formula $(p \rightarrow q) \rightarrow (\neg p \rightarrow \neg q)$, which can be considered as the schema for invalid arguments like this: *If one has money, then one has friends. So if one has no money, then one has no friends.* Consider the truth table in (45):

(45) p	q	$\neg p$	$\neg q$	$p \rightarrow q$	$\neg p \rightarrow \neg q$	$(p \rightarrow q) \rightarrow (\neg p \rightarrow \neg q)$
1	1	0	0	1	1	1
1	0	0	1	0	1	1
0	1	1	0	1	0	0
0	0	1	1	1	1	1

It appears that $\nvDash (p \rightarrow q) \rightarrow (\neg p \rightarrow \neg q)$, since a 0 occurs in the third row of the truth table. This row is completely determined by the circumstance that $V(p) = 0$ and $V(q) = 1$, in the sense that for every valuation V with $V(p) = 0$ and $V(q) = 1$ we have $V((p \rightarrow q) \rightarrow (\neg p \rightarrow \neg q)) = 0$. For this reason we can say that $V(p) = 0$, $V(q) = 1$ is a counterexample to $(p \rightarrow q) \rightarrow (\neg p \rightarrow \neg q)$.

We must be very clear that in spite of this we cannot say whether a sentence of the form $(\phi \rightarrow \psi) \rightarrow (\neg \phi \rightarrow \neg \psi)$ is a tautology or not without more information about the ϕ and ψ. If, for example, we choose p for both ϕ and ψ, then we get the tautology $(p \rightarrow p) \rightarrow (\neg p \rightarrow \neg p)$, and if we choose $p \vee \neg p$ and q for ϕ and ψ, respectively, then we get the tautology $((p \vee \neg p) \rightarrow q) \rightarrow (\neg (p \vee \neg p) \rightarrow \neg q)$. But if we choose p and q for ϕ and ψ, respectively, then we arrive at the sentence $(p \rightarrow q) \rightarrow (\neg p \rightarrow \neg q)$, which, as we saw in (45), is not a tautology.

Exercise 9

Determine of the following formulas whether they are tautologies. If any is not, give a counterexample. (Why is this exercise formulated with p and q, and not with ϕ and ψ as in exercise 8?)

(i) $(p \rightarrow q) \rightarrow (q \rightarrow p)$ (iv) $((p \vee q) \wedge (\neg p \rightarrow \neg q)) \rightarrow q$
(ii) $p \vee (p \rightarrow q)$ (v) $((p \rightarrow q) \rightarrow p) \rightarrow ((p \rightarrow q) \rightarrow q)$
(iii) $(\neg p \vee \neg q) \rightarrow \neg (p \vee q)$ (vi) $((p \rightarrow q) \rightarrow r) \rightarrow (p \rightarrow (q \rightarrow r))$

Closely related to the tautologies are those sentences ϕ such that for every valuation V, $V(\phi) = 0$. Such formulas are called *contradictions*. Since they are never true, only to utter a contradiction is virtually to contradict oneself. Best known are those of the form $\phi \wedge \neg \phi$ (see figure (46)).

(46)

ϕ	$\neg\phi$	$\phi \wedge \neg\phi$
1	0	0
0	1	0

We can obtain many contradictions from

Theorem 2

If ϕ is a tautology, then $\neg\phi$ is a contradiction.

Proof: Suppose ϕ is a tautology. Then for every V, $V(\phi) = 1$. But then for every V it must hold that $(V\ \neg\phi) = 0$. So according to the definition, $\neg\phi$ is a contradiction. $\square$

So $\neg((\phi \wedge \psi) \leftrightarrow (\psi \wedge \phi))$, $\neg(\phi \rightarrow \phi)$, and $\neg(\phi \vee \neg\phi)$ are contradictions, for example. An analogous proof gives us

Theorem 3

If ϕ is a contradiction, then $\neg\phi$ is a tautology.

This gives us some more tautologies of the form $\neg(\phi \wedge \neg\phi)$, the *law of noncontradiction*. All contradictions are equivalent, just like the tautologies. Those formulas which are neither tautologies nor contradictions are called *(logical) contingencies*. These are formulas ϕ such that there is both a valuation V_1 with $V_1(\phi) = 1$ and a valuation V_2 with $V_2(\phi) = 0$. The formula ϕ has, in other words, at least one 1 written under it in its truth table and at least one 0. Many formulas are contingent. Here are a few examples: p, q, p $\wedge$ q, p $\rightarrow$ q, p $\vee$ q, etc. It should be clear that not all contingencies are equivalent to each other. One thing which can be said about them is:

Theorem 4

ϕ is a contingency iff $\neg\phi$ is a contingency.

Proof: (Another proof could be given from theorems 2 and 3, but this direct proof is no extra effort.)

$\Rightarrow$: Suppose ϕ is contingent. Then there is a V_1 with $V_1(\phi) = 1$ and a V_2 with $V_2(\phi) = 0$. But then we have $V_2(\neg\phi) = 1$ and $V_1(\neg\phi) = 0$, from which it appears that ϕ is contingent.

$\Leftarrow$: Proceeds just like $\Rightarrow$. $\square$

Exercise 10

Let ϕ be a tautology, ψ a contradiction, and χ a contingency. Which of the following sentences are (i) tautological, (ii) contradictory, (iii) contingent, (iv) logically equivalent to χ.
(1) $\phi \wedge \chi$; (2) $\phi \vee \chi$; (3) $\psi \wedge \chi$; (4) $\psi \vee \chi$; (5) $\phi \wedge \psi$; (6) $\phi \vee \psi$; (7) $\chi \rightarrow \psi$.

Exercise 11

(i)   Prove the following general assertions:
    (a) If $\phi \rightarrow \psi$ is a contradiction, then ϕ is a tautology and ψ a contradiction.
    (b) $\phi \wedge \psi$ is a tautology iff ϕ and ψ are both tautologies.

(ii)   Refute the following general assertion by giving a formula to which it does not apply.
    If $\phi \vee \psi$ is a tautology, then ϕ is a tautology or ψ is a tautology.

(iii) ◊ Prove the following general assertion:
    If ϕ and ψ have no propositional letters in common, then $\phi \vee \psi$ is a tautology iff ϕ is a tautology or ψ is a tautology.

Before we give the wrong impression, we should emphasize that propositional logic is not just the science of tautologies or inference. Our semantics can just as well serve to model other important intellectual processes such as *accumulation of information*. Valuations on some set of propositional letters may be viewed as (descriptions of) states of the world, or situations, as far as they are expressible in this vocabulary. Every formula then restricts attention to those valuations ('worlds') where it holds: its 'information content'. More dynamically, successive new formulas in a discourse narrow down the possibilities, as in figure (47).

(47)

In the limiting case a unique description of one actual world may result. Note the inversion in the picture: the more worlds there still are in the information range, the less information it contains. Propositions can be viewed here as transformations on information contents, (in general) reducing uncertainty.

Exercise 12 ◊

Determine the valuations after the following three successive stages in a discourse (see (47)):

    (1) $\neg(p \wedge (q \rightarrow r))$; (2) $\neg(p \wedge (q \rightarrow r))$, $(p \rightarrow r) \rightarrow r$; (3) $\neg(p \wedge (q \rightarrow r))$, $(p \rightarrow r) \rightarrow r$, $r \rightarrow (p \vee q)$.

2.6 Truth functions

The connectives were not introduced categorematically when we discussed the syntax of propositional logic, but syncategorematically. And parallel to this, they were not interpreted directly in §2.5, but contextually. We did not interpret $\wedge$ itself; we just indicated how $\phi \wedge \psi$ should be interpreted once interpretations are fixed for ϕ and ψ. It is, however, quite possible to interpret $\wedge$ and the other connectives directly, as *truth functions;* these are functions with truth values as not only their range but also their domain.

The connective $\wedge$, for example, can be interpreted as the function $f_\wedge$ such that $f_\wedge(1, 1) = 1$, $f_\wedge(1, 0) = 0$, $f_\wedge(0, 1) = 0$, and $f_\wedge(0, 0) = 0$. Analogously, as interpretations of $\vee$, $\rightarrow$, and $\leftrightarrow$, the functions $f_\vee$, $f_\rightarrow$, and $f_{\leftrightarrow}$ can be given, these being defined by:

$f_\vee(1, 1) = f_\vee(1, 0) = f_\vee(0, 1) = 1$ and $f_\vee(0, 0) = 0$.
$f_\rightarrow(1, 1) = f_\rightarrow(0, 1) = f_\rightarrow(0, 0) = 1$ and $f_\rightarrow(1, 0) = 0$.
$f_{\leftrightarrow}(1, 1) = f_{\leftrightarrow}(0, 0) = 1$ and $f_{\leftrightarrow}(1, 0) = f_{\leftrightarrow}(0, 1) = 0$.

Finally, $\neg$ can be interpreted as the unary truth function $f_\neg$ defined by $f_\neg(1) = 0$ and $f_\neg(0) = 1$. Then, for every V we have $V(\neg \phi) = f_\neg(V(\phi))$; and if $\circ$ is any one of our binary connectives, then for every V we have $V(\phi \circ \psi) = f_\circ(V(\phi), V(\psi))$.

The language of propositional logic can very easily be enriched by adding new truth-functional connectives, such as, for example, the connective ∞ with, as its interpretation, f_∞ defined by $f_\infty(1, 0) = f_\infty(0, 1) = 1$ and $f_\infty(1, 1) = f_\infty(0, 0) = 0$. Conversely, a connective can be introduced which is to be interpreted as any truth function one might fancy.

But it turns out that there is a sense in which all of this is quite unnecessary, since we already have enough connectives to express any truth functions which we might think up. Let us begin with the unary truth functions. Of these there are just four (see figures (48a–d)):

(48)

a. f_1		b. f_2		c. f_3		d. f_4	
x	$f_1(x)$	x	$f_2(x)$	x	$f_3(x)$	x	$f_4(x)$
1	1	1	1	1	0	1	0
0	1	0	0	0	1	0	0

Apparently f_1, f_2, f_3, and f_4 are the only candidates to serve as the interpretation of a truth-functional unary connective. Now it is easy enough to find formulas whose truth tables correspond precisely to those truth functions. Just take $p \vee \neg p$, p, $\neg p$, and $p \wedge \neg p$.

There are exactly sixteen binary truth functions, and as it is not difficult to see, the general expression for the number of n-ary truth functions is 2^{2^n}. Now it can be proved that all of these truth functions can be expressed by means of the connectives which we already have at our disposal. That is, there is a general method which generates, given the table of any truth function at all, a formula with this table as its truth table. That is, the following theorem can be proved:

Theorem 5 (*functional completeness of propositional logic*)

If f is an n-ary truth function, then there is a formula ϕ with n propositional variables $p_1, \ldots, p_n$ such that for every valuation V of $p_1, \ldots, p_n$, $V(\phi) = f(V(p_1), \ldots, V(p_n))$.

Sketch of a proof. We shall not give a general description of the method, but shall illustrate it with reference to the ternary truth function f given in truth table (49):

(49) x	y	z	f(x, y, z)
1	1	1	0
1	1	0	0
1	0	1	1
1	0	0	0
0	1	1	1
0	1	0	1
0	0	1	0
0	0	0	0

What we are looking for, to recapitulate, is a formula ϕ with propositional variables p, q, and r with table (49) as its truth table; ϕ is supposed to have the truth value 1 in three different rows of its truth table, namely, the third, fifth, and sixth rows. We now construct three formulas ϕ_1, ϕ_2, and ϕ_3 which have a 1 in just one row of their truth tables, in the third, fifth, and sixth rows, respectively—just the points where ϕ is supposed to have a 1, that is, ϕ_1 must be true if and only if p is true, q is untrue, and r is true. So for ϕ_1 we can just take the formula: $p \land \neg q \land r$. Similarly, we can choose $\neg p \land q \land r$ and $\neg p \land q \land \neg r$ as ϕ_2 and ϕ_3, respectively. Now for ϕ we just take the disjunction of ϕ_1, ϕ_2, and ϕ_3: $\phi = \phi_1 \lor \phi_2 \lor \phi_3 = (p \land \neg q \land r) \lor (\neg p \land q \land r) \lor (\neg p \land q \land \neg r)$; ϕ is indeed the formula we want, since it gets a 1 in the third row of its truth table because ϕ_1 does, in the fifth row because ϕ_2 does, and in the sixth row because ϕ_3 does, while there is a 0 in all the other rows because all of ϕ_1, ϕ_2, and ϕ_3 have a 0 there. It is clear that this procedure can be followed for all truth functions, independently of the number of places they may have (with the one exception of a truth table in which only 0 appears, but in that case we can choose any contradiction as our ϕ). □

A system of connectives which, like $\land$, $\lor$, and $\neg$, can express all truth functions is said to be *functionally complete*. Because the system comprising $\land$, $\lor$, and $\neg$ is functionally complete, the larger system comprising $\land$, $\lor$, $\neg$, $\rightarrow$, and $\leftrightarrow$ is too, so these five connectives are certainly enough to express every possible truth-functional connective.

It is not at all difficult, having come this far, to show that $\neg$ and $\lor$ form a complete truth-functional system on their own. We already know that every truth function can be expressed by means of $\wedge$, $\vee$, and $\neg$. Furthermore, $\phi \wedge \psi$ and $\neg(\neg\phi \vee \neg\psi)$ are equivalent for all formulas ϕ and ψ (see exercise 6f). Now for every truth function there is a formula χ with connectives $\wedge$, $\vee$, and $\neg$ which expresses it. What we now do is just replace each subformula of the form $\phi \wedge \psi$ by the equivalent formula $\neg(\neg\phi \vee \neg\psi)$. The ultimate result is a formula χ' with $\vee$ and $\neg$ as its only connectives equivalent to χ, which thus expresses the same truth function as χ.

Exercise 13

(a) Give a formula with only $\vee$ and $\neg$ which is equivalent to
$$(p \wedge \neg q \wedge r) \vee (\neg p \wedge q \wedge r) \vee (\neg p \wedge q \wedge \neg r).$$
(b) Show that $\neg$ forms, together with $\wedge$, a functionally complete set of connectives, and that $\neg$ with $\rightarrow$ does too. (This last combination was Frege's choice in his *Begriffsschrift*.)
(c) The connective $¥$ (the *Quine dagger*) can be defined according to the truth table. Show that $¥$ by itself is a complete set of connectives. (Hint: first try to express $\neg$ with only $¥$, and then $\vee$ with only $¥$ and $\neg$.) Which conjunction in natural language corresponds to $¥$?

ϕ	ψ	$(\phi \; ¥ \; \psi)$
1	1	0
1	0	0
0	1	0
0	0	1

Exercise 14 ◇

Determine the maximal number of logically nonequivalent formulas that can be constructed from two propositional letters p, q using material implication only.

Exercise 15 ◇

Call a binary truth function f *conservative* if always $f(x, y) = f(x, f_\wedge(x, y))$. Call a truth function *truly binary* if its truth table cannot be defined using only unary truth functions. Determine all propositional formulas with two propositional letters p and q with truly binary conservative truth functions.

We now return to the concepts of commutativity and associativity. From the perspective which we have just developed, the commutativity and associativity of $\vee$ and $\wedge$ amount, quite simply, to the commutativity and associativity of $f_\vee$ and $f_\wedge$. For all truth values x, y, and z we have: $f_\vee(x, y) = f_\vee(y, x)$ and $f_\wedge(x, y) = f_\wedge(y, x)$; $f_\vee(x, f_\vee(y, z)) = f_\vee(f_\vee(x, y), z)$; and $f_\wedge(x, f_\wedge(y, z)) = f_\wedge(f_\wedge(x, y), z)$. And these are not the only associative connectives, $\leftrightarrow$ and ∞ being two more examples (in contrast to $\rightarrow$ and $¥$). As far as $\leftrightarrow$ is concerned, this can easily be read in (50):

(50) ϕ	ψ	χ	$\phi \leftrightarrow \psi$	$(\phi \leftrightarrow \psi) \leftrightarrow \chi$	$\psi \leftrightarrow \chi$	$\phi \leftrightarrow (\psi \leftrightarrow \chi)$
1	1	1	1	1	1	1
1	1	0	1	0	0	0
1	0	1	0	0	0	0
1	0	0	0	1	1	1
0	1	1	0	0	1	0
0	1	0	0	1	0	1
0	0	1	1	1	0	1
0	0	0	1	0	1	0

The associativity of ∞ can also be proved from figure (50) by means of the equivalence of $\theta \infty \theta'$ and $\neg(\theta \leftrightarrow \theta')$, and that of $\neg\theta \infty \theta'$ and $\theta \leftrightarrow \theta'$ (see exercise 6f). The formula $(\phi \infty \psi) \infty \chi$ is equivalent to $\neg(\phi \leftrightarrow \psi) \infty \chi$ and thus also to $\neg\neg(\phi \rightarrow \psi) \leftrightarrow X$ and to $(\phi \leftrightarrow \psi) \leftrightarrow \chi$, and in view of the associativity of $\leftrightarrow$, to $\phi \leftrightarrow (\psi \leftrightarrow \chi)$, using commutativity of $\leftrightarrow$ and ∞, to $\phi \infty \neg(\psi \leftrightarrow \chi)$, and finally to $\phi \infty (\psi \infty \chi)$. Now it might seem natural to leave out the brackets in these expressions just as we did with $\wedge$ and $\vee$, and just to write $\phi \leftrightarrow \psi \leftrightarrow \chi$ and $\phi \infty \psi \infty \chi$. There is, however, one thing we would have to watch out for. We would be inclined to read $\phi \leftrightarrow \psi \leftrightarrow \chi$ as ϕ *iff* ψ *and* ψ *iff* χ (in other words, $\phi \leftrightarrow \psi \leftrightarrow \chi$ iff $V(\phi) = V(\psi) = V(\chi)$) and thus to assume that $\vDash \phi \leftrightarrow \psi \leftrightarrow \chi$ just in case ϕ, ψ, and χ are logically equivalent; and we would be inclined to read $\phi \infty \psi \infty \chi$ as *either ϕ, ψ, or χ*. But it is apparent from truth table (50) that this would be a mistake. What the above has shown is that $\phi \leftrightarrow \psi \leftrightarrow \chi$ and $\phi \infty \psi \infty \chi$ are, in fact, equivalent. This also shows that the natural language conjunction *either . . . or . . . or* is essentially ternary, and cannot be thought of as two applications of a binary, truth-functional connective; this in contrast to the inclusive *or . . . or* which can be constructed in this manner. Similarly, it can be shown that *either . . . , . . . , . . . or* is essentially quaternary, etc.

2.7 Coordinating and subordinating connectives

From a syntactic point of view, the connectives of propositional logic are *co-ordinating:* they combine two formulas in one new formula in which they both have the same role to play. And the conjunctions in natural language which correspond to the logical conjunction and disjunction, *and* and *or,* are coordinating conjunctions too. But this does not apply to the conjunction corresponding to implication, *if(. . . , then),* which from a syntactic point of view is said to be *subordinating.* Together with a sentence A this conjunction forms phrases *if A* which may modify other sentences B to form new sentences *if A then B.*

We saw in §2.6 that connectives can be interpreted directly by means of truth functions. Given this, it is also possible to introduce subordinating connectives into a propositional language. In this paragraph we shall treat the implication as a subordinating connective, and we shall do this in such a way that the meaning of formulas with the subordinating implication is the same as that of the corresponding formulas with the coordinating implication. The advantage is that we thus achieve a better agreement between the conjunctions of natural language and the connectives in our logical languages.

In what follows we shall give a definition of the languages for propositional logic which to some extent departs from the usual one. We do this not only in order to introduce subordinating connectives but also in order to show how the principle of the compositionality of meaning can be made explicit. This principle can be formulated as follows: the meaning of a composite expression is uniquely determined by the meanings of the expressions of which it is composed. This presupposes that the meanings of all noncomposite expressions have been specified and that the syntactic rules are interpreted. By this we mean that it must be clear how the meaning of a composite expression formed by any given rule depends on the meanings of the expressions from which it has been formed. Now in the syntax of languages for propositional logic it is usual not to treat the connectives as independent expressions but to introduce them syncategorematically and to interpret them contextually. This may seem to contradict the principle of the compositionality of meaning, but that is not the case. The meaning of, for example, the connective $\wedge$ is, as it were, hidden in the syntactic rule by means of which $\wedge$ is syncategorematically introduced. You could say that the principle is implicitly present.

The role of the principle can be made more explicit by interpreting the connectives directly, by means of truth functions. It then seems natural also to treat them as independent expressions of the language. If we do that, then propositional languages will have at least two different categories of expressions: connectives and formulas. But the connectives do not form a homogeneous group. The conjunction and the disjunction are binary: they bind two formulas together as one new formula, whereas negation is unary: it turns a single formula into another when placed in front of it. Thus we have three categories of expressions: formulas, unary connectives, and binary connectives. If in addition to this, the implication is introduced as a subordinating connective, then a fourth category originates. The subordinating implication turns a formula into an expression which functions just like negation, in the sense that it turns a single formula into another when placed in front of it. Together with such a formula, the subordinating implication forms, in other words, a composite unary connective. So, in two of these four categories we have, besides the basic or noncomposite expressions, composite expressions: in the category of formulas and in the category of unary connectives.

Before we give a precise definition, we make a short comment on brackets. In definition 1 in §2.3 we stated that $(\phi \wedge \psi)$ and $\neg \phi$ are formulas if ϕ and ψ are, only to leave off the brackets at a later stage. Another method would be to place brackets like this: $(\phi) \wedge (\psi)$, and $\neg(\phi)$. This guarantees the unambiguity of formulas too, and if the brackets around propositional letters are omitted, then the result is just the same; for example, (p ∧ q) becomes (p) ∧ (q) and after removing the brackets we have p ∧ q once again. But if the language is extended by adding subordinating connectives, then this way of dealing with brackets increases readability.

We now give the alternative definition for languages for propositional logic. The *vocabulary* contains, besides the brackets, expressions which can be put into the following four categories:

(i)   formulas: the propositional letters are the basic expressions in this category;
(ii)   unary connectives: the basic expression is the negation ¬;
(iii)   coordinating binary connectives: the basic expressions are the conjunction ∧ and the disjunction ∨;
(iv)   subordinating connectives: the basic expression is the implication ↦.

The *syntax* has the following rules, which define what expressions the different categories contain:

(i)   A basic expression in any category is an expression in that category.
(ii)   If φ is a formula and | is a subordinating connective, then |(φ) is a unary connective.
(iii)   If φ is a formula and + is a unary connective, then +(φ) is a formula.
(iv)   If φ and ψ are formulas and ∘ is a binary connective, then (φ) ∘ (ψ) is a formula.
(v)   Categories contain only those expressions they are required to by some finite number of applications of clauses (i)–(iv).

Clause (ii) enables us to construct composite unary connectives. A few examples of unary connectives are given in (51):

(51)   *unary connective*   *meaning*
        ↦p   if p (then)
        ↦(p ∧ q)   if p and q (then)
        ¬   not
        ↦(p ∨ (q ∧ r))   if p or (q and r) (then)
        ↦(↦pq)   if (q if p) (then)

Clause (iii) enables us to construct negations of formulas, like ¬p and ¬(p ∧ q), by means of the noncomposite connective ¬. But besides this, it also enables us to construct new formulas by means of the new composite unary connectives. Some examples are given in (52):

(52)

subordinating	meaning	coordinating
↦pq	if p (then) q	p → q
↦(p ∧ q)q	if p and q (then) q	(p ∧ q) → q
↦p(p ∨ q)	if p (then) p or q	p → (p ∨ q)

¬(↦pq)	it is not the case that if p (then) q	¬(p → q)
(↦pq) ∧ (↦qp)	if p (then) q and if q (then) p	(p → q) ∧ (q → p)
↦p(↦qr)	if p (then) if q (then) r	p → (q → r)

The corresponding formulas with the coordinating connective → are given in the last column of (52).

Now that we have modified the syntax, we must adjust the semantics to fit. A prerequisite is that the new formulas of form ↦(ϕ)(ψ) must receive exactly the same interpretation as the original formulas of form $\phi \to \psi$. In accordance with the principle of compositionality, the semantic interpretation goes as follows: (a) the basic expressions are interpreted; (b) for each syntactic clause which combines expressions with each other (these are just the clauses (ii), (iii), and (iv)), we specify how the interpretation of the combination is to be obtained from the interpretations of the expressions thus combined. Since besides the usual propositional letters the basic expressions now include the connectives ¬, ∧, ∨, and ↦, these must also be interpreted. This means that an interpretation V which only works on formulas will no longer do. We need a general interpretation function I with not only formulas but also basic and composite connectives in its domain.

In §2.6, where it was shown that connectives can be interpreted directly, implicit use was made of the sort of interpretation function we have in mind. There the unary connectives were interpreted as unary truth functions, as functions which take truth values as their arguments and give truth values as their values. The binary coordinating connectives were interpreted as binary truth functions, functions which accept ordered pairs of truth values as their arguments and give truth values as their values. The interpretation which the interpretation function I gives to the basic expressions in these categories can now be given as follows:

$$(53) \quad \begin{aligned} I(\neg) &= f_\neg \\ I(\wedge) &= f_\wedge \\ I(\vee) &= f_\vee \end{aligned}$$

The truth functions $f_\neg$, $f_\wedge$, and $f_\vee$ are defined as in §2.6. The interpretation function I also functions as a valuation, that is, it attributes truth values to the propositional letters. So now we have given the interpretation of all the basic expressions except one: the subordinating connective ↦. Before discussing its interpretation, let us first state how the interpretations of the wholes formed by syntactic clauses (ii) and (iv) depend on the interpretations given to the parts from which they have been formed. First clause (iv):

$$(54) \quad \text{If } \phi \text{ and } \psi \text{ are formulas and } \circ \text{ is a binary connective, then}$$
$$I((\phi) \circ (\psi)) = I(\circ)(I(\phi), I(\psi)).$$

For example, on the basis of (54) and (53), $I(p \wedge q) = I(\wedge)(I(p), I(q)) = f_\wedge(I(p), I(q))$.

The interpretation of formulas formed by means of rule (iii) is as follows:

(55) $I(+(\phi)) = I(+)(I(\phi))$

For example, (55) and (53) determine that $I(\neg p) = I(\neg)(I(p)) = f_\neg(I(p))$.

Besides the basic expression $\neg$, however, we also have composite expressions of the form $\mapsto(\phi)$ in the category of unary connectives. The latter expressions are formed by means of syntactic clause (ii), and this brings us to the matter of the interpretation of this rule or, to put it more precisely, to the expressions which can be formed by means of this rule. These expressions are all unary connectives, which must thus be given a semantic interpretation as unary truth functions. According to the principle of semantic compositionality, the interpretation of a composite expression depends on the interpretations of the expressions of which it is composed. That means that the unary truth function which is the interpretation of $\mapsto(\phi)$ must depend on the interpretation of ϕ, that is, on ϕ's truth value. So this brings us to the interpretation of $\mapsto$ itself. $I(\mapsto)$ is not itself a truth function. It must be a function $g_\mapsto$ mapping truth values onto unary truth functions. But we want formulas of the form $\mapsto(\phi)(\psi)$ to mean the same thing as the old formulas of the form $\phi \to \psi$, so this doesn't leave us much choice as to the function $g_\mapsto$. If the antecedent of an implication is false, then the implication must as a whole be true, no matter what the truth value of the consequent is. And if its antecedent is true, then the truth value of the implication as a whole is equal to that of its consequent. This means that $g_\mapsto$ must be defined as follows:

(56) $g_\mapsto(0) = f_1$
$g_\mapsto(1) = f_{id}$

f_1 and f_{id} are the following unary truth functions:

(57) $f_1(0) = f_1(1) = 1$
(58) $f_{id}(0) = 0;\ f_{id}(1) = 1$

The interpretation of the basic expression $\mapsto$ is given by:

(59) $I(\mapsto) = g_\mapsto$

And the interpretation of syntactic rule (ii) is then:

(60)   If ϕ is a formula and $|$ is a subordinating connective, then
$I(|(\phi)) = I(|)(I(\phi))$.

So now the interpretation of syntactic clause (iii), given in (55), is complete too, and we have, for example:

$I(\mapsto pq) = I(\mapsto p)(I(q)) = (I(\mapsto)(I(p)))(I(q)) = (g_\mapsto(I(p)))(I(q))$.

We shall now review the different parts of the semantic interpretation. An interpretation is a function I such that:

(i)   (a) $I(p) = 0$ or 1 for all propositional letters in the vocabulary,
     (b) $I(\neg) = f_\neg$;
     (c) $I(\wedge) = f_\wedge$;
     (d) $I(\vee) = f_\vee$;
     (e) $I(\mapsto) = g_\mapsto$.

(ii)   If ϕ is a formula and $|$ is a subordinating connective, then $I(|(\phi)) = I(|)(I(\phi))$.

(iii)   If ϕ is a formula and $+$ is a unary connective, then $I(+(\phi)) = I(+)(I(\phi))$.

(iv)   If ϕ and ψ are formulas and $\circ$ is a binary connective, then $I((\phi) \circ (\psi)) = I(\circ)(I(\phi), I(\psi))$.

The interpretation function I thus functions as a valuation which attributes truth values to atomic formulas (clauses (iii) and (iv)) and to composite formulas (clauses (iii) and (iv)). But I attributes an interpretation to all the other expressions too, to the noncomposite connectives (clauses (ib–e)) and to the composite connectives (clause (ii)).

In order to see that formulas of the form $\mapsto(\phi)(\psi)$ are in fact interpreted in just the same way as formulas of the form $\phi \rightarrow \psi$ always were, we suppose that the binary connective $\rightarrow$ is also present, being interpreted according to:

(61) $I(\rightarrow) = f_\rightarrow$

where $f_\rightarrow$ is defined as in §2.6. We shall now show that for every interpretation function I we have $I(\mapsto(\phi)(\psi)) = I(\phi \rightarrow \psi)$. To this end we examine each of the four possible distributions of truth values among ϕ and ψ, in each case satisfying ourselves that the truth values of $\mapsto(\phi)(\psi)$ and $\phi \rightarrow \psi$ are identical.

(a) Suppose $I(\phi) = I(\psi) = 1$:
    then $I(\phi \rightarrow \psi) = I(\rightarrow)(I(\phi), I(\psi)) = f_\rightarrow(1, 1) = 1$;
    and $I(\mapsto(\phi)(\psi)) = I(\mapsto\phi)(I(\psi)) = (I(\mapsto)(I(\phi)))(I(\psi)) = (g_\rightarrow(1))(1) = f_{id}(1) = 1$.

(b) Suppose $I(\phi) = 1$ and $I(\psi) = 0$:
    then $I(\phi \rightarrow \psi) = \ldots = f_\rightarrow(1, 0) = 0$;
    and $I(\mapsto(\phi)(\psi)) = \ldots = (g_\rightarrow(1))(0) = f_{id}(0) = 0$.

(c) Suppose $I(\phi) = 0$ and $I(\psi) = 1$:
    then $I(\phi \rightarrow \psi) = \ldots = f_\rightarrow(0, 1) = 1$;
    and $I(\mapsto(\phi)(\psi)) = \ldots = (g_\rightarrow(0))(1) = f_1(0) = 1$.

(d) Suppose $I(\phi) = 0 = I(\psi) = 0$:
    then $I(\phi \rightarrow \psi) = \ldots = f_\rightarrow(0, 0) = 1$;
    and $I(\mapsto(\phi)(\psi)) = \ldots = (g_\rightarrow(0))(0) = f_1(0) = 1$.

What all this means of course is that from a logical point of view nothing is gained or lost by this alternative way of setting up propositional logic. But at least it does show that there are other ways of setting it up. One advantage of doing so is to emphasize the parallels between the language of propositional logic and the syntax of natural language. It also becomes clear that another syntax need not necessarily lead to another semantic interpretation, though of course the details of how the semantics is set up will have to be adjusted because of the direct relationship between the way a formula is constructed and the way its interpretation is constructed. Another advantage, which doesn't really have much to do with subordinating and coordinating connectives, is the following: By not introducing the connectives syncategorematically but as independent expressions with their own semantic interpretations, the way the principle of compositionality works is more clearly displayed.

Exercise 16

How can the binary connective ∧ (conjunction) be treated 'stepwise' in the same way as implication?

3 Predicate Logic

3.1 Atomic Sentences

A language for predicate logic, as before, consists of logical constants, logical variables, and auxiliary symbols. Among the logical constants we have the familiar connectives, and brackets are still to be found among the auxiliary signs, but both categories will be expanded by the introduction of various new symbols. The propositional letters have disappeared, since the idea of predicate logic is to subject simple statements to a deeper analysis. The simple statements we are thinking of are, first of all, individual statements with a clear subject-predicate structure, like:

(1)   Plato is a man.

(2)   Socrates is mortal.

(3)   The chicken is cackling.

(4)   This kettle leaks.

Each of the sentences has one part which refers to a property (being a man, being mortal, cackling, and leaking) and another part which refers to some entity (Plato, Socrates, the chicken, and this kettle). Accordingly, in predicate logic we have (*individual*) *constants* which are always interpreted in such a way that they refer to an entity (that is, an individual or an object) and *predicate constants* or *predicate letters* which are always interpreted such that they refer to all kinds of properties which entities (of some particular sort) may or may not have. Note that individual constants and predicate constants are *logical* variables (see §1.3). We shall use lowercase letters for individual constants, for the time being a–v, though later we shall restrict ourselves to the letters a, b, and c. We shall use capital letters for predicate letters, and both will have subscripts where necessary. A well-formed formula corresponding to a sentence can be made by prefixing a predicate letter to a constant. If we have some particular interpretation of the sentences in mind, then we may choose suggestive letters. So (1)–(4) might, for example, be represented as M_1p_1, M_2s, Cc, and Lk, respectively.

Until the end of the nineteenth century, statements with the subject-predicate structure were the only individual statements which were taken seriously. Besides these, however, there are other kinds of individual statements which from a logical point of view cannot profitably be analyzed in terms of subjects and predicates. Sentences which say that two entities bear some particular relationship to each other are a case in point. Here are some examples:

(5)   Casper is bigger than John.

(6)   Peter is plucking the chicken.

(7)   Alcibiades admires Socrates.

There are, of course, instances in which it is useful to distinguish subjects and predicates in such sentences. For example, in linguistics, (5) is often parsed as consisting of a subject, *Casper,* and a predicate, *is bigger than John.* But if one is interested in studying reasoning, then another approach seems preferable, at least for the moment (there are richer logical systems, like higher-order logic with lambda abstraction [see vol. 2], which allow an approach closer to the subject-predicate analysis). For example:

(8)   Casper is bigger than John.
       John is bigger than Peter.
       _____
       Casper is bigger than Peter.

This is a valid argument, given the meaning of *is bigger than.* However, that cannot be shown if we analyze the premises and conclusion in the subject-predicate schema. For the premises would then contain a different predicate, referring to a different property. The first premise would be translated as Jc, with c translating *Casper,* and J standing for *is bigger than John,* whereas the second would come out as Pj, with j for *John* and P for *is bigger than Peter,* and the conclusion would read Pc. But the argument schema:

Jc
Pj
___
Pc

cannot be shown to be valid. What we need is an analysis of (8) which treats the relation *is bigger than* as a logical unit of its own. For it is a general property of the relation *is bigger than* which makes (8) valid: that where the first of three things is bigger than the second, and the second is bigger than the third, the first will always also be bigger than the third. So in order to show the validity of (8), we need to be able to express this general property of *is bigger than,* to treat it as an extra (hidden) premise of the argument in (8) (see §4.1). And we need to be able to express that in the premises and the conclusion of (8), this is the relation that is involved.

For this reason, languages of predicate logic also include symbols which stand for relations between two entities. Sentences (5), (6), and (7) can thus be translated as B_1cj, Pp_2c, and Aas, respectively; B, P, and A are the translations of *being bigger than, plucking,* and *admiring,* respectively. And (8) can now be turned into the schema:

$$B_1cj$$
$$B_1jp$$
$$\overline{}$$
$$B_1cp$$

This can be shown to be valid, once we add the extra premise mentioned above, which can also be expressed by using the apparatus of predicate logic. We can also use symbols for relations between three entities (like *lies between . . . and*), and so on. All of these symbols are called predicate constants, or predicate letters. Each predicate letter has its own fixed arity: there are unary predicate letters which stand for the properties of entities, there are binary predicate letters which stand for relations between pairs of entities, and so on. In general, n-ary predicates may be introduced for any whole number n larger than zero.

An *atomic sentence* is obtained by writing n (not necessarily different) constants after an n-ary predicate letter. If A is a quaternary predicate letter, for instance, and a, b, c, and d are constants, then Aabcd, Adabc, Addaa, and Abbbc are all atomic sentences. The notation with the predicate letter first is called, as with functions, prefix notation. There are a few relations which are conventionally written in infix notation, one of these being the identity relation, for which we shall introduce the logical constant $=$ shortly. We write $a = b$ and not $=$ab.

The order of the entities can make a difference for some relations: if Casper is bigger than John, then John is not bigger than Casper. So the order in which the constants are placed after a predicate letter is important: B_1cj and B_1jc express different things. This must not be forgotten when writing keys to translations of natural language sentences: (9), for example, is insufficient as a key.

(9) B_2: lies between
b: Breda, t: Tilburg, e: Eindhoven

This is because it is not clear from (9) whether the formula B_2bte stands for sentence (10) or sentence (11).

(10)   Tilburg is between Breda and Eindhoven

(11)   Breda is between Tilburg and Eindhoven

So apparently we have to find some way to fix the order of the entities in keys to translations. *Variables* are useful for this purpose. Variables are referred to by x, y, z, and w, and subscripts may be added if we run out of letters. Variables will be seen to have an even more important role to play when we come to the analysis of expressions which quantify. In themselves, variables never have a meaning; they just mark places in sentences. We can use this in giving keys to translations. Instead of (9) we use (12):

(12) B_2xyz: x is between y and z.
       b: Breda; t: Tilburg; e: Eindhoven

Unlike (9), (12) leaves no ambiguities in the meanings of sentences which can be formed from these letters; B_2bte is the translation of (11), and B_2tbe is that of (10). The less explicit keys in the above can now be given in the following form:

(13) Lx : x leaks j : John
       M_1x : x is a man p_1 : Plato
       M_2x : x is mortal p_2 : Peter
       Cx : x is cackling s : Socrates
       B_1xy : x is bigger than y c_1 : the chicken
       Pxy : x is plucking y k : this kettle
       Axy : x admires y c_2 : Casper
                                      a : Alcibiades

The key (13) gives all the translations we had for the sentences (1)–(7).

   We now return to B_2 in order to emphasize that variables do not have any meaning of their own but simply serve as markers.

(14) B_2yxz: y is between x and z.

(15) B_2zxy: z is between x and y.

(16) B_2zyx: z is between y and x.

(17) B_2xyz: y is between x and z.

Key (14) is just the same as (12): (12) and (14) give identical readings to atomic sentences B_2bte, B_2tbe, and so on. And both (15) and (16) give the same results as (12) and (14) too. But key (17) is essentially different, since it gives B_2bte as the translation of (10) and B_2tbe as the translation of (11).

   Combining key (13) with the use of the connectives of propositional logic, we can translate some more complicated sentences from natural language, as can be seen in (18):

(18)   *Sentence*   *Translation*
       (a) John is bigger than Peter or Peter is $Bjp_2 \lor Bp_2j$
           bigger than John.
       (b) If the chicken is cackling, then $Cc_1 \rightarrow Pc_2c_1$
           Casper is plucking it.
       (c) If John is cackling, then Casper is $Cj \rightarrow B_1c_2j$
           bigger than John.
       (d) If Peter admires Casper, then he is $Ap_2c_2 \rightarrow \neg Pp_2c_2$
           not plucking him.

(e) Alcibiades admires himself.	Aaa
(f) Casper and John are plucking each other.	$Pjc_2 \wedge Pc_2j$
(g) If Socrates is a man, then he is mortal.	$M_1s \rightarrow M_2s$
(h) Socrates is a mortal man.	$M_1s \wedge M_2s$

In (18) we also see how words which refer back to entities already mentioned, like personal and reflexive pronouns, can be handled in predicate logic. Possessive pronouns are a bit more difficult. Expressions beginning with a possessive pronoun generally refer to some particular object; the context determines which one. As such they are just like expressions beginning with *the, this,* etc., and all such expressions will in the meantime be translated as individual constants without being subjected to any further analysis. In §5.2, where we discuss so-called definite descriptions, we shall have more to say about them.

Sentences (b), (d), and (g) in (18) of course all have readings for which the given translations are incorrect; contexts can be thought of in which *it* and *he* refer to entities other than *the chicken, Casper, Peter,* and *Socrates.* In translating these kinds of sentences, we just choose the most natural interpretation.

Unlike the theory of types, which will be discussed in volume 2, predicate logic does not enable us to distinguish between (18e) and *Alcibiades admires Alcibiades.* Sentences (19) and (20) cannot be distinguished either:

(19) If Onno teases Peter, then he pleases him.

(20) If Onno teases Peter, then Onno pleases Peter.

Both (19) and (20), given the obvious translation key, are rendered as Top → Pop.

Note that the simple sentence (18h) has been translated as the conjunction of two atomic sentences. This is in order to make the logical properties of the sentence as explicit as possible, which is the aim of such translations. Logically speaking, sentence (18h) expresses two things about Socrates: that he is a man and that he is mortal.

Exercise 1

Translate the following sentences into predicate logic. Preserve as much of the structure as possible, and in each case give the key.
a. John is nicer than Peter.
b. Charles is nice, but Elsa isn't.
c. Peter went with Charles on Marion's new bicycle to Zandvoort.
d. If Peter didn't hear the news from Charles, he heard it from Elsa.
e. Charles is boring or irritating.
f. Marion is a happy woman.
g. Bee is a best-selling author.
h. Charles and Elsa are brother and sister or nephew and niece.
i. John and Peter are close friends.

j. John admires himself.

k. If John gambles, then he will hurt himself.

l. Although John and Mary love each other deeply, they make each other very unhappy.

3.2 Quantifying Expressions: Quantifiers

Besides connectives, predicate logic also deals with quantifying expressions. Consider a sentence like:

(21)   All teachers are friendly.

Aristotle saw a sentence like this as a relationship between two predicates: in this case between *being a teacher* and *being friendly*. He distinguished four different ways of linking two predicates A and B. Besides *all A are B*, of which the above is an instance, he had *some A are B*, *all A are not-B*, and *some A are not-B*.

If you just consider properties, then this works quite nicely. But as soon as you move from predicates to relations, and from simple quantification to sentences in which more than one quantifying expression appears, things become more difficult. It would not be easy to say what kind of relationship is expressed by sentence (22) between the relation *admires* and the people being talked about:

(22)   Everyone admires someone.

And even if we could manage this sentence somehow, there are always even more complex ones, like (23) and (24):

(23)   Everyone admires someone who admires everyone.

(24)   No one admires anyone who admires everyone who admires someone.

It would seem that we are in need of a general principle with which the role of quantifying expressions can be analyzed.

Let us first examine sentences in which just a single predicate appears.

(25)   Peter is friendly.

(26)   No one is friendly.

We translate (25) as Vp: the entity which we refer to as p is said to possess the property which we refer to as V. Now it would not be correct to treat (26) the same way, using a constant *n* for the x in Vx. There simply isn't anyone called *no one* of whom we could say, truthfully or untruthfully, that he is friendly. Expressions whose semantic functions are as different as *Peter* and *no one* cannot be dealt with in the same way. It happens that the syntactic characteristics of *Peter* and *no one* are not entirely the same in natural language either.

Compare, for example, the phrases *none of you* and *Peter of you*, or *no one except John* and *Peter except John*.

In (25) it is said of Peter that he has a particular property. We could also turn things around and say that the predicate *friendly* is said to have the property of applying to Peter. This is not the way things are done in predicate logic, but there are richer logical systems which work this way, which can be an advantage in the logical analysis of natural language (see vol. 2). It seems more natural to turn things around in dealing with (26), since there is no one to whom the property of being friendly is attributed, and it is thus better to say that this sentence states something about the property *friendly*, namely, that it applies to none of the entities to which it might in principle apply. Likewise, in a sentence such as

(27)   Someone is friendly.

we also have a statement about the property *friendly*, namely, that there is at least one among the entities to which it might in principle apply to which it does in fact apply. Instead of having to say *the entities to which the predicates might in principle apply*, we can make things easier for ourselves by collectively calling these entities the *universe of discourse*. This contains all the things which we are talking about at some given point in time. The sentence

(28)   Everyone is friendly.

can with this terminology be paraphrased as: every entity in the domain of discourse has the property *friendly*. The domain is in this case all human beings, or some smaller group of human beings which is fixed in the context in which the sentence appears. Note that the choice of domain can affect the truth values of sentences. It is highly probable that sentence (28) is untrue if we include every single human being in our domain of discourse, but there are certainly smaller groups of human beings for whom (28) is true.

We shall introduce two new symbols into the formal languages, the *universal quantifier* $\forall$ and the *existential quantifier* $\exists$. Each quantifier always appears together with a variable. This combination of a quantifier plus a variable (for example, $\forall x$ or $\exists y$) is conveniently also referred to as a quantifier (universal or existential). $\forall x$ . . . means: for every entity x in the domain we have . . . ; and $\exists x$ . . . means: there is at least one entity in the domain such that . . . ; $\forall x\phi$ is called the *universal generalization* of ϕ, and $\exists x\phi$ is its *existential generalization*.

We are now in a position to translate (28) as $\forall x V x$ (or equivalently, as $\forall y V y$ or as $\forall z V z$, since variables have no meaning of their own), to translate (27) as $\exists x V x$ (or as $\exists y V y$ or $\exists z V z$), (26) as $\neg\exists x V x$, and *everyone is unfriendly* as $\forall x \neg V x$.

It turns out that under this interpretation *no one is friendly* and *everyone is unfriendly* have the same meaning, since $\neg\exists x V x$ and $\forall x \neg V x$ are equivalent sentences in predicate logic. Later we shall find this analysis of *everyone* and *someone* a bit simplistic, but it will do for the cases we have discussed.

We will now build up the translation of (22), an example of a sentence which contains two quantifying expressions, in several steps. We use the key

(29)   Axy: x admires y.

We replace the x in *x admires y* by *Plato* and thus obtain a *propositional function:*

(30)   Plato admires y.

This would be translated as Apy and expresses the property of *being admired by Plato*. If we wish to say that someone has this property, this can be done by translating

(31)   Plato admires someone.

as ∃yApy. Replacing *Plato* by *x* in (31), we obtain the propositional function

(32)   x admires someone.

This again expresses a property, namely, that of *admiring someone,* and would be translated as ∃yAxy. Finally, by universally quantifying this formula we obtain the formula ∀x∃yAxy, which says that everyone in the domain has the property expressed by (32). So ∀x∃yAxy will serve as a translation of (22); (23) and (24) are best left until we have dealt with the notion of *formulas of predicate logic.*

We shall first discuss how the four forms which Aristotle distinguished can be represented by means of quantifiers. The following can be formed with *teacher* and *friendly* ((33) = (21)):

(33)   All teachers are friendly.

(34)   Some teachers are friendly.

(35)   All teachers are unfriendly.

(36)   Some teachers are unfriendly.

The material implication, as the reader may already suspect from what was said when it was first introduced, is rather useful in translating (33). For if (33) is true, then whatever Peter does for a living, we can be quite sure that (37) is true.

(37)   If Peter is a teacher, then Peter is friendly.

In (37), the *if . . . then* is understood to be the material implication. This can be seen very simply. If he happens to be a teacher, then, assuming (33) to be true, he must also be friendly, so (37) is true. And if he does not happen to be a teacher, then according to the truth table, (37) must be true too, whether he is friendly or not.

If, on the other hand, (33) is not true, then there must be at least one unfriendly teacher, say John, and then (38) is untrue.

(38)   If John is a teacher, then John is friendly.

It should now be clear that (33) is true just in case it is true that for every person x, if x is a teacher, then x is friendly. This means that we now have the following translation for (33):

(39) $\forall x(Tx \rightarrow Fx)$

The reader should be warned at this stage that (39) would also be true if there were no teachers at all. This does not agree with what Aristotle had to say on the matter, since he was of the opinion that *all A are B* implies that there are at least some As. He allowed only nonempty 'terms' in his syllogisms.

Sentence (34) would be translated into predicate logic as (40):

(40) $\exists x(Tx \wedge Fx)$

Translation (40) is true if and only if there is at least one person in the domain who is a teacher and who is friendly. Some nuances seem to be lost in translating (34) like this; (34) seems to say that there are more friendly teachers than just one, whereas a single friendly teacher is all that is needed for (40) to be true. Also, as a result of the communtativity of $\wedge$, (40) means the same as (41), which is the translation of (42):

(41) $\exists x(Tx \wedge Fx)$

(42)   Some friendly people are teachers.

It could be argued that it is unrealistic to ignore the asymmetry which is present in natural language. But for our purposes, this translation of (34) will do. In §3.7 we will see that it is quite possible to express the fact that there are several friendly teachers by introducing the relation of identity. Sentences (35) and (36) are now no problem; (36) can be rendered as (43), while (35) becomes (44).

(43) $\exists x(Tx \wedge \neg Fx)$

(44) $\forall x(Tx \rightarrow \neg Fx)$

Sentences (45) and (46) mean the same as (35), and both can be translated as (47):

(45)   No teachers are friendly.

(46)   It is not the case that some teachers are friendly.

(47) $\neg \exists x(Tx \wedge Fx)$

Indeed, the precise formulation of the semantics of predicate logic is such that (44) and (47) are equivalent. The definitions of the quantifiers are such that $\forall x \neg \phi$ always means the same as $\neg \exists x \phi$. This is reflected in the fact that (48) and (49) have the same meaning:

(48)   Everyone is unfriendly.

(49)   No one is friendly.

This means that (47) must be equivalent to $\forall x \neg (Tx \wedge Fx)$. And according to propositional logic, this formula must once again be equivalent to (44), since $\neg(\phi \wedge \psi)$ is equivalent to $\phi \rightarrow \neg\psi$.

Exercise 2

Translate the following sentences into predicate logic. Preserve as much of the structure as possible and give in each case the key and the domain of discourse.
a. Everybody loves Marion.
b. Some politicians are honest.
c. Nobody is a politician and not ambitious.
d. It is not the case that all ambitious people are not honest.
e. All blond authors are clever.
f. Some best-selling authors are blind.
g. Peter is an author who has written some best-selling books.

3.3 Formulas

Certain problems arise in defining the formulas of predicate logic which we didn't have with propositional logic. To begin with, it is desirable that the notions of *sentence* and of *formula* do not coincide. We wish to have two kinds of formulas: those which express propositions, which may be called *sentences,* and those which express properties or relations, which may be called *propositional functions.* So we shall first give a general definition of *formula* and then distinguish the sentences among them.

Another point is that it is not as obvious which expressions are to be accepted as formulas as it was in the case of propositional logic. If A and B are unary predicate letters, then $\forall x Ax$, $\forall y(Ay \rightarrow By)$, and $Ax \wedge By$ are clearly the sorts of expressions which we wish to have among the formulas. But what about $\forall x Ay$ and $\forall x(Ax \wedge \exists x Bx)$? One decisive factor in choosing a definition is simplicity. A simple definition makes it easier to think about formulas in general and facilitates general statements about them. If ϕ is a formula, we simply choose to accept $\forall x \phi$ and $\exists x \phi$ as formulas too. We shall see that the eventuality that the variable x does not even occur in ϕ need not cause any complications in the interpretation of $\forall x \phi$ and $\exists x \phi$: $\forall x Ay$ is given the same interpretation as Ay, and the same applies to $\exists x Ay$. In much the same way, $\forall x(Ax \wedge \exists x Bx)$ receives the same interpretation as $\forall x(Ax \wedge \exists y By)$. We shall see that all formulas which may be recognized as such admit of interpretation. This is primarily of theoretical importance. When translating formulas from natural language into predicate logic, we shall of course strive to keep the formulas as easily readable as possible.

Each language L of predicate logic has its own stock of constants and predicate letters. Each of the predicate letters has its own fixed arity. Besides these, there are also the symbols which all languages of predicate logic have in common: the connectives, the quantifiers ∀ and ∃, and as auxiliary signs, the brackets and an infinite supply of variables. Any given formula will, of course, contain only a finite number of the latter, but we do not wish to place an upper limit on the length of formulas, and we therefore can't have any finite upper limit to the number of variables either. Together these symbols form the *vocabulary* of L. Given this vocabulary, we define the formulas of language L as follows (compare definition 1 in §2.3):

Definition 1

(i)   If A is an *n*-ary predicate letter in the vocabulary of L, and each of $t_1, \ldots, t_n$ is a constant or a variable in the vocabulary of L, then $At_1, \ldots, t_n$ is a formula in L.

(ii)   If ϕ is a formula in L, then $\neg\phi$ is too.

(iii) If ϕ and ψ are formulas in L, then so are $(\phi \land \psi)$, $(\phi \lor \psi)$, $(\phi \to \psi)$, and $(\phi \leftrightarrow \psi)$.

(iv)   If ϕ is a formula in L and x is a variable, then $\forall x\phi$ and $\exists x\phi$ are formulas in L.

(v)   Only that which can be generated by the clauses (i)–(iv) in a finite number of steps is a formula in L.

Clause (i) yields the *atomic formulas*. These are formulas like Bxyz, Mp, and Apx. Formulas formed according to (iv) are called *universal* and *existential* formulas, respectively.

Just as in propositional logic, we leave off the outer brackets of formulas and just talk about predicate-logical formulas where it doesn't matter what language L we are dealing with. Here too there is a characteristic construction tree associated with each formula. Formula (51), for instance, has the construction tree represented in figure (50):

(50)   ¬∃x∃y(∀z(∃wAzw → Ayz) ∧ Axy)   (ii)
                                        |
                 ∃x∃y(∀z(∃wAzw → Ayz) ∧ Axy)   (iv, ∃)
                                        |
                  ∃y(∀z(∃wAzw → Ayz) ∧ Axy)   (iv, ∃)
                                        |
                     ∀z(∃wAzw Ayz) ∧ Axy   (iii, ∧)
                   ┌────────────────────┴──────┐
         ∀z(∃wAzw → Ayz) (iv, ∀)   Axy   (i)
                    |
          ∃wAzw → Ayz   (iii, →)
            ┌────────┴────────┐
       ∃wAzw   (iv, ∃)   Ayz   (i)
          |
       Azw   (i)

(51)   ¬∃x∃y(∀z(∃wAzw → Ayz) ∧ Axy)

This tree could be added to in order to show how the atomic formulas appearing in it have been built up from predicate letters, variables, and constants, as in figure (52):

(52)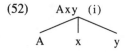

But for our purposes these details are unnecessary. Just as in propositional logic, the subformulas of a formula are those formulas which appear in its construction tree. Formula (51) has, for example, itself, ∃x∃y(∀z(∃wAzw → Ayz) ∧ Axy), ∃y(∀z(∃wAzw → Ayz) ∧ Axy), ∀z(∃wAzw → Ayz) ∧ Axy, ∀z(∃wAzw → Ayz), Axy, ∃wAzw → Ayz, ∃wAzw, Azw, and Ayz as its subformulas. And just as in propositional logic, it can be shown that the subformulas of a formula φ are just those strings of consecutive symbols taken from φ which are themselves formulas.

In order to decide which formulas are to be called sentences, but also in order to be able to interpret formulas in the first place, it is essential to be able to say how much of a given formula is governed by any quantifier appearing in it. We shall deal with this in the next few definitions.

Definition 2

If ∀xψ is a subformula of φ, then ψ is called the *scope* of this particular occurrence of the quantifier ∀x in φ. The same applies to occurrences of the quantifier ∃x.

As a first example, the scopes of the quantifiers occurring in (51) have been summarized in (53):

(53)   *Quantifier*   *Scope*

    ∃w   Azw

    ∀z   ∃wAzw → Ayz

    ∃y   ∀z(∃wAzw → Ayz) ∧ Axy

    ∃x   ∃y(∀z(∃wAzw → Ayz) ∧ Axy)

We distinguish between different *occurrences* of a quantifier in definition 2 because there are formulas like (54):

(54)   ∀xAx ∧ ∀xBx

In (54), one and the same quantifier appears more than once. The first occurrence of ∀x in (54) has Ax as its scope, while the second occurrence has Bx as its scope. What this means is that the first occurrence of ∀x only governs the x in Ax, while the second occurrence governs the x in Bx. We shall now incorporate this distinction into the following general definition:

Definition 3

(a) An occurrence of a variable x in the formula ϕ (which is not part of a quantifier) is said to be *free in* ϕ if this occurrence of x does not fall within the scope of a quantifier $\forall$x or a quantifier $\exists$x appearing in ϕ.

(b) If $\forall$xψ (or $\exists$xψ) is a subformula of ϕ and x is free in ψ, then this occurrence of x is said to be *bound* by the quantifier $\forall$x (or $\exists$x).

It will be clear that either an occurrence of a variable x in a formula is free or it is bound by a quantifier $\forall$x or $\exists$x.

Definition 3 is a little more complicated than may seem necessary, and this is because we allow formulas such as $\forall$x(Ax $\wedge$ $\exists$xBx). In this formula, the x in Bx is bound by the $\exists$x, while the x in Ax is bound by the $\forall$x. According to definition 2, the x in Bx also occurs within the scope of the $\forall$x. But this occurrence of x is not bound by the $\forall$x, because it is not free in Ax $\wedge$ $\exists$xBx, the scope of $\forall$x, which is what clause (b) of definition 3 requires. In practice we will tend to avoid situations in which bound variables occur within the scope of quantifiers with the same variable, but definition 1 does not exclude them. The funny thing about the other strange formula we have mentioned, $\forall$xAy, is that the quantifier $\forall$x does not bind any variables at all. These kinds of formulas we shall tend to avoid as well, but definition 1 does not exclude them either.

Now we can define what we mean by *sentence* in predicate logic:

Definition 4

A *sentence* is a formula in L which lacks free variables.

$\forall$xAy is not a sentence, for example, because the occurrence of the variable y is free; $\forall$x(Ax $\wedge$ $\exists$xBx) is a sentence, but Ax $\wedge$ $\exists$xBx is not, since the first occurrence of x is free.

Exercise 3

For each of the following formulas of the predicate calculus, indicate:

(a) whether it is a negation, a conjunction, a disjunction, an implication, a universal formula, or an existential formula;

(b) the scope of the quantifiers;

(c) the free variables;

(d) whether it is a sentence.

(i) $\exists$x(Axy $\wedge$ Bx)	(vii) $\neg$Bx $\rightarrow$ ($\neg\forall$y($\neg$Axy $\vee$ Bx) $\rightarrow$ Cy)
(ii) $\exists$xAxy $\wedge$ Bx	(viii) $\exists$x(Axy $\vee$ By)
(iii) $\exists$x$\exists$yAxy $\rightarrow$ Bx	(ix) $\exists$xAxx $\vee$ $\exists$yBy
(iv) $\exists$x($\exists$yAxy $\rightarrow$ Bx)	(x) $\exists$x($\exists$yAxy $\vee$ By)
(v) $\neg\exists$x$\exists$yAxy $\rightarrow$ Bx	(xi) $\forall$x$\forall$y((Axy $\wedge$ By) $\rightarrow$ $\exists$wCxw)
(vi) $\forall$x$\neg\exists$yAxy	(xii) $\forall$x($\forall$yAyx $\rightarrow$ By)
	(xiii) $\forall$x$\forall$yAyy $\rightarrow$ Bx

As we have mentioned, a formula with free variables is called a *propositional function*. If we take the formula Tx → Fx with its one free variable x and replace x with the constant j, then we obtain a sentence, namely, Tj → Fj. So Tx → Fx can indeed be seen as a function: it has as its domain the constants of the language L which we are working in, and the sentences in L as its range. If c is a constant, then the value of the propositional function Tx → Fx with c as its argument is the sentence Tc → Fc. Analogously, the function corresponding to a formula with two free variables is binary. For example, formula (55), the translation of *y admires all those whom x admires*, has sentence (56) as its value when fed the arguments p and j:

(55) $\forall z(Axz \to Ayz)$

(56) $\forall z(Apz \to Ajz)$

This is the translation of *John admires all those whom Peter admires*. The following notation is often useful in this connection. If ϕ is a formula, c is a constant, and x is a variable, then $[c/x]\phi$ is the formula which results when all free occurrences of x in ϕ are replaced with occurrences of c. The examples given in table (57) should make this clear. The formulas $[y/x]\phi$ and $[x/c]\phi$ can be defined in exactly the same way.

(57) ϕ	$[c/x]\phi$
Axy	Acy
Axx	Acc
$\forall$xAxx	$\forall$xAxx
Ay	Ay
Acx	Acc
Axx $\wedge$ $\exists$xBx	Acc $\wedge$ $\exists$xBx
$\forall$xBy	$\forall$xBy
$\exists$x$\exists$yAxy → Bx	$\exists$x$\exists$yAxy → Bc
$\forall$x$\forall$yAyy → Bx	$\forall$x$\forall$yAyy → Bc

Exercise 4

The *quantifier depth* of a predicate-logical formula is the maximal length of a 'nest' of quantifiers $Q_1x(\ldots (Q_2y(\ldots (Q_3z(\ldots$ occurring in it. E.g., both $\exists x\forall yRxy$ and $\exists x(\forall yRxy \wedge \exists zSxz)$ have quantifier depth 2. Give a precise definition of this notion using the inductive definition of formulas.

3.4 Some more quantifying expressions and their translations

Besides the expressions *everyone, someone, all, some, no one*, and *no* which we have discussed, there are a few other quantifying expressions which it is relatively simple to translate into predicate logic. To begin with, *every* and *each* can be treated as *all*, while *a few* and *one or more* and *a number of* can be treated as *some*. In addition, translations can also be given for *everything, something,* and *nothing.* Here are a few examples:

(58) Everything is subject to decay.

Translation: $\forall x Vx$.
Key: Vx: x is subject to decay.
Domain: everything on earth.

(59) John gave something to Peter.

Translation: $\exists x(Tx \land Gjxp)$.
Key: Tx: x is a thing; $Gxyz$: x gave y to z.
Domain: people and things.

The translation of (59) is perhaps a bit more complicated than seems necessary; with a domain containing both people and things, however, $\exists xGjxp$ would translate back into English as: *John gave Peter someone or something.* We say that the quantifier $\exists x$ is *restricted to* T in $\exists x(Tx \land Gjxp)$. Suppose we wish to translate a sentence like

(60) Everyone gave Peter something.

Then these problems are even more pressing. This cannot as it is be translated as $\forall y \exists x(Tx \land Gyxp)$, since this would mean: *everyone and everything gave Peter one or more things.* The quantifier $\forall y$ will have to be restricted too, in this case to P (key: Px: x is a person). We then obtain:

(61) $\forall y(Py \rightarrow \exists x(Tx \land Gyxp))$

When restricted to A, a quantifier $\exists x$ becomes $\exists x(Ax \land$; and a quantifier $\forall x$ becomes $\forall x(Ax \rightarrow$. The reasons for this were explained in the discussion of *all* and *some.* Sentence (61) also serves as a translation of:

(62) All people gave Peter one or more things.

Here is an example with *nothing:*

(63) John gave Peter nothing.

Sentence (63) can be seen as the negation of (59) and can thus be translated as $\neg\exists x(Tx \land Gjxp)$.

The existential quantifier is especially well suited as a translation of *a(n)* in English.

(64) John gave Peter a book.

Sentence (64), for example, can be translated as $\exists x(Bx \land Gjxp)$; Bx: x is a book, being added to the key. This shows that $\exists x(Tx \land Gjxp)$ can also function as a translation of

(65) John gave Peter a thing.

This means that the sentence *John gave Peter a book* is true just in case *John gave Peter one or more books* is. In *John gave Peter a book,* there is a strong suggestion that exactly one book changed hands, but the corresponding suggestion is entirely absent in sentences (66) and (67), for example.

(66)   Do you have a pen?

(67)   He has a friend who can manage that.

We conclude that semantically speaking, the existential quantifier is a suitable translation for the indefinite article. Note that there is a usage in which *a(n)* means something entirely different:

(68)   A whale is a mammal.

Sentence (68) means the same as *Every whale is a mammal* and must therefore be translated as $\forall x(Wx \rightarrow Mx)$, with Wx: x is a whale, Mx: x is a mammal as the key and all living creatures as the domain. This is called the generic usage of the indefinite article *a(n)*.

Not all quantifying expressions can be translated into predicate logic. Quantifying expressions like *many* and *most* are cases in point. Subordinate clauses with *who* and *that,* on the other hand, often can. Here are some examples with *who*.

(69)   He who is late is to be punished.

Translation: $\forall x(Lx \rightarrow Px)$
Key: Lx: x is late; Px: x is to be punished.
Domain: People

(70)   Boys who are late are to be punished.

Translation: $\forall x((Bx \land Lx) \rightarrow Px)$, or, given the equivalence of $(\phi \land \psi) \rightarrow \chi$ and $\phi \rightarrow (\psi \rightarrow \chi)$ (see exercise 5o in §2.5), $\forall x(Bx \rightarrow (Lx \rightarrow Px))$. Bx: x is a boy must be added to the key to the translation.

The *who* in (69) can without changing the meaning be replaced by *someone who,* as can be seen by comparing (69) and (71):

(71)   Someone who is late is to be punished.

This must, of course, not be confused with

(72)   Someone, who is late, is to be punished.

Sentences (71) and (69) are synonymous; (71) and (72) are not. In (71), with the restrictive clause *who is late,* the *someone* must be translated as a universal quantifier; whereas in (72), with its appositive relative clause, it must be translated as an existential quantifier, as is more usual. Sentence (71) is thus translated as $\forall x(Lx \rightarrow Px)$, while (72) becomes $\exists x(Lx \land Px)$.

Combining personal and reflexive pronouns with quantifying expressions opens some interesting possibilities, of which the following is an example:

(73)   Everyone admires himself.

Sentence (73) can be translated as $\forall x Axx$ if the domain contains only humans, while $\forall x(Hx \to Axx)$ is the translation for any mixed domain.

(74)   John has a cat which he spoils.

   Translation: $\exists x(Hjx \wedge Cx \wedge Sjx)$.
   Key: Hxy: x has y; Cx: x is a cat; Sxy: x spoils y.
   Domain: humans and animals.

(75)   Everyone who visits New York likes it.

   Translation: $\forall x((Hx \wedge Vxn) \to Lxn)$.
   Key: Hx: x is human; Vxy: x visits y; Lxy: x likes y.
   Domain: humans and cities.

(76)   He who wants something badly enough will get it.

Sentence (76) is complicated by the fact that *it* refers back to *something*. Simply rendering *something* as an existential quantifier results in the following incorrect translation:

(77) $\forall x((Px \wedge \exists y(Ty \wedge Wxy)) \to Gxy)$

   Key: Px: x is a person; Tx: x is a thing; Wxy: x wants y badly enough; Gxy: x will get y.
   Domain: people and things.

   This translation will not do, since Gxy does not fall within the scope of $\exists y$, so the y in Gxy is free. Changing this to (78) will not help at all:

(78) $\forall x(Px \wedge \exists y(Ty \wedge (Wxy \to Gxy)))$

This is because what (78) says is that for every person, there is something with a given property, which (76) does not say at all. The solution is to change (76) into

(79)   For all persons x and things y, if x wants y badly enough then x will get y.

This can then be translated into predicate logic as

(80) $\forall x(Px \to \forall y(Ty \to (Wxy \to Gxy)))$

Sentences (81) and (82) are two other translations which are equivalent to (80):

(81) $\forall x \forall y((Px \wedge Ty \wedge Wxy) \to Gxy)$

(82) $\forall y(Ty \to \forall x(Px \to (Wxy \to Gxy)))$

Actually, officially we do not know yet what *equivalence* means in predicate logic; we come to that in §3.6.4. So strictly speaking, we are not yet entitled to leave off the brackets and write (Px ∧ Ty ∧ Wxy) as we did in (81). We will come to this as well. By way of conclusion, we now return to (83) and (84) (=(23) and (24)):

(83)   Everyone admires someone who admires everyone.

(84)   No one admires anyone who admires everyone who admires someone.

The most natural reading of (83) is as (85):

(85)   Everyone admires at least one person who admires everyone.

The translation of (85) is put together in the following 'modular' way:

y admires everyone: ∀zAyz;
x admires y, and y admires everyone: Axy ∧∀zAyz;
there is at least one y whom x admires, and y admires everyone: ∃y(Axy ∧ ∀zAyz).
for each x there is at least one y whom x admires, and y admires everyone: ∀x∃y(Axy ∧ ∀zAyz).

As a first step toward rendering the most natural reading of (84), we translate the phrase *y admires everyone who admires someone* as ∀z(∃wAzw →Ayz). We then observe that (84) amounts to denying the existence of x and y such that both *x admires y* and *y admires everyone who admires someone* hold. Thus, one suitable translation is given by formula ¬∃x∃y(∀z(∃wAzw ∧ Ayz) ∧ Axy), which we met before as formula (51), and whose construction tree was studied in figure (50).

Perhaps it is unnecessary to point out that these translations do not pretend to do justice to the grammatical forms of sentences. The question of the relation between grammatical and logical forms will be discussed at length in volume 2.

Exercise 5

Translate the following sentences into predicate logic. Retain as much structure as possible and in each case give the key and the domain.

(i)   Everything is bitter or sweet.
(ii)   Either everything is bitter or everything is sweet.
(iii)   A whale is a mammal.
(iv)   Theodore is a whale.
(v)   Mary Ann has a new bicycle.
(vi)   This man owns a big car.
(vii)   Everybody loves somebody.
(viii)   There is somebody who is loved by everyone.

(ix)   Elsie did not get anything from Charles.

(x)   Lynn gets some present from John, but she doesn't get anything from Peter.

(xi)   Somebody stole or borrowed Mary's new bike.

(xii)   You have eaten all my cookies.

(xiii)   Nobody is loved by no one.

(xiv)   If all logicians are smart, then Alfred is smart too.

(xv)   Some men and women are not mature.

(xvi)   Barking dogs don't bite.

(xvii)   If John owns a dog, he has never shown it to anyone.

(xviii) Harry has a beautiful wife, but she hates him.

(xix)   Nobody lives in Urk who wasn't born there.

(xx)   John borrowed a book from Peter but hasn't given it back to him.

(xxi)   Some people are nice to their bosses even though they are offended by them.

(xxii)   Someone who promises something to somebody should do it.

(xxiii) People who live in Amherst or close by own a car.

(xxiv)   If you see anyone, you should give no letter to her.

(xxv)   If Pedro owns donkeys, he beats them.

(xxvi)   Someone who owns no car does own a motorbike.

(xxvii) If someone who cannot make a move has lost, then I have lost.

(xxviii) Someone has borrowed a motorbike and is riding it.

(xxix)   Someone has borrowed a motorbike from somebody and didn't return it to her.

(xxx)   If someone is noisy, everybody is annoyed.

(xxxi)   If someone is noisy, everybody is annoyed at him.

Exercise 6 ◇

In natural language there seem to be linguistic restrictions on how deeply inside subordinate expressions a quantifier can bind. Let us call a formula *shallow* if no quantifier in it binds free variables occurring within the scope of more than one intervening quantifier. For instance, $\exists x Px$, $\exists x \forall y Rxy$ are shallow, whereas $\exists x \forall y \exists z Rxyz$ is not. Which of the following formulas are shallow or intuitively equivalent to one which is shallow?

(i) $\exists x(\forall y Rxy \rightarrow \forall z Szx)$

(ii) $\exists x \forall y(Rxy \rightarrow \forall z Tzxy)$

(iii) $\exists x(\forall y \exists u Ruy \rightarrow \forall z Szx)$

(iv) $\exists x \forall y \forall z(Rxy \wedge Sxz)$

3.5 Sets

Although it is strictly speaking not necessary, in §3.6 we shall give a set-theoretical treatment of the semantics of predicate logic. There are two reasons for this. First, it is the usual way of doing things in the literature. And second, the concept of a set plays an essential role in the semantics of logical systems which are more complex than predicate logic (and which we shall come to in volume 2).

Actually, we have already run across sets in the domains and ranges of functions. To put it as generally as possible, a *set* is a collection of entities. There is a sense in which its membership is the only important thing about a set, so it does not matter how the collection was formed, or how we can discover what entities belong to it. Take the domain of a function, for instance. Whether or not this function attributes a value to any given entity depends on just one thing—the membership of this entity in the domain. The central importance of membership is expressed in the *principle of extensionality* for sets. According to this principle, a set is completely specified by the entities which belong to it. Or, in other words, no two different sets can contain exactly the same members. For example, the set of all whole numbers larger than 3 and smaller than 6, the set containing just the numbers 4 and 5, and the set of all numbers which differ from 4.5 by exactly 0.5 are all the same set. An entity a which belongs to a set A is called an *element* or a *member* of A. We say that A *contains* a (as an element). This is written $a \in A$. We write $a \notin A$ if a is not an element of A.

Finite sets can be described by placing the names of the elements between set brackets: so $\{4, 5\}$ is the set described above, for example; $\{0, 1\}$ is the set of truth values; $\{p, q, p \rightarrow q, \neg(p \rightarrow q)\}$ is the set of all subformulas of $\neg(p \rightarrow q)$; $\{x, y, z\}$ is the set of all variables which are free in the formula $\forall w((Axw \wedge Byw) \rightarrow Czw)$. So we have, for example $0 \in \{0, 1\}$ and $y \in \{x, y, z\}$. There is no reason why a set may not contain just a single element, so that $\{0\}$, $\{1\}$, and $\{x\}$ are all examples of sets. Thus $0 \in \{0\}$, and to put it generally, $a \in \{0\}$ just in case $a = 0$. It should be noted that a set containing some single thing is not the same as that thing itself; in symbols, $a \neq \{a\}$. It is obvious that $2 \neq \{2\}$, for example, since 2 is a number, while $\{2\}$ is a set. Sets with no elements at all are also allowed; in view of the principle of extensionality, there can be only one such empty set, for which we have the notation $\varnothing$. So there is no a such that $a \in \varnothing$. Since the only thing which matters is the membership, the order in which the elements of a set are given in the brackets notation is irrelevant. Thus $\{4, 5\} = \{5, 4\}$ and $\{z, x, y\} = \{x, y, z\}$, for example. Nor does it make any difference if some elements are written more than once: $\{0, 0\} = \{0\}$ and $\{4, 4, 5\} = \{4, 5\}$. A similar notation is also used for some infinite sets, with an expression between the brackets which suggests what elements are included. For example, $\{1, 2, 3, 4, \ldots\}$ is the set of positive whole numbers; $\{0, 1, 2, 3, \ldots\}$ is the set of *natural numbers;* $\{\ldots -2, -1, 0, 1, 2, \ldots\}$ is the set of all whole numbers; $\{0, 2, 4, 6, \ldots\}$ is the set of even natural numbers; and $\{p, \neg p, \neg\neg p, \neg\neg\neg p, \ldots\}$ is the set of all formulas in which only p and $\neg$ occur. We shall refer to the set of natural numbers as N for convenience, to the whole numbers as Z, and (at least in this section) to the even numbers as E.

If all of the elements of a set A also happen to be elements of a set B, then we say that A is a *subset* of B, which is written $A \subseteq B$. For example, we have $\{x, z\} \subseteq \{x, y, z\}$; $\{0\} \subseteq \{0, 1\}$; $E \subseteq N$, and $N \subseteq Z$. Two borderline cases of this are $A \subseteq A$ for every set A and $\varnothing \subseteq A$ (since the empty set has no elements at all, the requirement that all of its elements are elements of A is fulfilled vacuously). Here are a few properties of $\in$ and $\subseteq$ which can easily be verified:

(86) if $a \in A$ and $A \subseteq B$, then $a \in B$
      if $A \subseteq B$ and $B \subseteq C$, then $A \subseteq C$
      $a \in A$ iff $\{a\} \subseteq A$
      $a \in A$ and $b \in A$ iff $\{a, b\} \subseteq A$
      if $A \subseteq B$ and $B \subseteq A$, then $A = B$

The last of these, which says that two sets that are each other's subsets are equal, emphasizes once more that it is the membership of a set which determines its identity.

Often we will have cause to specify a subset of some set A by means of a property G, by singling out all of A's elements which have this property G. The set of natural numbers which have the property of being both larger than 3 and smaller than 6 is, for example, the set $\{4, 5\}$. Specifying this set in the manner just described, it would be written as $\{4, 5\} = \{x \in N \mid x > 3$ and $x < 6\}$. The general notation for the set of all elements of A which have the property G is $\{x \in A \mid G(x)\}$. A few examples have been given as (87):

(87) $N = \{x \in Z \mid x \geqslant 0\}$
      $E = \{x \in N \mid \text{there is an } y \in N \text{ such that } x = 2y\}$
      $\{0\} = \{x \in \{0, 1\} \mid x + x = x\}$
      $\{0, 1, 4, 9, 16, 25, \ldots\} = \{x \in N \mid \text{there is an } y \in N \text{ such that}$
        $x = y^2\}$
      $\varnothing = \{x \in \{4, 5\} \mid x + x = x\}$
      $\{0, 1\} = \{x \in \{0, 1\} \mid x \times x = x\}$
      $\{p \to q\} = \{\phi \in \{p, q, p \to q, \neg(p \to q)\} \mid \phi \text{ is an implication}\}$

The above specification of E is also abbreviated as: $\{2y \mid y \in N\}$. Analogously, we might also write $\{y^2 \mid y \in N\}$ for the set $\{0, 1, 4, 9, 16, 25, \ldots\}$. Using this notation, the fact that f is a function from A *onto* B can easily be expressed by $\{f(a) \mid a \in A\} = B$. Another notation for the set of entities with some property G is $\{x \mid G(x)\}$. We can, by way of example, define $P = \{X \mid X \subseteq \{0, 1\}\}$; in which case P is set $\{\varnothing, \{0\}, \{1\}, \{0, 1\}\}$. Note that sets are allowed to have other sets as members.

The *union* $A \cup B$ of two sets A and B can now be defined as the set $\{x \mid x \in A \lor x \in B\}$. So $A \cup B$ is the set of all things which appear in either or both of A and B. Analogously, the *intersection* A ∩ B of A and B is defined as $\{x \mid x \in A \wedge x \in B\}$, the set of all things which appear in both A and B. By means of Venn diagrams, A ∪ B and A ∩ B can be represented graphically as in figures (88) and (89), respectively.

(88) A   B

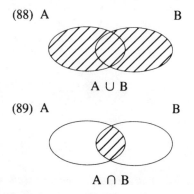

A ∪ B

(89) A   B

A ∩ B

Defining sets by means of $\{x \mid G(x)\}$ can, however, cause considerable difficulty if no restrictions are placed on the reservoir from which the entities satisfying G are to be drawn. In fact, if we assume that $\{x \mid G(x)\}$ is always a set for every property G, then we get caught in the *Russell paradox,* which caused a great deal of consternation in mathematics around the turn of the century. A short sketch of the paradox now follows. Given the above assumption, we have to accept $\{x \mid x = x\}$ as a set. V is the universal set containing everything, since every entity is equal to itself. Now if V contains everything, then in particular, $V \in V$; so $x \in x$ is a property which some special sets like V have, but which most sets do not have; $0 \notin 0$ because 0 is not a set; $\{0\} \notin \{0\}$ because $\{0\}$ has just one element, 0, and $0 \neq \{0\}$; $N \notin N$, since N has only whole numbers as its elements, and not sets of these, etc. Now consider the set R of all these entities, which according to our assumption, is defined by $R = \{x \mid x \notin x\}$. Then either R is an element of itself or not, and this is where the paradox comes in. If we suppose that $R \in R$, then R must have the property which determines membership in R, whence $R \notin R$. So apparently $R \in R$ is impossible. But if $R \notin R$, then R has the property which determines membership in R, and so it must be the case that $R \in R$. So $R \notin R$ is also impossible.

In modern set theory, axioms determine which sets can be defined by means of which others. In this manner, many sets may be defined in the manner of $\{x \mid G(x)\}$, without giving rise to the Russell paradox. One price which must be paid for this is that the class $V = \{x \mid x = x\}$ can no longer be accepted as a set: it is too big for this. This is one of the reasons why we cannot simply include everything in our domain when translating into predicate logic.

There are occasions when the fact that the order of elements in a set does not matter is inconvenient. We sometimes need to be able to specify the sequential order of a group of entities. For this reason, we now introduce the notion of *finite sequences* of entities. The finite sequence beginning with the numeral 4, ending with 5, and containing just two entities, for example, is written as $\langle 4, 5 \rangle$. Thus, we have $\langle 4, 5 \rangle \neq \langle 5, 4 \rangle$ and $\langle z, x, y \rangle \neq \langle x, y, z \rangle$. Other than with sets, with finite sequences it makes a difference if an entity appears a number of times: $\langle 4, 4, 5 \rangle \neq \langle 4, 5 \rangle$ and $\langle 4, 4, 4 \rangle \neq \langle 4, 4 \rangle$: the length of the sequences $\langle 4, 4, 5 \rangle$ and $\langle 4, 4, 4 \rangle$ is 3, while the length of $\langle 4, 5 \rangle$ and $\langle 4, 4 \rangle$ is 2, the length of a sequence being the number of entities appearing in it. Finite sequences of two entities are also called *ordered pairs,* finite sequences of three entities are called ordered triples, and ordered sequences of n entities are called ordered n-tuples. The set of all ordered pairs which can be formed from a set A is written A^2, A^3 is written for that of all ordered 3-tuples, and so on. More formally: $A^2 = \{\langle a, b \rangle | a \in A \text{ and } b \in A\}$; $A^3 = \{\langle a_1, a_2, a_3 \rangle | a_1 \in A \text{ and } a_2 \in A \text{ and } a_3 \in A\}$, and so on. For example, $\langle 2, 3 \rangle \in N^2$ and $\langle 1, 1, 1 \rangle \in N^3$ and $\langle -1, 2, -3, 4 \rangle \in Z^4$. The general notation A^n is used for the set of ordered n-tuples of elements of A; A^1 and A are identical.

This enables us to treat a binary function f with A as its domain as a unary function with A^2 as its domain. Instead of writing f(a, b), we can then write: $f(\langle a, b \rangle)$.

3.6 The Semantics of Predicate logic

The semantics of predicate logic is concerned with how the meanings of sentences, which just as in propositional logic, amount to their truth values, depend on the meanings of the parts of which they are composed. But since the parts need not themselves be sentences, or even formulas—they may also be predicate letters, constants, or variables—we will not be able to restrict ourselves to truth values in interpreting languages of predicate logic. We will need functions other than the valuations we encountered with in propositional logic, and ultimately the truth values of sentences will have to reduce to the interpretations of the constants and predicate letters and everything else which appears in them. Valuations, however, retain a central role, and it is instructive to start off just with them and to build up the rest of the apparatus for the interpretation of predicate logic from there. One first attempt to do this is found in the following definition, in which valuations are extended to the languages of predicate logic. It turns out that this is in itself not enough, so remember that the definition is only preliminary.

Definition 5

A valuation for a language L of predicate logic is a function with the sentences in L as its domain and $\{0, 1\}$ as its range, and such that:

(i) $V(\neg \phi) = 1$ iff $V(\phi) = 0$;
(ii) $V(\phi \wedge \psi) = 1$ iff $V(\phi) = 1$ and $V(\psi) = 1$;
(iii) $V(\phi \vee \psi) = 1$ iff $V(\phi) = 1$ or $V(\psi) = 1$;

(iv) $V(\phi \rightarrow \psi) = 1$ iff $V(\phi) = 0$ or $V(\psi) = 1$;
(v) $V(\phi \leftrightarrow \psi) = 1$ iff $V(\phi) = V(\psi)$;
(vi) $V(\forall x\phi) = 1$ iff $V([c/x]\phi) = 1$ for all constants c in L;
(vii) $V(\exists x\phi) = 1$ iff $V([c/x]\phi) = 1$ for at least one constant c in L.

The idea is that $\forall x\phi$ is true just in case $[c/x]\phi$ is true for every c in L, and that $\exists x\phi$ is true just in case $[c/x]\phi$ is true for at least one c in L. This could be motivated with reference to (90) and (91). For (90) is true just in case every substitution of the name of an individual human being into the open space in (91) results in a true sentence. And (92) is true just in case there is at least one name the substitution of which into (91) results in a true sentence.

   (90)   Everyone is friendly.

   (91)   . . . is friendly.

   (92)   Someone is friendly.

One thing should be obvious right from the start: in formal semantics, as in informal semantics, it is necessary to introduce a *domain of discourse*. For (90) may very well be true if the inhabitants of the Pacific state of Hawaii are taken as the domain, but untrue if all human beings are included. So in order to judge the truth value of (90), it is necessary to know what we are talking about, i.e., what the domain of discourse is. Interpretations of a language L of predicate logic will therefore always be with reference to some domain set D. It is usual to suppose that there is always at least one thing to talk about—so by convention, the domain is not empty.

3.6.1 *Interpretation Functions*

We will also have to be more precise about the relationship between the constants in L and the domain D. For if we wish to establish the truth value of (90) in the domain consisting of all inhabitants of Hawaii, then the truth value of *Liliuokalani is friendly* is of importance, while the truth value of *Gorbachev is friendly* is of no importance at all, since Liliuokalani is the name of an inhabitant of Hawaii (in fact she is, or at least was, one of its queens), while Gorbachev, barring unlikely coincidences, is not. Now it is a general characteristic of a proper name in natural language that it refers to some fixed thing. This is not the case in formal languages, where it is necessary to stipulate what the constants refer to. So an interpretation of L will have to include a specification of what each constant in L refers to. In this manner, constants refer to entities in the domain D, and as far as predicate logic is concerned, their meanings can be restricted to the entities to which they refer. The interpretation of the constants in L will therefore be an attribution of some entity in D to each of them, that is, a function with the set of constants in L as its domain and D as its range. Such functions are called *interpretation functions*.

I(c) is called the *interpretation* of a constant c, or its *reference* or its *denotation,* and if e is the entity in D such that I(c) = e, then c is said to be one of e's *names* (e may have several different names).

Now we have a domain D and an interpretation function I, but we are not quite there yet. It could well be that

(93)   Some are white.

is true for the domain consisting of all snowflakes without there really being any English sentence of the form *a is white* in which *a* is the name of a snowflake. For although snowflakes tend to be white, it could well be that none of them has an English name. It should be clear from this that definition 5 does not work as it is supposed to as soon as we admit domains with unnamed elements. So two approaches are open to us:

A. We could stick to definition 5 but make sure that all objects in our domains have names. In this case, it will sometimes be necessary to add constants to a language if it does not contain enough constants to give a unique name to everything in some domain that we are working with.

B. We replace definition 5 by a definition which will also work if some entities lack names.

We shall take both approaches. Approach B seems preferable, because of A's intuitive shortcomings: it would be strange if the truth of a sentence in predicate logic were to depend on a contingency such as whether or not all of the entities being talked about had a name. After all, the sentences in predicate logic do not seem to be saying these kinds of things about the domains in which they are interpreted. But we shall also discuss A, since this approach, where it is possible, is simpler and is equivalent to B.

3.6.2 *Interpretation by Substitution*

First we shall discuss **approach A,** which may be referred to as *the interpretation of quantifiers by substitution.* We shall now say more precisely what we mean when we say that each element in the domain has a name in L. Given the terminology introduced in §2.4, we can be quite succinct: the interpretation function I must be a function from the constants in L *onto* D. This means that for every element d in D, there is at least one constant c in L such that I(c) = d, i.e., c is a name of d. So we will only be allowed to make use of the definition if I is a function onto D.

But even this is not wholly satisfactory. So far, the meaning of predicate letters has only been given syncategorematically. This can be seen clearly if the question is transplanted into natural language: definition 5 enables us to know the meaning of the word *friendly* only to the extent that we know which sentences of the form *a is friendly* are true. If we want to give a direct, categorematic interpretation of *friendly,* then the interpretation will have to be such that the truth values of sentences of the form *a is friendly* can be deduced from it. And that is the requirement that can be placed on it, since we have restricted the meanings of sentences to their truth values. As a result, the only thing which matters as far as sentences of the form *a is friendly* are concerned is their truth values. An interpretation which establishes which people are friendly and which are not will satisfy this requirement. For example, *Gorbachev is friendly* is true just in case Gorbachev is friendly, since *Gorbachev* is one name for the man Gorbachev. Thus we can establish which people are friendly and which are not just by taking the set of all friendly people in our domain as the interpretation of *friendly*. In general then, as the interpretation I(A) of a unary predicate letter A we take the set of all entities e in D such that for some constant a, Aa is true and I(a) = e. So I(A) = {I(a) | Aa is true} or, in other words, Aa is true just in case I(a) ∈ I(A).

Interpreting A as a set of entities is not the only approach open to us. We might also interpret A as a property and determine whether a given element of D has this property. Indeed, this seems to be the most natural interpretation. If it is a predicate letter, we would expect A to refer to a property. What we have done here is to take, not properties themselves, but the sets of all things having them, as the interpretations of unary predicate letters. This approach may be less natural, but it has the advantage of emphasizing that in predicate logic the only thing we need to know in order to determine the truth or falsity of a sentence asserting that something has some property is which of the things in the domain have that property. It does not matter, for example, how we know this or whether things could be otherwise. As far as truth values are concerned, anything else which may be said about the property is irrelevant. If the set of friendly Hawaiians were to coincide precisely with the set of bald ones, then in this approach, *friendly* and *bald* would have the same meaning, at least if we took the set of Hawaiians as our domain. We say that predicate letters are *extensional* in predicate logic. It is characteristic of modern logic that such restrictions are explored in depth and subsequently relaxed. More than extensional meaning is attributed to expressions, for example, in *intensional* logical systems, which will be studied in volume 2.

To continue with approach A, and assuming that I is a function onto D as far as the constants are concerned, we turn to the interpretations of binary predicate letters. Just as with unary predicates, the interpretation of any given binary predicate B does not have to do anything more than determine the d and e in D for which Bab is true if I(a) = d and I(b) = e. This can be done by interpreting B as a set of ordered pairs ⟨d, e⟩ in D^2 and taking Bab to be true if I(a) = d and I(b) = e. The interpretation must consist of ordered pairs, because the order of a and b matters. The interpretation of B is, in other words, a subset of D^2, and we have I(B) = {⟨I(a), I(b)⟩ | Bab is true} or equivalently, Bab is true just in case ⟨I(a), I(b)⟩ ∈ I(B). Here too it may seem more intuitive to interpret B as a relation on D and to say that Bab is true if and only if I(a) and I(b) bear this relation to each other. For reasons already mentioned, however, we prefer the extensional approach and interpret a binary predicate letter not as a relation itself but as the set of ordered pairs of domain elements which (in the order they have in the pairs) have this relation to each other. And we thus have the principle of extensionality here too: two relations which hold for the same ordered pairs are identical. Ternary predicates and predicates of all higher arities are given an analogous treatment. If C is a ternary predicate letter, then I(C) is a subset of D^3, and if C is an n-ary predicate, then I(C) is a subset of D^n. We shall now summarize all of this in the following two definitions:

Definition 6

A *model* **M** for a language L of predicate logic consists of a domain D (this being a nonempty set) and an interpretation function I which is defined on the set of constants and predicate letters in the vocabulary of L and which conforms to the following requirements:

(i)   if c is a constant in L, then $I(c) \in D$;
(ii)   if B is an n-ary predicate letter in L, then $I(B) \subseteq D^n$.

Definition 7

If **M** is a model for L whose interpretation function I is a function of the constants in L onto the domain D, then V_M, *the valuation V based on* **M**, is defined as follows:

(i)   If $Aa_1 \ldots a_n$ is an atomic sentence in L, then $V_M(Aa_1 \ldots a_n) = 1$ if and only if $\langle I(a_1), \ldots, I(a_n) \rangle \in I(A)$.
(ii) $V_M(\neg\phi) = 1$ iff $V_M(\phi) = 0$.
(iii) $V_M(\phi \wedge \psi) = 1$ iff $V_M(\phi) = 1$ and $V_M(\psi) = 1$.
(iv) $V_M(\phi \vee \psi) = 1$ iff $V_M(\phi) = 1$ or $V_M(\psi) = 1$.
(v) $V_M(\phi \rightarrow \psi) = 1$ iff $V_M(\phi) = 0$ or $V_M(\psi) = 1$.
(vi) $V_M(\phi \leftrightarrow \psi) = 1$ iff $V_M(\phi) = V_M(\psi)$.
(vii) $V_M(\forall x\phi) = 1$ iff $V_M([c/x]\phi) = 1$ for all constants c in L.
(viii) $V_M(\exists x\phi) = 1$ iff $V_M([c/x]\phi) = 1$ for at least one constant c in L.
If $V_M(\phi) = 1$, then ϕ is said to be *true* in model **M**.

If the condition that I be a function onto D is not fulfilled, then approach B will still enable us to define a suitable valuation function V_M, though this function will no longer fulfill clauses (vii) and (viii) of definition 7. Before showing how this can be done, we shall first give a few examples to illustrate method A.

Example 1

We turn the key to a translation into a model.
Key: Lxy: x loves y; domain: Hawaiians.
We take H, the set of all Hawaiians, as the domain of model **M**. Besides the binary predicate L, our language must contain enough constants to give each

Hawaiian a name; $a_1, \ldots, a_{1,000,000}$ should be enough. Now for each i from 1 to 1,000,000 inclusive, a_i must be interpreted as a Hawaiian: $I(a_i) \in H$, and this in such a way that for each Hawaiian h there is some a_h which is interpreted as that Hawaiian, that is, for which $I(a_h) = h$. The interpretation of L is the following subset of H^2, i.e., the set of pairs of Hawaiians: $\{\langle d, e\rangle | d$ loves e$\}$. Lets us now determine the truth value of $\exists x \exists y(Lxy \wedge Lyx)$, which is the translation of *some people love each other*. Suppose that John loves Mary, that Mary's love for John is no less, that $I(a_{26})$ is Mary, and that $I(a_{27})$ is John. Then $\langle I(a_{26}), I(a_{27})\rangle \in I(L)$, and $\langle I(a_{27}), I(a_{26})\rangle \in I(L)$. According to definition 7i, we have $V_M(La_{26}a_{27}) = 1$ and $V_M(La_{27}a_{26}) = 1$, so that according to definition 7iii, we have $V_M(La_{26}a_{27} \wedge La_{27}a_{26}) = 1$. One application of definition 7viii now gives us $V_M(\exists y(La_{26}y \wedge Lya_{26})) = 1$, and a second gives us $V_M(\exists x \exists y(Lxy \wedge Lyx)) = 1$. Of course, it doesn't matter at all which constants are interpreted as which people. We could have shown that $V_M(\exists x \exists y(Lxy \wedge Lyx)) = 1$ just as well if $I(a_2)$ had been John and $I(a_9)$ had been Mary. This is a general fact: the truth of a sentence lacking constants is in any model independent of the interpretations of the constants in that model— with the proviso that everything in the domain has a name. A comment such as this should of course be proved, but we do not have the space here.

It is perhaps worth pointing out at this stage that semantics is not really concerned with finding out which sentences are in fact true and which are false. One's ideas about this are unlikely to be influenced much by the analysis given here. Essentially, semantics is concerned with *the ways the truth values of sentences depend on the meanings of their parts and the ways the truth values of different sentences are related*. This is analogous to the analysis of the notion of grammaticality in linguistics. It is assumed that it is clear which expressions are grammatical and which are not; the problem is to conceive a systematic theory on the subject.

The following examples contain a few extremely simple mathematical structures. We shall leave off the index **M** in V_M if it is clear what model the valuation is based on.

Example 2

The language we will interpret contains three constants, a_1, a_2, and a_3, and the binary predicate letter R. The domain D of the model is the set of points $\{P_1, P_2, P_3\}$ represented in figure (94).

(94)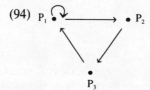

The constants are interpreted as follows: $I(a_1) = P_1$; $I(a_2) = P_2$; and $I(a_3) = P_3$. The interpretation of R is the relation holding between any two not necessarily different points with an arrow pointing from the first to the second. So the following interpretation of R can be read from figure (94): I(R) = $\{\langle P_1, P_1\rangle, \langle P_1, P_2\rangle, \langle P_2, P_3\rangle, \langle P_3, P_1\rangle\}$. Representing this by means of a key, Rxy: there is an arrow pointing from x to y. It is directly obvious that $V(Ra_1a_2) = 1$, $V(Ra_2a_3) = 1$, $V(Ra_3a_1) = 1$, and $V(Ra_1a_1) = 1$; in all other cases, $V(Rbc) = 0$, so that, for example, $V(Ra_2a_1) = 0$ and $V(Ra_3a_3) = 0$. We shall now determine the truth value of $\forall x\exists yRxy$ (which means *every point has an arrow pointing away from it*).

(a) $V(\exists yRa_1y) = 1$ follows from $V(Ra_1a_2) = 1$ with definition 7viii;
(b) $V(\exists yRa_2y) = 1$ follows from $V(Ra_2a_3) = 1$ with definition 7viii;
(c) $V(\exists yRa_3y) = 1$ follows from $V(Ra_3a_1) = 1$ with definition 7viii.

From (a), (b), and (c), we can now conclude that $V(\forall x\exists yRxy) = 1$ with definition 7vii. The truth value of $\forall x\exists yRyx$ (which means *every point has an arrow pointing to it*) can be determined in just the same way:

(d) $V(\exists yRya_1) = 1$ follows from $V(Ra_1a_1) = 1$ with definition 7viii;
(e) $V(\exists yRya_2) = 1$ follows from $V(Ra_1a_2) = 1$ with definition 7viii;
(f) $V(\exists yRya_3) = 1$ follows from $V(Ra_2a_3) = 1$ with definition 7viii.

From (d), (e), and (f), we conclude that $V(\forall x\exists yRyx) = 1$ with definition 7vii.

Finally, we shall determine the truth value of $\exists x\forall yRxy$ (which means: *there is a point from which arrows go to all other points*):

(g) $V(\forall yRa_1y) = 0$ follows from $V(Ra_1a_3) = 0$ with definition 7vii;
(h) $V(\forall yRa_2y) = 0$ follows from $V(Ra_2a_2) = 0$ with definition 7vii;
(i) $V(\forall yRa_3y) = 0$ follows from $V(Ra_3a_3) = 0$ with definition 7vii.

From (g), (h), and (i), we can now conclude that $V(\exists x\forall yRxy) = 0$ with definition 7viii.

Example 3

We consider a language with a unary predicate letter E, a binary predicate letter L, and constants $a_0, a_1, a_2, a_3, \ldots$. We take N, the set $\{0, 1, 2, 3, \ldots\}$ of natural numbers, as our domain. We choose $V(a_i) = i$ for every i and interpret E as the set of even numbers, so that $I(E) = \{0, 2, 4, 6, \ldots\}$. We interpret L as $<$, so that $I(L) = \{\langle m, n\rangle | m \text{ less than } n\}$. As true sentences we then have, for example, Ea_2, La_4a_5, and $\forall x\exists y(Lxy \wedge \neg Ey)$ (these mean *2 is even*, *4 is less than 5*, and *for every number there is a larger number which is odd*, respectively). We shall expand on the last of these. Consider any number m. This number must be either even or odd.

If m is even, then m + 1 is odd, so that $V(Ea_{m+1}) = 0$ and $V(\neg Ea_{m+1}) = 1$. We also have $V(La_ma_{m+1}) = 1$, since $m < m + 1$. From this we may conclude that $V(La_ma_{m+1} \wedge \neg Ea_{m+1}) = 1$, and finally that $V(\exists y(La_my \wedge \neg Ey)) = 1$.

If, on the other hand, m is odd, then m + 2 is odd too, so that $V(Ea_{m+2}) = 0$ and $V(\neg Ea_{m+2}) = 1$. We also have $V(La_ma_{m+2}) = 1$, since $m < m + 2$, and thus $V(La_m a_{m+2} \wedge \neg Ea_{m+2}) = 1$, so that we have $V(\exists y(La_m y \wedge \neg Ey)) = 1$ in this case as well. Since this line of reasoning applies to an arbitrary number m, we have for every a_m: $V(\exists y(La_m y \wedge \neg Ey)) = 1$. Now we have shown that $V(\forall x \exists y(Lxy \wedge \neg Ey)) = 1$.

(95)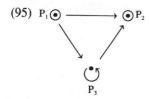

Exercise 7

Model **M** is given in figure (95). The language has three constants a_1, a_2, and a_3 interpreted as the points P_1, P_2, and P_3, a unary predicate letter A interpreted as the predicate that applies to a point if it has a circle around it, and a binary predicate letter R to be interpreted as in example 2.

(a) Describe exactly the interpretation function I of the model **M**.
(b) Determine on the basis of their meaning the truth or falsity of the following sentences on model **M** and then justify this in detail, using definition 7:

(i) $\exists x \exists y \exists z(Rxy \wedge Ay \wedge Rxz \wedge \neg Az)$.
(ii) $\forall x Rxx$.
(iii) $\forall x(Rxx \leftrightarrow \neg Ax)$.
(iv) $\exists x \exists y(Rxy \wedge \neg Ax \wedge \neg Ay)$.
(v) $\forall x(Rxx \rightarrow \exists y(Rxy \wedge Ay))$.
(vi) $\forall x(Ax \rightarrow \exists y\, Rxy)$.
(vii) $\exists x \exists y(Rxy \wedge \neg Ryx \wedge \exists z(Rxz \wedge Rzy))$.

3.6.3 *Interpretation by means of assignments*

We have now come to the explication of **approach B.** To recapitulate: we have a language L, a domain D, and an interpretation function I which maps all of L's constants into D but which is not necessarily a function *onto* D. That is, we have no guarantee that everything in the domain has some constant as its name. This means that the truth of sentences $\exists x \phi$ and $\forall x \phi$ can no longer be reduced to that of sentences of the form $[c/x]\phi$. Actually, this reduction is not that attractive anyway, if we wish to take the principle of compositionality strictly. This principle requires that the meaning (i.e., the truth value) of an expression be reducible to that of its composite parts. But sentences $\exists x \phi$ and $\forall x \phi$ do not have sentences of the form $[c/x]\phi$ as their component parts, because they are obtained by placing a quantifier in front of a formula ϕ, which normally has a free variable x and therefore is not even another sentence. What this means is that we will have to find some way to attach meanings to formulas in general; we can no longer restrict ourselves to the special case of sentences.

We have reserved the name *propositional function* for formulas with free variables, in part because sentences can be obtained by replacing the free variables with constants, and in part because a formula with free variables does not seem to express a proposition but rather a property or a relation. But we could also take a different view and say that formulas with free variables express propositions just as much as sentences do, only these propositions are about unspecified entities. This would be why they are suited to express properties and relations.

In order to see how a meaning can be attached to these kinds of formulas, let us return again to (96) (=(93)):

(96)   Some are white.

This was to be interpreted in the domain consisting of all snowflakes. What we want to do is determine the truth value of (96) with reference to the meaning of *x is white* interpreted in the domain consisting of all snowflakes. Now x, as we have emphasized, has no meaning of its own, so it must not refer to some fixed entity in the domain as if it were a constant. This may be compared with the way pronouns refer in sentences like *he is white* and *she is black*. But precisely for this reason, it may make sense to consider x as the *temporary* name of some entity. The idea is to consider model **M** together with an extra attribution of denotations to x and all the other variables; x will receive a temporary interpretation as an element in D. It is then quite easy to determine the truth value of (96): (96) is true if and only if there is some attribution of a denotation in the domain of all snowflakes to x, such that *x is white* becomes a true sentence. In other words, (96) is true just in case there is some snowflake which, if it is given the name x, will turn *x is white* into a true sentence—and that is exactly what we need.

The meaning of

(97)   They are all black.

in the domain consisting of all snowflakes can be handled in much the same way: (97) is true if and only if *every* attribution of a denotation to x in this domain turns *x is black* into a true sentence. Analyzing this idea brings up more technical problems than most things we have encountered so far.

In order to determine the truth value of a sentence like ∃x∃y(Hxy ∧ Hyx), it is necessary to work back (in two steps) to the meaning of its subformula Hxy ∧ Hyx, which has two free variables. Obviously since no limitation is placed on the length of formulas, such subformulas can contain any number of free variables. This means that we must deal with the meanings of formulas with any number of free variables in order to determine the truth values of sentences. What matters is the truth value of a formula once all of its free variables have been given a temporary denotation, but it turns out that it is

easiest to give all free variables a denotation at the same time. It is un-
necessarily difficult to keep track of what free variables each formula has and
to assign denotations to them. What we do is use certain functions called *assignments* which have the set of all variables in the language as their domain,
and D, the domain of the model, as their range.

We will now describe the truth values a model **M** gives to the formulas of L
under an assignment g by means of a valuation function $V_{M,g}$. This function
will be defined by modifying conditions (i)–(viii) of definition 7 above.

The complications begin with clause (i). There is no problem as long as we
deal with an atomic formula containing only variables and no constants: we
are then dealing with $V_{M,g}(Ax_1 \ldots x_n)$, and it is clear that we wish to have
$V_{M,g}(Ax_1 \ldots x_n) = 1$ if and only if $\langle g(x_1), \ldots, g(x_n)\rangle \in I(A)$, since the
only difference from the earlier situation is that we have an assignment g attributing denotations to variables instead of an interpretation I attributing
denotations to constants. But it becomes more difficult to write things up
properly for formulas of the form $At_1 \ldots t_n$, in which $t_1, \ldots, t_n$ may be
either constants or variables. What we do is introduce *term* as the collective
name for the constants and variables of L. We first define what we mean by
$[\![t]\!]_{M,g}$, the interpretation of a term t in a model **M** under an assignment g.

Definition 8

$[\![t]\!]_{M,g} = I(t)$ if t is a constant in L, and
$[\![t]\!]_{M,g} = g(t)$ if t is a variable.

Now we can generalize (i) in definition 7 to:

$$V_{M,g}(At_1 \ldots t_n) = 1 \text{ iff } \langle [\![t_1]\!]_{M,g}, \ldots, [\![t_n]\!]_{M,g}\rangle \in I(A).$$

It is clear that the value of $V_{M,g}(At_1 \ldots t_n)$ does not depend on the value of
g(y) if y does not appear among the terms $t_1, \ldots, t_n$.

Clauses (ii) to (vi) in definition 7 can be transferred to the definition of $V_{M,g}$
without modification. The second clause we have to adapt is (viii), the clause
for $V_{M,g}(\exists y\phi)$. Note that ϕ may have free variables other than y. Let us return
to the model given in example 1, only this time for a language lacking constants. We take Lxy as our ϕ. Now how is $V_{M,g}(\exists yLxy)$ to be defined? Under
an assignment g, x is treated as if it denotes g(x), so $\exists yLxy$ means that g(x)
loves someone. So the definition must result in $V_{M,g}(\exists yLxy) = 1$ if and only if
there is a $d \in H$ such that $\langle g(x), d\rangle \in I(L)$. The idea was to reduce the meaning of $\exists yLxy$ to the meaning of Lxy. But we cannot take $V_{M,g}(\exists yLxy) = 1$ if
and only if $V_{M,g}(Lxy) = 1$, since $V_{M,g}(Lxy) = 1$ if and only if $\langle g(x), g(y)\rangle \in$
I(L), that is, if and only if g(x) loves g(y). For it may well be that g(x) loves
someone without this someone being g(y). The existential quantifier forces us
to consider assignments other than g which only differ from g in the value
which they assign to y, since the denotation of x may clearly not be changed.

On the one hand, if there is an assignment g' which differs from g only in the value it assigns to y and such that $V_{M,g'}(Lxy) = 1$, then $\langle g'(x), g'(y) \rangle \in I(L)$, and thus, because $g(x) = g'(x)$, $\langle g(x), g'(y) \rangle \in I(L)$. So for some $d \in H$, $\langle g(x), d \rangle \in I(L)$. On the other hand, if there is some $d \in H$ such that $\langle g(x), d \rangle \in I(L)$, then it can easily be seen that there is always an assignment g' such that $V_{M,g'}(Lxy) = 1$. Choose g', for example, the assignment obtained by taking g and then just changing the value assigned to y to d. Then $\langle g'(x), g'(y) \rangle \in I(L)$, and so $V_{M,g'}(Lxy) = 1$. This argument can be repeated for any given formula, so now we can give a first version of the new clause for existential formulas. It is this: $V_{M,g}(\exists yLxy) = 1$ if and only if there is a g' which differs from g only in its value for y and for which $V_{M,g'}(Lxy) = 1$. So g' is uniquely determined by g, and the value g' is assigned to the variable y. This means that we can adopt the following notation: we write $g[y/d]$ for g' if this assignment assigns d to y and assigns the same values as g to all the other variables. (Note that c in the notation $[c/x]\phi$ refers to a constant in L, whereas the d in $g[y/d]$ refers to an entity in the domain; the first expression refers to the result of a syntactic operation, and the second does not.) The assignments $g[y/d]$ and g tend to differ. But that is not necessarily the case, since they are identical if $g(y) = d$. So now we can give the final version of the new clause for existential formulas. It is this:

$$V_{M,g}(\exists y\phi) = 1 \text{ iff there is a } d \in D \text{ such that } V_{M,g[y/d]}(\phi) = 1.$$

A similar development can be given for the new clause for the universal quantifier. So now we can complete this discussion of the B approach by giving the following definition. It is well known as Tarski's truth definition, in honor of the mathematician A. Tarski who initiated it; it is a generalization of definition 7. Although clauses (ii)–(vi) are not essentially changed, we give the definition in full for ease of reference.

Definition 9

If **M** is a model, D is its domain, I is its interpretation function, and g is an assignment into D, then

(i) $V_{M,g}(At_1 \ldots t_n) = 1$ iff $\langle [\![t_1]\!]_{M,g}, \ldots, [\![t_n]\!]_{M,g} \rangle \in I(A)$;

(ii) $V_{M,g}(\neg\phi) = 1$ iff $V_{M,g}(\phi) = 0$;

(iii) $V_{M,g}(\phi \wedge \psi) = 1$ iff $V_{M,g}(\phi) = 1$ and $V_{M,g}(\psi) = 1$;

(iv) $V_{M,g}(\phi \vee \psi) = 1$ iff $V_{M,g}(\phi) = 1$ or $V_{M,g}(\psi) = 1$;

(v) $V_{M,g}(\phi \rightarrow \psi) = 1$ iff $V_{M,g}(\phi) = 0$ or $V_{M,g}(\psi) = 1$;

(vi) $V_{M,g}(\phi \leftrightarrow \psi) = 1$ iff $V_{M,g}(\phi) = V_{M,g}(\psi)$;

(vii) $V_{M,g}(\forall x\phi) = 1$ iff for all $d \in D$, $V_{M,g[x/d]}(\phi) = 1$;

(viii) $V_{M,g}(\exists x\phi) = 1$ iff there is at least one $d \in D$ such that $V_{M,g[x/d]}(\phi) = 1$.

We now state a few facts about this definition which we shall not prove. First, the only values of g which $V_{M,g}(\phi)$ is dependent on are the values which g

assigns to variables which occur as free variables in ϕ; so ϕ has the same value for every g in the extreme case in which ϕ is a sentence. This means that for sentences ϕ we can just write $V_M(\phi)$. Consequently, it holds for sentences ϕ that if ϕ is true with respect to some g, then it is true with respect to all g. If all elements of the domain of **M** have names, then for any sentence ϕ, approach A and approach B give the same values for $V_M(\phi)$. In such cases then, either can be taken. We shall now return to the examples given in connection with approach A, and reconsider them with B.

Example 1

There is just a single binary predicate letter L in the language; the domain is H, the set of all Hawaiians; $I(L) = \{\langle d, e \rangle \in H^2 \,|\, d \text{ loves } e\}$, and John and Mary are two members of the domain who love one another. We now define $g(x) =$ John and $g(y) =$ Mary; we complete g by assigning the other variables at random. Then $V_{M,g}(Lxy) = 1$, since $\langle [\![x]\!]_{M,g}, [\![y]\!]_{M,g} \rangle = \langle g(x), g(y) \rangle = \langle \text{John}, \text{Mary} \rangle \in I(L)$. Analogously, $V_{M,g}(Lyx) = 1$, so that we also have $V_{M,g}(Lxy \wedge Lyx) = 1$. This means that $V_{M,g}(\exists y(Lxy \wedge Lyx)) = 1$, since $g = g[y/\text{Mary}]$, and that $V_{M,g}(\exists x\exists y(Lxy \wedge Lyx)) = 1$ too, since $g = g[x/\text{John}]$.

Example 2

There is just a single binary predicate letter R in the language; the domain is $\{P_1, P_2, P_3\}$; $I(R) = \{\langle P_1, P_2 \rangle, \langle P_1, P_1 \rangle, \langle P_2, P_3 \rangle, \langle P_3, P_1 \rangle\}$. Now for an arbitrary g we have:

if $g(x) = P_1$, then $V_{M,g[y/P_2]}(Rxy) = 1$, since $\langle P_1, P_2 \rangle \in I(R)$;
if $g(x) = P_2$, then $V_{M,g[y/P_3]}(Rxy) = 1$, since $\langle P_2, P_3 \rangle \in I(R)$;
if $g(x) = P_3$, then $V_{M,g[y/P_1]}(Rxy) = 1$, since $\langle P_3, P_1 \rangle \in I(R)$.

This means that for every g there is a $d \in \{P_1, P_2, P_3\}$ such that $V_{M,g[y/d]}(Rxy) = 1$. This means that $V_{M,g}(\exists yRxy) = 1$. Since this holds for an arbitrary g, we may conclude that $V_{M,g[x/d]}(\exists yRxy) = 1$ for every $d \in D$. We have now shown that $V_{M,g}(\forall x\exists yRxy) = 1$. That $V_{M,g}(\forall x\exists yRyx) = 1$ can be shown in the same way.

Now for the truth value of $\exists x\forall yRxy$. For arbitrary g, we have:

if $g(x) = P_1$, then $V_{M,g[y/P_3]}(Rxy) = 0$, since $\langle P_1, P_3 \rangle \notin I(R)$;
if $g(x) = P_2$, then $V_{M,g[y/P_2]}(Rxy) = 0$, since $\langle P_2, P_2 \rangle \notin I(R)$;
if $g(x) = P_3$, then $V_{M,g[y/P_3]}(Rxy) = 0$, since $\langle P_3, P_3 \rangle \notin I(R)$.

This means that for every g there is a $d \in \{P_1, P_2, P_3\}$ such that $V_{M,g[y/d]}(Rxy) = 0$. From this it is clear that for every g we have $V_{M,g}(\forall yRxy) = 0$, and thus that for every $d \in D$, $V_{M,g[y/d]}(\forall yRxy) = 0$; and this gives $V_{M,g}(\exists x\forall yRxy) = 0$.

Example 3

The language contains a unary predicate letter E and a binary predicate letter L. The domain of our model **M** is the set N, $I(E) = \{0, 2, 4, 6, \ldots\}$, and $I(L)$

$= \{\langle m, n \rangle | m < n\}$. Now let g be chosen at random. Then there are two possibilities:

(a) g(x) is an even number. In that case g(x) + 1 is odd, so that g(x) + 1 $\notin$ I(E), from which it follows that $V_{M,g[y/g(x)+1]}(Ey) = 0$ and that $V_{M,g[y/g(x)+1]}(\neg Ey) = 1$. Furhermore, $\langle g(x), g(x) + 1 \rangle \in I(L)$, and therefore $V_{M,g[y/g(x)+1]}(Lxy) = 1$, so that we have $V_{M,g[y/g(x)+1]}(Lxy \land \neg Ey) = 1$.

(b) g(x) is an odd number. In that case, g(x) + 2 is an odd number too. From this it follows, as in (a), that $V_{M,g[y/g(x)+2]}(Lxy \land \neg Ey) = 1$. In both cases, then, there is an n $\in$ N such that $V_{M,g[y/n]}(Lxy \land \neg Ey) = 1$. This means that for every g, $V_{M,g}(\exists y(Lxy \land \neg Ey)) = 1$, from which it is clear that $V_{M,g}(\forall x \exists y(Lxy \land \neg Ey)) = 1$.

Exercise 8

Work out exercise 7bi, iii, and v again, now according to approach B (definition 9).

3.6.4 *Universal Validity*

In predicate logic as in propositional logic, we speak of *contradictions*, these being sentences ϕ such that $V_M(\phi) = 0$ for all models M in the language from which ϕ is taken. Here are some examples of contradictions: $\forall x(Ax \land \neg Ax)$, $\forall xAx \land \exists y\neg Ay$, $\exists x \forall y(Ryx \leftrightarrow \neg Ryy)$ (the last one is a formalization of Russell's paradox).

Formulas ϕ such that $V_M(\phi) = 1$ for all models M for the language from which ϕ is taken are called *universally valid* formulas (they are not normally called tautologies). That ϕ is universally valid is written as $\vDash \phi$. Here are some examples of universally valid formulas (more will follow later): $\forall x(Ax \lor \neg Ax)$, $\forall x(Ax \land Bx) \rightarrow \forall xAx$, $(\forall x(Ax \lor Bx) \land \exists x\neg Ax) \rightarrow \exists xBx$.

And in predicate logic as in propositional logic, sentences ϕ and ψ are said to be *equivalent* if they always have the same truth values, that is, if for every model M for the language from which ϕ and ψ are taken, $V_M(\phi) = V_M(\psi)$. On approach B, this can be generalized to: two formulas ϕ and ψ are equivalent if for every model M for the language from which they are taken and every assignment g into M, $V_{M,g}(\phi) = V_{M,g}(\psi)$. As an example of a pair of equivalent sentences, we have $\forall xAx$, $\forall yAy$, as can easily be checked. More generally, are $\forall x\phi$ and $\forall y([y/x]\phi)$ always equivalent? Not when y occurs free in ϕ; obviously $\exists xLxy$ is not equivalent to $\exists yLyy$: somebody may love y without anybody loving him- or herself.

It might be thought though, that $\forall x\phi$ and $\forall y([y/x]\phi)$ are equivalent for any ϕ in which y does not occur free. This is, however, not the case, as can be seen from the fact that $\forall x\exists yAxy$ and $\forall y\exists yAyy$ are not equivalent. In $\forall y\exists yAyy$, the quantifier $\forall y$ does not bind any variable y, and therefore $\forall y\exists yAyy$ is equivalent to $\exists yAyy$. But clearly $\forall x\exists yAxy$ can be true without $\exists yAyy$ being true. Everyone has a mother, for example, but there is no one who is his or her own mother. The problem, of course, is that y has been substituted for a free variable x within the range of the quantifier ∀y. If we want to turn the above into a theorem, then we need at least one restriction saying that this may not occur. The following definition enables us to formulate such restrictions more easily:

Definition 10

y is *free* (*for substitution*) *for x in* ϕ if x does not occur as a free variable within the scope of any quantifier ∀y or ∃y in ϕ.

For example, y will clearly be free for x in ϕ if y doesn't appear in ϕ. In general, it is not difficult to prove (by induction on the complexity of ϕ) that for ϕ in which y does not occur free, ϕ and $\forall y([y/x]\phi)$ are indeed equivalent if y is free for x in ϕ.

In predicate logic as in propositional logic, substituting equivalent subformulas for each other does not affect equivalence. We will discuss this in §4.2, but we use it in the following list of pairs of equivalent formulas:

(a) $\forall x \neg \phi$ is equivalent to $\neg \exists x \phi$. This is apparent from the fact that $V_{M,g}(\forall x \neg \phi) = 1$ iff for every $d \in D_M$, $V_{M,g[x/d]}(\neg \phi) = 1$; iff for every $d \in D_M$, $V_{M,g[x/d]}(\phi) = 0$; iff it is not the case that there is a $d \in D_M$ such that $V_{M,g[x/d]}(\phi) = 1$; iff it is not the case that $V_{M,g}(\exists x \phi) = 1$; iff $V_{M,g}(\exists x \phi) = 0$; iff $V_{M,g}(\neg \exists x \phi) = 1$.

(b) $\forall x \phi$ is equivalent to $\neg \exists x \neg \phi$, since $\forall x \phi$ is equivalent to $\forall x \neg \neg \phi$, and thus, according to (a), to $\neg \exists x \neg \phi$ too.

(c) $\neg \forall x \phi$ is equivalent to $\exists x \neg \phi$, since $\exists x \neg \phi$ is equivalent to $\neg \neg \exists x \neg \phi$, and thus, according to (b), to $\neg \forall x \phi$ too.

(d) $\neg \forall x \neg \phi$ is equivalent to $\exists x \phi$. According to (c), $\neg \forall x \neg \phi$ is equivalent to $\exists x \neg \neg \phi$, and thus to $\exists x \phi$.

(e) $\forall x (Ax \wedge Bx)$ is equivalent to $\forall x Ax \wedge \forall x Bx$, since $V_{M,g}(\forall x (Ax \wedge Bx)) = 1$ iff for every $d \in D_M$: $V_{M,g[x/d]}(Ax \wedge Bx) = 1$; iff for every $d \in D_M$: $V_{M,g[x/d]}(Ax) = 1$ and $V_{M,g[x/d]}(Bx) = 1$; iff for every $d \in D_M$: $V_{M,g[x/d]}(Ax) = 1$, while for every $d \in D_M$: $V_{M,g[x/d]}(Bx) = 1$; iff $V_{M,g}(\forall x Ax) = 1$ and $V_{M,g}(\forall x Bx) = 1$; iff $V_{M,g}(\forall x Ax \wedge \forall x Bx)) = 1$.

(f) $\forall x (\phi \wedge \psi)$ is equivalent to $\forall x \phi \wedge \forall x \psi$. This is a generalization of (e), and its proof is the same.

(g) $\exists x (\phi \vee \psi)$ is equivalent to $\exists x \phi \vee \exists x \psi$, since $\exists x (\phi \vee \psi)$ is equivalent to $\neg \forall x \neg (\phi \vee \psi)$, and thus to $\neg \forall x (\neg \phi \wedge \neg \psi)$ (de Morgan) and thus, according to (f), to $\neg (\forall x \neg \phi \wedge \forall x \neg \psi)$, and thus to $\neg \forall x \neg \phi \vee \neg \forall x \neg \psi$ (de Morgan), and thus, according to (d), to $\exists x \phi \vee \exists x \psi$.

N.B. $\forall x (\phi \vee \psi)$ is not necessarily equivalent to $\forall x \phi \vee \forall x \psi$. For example, each is male or female in the domain of human beings, but it is not the case that either all are male or all are female. $\exists x (\phi \wedge \psi)$ and $\exists x \phi \wedge \exists x \psi$ are not necessarily equivalent either. What we do have, and can easily prove, is:

(h) $\forall x(\phi \lor \psi)$ is equivalent to $\phi \lor \forall x\psi$ if x is not free in ϕ, and to $\forall x\phi \lor \psi$ if x is not free in ψ. Similarly:

(k) $\exists x(\phi \land \psi)$ is equivalent to $\exists x\phi \land \psi$ if x is not free in ψ, and to $\phi \land \exists x\phi$ if x is not free in ϕ.

(l) $\forall x(\phi \rightarrow \psi)$ is equivalent to $\phi \rightarrow \forall x\psi$ if x is not free in ϕ, since $\forall x(\phi \rightarrow \psi)$ is equivalent to $\forall x(\neg\phi \lor \psi)$ and thus, according to (h), to $\neg\phi \lor \forall x\psi$, and thus to $\phi \rightarrow \forall x\psi$. An example: *For everyone it holds that if the weather is fine, then he or she is in a good mood* means the same as *If the weather is fine, then everyone is in a good mood.*

(m) $\forall x(\phi \rightarrow \psi)$ is equivalent to $\exists x\phi \rightarrow \psi$ if x is not free in ψ, since $\forall x(\phi \rightarrow \psi)$ is equivalent to $\forall x(\neg\phi \lor \psi)$ and thus, according to (h), to $\forall x\neg\phi \lor \psi$, and thus, according to (a), to $\neg\exists x\phi \lor \psi$, and thus to $\exists x\phi \rightarrow \psi$. An example: *For everyone it holds that if he or she puts a penny in the slot, then a package of chewing gum drops out* means the same as *If someone puts a penny in the machine, then a package of chewing gum rolls out.*

(n) $\exists x\exists y(Ax \land By)$ is equivalent to $\exists xAx \land \exists yBy$, since $\exists x\exists y(Ax \land By)$ is equivalent to $\exists x(Ax \land \exists yBy)$, given (k), and with another application of (k), to $\exists xAx \land \exists yBy$.

(o) $\exists x\phi$ is equivalent to $\exists y([y/x]\phi)$ if y does not occur free in ϕ and y is free for x in ϕ, since $\exists x\phi$ is equivalent to $\neg\forall x\neg\phi$, according to (d). This in turn is equivalent to $\neg\forall y([y/x]\neg\phi)$, for y is free for x in ϕ if y is free for x in $\neg\phi$. And $\neg\forall y(\exists y/x]\neg\phi)$, finally, is equivalent to $\exists y([y/x]\phi)$ by (d), since $\neg([y/x]\phi)$ and $[y/x]\neg\phi$ are one and the same formula.

(p) $\forall x\forall y\phi$ is equivalent to $\forall y\forall x\phi$, as can easily be proved.

(q) $\exists x\exists y\phi$ is equivalent to $\exists y\exists x\phi$, on the basis of (d) and (p).

(r) $\exists x\exists yAxy$ is equivalent to $\exists x\exists yAyx$. According to (o), $\exists x\exists yAxy$ is equivalent to $\exists x\exists zAxz$, with another application of (o), to $\exists w\exists zAwz$, with (q), to $\exists z\exists wAwz$, and applying (o) another two times, to $\exists x\exists yAyx$.

In predicate logic too, for sentences ϕ and ψ, $\vDash\phi \leftrightarrow \psi$ iff ϕ and ψ are equivalent. And if $\vDash\phi \leftrightarrow \psi$, then both $\vDash\phi \rightarrow \psi$ and $\vDash\psi \rightarrow \phi$. But it is quite possible that $\vDash\phi \rightarrow \psi$ without ϕ and ψ being fully equivalent.

Here are some examples of universally valid formulas (proofs are omitted):

(i)	$\forall x\phi \rightarrow \exists x\phi$	(vi)	$\exists x\forall y\phi \rightarrow \exists y\forall x\phi$
(ii)	$\forall x\phi \rightarrow [t/x]\phi$	(vii)	$\forall xAxx \rightarrow \forall x\exists yAxy$
(iii)	$[t/x]\phi \rightarrow \exists x\phi$	(viii)	$\exists x\forall yAxy \rightarrow \exists xAxx$
(iv)	$(\forall x\phi \land \forall x\psi) \rightarrow \forall x(\phi \land \psi)$	(ix)	$\forall x(\phi \rightarrow \psi) \rightarrow (\forall x\phi \rightarrow \forall x\psi)$
(v)	$\exists x(\phi \land \psi) \rightarrow (\exists x\phi \land \exists x\psi)$	(x)	$\forall x(\phi \rightarrow \psi) \rightarrow (\exists x\phi \rightarrow \exists x\psi)$

Exercise 9

Prove of (i), (ii), (v) and (vii) of the above formulas that they are universally valid: prove (i) and (v) using approach A, assuming that all elements of a model have a name; prove (ii) and (vii) using approach B.

Exercise 10 ◇

Find as many implications and nonimplications as you can in the set of all possible formulas of the form Rxy prefixed by two quantifiers Q_1x, Q_2y (not necessarily in that order).

3.6.5 *Rules*

In order to discover universally valid formulas we may use certain *rules*. First, there is *modus ponens:*

(i)   If $\models\phi$ and $\models\phi\to\psi$, then $\models\psi$.

It is not difficult to see that this rule is correct. For suppose that $\models\phi$ and $\models\phi\to\psi$, but that $\not\models\psi$. It follows from $\not\models\psi$ that there is some model **M** with $V_M(\psi)=0$, and it follows from $\models\phi$ that $V_M(\phi)=1$, and thus that $V_M(\phi\to\psi)=0$, which contradicts $\models\phi\to\psi$. Here are some more rules:

(ii)   If $\models\phi$ and $\models\psi$, then $\models\phi\wedge\psi$.
(iii)   If $\models\phi\wedge\psi$, then $\models\phi$.
(iv)   If $\models\phi$, then $\models\phi\vee\psi$.
(v)   If $\models\phi\to\psi$, then $\models\neg\psi\to\neg\phi$.
(vi) $\models\neg\neg\phi$ iff $\models\phi$.

Such rules can be reduced to modus ponens. Take (v), for example, and suppose $\models\phi\to\psi$. It is clear that $\models(\phi\to\psi)\to(\neg\psi\to\neg\phi)$, since this formula has the form of a propositional tautology (theorem 13 in §4.2.2 shows that substitutions into tautologies like this are universally valid). Then with modus ponens it follows that $\models\neg\psi\to\neg\phi$. Here is a different kind of rule:

(vii) $\models\phi$ iff $\models\forall x([x/c]\phi)$, if x is free for c in ϕ.

Intuitively this is clear enough: if ϕ is universally valid and c is a constant appearing in ϕ, then apparently the truth of ϕ is independent of the interpretation given to c (ϕ holds for an 'arbitrary' c), so we might as well have a universal quantification instead of c.

  Proof of (vii):

  $\Leftarrow$: Suppose $\models\forall x([x/c]\phi)$. From example (ii) at the end of §3.6.4, we may conclude that $\models\forall x([x/c]\phi)\to[c/x][x/c]\phi$, and $[c/x][x/c]\phi$ is the same formula as ϕ (since x is free for c in ϕ). Now $\models\phi$ follows with modus ponens.
  $\Rightarrow$: Suppose $\models\phi$, while $\not\models\forall x([x/c]\phi)$. Then apparently there is a model **M** with $V_M([x/c]\phi)=0$. This means that there is an assignment g into **M** such that $V_{M,g}([x/c]\phi)=0$. If we now define **M'** such that **M'** is the same as **M** (the same domain, the same interpretations), except that $I_{M'}(c)=g(x)$, then it is clear that

$V_{M'}(\phi) = 0$, since x appears as a free variable in $[x/c]\phi$ at precisely the same points at which c appears in ϕ, because x is free for c in ϕ. This, however, cannot be the case, since ϕ is universally valid, so $\nvDash \forall x([x/c]\phi)$ cannot be the case either. $\square$

Rule (vii) now opens all kinds of possibilities. From $\vDash (Ac \wedge Bc) \rightarrow Ac$ (by substitution into a taulogy), it now follows that $\vDash \forall x((Ax \wedge Bx) \rightarrow Ax)$. And applying (ix) in §3.6.4 and modus ponens to this result, we obtain $\vDash \forall x(Ax \wedge Bx) \rightarrow \forall x Ax$.

3.7 Identity

It is often useful in languages for predicate logic to have a binary predicate letter which expresses *identity,* the *equality* of two things. For this reason, we now introduce a new logical constant, $=$, which will always be interpreted as the relation of identity. The symbol $=$, of course, has been used many times in this book as an informal equality symbol derived from natural language or, if the reader prefers, as a symbol which is commonly added to natural language in order to express equality. We will continue to use $=$ in this informal way, but this need not lead to any confusion.

A strong sense of the notion *identity* is intended here: by a $=$ b we do not mean that the entities to which a and b refer are identical in the sense that they resemble each other very closely, like identical twins, for example. What we mean is that they are the same, so that a $=$ b is true just in case a and b refer to the same entity. To put this in terms of valuations, we want $V_M(a = b) = 1$ in any model **M** just in case I(a) = I(b). (The first $=$ in the sentence was in a formal language, the object language; the other two were in natural language, the metalanguage.)

The right valuations can be obtained if we stipulate that I will always be such that: $I(=) = \{\langle d, e \rangle \in D^2 | d = e\}$, or a shorter notation: $I(=) = \{\langle d, d \rangle | d \in D\}$. Then, with approach A, we have $V_M(a = b) = 1$ iff $\langle I(a), I(b) \rangle \in I(=)$ iff I(a) = I(b). And with method B, we have $V_{M,g}(a = b) = 1$ iff $\langle [\![a]\!]_{M,g}, [\![b]\!]_{M,g} \rangle \in I(=)$ iff $[\![a]\!]_{M,g} = [\![b]\!]_{M,g}$ iff I(a) = I(b).

The identity symbol can be used for more than just translations of sentences like *The morning star is the evening star* and *Shakespeare and Bacon are one and the same person.* Some have been given in (98):

(98)

Sentence	Translation
John loves Mary, but Mary loves someone else.	$Ljm \wedge \exists x(Lmx \wedge x \neq j)$
John does not love Mary but someone else.	$\neg Ljm \wedge \exists x(Ljx \wedge x \neq m)$

John loves no one but Mary.	$\forall x(Ljx \leftrightarrow x = m)$
No one but John loves Mary.	$\forall x(Lxm \leftrightarrow x = j)$
John loves everyone except Mary.	$\forall x(Ljx \leftrightarrow x \neq m)$
Everyone loves Mary except John.	$\forall x(Lxm \leftrightarrow x \neq j)$

The keys to the translations are the obvious ones and have been left out. In all cases, the domain is one with just people in it. We shall always write s ≠ t instead of ¬(s = t).

If the domain in the above examples were to include things other than people, then $\forall x(Hx \rightarrow$ would have to be substituted for $\forall x$ in all the translations, and $\exists x(Hx \wedge$ for $\exists x$. Quite generally, if a sentence says that of all entities which have some property A, only a bears the relation R to b, then that sentence can be translated as $\forall x(Ax \rightarrow (Rxb \leftrightarrow x = a))$; but if a sentence states that all entities which have A bear R to b except the one entity a, then that sentence can be translated as $\forall x(Ax \rightarrow (Rxb \leftrightarrow x \neq a))$. We can also handle more complicated sentences, such as (99):

(99)   Only John loves no one but Mary.

Sentence (99) can be rendered as $\forall x(\forall y(Lxy \leftrightarrow y = m) \leftrightarrow x = j)$. That this is correct should be fairly clear if it is remembered that $\forall y(Lxy \leftrightarrow y = m)$ says that x loves no one but Mary.

One of Frege's discoveries was that the meanings of numerals can be expressed by means of the quantifiers of predicate logic and identity. The principle behind this is illustrated in (100), the last three rows of which contain sentences expressing the numerals *one*, *two*, and *three*. For any natural number *n*, we can express the proposition that there are *at least n* things which have some property A by saying that there are *n* mutually different things which have A. That there are *at most n* different things which have A can be expressed by saying that of any *n* + 1 (not necessarily different) things which have A, at least two must be identical. That there are *exactly n* entities with A can now be expressed by saying that there are at least, and at most, *n* entities with A. So, for example, $\exists xAx \wedge \forall x\forall y((Ax \wedge Ay) \rightarrow x = y)$ can be used to say that there is exactly one x such that Ax. But shorter formulas that have the same effect can be found if we follow the procedure illustrated in (100). We say that there are *n* different entities and that any entity which has the property A must be one of these.

(100)

There is at least one x such that Ax.	$\exists xAx$

There are at least two (different) x such that Ax.	$\exists x \exists y(x \neq y \wedge Ax \wedge Ay)$
There are at least three (different) x such that Ax.	$\exists x \exists y \exists z(x \neq y \wedge x \neq z \wedge y \neq z \wedge Ax \wedge Ay \wedge Az)$
There is at most one x such that Ax.	$\forall x \forall y((Ax \wedge Ay) \rightarrow x = y)$
There are at most two (different) x such that Ax.	$\forall x \forall y \forall z((Ax \wedge Ay \wedge Az) \rightarrow (x = y \vee x = z \vee y = z))$
There are at most three (different) x such that Ax.	$\forall x \forall y \forall z \forall w((Ax \wedge Ay \wedge Az \wedge Aw) \rightarrow (x = y \vee x = z \vee x = w \vee y = z \vee y = w \vee z = w))$
There is exactly one x such that Ax.	$\exists x \forall y(Ay \leftrightarrow y = x)$
There are exactly two x such that Ax.	$\exists x \exists y(x \neq y \wedge \forall z(Az \leftrightarrow (z = x \vee z = y)))$
There are exactly three x such that Ax.	$\exists x \exists y \exists z(x \neq y \wedge x \neq z \wedge y \neq z \wedge \forall w(Aw \leftrightarrow (w = x \vee w = y \vee w = z)))$

This procedure is illustrated for a unary predicate letter A, but it works just as well for formulas ϕ. The formula $\exists x \forall y([y/x]\phi \leftrightarrow y = x)$, for example, says that there is exactly one thing such that ϕ, with the proviso that y must be a variable which is free for x in ϕ and does not occur free in ϕ. Sometimes a special notation is used for a sentence expressing *There is exactly one x such that* ϕ, $\exists x \forall y([y/x]\phi \leftrightarrow y = x)$ being abbreviated as $\exists!x\phi$.

We now give a few examples of sentences which can be translated by means of $=$. We do not specify the domains, since any set which is large enough will do.

(101) There is just one queen.
   Translation: $\exists x \forall y (Qy \leftrightarrow y = x)$.
   Key: Qx: x is a queen.

(102) There is just one queen, who is the head of state.
   Translation: $\exists x(\forall y(Qy \leftrightarrow y = x) \wedge x = h)$.
   Key: Qx: x is a queen; h: the head of state.
   (This should be contrasted with $\exists!x(Qx \wedge x = h)$, which expresses that only one person is a governing queen, although there may be other queens around.)

(103) Two toddlers are sitting on a fence.
   Translation: $\exists x(Fx \wedge \exists y_1 \exists y_2(y_1 \neq y_2 \wedge \forall z((Tz \wedge Szx) \leftrightarrow$

$(z = y_1 \lor z = y_2))))$.
Key: Tx: x is a toddler; Sxy: x is sitting on y; Fx: x is a fence.

(104)   If two people fight for something, another will win it.
Translation: $\forall x \forall y \forall z ((Px \land Py \land x \neq y \land Tz \land Fxyz) \rightarrow \exists w (Pw \land w \neq x \land w \neq y \land Wwz))$.
Key: Px: x is a person; Tx: x is a thing; Fxyz: x and y fight for z; Wxy: x wins y.

Exercise 11

(a)   No man is more clever than himself.
(b)   For every man there exists another who is more clever.
(c)   There is some man who is more clever than everybody except himself.
(d)   There is somebody who is more clever than anybody except himself, and that is the prime minister.
(e)   There are at least two queens.
(f)   There are at most two queens.
(g)   There are no queens except Beatrix.
(h)   If two people make an exchange, then one of the two will be badly off.
(i)   Any person has two parents.
(j)   Mary only likes men.
(k)   Charles loves no one but Elsie and Betty.
(l)   Charles loves none but those loved by Betty.
(m)   Nobody understands somebody who loves nobody except Mary.
(n)   I help only those who help themselves.
(o)   Everybody loves exactly one person.
(p)   Everybody loves exactly one other person.
(q)   Everybody loves a different person.
(r)   All people love only themselves.
(s)   People who love everybody but themselves are altruists.
(t)   Altruists love each other.
(u)   People who love each other are happy.

Exercise 12

(a)   In many books, the dependencies between the different chapters or sections is given in the introduction by a figure. An example is figure a taken from Chang and Keisler's *Model Theory* (North-Holland, 1973). One can read figure a as a model having as its domain the set of sections {1.1, 1.3, . . . , 5.4, 5.5} in which the binary predicate letter R has been interpreted as dependency, according to the key: Rxy: y depends on x. Section 4.1, for example, depends on §3.1, but also on §§2.1, 1.4, and 1.3. For example, $\langle 2.1, 3.1 \rangle \in I(R)$, and $\langle 1.4, 5.3 \rangle \in I(R)$, but $\langle 2.2, 4.1 \rangle \notin I(R)$.

Determine the truth values of the sentences below in the model on the basis of their meaning. Do not give all details. (With method A that is not possible anyway, since the entities in the model have not been named.)

a.

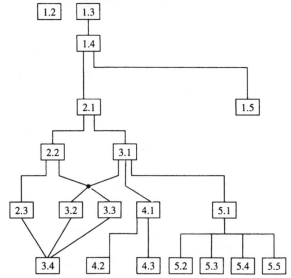

(i) $\exists x Rxx$

(ii) $\exists x \exists y (x \neq y \wedge Rxy \wedge Ryx)$

(iii) $\exists x (\neg \exists y Ryx \wedge \neg \exists y Rxy)$

(iv) $\exists x \exists y (x \neq y \wedge \forall z (\neg \exists w Rzw \leftrightarrow (z = x \vee z = y)))$

(v) $\exists x \exists y \exists z (y \neq z \wedge \forall w (Rxw \leftrightarrow (w = y \vee w = z)))$

(vi) $\exists x \exists y (x \neq y \wedge \exists z Rxz \wedge \exists z Ryz \wedge \forall z (Rxz \leftrightarrow Ryz))$

(vii) $\exists x_1 \exists x_2 \exists x_3 \exists x_4 \exists x_5 \exists x_6 \exists x_7 (Rx_1 x_2 \wedge Rx_2 x_3 \wedge Rx_3 x_4 \wedge Rx_4 x_5 \wedge Rx_5 x_6 \wedge Rx_6 x_7)$

(viii) $\forall x_1 \forall x_2 \forall x_3 ((x_1 \neq x_2 \wedge x_1 \neq x_3 \wedge x_2 \neq x_3 \wedge \neg Rx_1 x_2 \wedge \neg Rx_2 x_1 \wedge \neg Rx_1 x_3 \wedge \neg Rx_3 x_1 \wedge \neg Rx_2 x_3 \wedge \neg Rx_3 x_2) \to \neg \exists y (Rx_1 y \wedge Rx_2 y \wedge Rx_3 y))$

(ix) $\forall x \forall y ((x \neq y \wedge \neg Rxy \wedge \neg Ryx) \to \neg \exists z \exists w (z \neq w \wedge \neg Rzw \wedge \neg Rwz \wedge Rxz \wedge Ryz \wedge Rxw \wedge Ryw))$

(b) Consider the model given in figure b. Its domain consists of the points and the lines in the figure. Hence $D = \{P_1, P_2, P_3, P_4, P_5, l_1, l_2, l_3, l_4\}$. The language contains the unary predicate letter P with the points as its interpretation; the unary predicate letter L with the lines as its interpretation; the binary predicate letter O with, as its interpretation, *lie on* (key: Oxy: the point x lies on the line y); and the ternary predicate letter B with, as its interpretation, *lie between* (key: Bxyz: y lies between x and z, i.e., $I(B) = \{\langle P_1, P_2, P_4 \rangle, \langle P_4, P_2, P_1 \rangle, \langle P_3, P_4, P_5 \rangle, \langle P_5, P_4, P_3 \rangle\}$).

b.
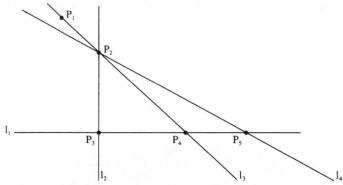

As in (a), determine the truth value in the model of the sentences below on the basis of their meaning.

(i) $\forall x(Lx \leftrightarrow \exists yOyx)$

(ii) $\forall x\forall y((Lx \land Ly) \rightarrow \exists z(Pz \land Ozx \land Ozy))$

(iii) $\forall x\forall y((Px \land Py) \rightarrow \exists z(Lz \land Oxz \land Oyz))$

(iv) $\exists x\exists y\forall z(Pz \rightarrow (Ozx \lor Ozy))$

(v) $\exists x\exists y_1\exists y_2\exists y_3 (y_1 \neq y_2 \land y_1 \neq y_3 \land y_2 \neq y_3 \land \forall z((Pz \land Ozx)$
       $\leftrightarrow (z = y_1 \lor z = y_2 \lor z = y_3)))$

(vi) $\exists x_1\exists y_1\exists x_2\exists y_2(x_1 \neq x_2 \land y_1 \neq y_2 \land Ox_1y_1 \land Ox_1y_2 \land Ox_2y_1 \land$
       $Ox_2y_2)$

(vii) $\forall x\forall y\forall z(Bxyz \rightarrow Bzyx)$

(viii) $\forall x(Lx \rightarrow \exists y\exists z\exists w(Oyx \land Ozx \land Owx \land Byzw))$

(ix) $\forall x\forall y\forall z((x \neq y \land x \neq z \land y \neq z \land \exists w(Oxw \land Oyw \land Ozw)) \rightarrow$
       $(Bxyz \lor Byzx \lor Bzxy))$

(x) $\forall x(\exists y_1\exists y_2(y_1 \neq y_2 \land Oxy_1 \land Oxy_2) \rightarrow \exists z_1\exists z_2Bz_1xz_2)$

Exercise 13

There is actually a great deal of flexibility in the semantic schema presented here. Although the main emphasis has been on the case where a formula ϕ is interpreted in a given model ('verification'), there are various other modes of employment. For instance, given only some formula ϕ, one may ask for all models where it holds. Or conversely, given some model **M,** one may try to describe exactly those formulas that are true in it. And given some formulas and some nonlinguistic situation, one may even try to set up an interpretation function that makes the formulas true in that situation: this happens when we learn a foreign language. For instance, given a domain of three objects, what different interpretation functions will verify the following formula?

$\forall x\forall y(Rxy \lor Ryx \lor x = y) \land \forall x\forall y(Rxy \rightarrow \neg Ryx)$

Exercise 14 ◇

Formulas can have different numbers of models of different sizes. Show that

(i) $\exists x\forall y(Rxy \leftrightarrow \neg Ryy)$ has no models.

(ii)   ∀x∀y(Rxy ∨ Ryx ∨ x = y) ∧ ∀x∀y(Rxy ↔ ¬(Px ↔ Py)) has only finite models of size at most two.

(iii)   ∀x∃yRxy ∧ ∀x¬Rxx ∧ ∃x∀y¬Ryx ∧ ∀x∀y∀z((Rxz ∧ Ryz) → x = y) has only models with infinite domains.

Exercise 15 ◇

Describe all models with finite domains of 1, 2, 3, . . . objects for the conjunction of the following formulas:

∀x¬Rxx
∀x∃yRxy
∀x∀y∀z((Rxy ∧ Rxz) → y = z)
∀x∀y∀z((Rxz ∧ Ryz) → x = y)

Exercise 16 ◇

In natural language (and also in science), discourse often has changing domains. Therefore it is interesting to study what happens to the truth of formulas in a model when that model undergoes some transformation. For instance, in semantics, a formula is sometimes called *persistent* when its truth is not affected by enlarging the models with new objects. Which of the following formulas are generally persistent?

(i)   ∃xPx
(ii)   ∀xPx
(iii)   ∃x∀yRxy
(iv)   ¬∀x∀yRxy

3.8 Some Properties of Relations

In §3.1 we stated that if the first of three objects is larger than the second, and the second is in turn larger than the third, then the first object must also be larger than the third; and this fact can be expressed in predicate logic. It can, for example, be expressed by the formula ∀x∀y∀z((Lxy ∧ Lyz) → Lxz), for in any model **M** in which L is interpreted as the relation *larger than,* it will be the case that $V_M(∀x∀y∀z((Lxy ∧ Lyz) → Lxz)) = 1$. It follows directly from the truth definition that this is true just in case, for any d_1, d_2, $d_3 ∈ D$, if $⟨d_1, d_2⟩ ∈ D$ and $⟨d_2, d_3⟩ ∈ D$, then $⟨d_1, d_3⟩ ∈ D$. A relation I(R) in a model **M** is said to be *transitive* if ∀x∀y∀z((Rxy ∧ Ryz) → Rxz) is true in **M**. So *larger than* is a transitive relation. The relations *just as large as* and = are other examples of transitive relations. For the sentence ∀x∀y∀z((x = y ∧ y = z) → x = z) is true in every model.

There is also a difference between *just as large as* (translated as H) and =, on the one hand, and *larger than*, on the other: ∀x∀y(Hxy → Hyx) and ∀x∀y(x = y → y = x) are always true, but ∀x∀y(Lxy → Lyx) is never true. Apparently the order of the elements doesn't matter with *just as large as* and =, but does matter with *larger than*. If ∀x∀y(Rxy → Ryx) is true in a model

M, then we say that I(R) is *symmetric(al)* in **M;** so *just as large as* and = are symmetric relations. If ∀x∀y(Rxy → ¬Ryx) is true in a model **M,** then we say that I(R) is *asymmetric(al)* in **M.** *Larger than* is an *asymmetric(al)* relation. Not every relation is either symmetric or asymmetric; the *brother of* relation, for example, is neither: if John is one of Robin's brothers, then Robin may or may not be one of John's brothers, depending on whether Robin is male or female.

A relation I(R) is said to be *reflexive* in **M,** just in case ∀xRxx is true in **M.** The relations *just as large as* and =, once again, are reflexive, since everything is just as large as and equal to itself. On the other hand, nothing is larger than itself; we say that I(R) is *irreflexive* in **M** just in case ∀x¬Rxx is true in **M,** so that *larger than* is an irreflexive relation.

There are other comparatives in natural language which are both asymmetrical and irreflexive, such as *thinner than* and *happier than,* for example. Other comparatives, like *at least as large as* and *at least as happy as,* are neither symmetrical nor asymmetrical, though they are both reflexive and transitive. The relations > and ≥ between numbers are analogous to *larger than* and *at least as large as:* > is transitive, asymmetrical, and irreflexive, whereas ≥ is transitive and neither symmetrical nor asymmetrical.

But ≥ has one additional property: if I(R) is ≥, then ∀x∀y((Rxy ∧ Ryx) → x = y) is always true. Relations like this are said to be *antisymmetric(al).* *At least as large as* is not antisymmetric, since John and Robin can each be just as large as the other without being the same person.

Finally, we say that a relation I(R) is *connected* in a model **M** just in case ∀x∀y(Rxy ∨ x = y ∨ Ryx) is true in **M.** The relations > and ≥ are connected. The relations ≥, *at least as large as,* and > are too, but note that *larger than* is not connected.

These properties of relations can be illustrated as follows. Just as in example 2 in §3.6.2, we choose the points in a figure as the domain of a model and we interpret R such that ⟨d, e⟩ ∈ I(R) iff there is an arrow pointing from d to e. Then (105) gives what all of the different properties mean for the particular relation I(R). For ease of reference we also include the defining predicate logical formula.

(105)

I(R) is symmetric.	∀x∀y(Rxy → Ryx)	If an arrow connects two points in one direction, then there is an arrow in the other direction too.
I(R) is asymmetric.	∀x∀y(Rxy → ¬Ryx)	Arrows do not go back and forth between points.
I(R) is reflexive.	∀xRxx	Every point has an arrow pointing to itself.
I(R) is irreflexive.	∀x¬Rxx	No point has an arrow pointing to itself.

I(R) is transitive.	$\forall x\forall y\forall z((Rxy \wedge Ryz) \rightarrow Rxz)$	If an arrow points from the first of three points to the second, and an arrow points from the second to the third, then there is an arrow pointing from the first to the third.
I(R) is antisymmetric.	$\forall x\forall y((Rxy \wedge Ryx) \rightarrow x = y)$	Arrows do not go back and forth between different points.
I(R) is connected.	$\forall x\forall y(Rxy \vee x = y \vee Ryx)$	Any two different points are connected by at least one arrow.

The last two cases in (105) will be clearer if it is realized that antisymmetry can just as well be expressed by $\forall x\forall y(x \neq y \rightarrow (Rxy \rightarrow \neg Ryx))$, and connectedness by $\forall x\forall y(x \neq y \rightarrow (Rxy \vee Ryx))$. The difference between asymmetry and antisymmetry is that asymmetry implies irreflexivity. This is apparent from the formulation given above: if an arrow were to run from one point to itself, then there would automatically be an arrow running 'back'. In formulas: if $\forall x\forall y(Rxy \rightarrow \neg Ryx)$ is true in a model, then $\forall x(Rxx \rightarrow \neg Rxx)$ is true too. And this last formula is equivalent to $\forall x\neg Rxx$.

Finally, we observe that all the properties mentioned here make sense for arbitrary binary relations, whether they serve as the interpretation of some binary predicate constant or not. With respect to natural language expressions of relations, a word of caution is in order. The exact properties of a relation in natural language depend on the domain of discourse. Thus *brother of* is neither symmetric nor asymmetric in the set of all people, but is symmetric in the set of all male people. And *smaller than* is connected in the set of all natural numbers but not in the set of all people.

Exercise 17

Investigate the following relations as to their reflexivity, irreflexivity, symmetry, asymmetry, antisymmetry, transitivity, and connectedness:
(i)   the grandfather relation in the set of all people;
(ii)   the ancestor relation in the set of all people;
(iii)   the relation *smaller than* in the set of all people;
(iv)   the relation *as tall as* in the set of all people;
(v)   the relation *exactly one year younger than* in the set of all people;
(vi)   the relation *north of* in the set of all sites on earth;
(vii)   the relation *smaller than* in the set of all natural numbers;
(viii)   the relation *divisible by* in the set of all natural numbers;
(ix)   the relation *differs from* in the set of all natural numbers.

Exercise 18

There are certain natural *operations* on binary relations that transform them into other relations. One example is *negation,* which turns a relation H into its complement, −H; another is *converse,* which turns a relation H into H̆ = {⟨x, y⟩|⟨y, x⟩ ∈ H}. Such operations may or may not preserve the special properties of the relations defined above. Which of the following are preserved under negation or converse?
(i)   reflexivity
(ii)   symmetry
(iii)   transitivity

3.9 Function symbols

A function is a special kind of relation. A function r from D into D can always be represented as a relation R defined as follows: ⟨d, e⟩ ∈ I(R) iff r(d) = e. And then ∀x∃!yRxy is true in the model in question. Conversely, if ∀x∃!yRxy is true in some model for a binary relation R, then we can define a function r which assigns the unique e such that ⟨d, e⟩ ∈ I(R) to any domain element d. So unary functions can be represented as binary relations, *n*-ary functions as *n*+1-ary relations. For example, the sum function + can be represented by means of a ternary predicate letter P. Given a model with the natural numbers as its domain, we then define I(P) such that ⟨n_1, n_2, n_3⟩ ∈ I(P) iff n_1 + n_2 = n_3. Then, for example, ⟨2, 2, 4⟩ ∈ I(P) and ⟨2, 2, 5⟩ ∉ I(P).

The commutativity of addition then amounts to the truth of ∀x∀y∀z(Pxyz → Pyxz) in the model. Associativity is more difficult to express. But it can be done; it is done by the following sentence: ∀x∀y∀z∀w_1∀w_2∀w_3((Pxyw_1 ∧ Pw_1zw_2 ∧ Pyzw_3) → Px$w_3$$w_2$). This is represented graphically in figure (106):

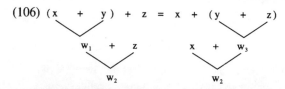

It is clear that expressing the properties of functions by means of predicate letters leads to formulas which are not very readable. It is for this reason that special symbols which are always interpreted as functions are often included in predicate languages, the *function symbols.*

Function symbols, like predicate letters, come in all kinds of arities: they may be unary, binary, ternary, and so forth. But whereas an *n*-ary predicate letter followed by *n* terms forms an atomic formula, an *n*-ary function symbol followed by *n* terms forms another term, an expression which refers to some entity in the domain of any model in which it is interpreted, just as constants and variables do. Such expressions can therefore play the same roles as constants and variables, appearing in just the same positions in formulas as constants and variables do.

If the addition function on natural numbers is represented by means of the binary function symbol p, then the commutativity and associativity of addition are conveniently expressed by:

(107) $\forall x \forall y (p(x, y) = p(y, x))$

(108) $\forall x \forall y \forall z (p(p(x, y), z) = p(x, p(y, z)))$

So now we have not only simple terms like constants and variables but also composite terms which can be constructed by prefixing function symbols to the right number of other terms. For example, the expressions p(x, y), p(y, x), p(p(x, y), z), p(x, p(y, z)), and p(y, z) appearing in (107) and (108) are all composite terms. Composite terms are built up from simpler parts in much the same way as composite formulas, so they too can be given an inductive definition:

Definition 11

(i)   If t is a variable or constant in L, then t is a term in L.
(ii)   If f is an n-ary function symbol in L and $t_1, \ldots , t_n$ are terms in L, then $f(t_1, \ldots , t_n)$ is a term in L too.

The definition of the formulas of L does not have to be adapted. Their semantics becomes slightly more complicated, since we now have to begin by interpreting terms. Naturally enough, we interpret an n-ary function symbol f as some n-ary function I(f) which maps D^n, the set of all n-tuples of elements of the domain D of some model we are working with, into D. Variables and constants are interpreted just as before, and the interpretations of composite terms can be calculated by means of the clause:

$$[\![f(t_1, \ldots , t_n)]\!]_{M,g} = (I(f))(\langle [\![t_1]\!]_{M,g}, \ldots , [\![t_n]\!]_{M,g} \rangle).$$

So now we can see why the idea behind definition 8 is useful: it makes generalizing so much easier. In approach A, by the way, we only have to consider terms without variables, in which case $[\![t]\!]_M$ can be defined instead of $[\![t]\!]_{M,g}$.

Our account of predicate logic so far has been biased toward *predicates* of and *relations* among individual objects as the logically simple expressions. In this we followed natural language, which has few (if any) basic, i.e., lexical functional expressions. Nevertheless, it should be stressed that in many applications of predicate logic to *mathematics,* functions are the basic notion rather than predicates. (This is true, for instance, in many fields of algebra.) Moreover, at a higher level, there is much functional behavior in natural language too, as we shall see in a later chapter on type theory (see vol. 2).

4   Arguments and Inferences

4.1 Arguments and Argument Schemata

So far we have mainly been concerned with the truth of sentences. To this end we have constructed a formal language, that of predicate logic, and have shown how to translate (certain kinds of) natural language sentences into it. We have also developed conditions which determine the truth or falsity of given sentences in predicate logic under given circumstances, that is, in any given models. Not that we had any particular sentences in mind whose truth or falsity we wished to assess. Our idea was to show how the truth value of a sentence depends on the meanings of the parts from which it is built up.

We shall now turn to another, related matter: the ways that accepting certain sentences can commit one to accept other sentences. This is an important facet of the more general question of the interdependencies between the meanings of sentences.

It is quite common, in everyday language, to accept a sentence just because one has previously accepted certain other sentences from which it follows by some kind of argument. The simplest arguments are those in which a number of previously accepted sentences (the *assumptions,* or premises) are followed by an expression such as *thus* and then a new sentence (the argument's *conclusion*). We saw some examples of arguments in §1.1. In chapters 2 and 3 we translated sentences derived from natural language into formal language, and now we shall do the same for arguments. But we shall stick to these simple kinds of arguments, since so many factors determine the forms of arguments and the extent to which they are found convincing that a general treatment would seem still to be beyond our reach. You could say that we restrict ourselves in logic to the results which an argument yields, which is in a way another *extensionalization:* the only thing which really matters about an argument is whether or not its conclusion is justified by its assumptions. Translating the assumptions of a given argument into predicate logic as the sentences $\phi_1, \ldots, \phi_n$ and its conclusion as the sentence ψ, we obtain an *argument schema* $\phi_1, \ldots, \phi_n/\psi$. It has $\phi_1, \ldots, \phi_n$ as its premises and ψ as its conclusion. If accepting $\phi_1, \ldots, \phi_n$ commits one to accepting ψ, then this argument schema is said to be *valid*, and ψ is said to be a *logical consequence* of $\phi_1, \ldots, \phi_n$. An informal argument is also said to be valid if it can be translated into a valid argument schema.

The logical constants appearing in the formulas of an argument schema are the only symbols whose meaning determines whether it is valid or not. This can result in some intuitively valid schemata being pronounced invalid, since expressions other than logical constants can hide aspects of meaning which lend arguments intuitive credibility. This can be avoided, for example, by making the hidden meanings explicit in additional premises. Indeed, we saw an example of just this in the discussion of argument (8) in §3.1, here re-numbered as argument (1).

(1)   Casper is bigger than John.
        John is bigger than Peter.
        _____
        Casper is bigger than Peter.

A direct translation results in an argument schema which (as we shall see) is invalid: Bcj,Bjp/Bcp. But adding the transitivity of *bigger than*, mentioned in that discussion, results in the following argument schema, which (as we shall see) *is* valid: Bcj,Bjp,∀x∀y∀z((Bxy ∧ Byz) → Bxz)/Bcp.

There are two essentially different approaches to the notion of validity as it applies to argument schemata. The first of these is the *semantic* approach, which involves the interpretation of the sentences of predicate logic and thus concepts like models and truth. This approach will be developed systematically in §4.2, but it can do no harm to anticipate by giving the obvious definition of (semantic) validity for argument schemata in predicate logic.

Definition 1

$\phi_1, \ldots, \phi_n/\psi$ is *semantically valid* if for all models **M** which interpret all the predicate letters and constants and any function symbols appearing in $\phi_1, \ldots, \phi_n, \psi$ and for which $V_M(\phi_1) = \ldots = V_M(\phi_n) = 1$, we also have $V_M(\psi) = 1$.

In other words, $\phi_1, \ldots, \phi_n/\psi$ is (semantically) valid if it is not possible that both $V_M(\phi_1) = \ldots = V_M(\phi_n) = 1$ and $V_M(\psi) = 0$. Accepting the *truth* of $\phi_1, \ldots, \phi_n$ thus commits one to accepting the truth of ψ. Where $\phi_1, \ldots, \phi_n/\psi$ does not contain any premises, so that $n = 0$, the validity of the argument schema depends on whether or not ψ can be concluded anyway, from nothing at all. Then the definition reduces to: $/\psi$ is semantically valid iff ψ is universally valid (in propositional logic: a tautology).

The second line of approach to the notion of validity is via syntactic methods. Although semantic methods tend to give one a better understanding (and tend to be more fertile with regard to, for example, linguistic applications), no introduction to logic would be complete without a syntactic treatment of the notion of inference. The semantic notion of validity is based on universal quantification over that mysterious totality, the class of all models (there are infinitely many models, and models can themselves be infinitely large). The notion of meaning which we use in the syntactic approach is more instrumental: the meaning of some part of a sentence lies in the conclusions which, because precisely that part appears at precisely that place, can be drawn from that sentence. Against the background formed by such considerations, a very precise and finite list of small, almost entirely trivial steps of reasoning is drawn up. These steps can be linked to form the longer, formal chains of reasoning which are called *derivations*. Relations of syntactic inference are then of the form: $\phi_1, \ldots, \phi_n/\psi$ is *syntactically valid* iff there is a derivation of ψ from $\phi_1, \ldots, \phi_n$. The syntactic approach which we have chosen is that of *natural deduction*. It illustrates the instrumental point of view on the meaning of connectives and quantifiers most clearly. And this new point of view should also help to deepen our understanding of what the logical constants mean.

We will discuss the semantic and syntactic approaches in §§4.2 and 4.3, respectively. Then we will discuss important connections between the two in §4.4. It turns out that these two divergent methods ultimately lead to exactly the same argument schemata being pronounced valid. It is comforting to know that the semantic notion of validity, with its heavy ontological commitment, is parallel to simple combinatory methods which entirely avoid such abstract concepts (see §4.4).

We conclude this section with a few remarks on the connection between inference relations and the meaning of a sentence or a part of a sentence. Actually, the fact that, for example, ψ follows from ϕ (ϕ/ψ is valid) indicates a connection between the meanings of ϕ and ψ. But if not only does ϕ follow from ϕ but ϕ in turn follows from ψ, then there is a sense in which ϕ and ψ have the same meaning. In such cases ϕ and ψ are said to have the same *extensional meaning*. It is not too difficult to see (and it will be proved in theorem 3 in §4.2.2) that semantically speaking, this amounts to the equivalence of ϕ and ψ. Predicate logic has the property that ϕ and ψ can be freely substituted for each other without loss of extensional meaning as long as they are equivalent (i.e., as long as they have the same extensional meaning). We referred to this as the *principle of extensionality* for predicate logic. These remarks apply directly only to those sentences which share the same meaning in the strict, 'logical' sense. Pairs like (2) and (3) are a bit more complicated:

(2)   Casper is bigger than Peter.
       Peter is smaller than Casper.

(3)   Pierre is a bachelor.
       Pierre is an unmarried man.

We will discuss this briefly in §4.2.2.

4.2 Semantic Inference Relations

4.2.1 *Semantic validity*

Let us first review the definition of semantic validity, which we shall refer to simply as *validity*, in a slightly different manner. We give the definition for predicate logic first; the obvious restriction to propositional logic follows immediately.

Definition 2

(a) A model **M** is *suitable* for the argument schema $\phi_1, \ldots, \phi_n/\psi$ if all predicate letters, constants, and function symbols appearing in $\phi_1, \ldots, \phi_n$ or in ψ are interpreted in **M**.

(b) $\phi_1, \ldots, \phi_n/\psi$ is said to be *valid* (shorter notation: $\phi_1, \ldots, \phi_n \vDash \psi$) if for every model **M** which is suitable for $\phi_1, \ldots, \phi_n/\psi$ and such that $V_M(\phi_1) = \ldots = V_M(\phi_n) = 1$, $V_M(\psi) = 1$.

In that case we also say that ψ *is a semantic consequence of* $\phi_1, \ldots, \phi_n$. If $\phi_1, \ldots, \phi_n/\psi$ is not valid, then this may also be written as $\phi_1, \ldots, \phi_n \nvDash \psi$.

Note that the validity of $\phi_1, \ldots, \phi_n/\psi$ reduces to the universal validity of ψ if $n = 0$, and that the notation $\vDash$ is therefore no more than an expansion of the notation introduced in §3.6.4. The definition for propositional logic is slightly simpler:

Definition 3

For formulas $\phi_1, \ldots, \phi_n, \psi$ in propositional logic, $\phi_1, \ldots, \phi_n \vDash \psi$ holds just in case for all valuations V such that $V_M(\phi_1) = \ldots = V_M(\phi_n) = 1$, $V_M(\psi) = 1$.

We could of course restrict ourselves to valuations 'suitable' for $\phi_1, \ldots, \phi_n/\psi$, these being functions which map all the propositional letters appearing in $\phi_1, \ldots, \phi_n, \psi$ onto 0 or 1, but not necessarily all the others. In fact, that is more or less what is done in truth tables.

The validity of every argument schema in propositional logic can be decided by means of truth tables. We shall discuss schemata (4) and (5) as examples:

(4) $p \rightarrow (q \wedge r), q \rightarrow \neg r / \neg p$

(5) $\neg p \rightarrow (q \wedge \neg r), \neg q \rightarrow \neg r / p$

A truth table for (4) is given in (6):

(6) p	q	r	q ∧ r	p → (q ∧ r)	¬r	q → ¬r	/	¬p
1	1	1	1	1	0	0		
1	1	0	0	0	1	1		
1	0	1	0	0	0	1		
1	0	0	0	0	1	1		
0	1	1	1	1	0	0		
0	1	0	0	1	1	1	*	1
0	0	1	0	1	0	1	*	1
0	0	0	0	1	1	1	*	1

We only have to consider the valuation of the conclusion ¬p in those cases (marked with a *) in which the valuations of the premises p → (q ∧ r) and q → ¬r are both 1. Now ¬p has the value 1 in each of these three cases. So p → (q ∧ r), q → ¬r ⊨¬p.

The truth table for schema (5) is in (7):

(7)

p	q	r	¬p	¬r	q ∧ ¬r	¬p → (q ∧ ¬r)	¬q	¬q → ¬r	/	p
1	1	1	0	0	0	1	0	1	*	1
1	1	0	0	1	1	1	0	1	*	1
1	0	1	0	0	0	1	1	0		
1	0	0	0	1	0	1	1	1	*	1
0	1	1	1	0	0	0	0	1		
0	1	0	1	1	1	1	0	1	*	0
0	0	1	1	0	0	0	1	0		
0	0	0	1	1	0	0	1	1		

From the truth table it is apparent that if V is such that V(p) = 0, V(q) = 1, and V(r) = 0, then V(¬p → (q ∧ ¬r)) = V(¬q → ¬r) = 1 and V(p) = 0 hold for V. From this it is clear that ¬p → (q ∧ ¬r), ¬q → ¬r ⊭p. A valuation like V with V(p) = 0, V(q) = 1, and V(r) = 0 which shows that an argument schema is not valid is called a *counterexample* to that argument schema. (The given V is a counterexample to ¬p → (q ∧ ¬r), ¬q → ¬r/p, for example.)

Such a counterexample can always be turned into a real-life counterexample if one wishes, by replacing the propositional letters by actual sentences with the same truth values as the propositions they replace. In this case, for example:

p: New York is in the United Kingdom; q: London is in the United Kingdom; r: Moscow is in the United Kingdom.

Exercise 1

Determine whether the following argument schemata are valid. If a schema is invalid, give a counterexample.

(a) p ∧ q/p   (j) p, ¬p/q
(b) p ∧ q/q   (k) p → (q ∧ ¬q)/¬p
(c) p ∨ q/p   (l) p ∨ q, p → r, q → r/r
(d) p, q/p ∧ q   (m) p ∨ q, (p ∧ q) → r/r
(e) p/p ∨ q   (n) p ∨ q, p → q/q
(f) q/p ∨ q   (o) p ∨ q, p → q/p
(g) p/p ∧ q   (p) p → q, ¬q/¬p
(h) p, p → q/q   (q) p → q/¬p → ¬q
(i) p, q → p/q

One essential difference between propositional logic and predicate logic is this: some finite number of (suitable) valuations will always suffice to determine the validity of an argument schema in propositional logic, whereas an infinite number of models can be relevant to the validity of an argument schema in predicate logic; and the models can themselves be infinite as well. This suggests that there may well be no method which would enable us to determine in a finite number of steps whether any given argument schema in predicate logic is valid or not. The suspicion that no general method exists has been given a precise formulation and has been proved; this is surely one of the most striking results in modern logic (see Church's Theorem, §4.4). There are systematic methods for investigating the validity of argument schemata in predicate logic, incidentally, but these cannot guarantee a positive or negative result within a finite time for every argument schema. We will not discuss any of these systematic methods but will give a few examples which show that in practice things are not so bad as long as we stick to simple formulas.

For schemata of predicate calculus, counterexamples are also referred to as *countermodels*. As we mentioned in §3.6.3, we can restrict ourselves to models in which every element in the domain has a name. We do this in examples (a)–(h).

(a) To begin with, a simple invalid argument schema: $\exists xLx/\forall xLx$ (the translation of a natural argument schema like *There are liars. So everyone is a liar*).

Proof: (that the schema is not valid). We need for this purpose a model M with $V_M(\exists xLx) = 1$ and $V_M(\forall xLx) = 0$. Any such model is called a counterexample to, or countermodel for, the schema. In this case it is not difficult to construct a counterexample. For example, let $D = \{1, 2\}$, $I(L) = \{1\}$, $I(a_1) = 1$, and $I(a_2) = 2$. Then we have $V_M(\exists xLx) = 1$, since $V_M(La_1) = 1$ because $1 \in I(L)$. And on the other hand, $V_M(\forall xLx) = 0$, since $V_M(La_2) = 0$, because $2 \notin I(L)$. A more concrete countermodel M' built on the same lines is this. We assume that Anne is a liar and that Betty is not. We take $D_{M'} = \{$Anne, Betty$\}$, $I_{M'}(L) = \{$Anne$\}$ and also $I_{M'}(a_1) =$ Anne and $I_{M'}(a_2) =$ Betty. Then exactly the same reasoning as above shows that $V_{M'}(\exists xLx) = 1$, while $V_{M'}(\forall xLx) = 0$. It is even more realistic if M'' is defined with $D_{M''} =$ the set of all people and $I_{M''}(L) =$ the set of all liars. If we once again assume that Anne is a liar and Betty is not and introduce a vast number of other constants in order to give everyone else a name too, then much the same reasoning as above again gives $V_{M''}(\exists xLx) = 1$ and $V_{M''}(\forall xLx) = 0$. It should be fairly clear not only that abstract models are easier to handle but also that they help us to avoid smuggling in presuppositions. In what follows, then, the counterexamples will all be abstract models with sets of numbers as their domains.

(b) Now for a very simple example of a valid argument schema: $\forall xSx/Sa_1$ (for example, as the translation of *Everyone is mortal. Thus, Socrates is mortal*). We have to show that $V_M(Sa_1) = 1$ for every suitable model M such that $V_M(\forall xSx) = 1$. Let us assume that. Then for every constant a interpreted in M, $V_M(Sa) = 1$. The constant a_1 must be interpreted in M, since M is suitable for $\forall xSx/Sa_1$. So it must be the case that $V_M(Sa_1) = 1$. We have now proved that $\forall xSx \vDash Sa_1$.

(c) The valid schema $\forall x(Mx \rightarrow Sx)$, Ma_1/Sa_1 (a translation of *All men are mortal. Socrates is a man. Thus, Socrates is mortal,* for example) is slightly more complicated. Let **M** be suitable for this schema and $V_M(\forall x(Mx \rightarrow Sx)) = V_M(Ma_1) = 1$. Then $V_M(Ma \rightarrow Sa) = 1$ must hold for every constant a which is interpreted in **M,** so in particular we have $V_M(Ma_1 \rightarrow Sa_1) = 1$. Together with $V_M(Ma_1) = 1$, this directly implies that $V_M(Sa_1) = 1$. So we have now shown that $\forall x(Mx \rightarrow Sx)$, $Ma_1 \vDash Sa_1$.

(d) The schema $\forall x\exists yLxy/\exists y\forall xLxy$ (a translation of *Everybody loves somebody. Thus, there is somebody whom everybody loves*) is invalid. In order to demonstrate this we need a model **M** in which L is interpreted and such that $V_M(\forall x\exists yLxy) = 1$ while $V_M(\exists y\forall xLxy) = 0$. We choose D = $\{1, 2\}$, $I(a_1) = 1$, and $I(a_2) = 2$ and $I(L) = \{\langle 1, 2\rangle, \langle 2, 1\rangle\}$ (so we interpret L as the relation of inequality in D: the pairs $\langle 1, 1\rangle$ and $\langle 2, 2\rangle$ are absent in I(L)). Now we have $V_M(\forall x\exists yLxy) = 1$, because (i) $V_M(\exists yLa_1y) = 1$, since $V_M(La_1a_2) = 1$; and (ii) $V_M(\exists yLa_2y) = 1$, since $V_M(La_2a_1) = 1$. But on the other hand, we have $V_M(\exists y\forall xLxy) = 0$, because (iii) $V_M(\forall xLxa_1) = 0$, since $V_M(La_1a_1) = 0$; and (iv) $V_M(\forall xLxa_2) = 0$, since $V_M(La_2a_2) = 0$. So we have now shown that $\forall x\exists yLxy \nvDash \exists y\forall xLxy$. Interpreting L as the relation of equality also gives a counterexample, and in view of the translation, this is perhaps more realistic. The counterexample given in (d) can easily be modified in such a way as to give a counterexample to the argument schema in (e).

(e) $\forall x(Ox \rightarrow \exists y(By \land Lxy))/\exists y(By \land \forall x(Ox \rightarrow Lxy))$ (a translation of *All logicians are reading a book. Thus, there is a book which all logicians are reading,* for example). The counterexample given in (d) will also work as a counterexample for this schema, if we take $I(O) = D$ and $I(B) = D$. Technically, this is quite correct, but nevertheless one might have objections. The informal schema of which this purports to be a translation seems to implicitly presuppose that logicians are not books, and books are not logicians, and that there are more things in our world than just logicians and books. These implicit presuppositions can be made explicit by including premises which express them in the argument schema. The schema thus developed, $\forall x(Ox \rightarrow \neg Bx)$, $\exists x(\neg Ox \land \neg Bx)$, $\forall x(Ox \rightarrow \exists y(By \land Lxy))/\exists y(By \land \forall x(Ox \rightarrow Lxy))$, is no more valid than the original one. In a countermodel **M'** we now choose $D_{M'} = \{1, 2, 3, 4, 5\}$, $I(a_1) = 1$, $I(a_2) = 2$, etc., $I(O)=\{1, 2\}$, $I(B) = \{3, 4\}$, and $I(L) = \{\langle 1, 3\rangle, \langle 2, 4\rangle\}$. Then it is not too difficult to check that we do indeed have $V_{M'}(\forall x(Ox \rightarrow \neg Bx)) = V_{M'}(\exists x(\neg Ox \land \neg Bx)) = V_{M'}(\forall x(Ox \rightarrow \exists y(By \land Lxy)) = 1$, while $V_{M'}(\exists y(By \land \forall x(Ox \rightarrow Lxy)))=0$.

(f) $\exists y\forall xLxy/\forall x\exists yLxy$ (a translation of *There is someone whom everyone loves. Thus everyone loves someone,* for example). Unlike the *quantifier switch* in (d), this quantifier switch is valid. Suppose $V_M(\exists y\forall xLxy) = 1$. We have to show that then $V_M(\forall x\exists yLxy) = 1$.

According to the assumption, there is a constant a interpreted in **M** such that $V_M(\forall xLxa) = 1$. This means that $V_M(Lba) = 1$ for every constant b which is interpreted in **M**. Now for any such b, it must also hold that $V_M(\exists yLby) = 1$, so that $V_M(\forall x\exists yLxy) = 1$ is guaranteed and $\exists y\forall xLxy \vDash \forall x\exists yLxy$ is proved. The proof that reversing (e) results in a valid argument schema is a little more complicated but goes along the same lines.

(g) $\forall xMx/\exists xMx$ (a translation of *Everyone is mortal. Thus, someone is mortal,* for example). Suppose **M** is suitable for this schema and that $V_M(\forall xMx) = 1$. Then we have $V_M(Ma) = 1$ for every constant a which is interpreted in **M**. There must be some such constant, since we have agreed that domains may never be empty, while in our approach A every element in the domain has a name. So $V_M(\exists xMx) = 1$. We have now proved that the schema is valid: $\forall xMx \vDash \exists xMx$. The validity of this schema depends on our choice of nonempty domains. In addition, Aristotle considered only predicates with nonempty extensions. So in his logic—unlike modern logic—the following schema was valid.

(h) $\forall x(Hx \rightarrow Mx)/\exists x(Hx \wedge Mx)$ (a translation of *All men are mortal. Thus, some men are mortal,* for example). As a counterexample we have, for example, **M** with $D_M = \{1\}$, $I(H) = I(M) = \varnothing$, and $I(a_1) = 1$. For then we have $V_M(Ha_1 \rightarrow Ma_1) = 1$, so that $V_M(\forall x(Hx \rightarrow Mx)) = 1$, while $V_M(Ha_1 \wedge Ma_1) = 0$, so that $V_M(\exists x(Hx \wedge Mx)) = 0$. If this seems a bit strange, then it should be remembered that this schema can also be seen as a translation of the intuitively invalid schema *All unicorns are quadrupeds. Thus, there are unicorns which are quadrupeds.* Furthermore, the original translation involves the implicit presupposition that there are in fact 'men', in the archaic sense of human beings. This presupposition can be made explicit by adding a premise which expresses it, and the resulting argument schema, $\forall x(Hx \rightarrow Mx)$, $\exists xHx/\exists x(Hx \wedge Mx)$, is valid. In order to see this, let **M** be any model which is suitable for this schema and such that $V_M(\forall x(Hx \rightarrow Mx)) = 1$ and $V_M(\exists xHx) = 1$. We now have to show that $V_M(\exists x(Hx \wedge Mx)) = 1$. The second assumption gives us a constant a which is interpreted in **M** and for which $V_M(Ha) = 1$. From the assumption that $V_M(\forall x(Hx \rightarrow Mx)) = 1$ it follows that, in particular, $V_M(Ha \rightarrow Ma) = 1$, from which it follows with the truth table for $\rightarrow$ that $V_M(Ma) = 1$, and then with the truth table for $\wedge$ that $V_M(Ha \wedge Ma) = 1$. Now it follows directly that $V_M(\exists x(Hx \wedge Mx)) = 1$.

Exercise 2

Show that the argument schemata below are invalid by giving counterexamples.

(a) $\exists xAx, \exists xBx/\exists x(Ax \wedge Bx)$.

(b) $\forall x(Ax \vee Bx)/\forall xAx \vee \forall xBx$.

(c) $\forall x(Ax \rightarrow Bx), \exists xBx/\neg\exists xAx$.

(d) $\exists x(Ax \wedge Bx), \exists x(Bx \wedge Cx)/\exists x(Ax \wedge Cx)$.

(e) $\forall x(Ax \vee Bx), \exists x\neg Ax, \exists x\neg Bx, \forall x((Ax \wedge Bx) \rightarrow Cx)/\exists xCx$.

(f) $\neg\forall x(Ax \rightarrow Bx), \neg\forall xBx/\forall xAx$.

(g) $\forall x Ax / \exists x (Bx \wedge \neg Bx)$.
(h) $\forall x \exists y Rxy / \exists x Rxx$.
(i) $\forall x Rxx / \forall x \forall y Rxy$.
(j) $\exists x \forall y Rxy, \forall x Rxx / \forall x \forall y (Rxy \vee Ryx)$.
(k) $\forall x \exists y Rxy, \forall x (Rxx \leftrightarrow Ax) / \exists x Ax$.
(l) $\forall x \exists y Rxy, \forall x \forall y (Rxy \vee Ryx) / \forall x \forall y \forall z ((Rxy \wedge Ryz) \rightarrow Rxz)$.
(m) $\forall x \exists y Rxy, \forall x \forall y \forall z ((Rxy \wedge Ryz) \rightarrow Rxz) / \exists x Rxx$.
(n) $\forall x \forall y (Rxy \rightarrow Ryx), \forall x \forall y \forall z ((Rxy \wedge Ryz) \rightarrow Rxz) / \exists x Rxx$.
(o) $\exists x \exists y \forall z (x = z \vee y = z) / \forall x \forall y (x = y)$.
(p) $\forall x \exists y (x \neq y) / \exists x \exists y \exists z (x \neq y \wedge x \neq z \wedge y \neq z)$.
(q) $\forall x \exists y (Rxy \wedge x \neq y), \forall x \forall y \forall z ((Rxy \wedge Ryz) \rightarrow Rxz) / \forall x \forall y (x = y \vee Rxy$ $\vee Ryx)$.
(r) $\forall x (Ax \leftrightarrow \forall y Rxy), \exists x \forall y (Ay \leftrightarrow x = y) / \forall x \forall y ((Rxx \wedge Ryy) \rightarrow x = y)$.

4.2.2 *The Principle of Extensionality*

We shall now say some more about the principle of extensionality for predicate logic and the closely related substitutivity properties, which will to some extent be proved. The following theorem, which shows a link between arguments from premises to conclusions and material implications from antecedents to consequents, will serve as an introduction:

Theorem 1

(a) $\phi \models \psi$ iff $\models \phi \rightarrow \psi$
(b) $\phi_1, \ldots, \phi_n \models \psi$ iff $\phi_1, \ldots, \phi_{n-1} \models \phi_n \rightarrow \psi$

Proof: A proof of (b) will do, since (a) is a special case of (b).

(b) $\Rightarrow$: Suppose $\phi_1, \ldots, \phi_n \models \psi$. Suppose furthermore that for some suitable V (we shall leave out any references to the model which V originates from, if they are irrelevant) $V(\phi_1) = \ldots = V(\phi_{n-1}) = 1$. We have to show that $V(\phi_n \rightarrow \psi) = 1$ too. Suppose this is not the case. Then from the truth table for $\rightarrow$, $V(\phi_n) = 1$ and $V(\psi) = 0$. But that is impossible, since then all of $V(\phi_1), \ldots, V(\phi_n)$ would be 1, in which case it follows from $\phi_1, \ldots, \phi_n \models \psi$ that $V(\psi) = 1$ and not 0.

(b) $\Leftarrow$: Suppose $\phi_1, \ldots, \phi_{n-1} \models \phi_n \rightarrow \psi$. Suppose furthermore that for some suitable V, $V(\phi_1) = \ldots = V(\phi_n) = 1$. We have to show that then necessarily $V(\psi) = 1$. Now if $V(\phi_1) = \ldots = V(\phi_n) = 1$, then obviously $V(\phi_1) = \ldots = V(\phi_{n-1}) = 1$; according to the assumption, we then have $V(\phi_n \rightarrow \psi) = 1$, and with $V(\phi_n) = 1$ it follows that $V(\psi) = 1$. $\square$

One direct consequence of this theorem is that in order to determine what argument schemata are valid, it is sufficient to know what formulas are universally valid. This is spelled out in theorem 2:

Theorem 2

$\phi_1, \ldots, \phi_n \vDash \psi$ iff $\vDash \phi_1 \to (\phi_2 \to (\ldots \to (\phi_n \to \psi) \ldots))$ iff $\vDash (\phi_1 \wedge \ldots \wedge \phi_n) \to \psi$.

Proof: a repeated application of theorem 1. □

There is a theorem on material equivalence which parallels theorem 1 and which we have already encountered in propositional logic.

Theorem 3

The following assertions can be deduced from each other; they are equivalent:
(i) $\phi \vDash \psi$ and $\psi \vDash \phi$
(ii) ϕ is equivalent to ψ
(iii) $\vDash \phi \leftrightarrow \psi$

Proof: It suffices to prove: (i) $\Rightarrow$ (ii) $\Rightarrow$ (iii) $\Rightarrow$ (i).

(i) $\Rightarrow$ (ii): Assume (i). Suppose, first, that $V(\phi) = 1$. Then $V(\psi) = 1$ because $\phi \vDash \psi$. Now suppose that $V(\phi) = 0$. Then it is impossible that $V(\psi) = 1$, since in that case it would also follow from $\psi \vDash \phi$ that $V(\phi) = 1$, so $V(\psi) = 0$ too. Apparently $V(\phi) = V(\psi)$ under all circumstances, so that ϕ and ψ are equivalent by definition.

(ii) $\Rightarrow$ (iii): Assume (ii). We now have to prove that $V(\phi \leftrightarrow \psi) = 1$ for any suitable V. But that is immediately evident, since under all circumstances $V(\phi) = V(\psi)$.

(iii) $\Rightarrow$ (i): Assume (iii). Suppose now that for some V which is suitable for $\phi \vDash \psi$, $V(\phi) = 1$. Since $\phi \leftrightarrow \psi$ is universally valid, $V(\phi) = V(\psi)$ holds for all V. It follows that $V(\psi) = 1$, and we have thus proved that $\phi \vDash \psi$; $\psi \vDash \phi$ can be proved in exactly the same manner. □

This theorem can be strengthened in the same way that theorem 1 (a) is strengthened to theorem 1 (b):

Theorem 4

$(\phi_1, \ldots, \phi_n, \psi \vDash \chi$ and $\phi_1, \ldots, \phi_n, \chi \vDash \psi)$ iff $\phi_1, \ldots, \phi_n \vDash \psi \leftrightarrow \chi$.

The reader will be spared a proof.

We are now in a position to give a simple version of the promised theorem that equivalent formulas can be substituted for each other without loss of extensional meaning in predicate logic, just as in propositional logic. We shall formulate this theorem for sentences first, that is, for formulas without any free variables.

Theorem 5

If ϕ and ψ are equivalent, ϕ is a subformula of χ, and $[\psi/\phi]\chi$ is the formula obtained by replacing this subformula ϕ in χ by ψ, then χ and $[\psi/\phi]\chi$ are equivalent.

Sketch of a proof: A rigorous proof can be given by induction on (the construction of) χ. It is, however, clear (Frege's principle of compositionality!) that the truth value of ϕ has precisely the same effect on the truth value of χ as the truth value of ψ has on the truth value of $[\psi/\phi]\chi$. So if ϕ and ψ have the same truth values, then χ and $[\psi/\phi]\chi$ must too. $\square$

The same reasoning also proves the following, stronger theorem (in which ϕ, ψ, χ, $[\psi/\phi]\chi$ are the same as above):

Theorem 6 *(Principle of extensionality for sentences in predicate logic)*

$\phi \leftrightarrow \psi \vDash \chi \leftrightarrow [\psi/\phi]\chi$.

And one direct consequence of theorem 6 is:

Theorem 7

If $\phi_1, \ldots, \phi_n \vDash \phi \leftrightarrow \psi$, then $\phi_1, \ldots, \phi_n \vDash \chi \leftrightarrow [\psi/\phi]\chi$.

Proof: Assume that $\phi_1, \ldots, \phi_n \vDash \phi \leftrightarrow \psi$. And for any suitable V, let $V(\phi_1) = \ldots = V(\phi_n) = 1$. Then of course $V(\phi \leftrightarrow \psi) = 1$. According to theorem 6 we then have $V(\chi \leftrightarrow [\psi/\phi]\chi) = 1$, whence $\phi_1, \ldots, \phi_n \vDash \chi \leftrightarrow [\psi/\phi]\chi$ is proved. $\square$

Theorem 7 can be paraphrased as follows: if two sentences are equivalent (have the same extensional meaning) under given assumptions, then under the same assumptions, they may be substituted for each other without loss of extensional meaning. There is also a principle of extensionality for formulas in general; but first we will have to generalize theorem 3 so that we can use the equivalence of formulas more easily.

Theorem 8

If the free variables in ϕ and in ψ are all among $x_1, \ldots, x_n$, then ϕ and ψ are equivalent iff $\vDash \forall x_1 \ldots \forall x_n(\phi \leftrightarrow \psi)$.

Proof: The proof will only be given for $n = 1$, since the general case is not essentially different. We will write x for x_1.

$\Rightarrow$: Suppose ϕ and ψ are equivalent. Then by definition, for every suitable **M** and g, $V_{M,g}(\phi) = V_{M,g}(\psi)$. That is, for every suitable **M** and g, $V_{M,g}(\phi \leftrightarrow \psi) = 1$. But then, for every suitable M, g, and d $\in$ D_M, $V_{M,g[x/d]}(\phi \leftrightarrow \psi) = 1$. According to Tarski's truth definition, this means that for every suitable M and g, $V_{M,g}(\forall x(\phi \leftrightarrow \psi)) = 1$. And this is the conclusion we needed.

$\Leftarrow$: The above proof of $\Rightarrow$ also works in reverse. $\square$

We can now prove a principle of extensionality for formulas in predicate logic, just as we proved theorems 6 and 7. We give the theorems and omit their proofs. The conditions on ϕ, ψ, χ, and $[\psi/\phi]\chi$ are the same as above except that ϕ and ψ may now be formulas, with the proviso that their free variables are all among $x_1, \ldots, x_n$ (if ϕ and ψ are sentences, then $n = 0$).

Theorem 9 (*Principle of extensionality for predicate logic*)

$\forall x_1 \ldots \forall x_n(\phi \leftrightarrow \psi) \vDash \chi \leftrightarrow [\psi/\phi]\chi$

Theorem 10

If $\phi_1, \ldots, \phi_m \vDash \forall x_1 \ldots \forall x_n(\phi \leftrightarrow \psi)$, then $\phi_1, \ldots, \phi_m \vDash \chi \leftrightarrow [\psi/\phi]\chi$

Theorem 10 again expresses the fact that formulas with the same extensional meaning can be substituted for each other without loss of extensional meaning. Actually this theorem sanctions, for example, leaving off the brackets in conjunctions and disjunctions with more than two members (see §2.5). Theorems 9 and 10 can be generalized so that ϕ need not have precisely the variables $x_1, \ldots, x_n$ in χ. A more general formulation is, however, somewhat tricky, and for that reason will not be given.

We conclude our discussion of the principle of extensionality for predicate logic with a few examples. The formulas $\forall x(Ax \wedge Bx)$ and $\forall xAx \wedge \forall xBx$ are equivalent. From this it follows from theorem 3 that $\forall x(Ax \wedge Bx) \vDash \forall xAx \wedge \forall xBx$, that $\forall xAx \wedge \forall xBx \vDash \forall x(Ax \wedge Bx)$, and that $\vDash \forall x(Ax \wedge Bx) \leftrightarrow (\forall xAx \wedge \forall xBx)$. This last can be used for theorem 10, with n = 0. If we choose $\forall x(Ax \wedge Bx) \rightarrow \exists x\neg Cx$ as our χ, then it follows that $\forall x(Ax \wedge Bx) \rightarrow \exists x\neg Cx$ and $(\forall xAx \wedge \forall xBx) \rightarrow \exists x\neg Cx$ are equivalent. And so on.

The equivalence of $Ax \wedge Bx$ and $Bx \wedge Ax$ results, using theorem 8, in $\vDash \forall x((Ax \wedge Bx) \leftrightarrow (Bx \wedge Ax))$. Applying theorem 10 to this, we obtain the equivalence of $\forall x((Ax \wedge Bx) \rightarrow \exists yRxy)$ and $\forall x((Bx \wedge Ax) \rightarrow \exists yRxy)$. Equivalences other than the commutativity of $\wedge$ can also be applied, the associative laws for $\wedge$ and $\vee$, for example, which result in the fact that in predicate logic as in propositional logic, brackets can be left out both in strings of conjunctions and in strings of disjunctions. Here is an application of theorem 10 with m > 0: it is not difficult to establish that $\neg(\exists xAx \wedge \exists xBx) \vDash \forall x(Ax \vee Bx) \leftrightarrow (\forall xAx \vee \forall xBx)$. It follows that $\neg(\exists xAx \wedge \exists xBx) \vDash (\forall xCx \rightarrow \forall x(Ax \vee Bx)) \leftrightarrow (\forall xCx \rightarrow (\forall xAx \vee \forall xBx))$, to take just one arbitrary example.

Given the above, we are also in a position to say more about problems with extralogical meanings, which we have noticed in connection with pairs of sentences like (8) (= (2)):

(8)   Casper is bigger than Peter
       Peter is smaller than Casper

Having translated *x is bigger than y* into predicate logic as Bxy, and *x is smaller than y* as Sxy, we now take ∀x∀y(Bxy ↔ Syx) as a permanent assumption, since we are only interested in models **M** in which $V_M(∀x∀y(Bxy ↔ Syx)) = 1$. Under this assumption, Bxy and Syx are equivalent. Furthermore, according to theorem 10, Bzw and Swz are equivalent for arbitrary variables z and w, since ∀x∀y(Bxy ↔ Syx) ⊨ ∀z∀w(Bzw ↔ Swz). In fact, it is not too difficult to see that Bt_1t_2 and St_2t_1 are also equivalent for arbitrary terms t_1 and t_2, as in Ba_1a_2 and Sa_2a_1, for example, so that if *Casper* is translated as a_1 and *Peter* as a_2, both of the sentences in (8) have the same extensional meaning. An assumption like the one we are discussing is called a *meaning postulate*. The problem with (9) (=(3)):

(9)   Pierre is a bachelor.
       Pierre is an unmarried man.

can be resolved in much the same manner by taking ∀x((Mx ∧ ¬Wx) ↔ Bx) as our meaning postulate; the key to the translation is Bx: x is a bachelor; Wx: x is married; Mx: x is a man. What meaning postulates do is provide information about what words mean. They are comparable with dictionary definitions in which *bachelor,* for example, is defined as *unmarried man.* In mathematics, some axioms play the role of meaning postulates. For instance, the following axioms relate the meanings of some key notions in geometry. If we interpret Px as x is a point; Lx as x is a line; and Oxy as x lies on y, for example, the following geometrical axioms can be drawn up: ∀x∀y((Px ∧ Py ∧ x ≠ y) → ∃!z(Lz ∧ Oxz ∧ Oyz)), that is, given two different points, exactly one line can be drawn which passes through both, and ∀x∀y((Lx ∧ Ly ∧ x ≠ y) → ∀z∀w((Pz ∧ Pw ∧ Ozx ∧ Ozy ∧ Owx ∧ Owy) → z = w), that is, two different lines have at most one point in common.

    In addition to the principles discussed above, there are also principles of extensionality dealing with constants and variables, not in connection with truth values, of course, but in terms of elements in a domain. Constants, and variables too, by assignments, are interpreted as elements in a domain. Here are two examples of such theorems, without proofs:

Theorem 11

If s and t are terms lacking variables, then for the formula [t/s]φ obtained by substituting t for s in φ, we have: s = t ⊨ φ ↔ [t/s]φ.

Theorem 12

If s_1, s_2, and t are terms whose variables are all among x_1, . . . , x_n, then for the term $[s_2/s_1]t$ obtained by substituting s_2 for s_1 in t, we have: $\vDash \forall x_1$ . . . $\forall x_n(s_1 = s_2 \rightarrow [s_2/s_1]t = t)$.

Here are some applications of these theorems, in a language with p as a binary function symbol for the addition function: $a_4 = p(a_2, a_2) \vDash p(a_4, a_4) = p(p(a_2, a_2), p(a_2, a_2))$, and $\vDash \forall x \forall y \forall z(p(x, y) = p(y, x) \rightarrow p(p(x, y), z) = p(p(y, x), z))$.

We conclude this section by returning briefly to what we said in § 1.1: that substituting sentences for the variables of a valid argument schema is supposed to result in another valid argument schema. Predicate logic does indeed comply with this: substituting formulas for the predicate letters in valid argument schemata results in other, valid argument schemata. But there are complications having to do with bound and free variables which mean that restrictions have to be placed on the substitutions, so that giving a general formulation is difficult. We will just give an example: the substitution of predicate-logical formulas in purely propositional argument schemata:

Theorem 13

Assume that ϕ_1, . . . , $\phi_n \vDash \psi$ in propositional logic and that ϕ_1, . . . , ϕ_n and ψ contain no propositional letters except p_1, . . . , p_m. And let χ_1, . . . , χ_m be sentences in some predicate-logical language L, while ϕ_1', . . . , ϕ_n' and ψ' are obtained from ϕ_1, . . . , ϕ_n and ψ by (simultaneously) substituting χ_1 , . . . , χ_m for p_1, . . . , p_m. Then ϕ_1', . . . , $\phi_n' \vDash \psi'$ in predicate logic.

Proof: Suppose that ϕ_1, . . . , $\phi_n \vDash \psi$, but ϕ_1', . . . , $\phi_n' \nvDash \psi'$. Then there is a counterexample **M** which is responsible for the latter: $V_M(\phi_1') = . . . = V_M(\phi_n') = 1$ and $V_M(\psi') = 0$. Then a propositional counterexample to the former argument schema can be obtained by taking: $V(p_i) = V_M(\chi_i)$ for every i between 1 and m. Then it is clear that $V(\phi_1) = . . . = V(\phi_n) = 1$ but that $V(\psi) = 0$, since ϕ_1, . . . , ϕ_n and ψ are composed of p_1, . . . , p_m in exactly the same way as ϕ_1', . . . , ϕ_n' and ψ' are composed of χ_1, . . . , χ_m. We now have a counterexample to our first assumption ϕ_1, . . . , $\phi_n \vDash \psi$, so it cannot be the case that $\phi'_1, . . . , \phi'_n \nvDash \psi'$. $\square$

One simple consequence of theorem 13 is that substitution instances of propositional tautologies are universally valid formulas. Here are a few applications:

(a) $p \wedge q \vDash q \wedge p$, so, for example,
    $(r \vee s) \wedge (p \rightarrow q) \vDash (p \rightarrow q) \wedge (r \vee s)$ and
    $\forall x \exists y Axy \wedge \forall x \exists y Bxy \vDash \forall x \exists y Bxy \wedge \forall x \exists y Axy$

(b) $\models ((p \to q) \to p) \to p$, so, for example,

$\models (((p \to q) \to (q \to r)) \to (p \to q)) \to (p \to q)$ and

$\models ((\forall xAx \to \exists yBy) \to \forall xAx) \to \forall xAx$.

We conclude this section with an example of an argument schema drawn from predicate logic, for which formulating a general theorem like the above takes too much doing:

(c) $\forall x(Ax \lor Bx), \exists x\neg Ax \models \exists xBx$, so, for example,

$\forall x((Ax \land Bx) \lor (Ax \land Cx)), \exists x\neg(Ax \land Bx) \models \exists x(Ax \land Cx)$ and

$\forall x(\exists yAxy \lor \exists zBxz), \exists x\neg\exists yAxy \models \exists x\exists zBxz$.

4.3 Natural Deduction: A Syntactic Approach to Inference

4.3.1 *Introduction and Elimination Rules*

As we stated in §4.1, in the syntactic approach to the notion of inference, a finite list of small steps of reasoning is given, these assumed to be correct. Then rules are given which say how these small steps can be linked to form *derivations*, the formal counterparts of arguments. In the method of natural deduction, these steps can be seen as answers to the following questions, which can be asked for each of the connectives (they will later also be asked for the quantifiers):

(a) When can a formula with this connective as its main sign be drawn as a conclusion?

(b) What conclusions may be drawn from a formula with this connective as its main sign?

The steps of reasoning which answer (a) for a connective ∘ are given in the *introduction rule*, I∘, for that connective. The answer to (b) for a connective ∘ results in its *elimination rule*, E∘. For the connective $\land$, the answers to (a) and (b) are as follows:

(a) $\phi \land \psi$ may be drawn as a conclusion if both ϕ and ψ are available, either as assumptions already made or as conclusions already drawn.

(b) ϕ and ψ may both be drawn as conclusions from $\phi \land \psi$.

These considerations give rise to the following (as we shall presently see, somewhat simplistic) picture. A *derivation* is a finite, numbered list of formulas like this:

1. ϕ_1
.
.
.
n. ϕ_n

Next to each formula ϕ_i, a statement must be written saying how it was obtained, in some fixed code. Now there are just two different ways in which a formula ϕ_i may be obtained: either ϕ_i is an assumption, in which case we write *assumption* next to it; or ϕ_i was obtained from the formulas occurring above it by means of one of the accepted rules, in which case the name of the rule in question must be given, followed by the numbers of the formulas from which ϕ_i was obtained. The last formula ϕ_n is the *conclusion*, this being the formula which was derived. The *assumptions* of this derivation are those of the formulas ϕ_i next to which *assumption* is written. Letting $\phi_1, \ldots, \phi_m$ be the assumptions, we write $\phi_1, \ldots, \phi_m \vdash \phi_n$, and we say: *there is a derivation of ϕ_n from (the assumptions) $\phi_1, \ldots, \phi_m$*.

4.3.2 *Conjunction*

The rules for the connective $\wedge$ will be clear from the above. The *introduction rule* $I\wedge$, by means of which formulas with $\wedge$ as their main sign may be drawn as conclusions:

1.   .
                      .
                      .
                      .
m_1. ϕ
                      .
                      .
                      .
m_2. ψ
                      .
                      .
                      .
n. $\phi \wedge \psi$ $I\wedge, m_1, m_2$

In this rule, it does not matter which comes first, m_1 or m_2. The rule $I\wedge$ is used in the following very simple derivation of $p \wedge q$ from p and q:

1.	p	assumption
2.	q	assumption
3.	$p \wedge q$	$I\wedge, 1, 2$

Because of this derivation, then, we may assert that $p, q \vdash p \wedge q$. Here is a slightly more complicated derivation, in which $(r \wedge p) \wedge q$ is derived from p, q, and r by means of $I\wedge$:

1.	p	assumption
2.	q	assumption
3.	r	assumption

4.   r ∧ p   I∧, 3, 1
5.   (r ∧ p) ∧ q   I∧, 4, 2

Because of this derivation, then, we may assert that p, q, r ⊢ (r ∧ p) ∧ q.

Exercise 3

Show that
(a) p, q ⊢ q ∧ p;
(b) p, q, r ⊢ q ∧ (p ∧ r).

The *elimination rule* E∧ gives us two ways of drawing conclusions:

(i)   1. .
            .
            .
            .

        m. φ ∧ ψ
            .
            .
            .

        n. φ   E∧, m

(ii)   1. .
            .
            .
            .

        m. φ ∧ ψ
            .
            .
            .

        n. ψ   E∧, m

Here is a derivation of p from p ∧ q, as an example of an application of E∧.

1.   p ∧ q   assumption
2.   p   E∧, 1

From this it follows that p ∧ q ⊢ p. In the following derivation of q ∧ p from
p ∧ q, both I∧ and E∧ are applied:

1.   p ∧ q   assumption
2.   p   E∧, 1
3.   q   E∧, 1
4.   q ∧ p   I∧, 3, 2

From this it follows that p ∧ q ⊢ q ∧ p. As a final example, we have a somewhat longer derivation which shows that p ∧ (q ∧ r) ⊢ (p ∧ q) ∧ r.

1.	p ∧ (q ∧ r)	assumption
2.	p	E∧, 1
3.	q ∧ r	E∧, 1
4.	q	E∧, 3
5.	r	E∧, 3
6.	p ∧ q	I∧, 2, 4
7.	(p ∧ q) ∧ r	I∧, 6, 5

Although this derivation demonstrates that ∧ is associative, we will continue to write brackets in conjunctions with multiple membership. This is because it would otherwise be impossible to apply E∧, since E∧ only accepts conjunctions with exactly two members. In the syntactic approach we are now taking, we do not deal with the meanings of formulas but only with their forms. The same applies to the disjunction.

Exercise 4

Show that p ∧ (q ∧ r) ⊢ r ∧ p.

4.3.3 *Implication*

We shall now consider the connective →. The *elimination rule* E→ is easy enough: from $\phi \to \psi$, given that ϕ is also available, we may draw the conclusion that ψ (modus ponens).

1.	.	
	.	
	.	
	.	
m_1.	$\phi \to \psi$	
	.	
	.	
	.	
m_2.	ϕ	
	.	
	.	
	.	
n.	ψ	E→, m_1, m_2

As an example, we shall demonstrate that p → q, p ⊢ q:

1.	p → q	assumption
2.	p	assumption
3.	q	E→, 1, 2

And the following derivation of p ∧ q from p ∧ r, r → q uses all the rules we have seen so far:

1.	p ∧ r	assumption
2.	r → q	assumption
3.	p	E∧, 1
4.	r	E∧, 1
5.	q	E→, 2, 4
6.	p ∧ q	I∧, 3, 5

Exercise 5

Show that
(a) p → (q → r), p, q ⊢ r.
(b) p → (q ∧ r), r → s, p ⊢ s.

The *introduction rule* I→ complicates things a bit. Under what circumstances may a conclusion of the form $\phi \to \psi$ be drawn? Actually we have already drawn a number of conclusions of a very similar form in this book. As noted in connection with theorem 1 (in §2.5), the proof of a theorem *if A then B* generally begins with the assumption that *A*, followed by a demonstration that *B* inevitably follows. The introduction rule for the implication is analogous to this. In order to derive $\phi \to \psi$, we first take ϕ as an assumption and then try to derive ψ. If we can do this, then we may draw the conclusion that $\phi \to \psi$, but as of that moment we may no longer proceed on the assumption that ϕ. We say that assumption ϕ is *dropped* (or *withdrawn*). That is exactly what we did in the proof of theorem 1. First we assumed that *A*, and then we proved that *B*. Having done this, we were satisfied that *if A, then B* and turned to the proof of the second half of the theorem, *if B, then A*. But then we could no longer proceed on the assumption *A*, since that would be circular. The notation we use for the introduction rule I→ is as follows:

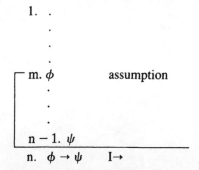

The line drawn in this derivation isolates that part of it which proceeds under the assumption ϕ, namely, the part numbered m to n − 1 inclusive. From n onwards, neither m nor any other of the numbers m + 1, . . . , n − 1 derived on the assumption that ϕ may be used. So this does not apply to the formula $\phi \to \psi$ itself, which was not derived from ϕ or any other formula in particular but from the fact that a piece of derivation like what is isolated by the line between rules m and n − 1 can be found. That is why $\phi \rightarrow \psi$ is not followed by the numbers of any formulas: it is clear from the line what part of the derivation the conclusion $\phi \rightarrow \psi$ is based on. The restriction that the rule I→ may only be used on the most recent assumption is natural enough, since otherwise assumptions would always be getting lost.

From now on we will write $\phi_1, \ldots, \phi_n \vdash \psi$ if there is a derivation with ψ as its last formula and with $\phi_1, \ldots, \phi_n$ as the assumptions *which have not been dropped*. It follows from the above that there are derivations that completely lack premises, these being derivations in which all of the assumptions are withdrawn along the way. One simple example of this is the following derivation, which shows that $\vdash (p \wedge q) \rightarrow p$:

1.	p ∧ q	assumption
2.	p	E∧, 1
3.	(p ∧ q) → p	I→

It can easily be seen that all assumptions made in this derivation have been withdrawn: we say that $(p \wedge q) \rightarrow p$ is *derivable without premises*. The following example demonstrates that $(p \wedge q) \rightarrow r \vdash (q \wedge p) \rightarrow r$:

1.	(p ∧ q) → r	assumption
2.	q ∧ p	assumption
3.	q	E∧, 2
4.	p	E∧, 2
5.	p ∧ q	I∧, 4, 3
6.	r	E→, 1, 5
7.	(q ∧ p) → r	I→

Assumption 2 is dropped with the application of I→ at 7. Assumption 1, on the other hand, is not dropped, so that this derivation is a derivation of 7 from 1: $(p \wedge q) \rightarrow r \vdash (q \wedge p) \rightarrow r$.

The following somewhat more complicated derivation without premises shows that $\vdash ((p \wedge q) \rightarrow r) \rightarrow (p \rightarrow (q \rightarrow r))$:

1.	(p ∧ q) → r	assumption
2.	p	assumption
3.	q	assumption
4.	p ∧ q	I∧, 2, 3
5.	r	E→, 1, 4
6.	q → r	I→
7.	p → (q → r)	I→
8.	((p ∧ q) → r) → (p → (q → r))	I→

How do we form such a derivation? We will go through it again in order to make this clear, documenting each step in turn.

The formula we want to derive is $((p \wedge q) \rightarrow r) \rightarrow (p \rightarrow (q \rightarrow r))$, a formula with $\rightarrow$ as its main sign. As a rule of thumb, we take the antecedent of the implication as an assumption and then try to derive its consequent, since the formula itself can be derived by means of rule I$\rightarrow$. So we begin with:

1. $(p \wedge q) \rightarrow r$ assumption

Now we must derive $p \rightarrow (q \rightarrow r)$, another formula with $\rightarrow$ as its main sign. So we do the same as we did above; we assume:

2.   p   assumption

We then derive $q \rightarrow r$, yet another formula with $\rightarrow$ as its main sign. So:

3.   q   assumption

We must now obtain r. Now we come to a stage in the derivation where we cannot just proceed on automatic pilot. We want to obtain r from 1, 2, and 3. The only place where r appears in the formulas is as the consequent in 1. So if we want to obtain r from that formula, we must somehow derive $p \wedge q$, the antecedent of 1, and then draw the conclusion that r by means of E$\rightarrow$. But that is easy enough:

4. $p \wedge q$ I$\wedge$, 2, 3

Now we can follow our plan and apply modus ponens (E$\rightarrow$):

5.   r   E$\rightarrow$, 1, 4

Now we have achieved our aim when we assumed q in 3: we have derived r. The idea behind our rule of thumb was that $q \rightarrow r$ can now be derived by applying I$\rightarrow$:

6. $q \rightarrow r$ I$\rightarrow$

So now we have achieved our aim in assuming p in 2:

7. $p \rightarrow (q \rightarrow r)$ I$\rightarrow$

And we have achieved our aim in assuming $(p \wedge q) \rightarrow r$ in 1:

8. $((p \wedge q) \rightarrow r) \rightarrow (p \rightarrow (q \rightarrow r))$ I$\rightarrow$.

Exercise 6

Show that
(a) $\vdash (p \rightarrow (q \rightarrow r)) \rightarrow ((p \wedge q) \rightarrow r)$.
(b) $\vdash (p \rightarrow (p \rightarrow q)) \rightarrow (p \rightarrow q)$.

Besides the introduction and elimination rules, we also introduce a *rule of repetition, Rep*, which enables us to repeat at a later stage in a derivation any formula we have obtained, under the obvious proviso that it is not an assumption which has since been withdrawn, or dependent on any such assumption:

1.   .
              .
              .
m. ϕ
              .
              .
              .
n. ϕ Rep, m

This rule does not in fact add anything to what we already had; it just enables us to derive some formulas more easily than would otherwise be the case. As an example, we now give a derivation without premises for p → (q → p).

1. p	assumption
2. q	assumption
3. p	Rep, 1
4. q → p	I→
5. p → (q → p)	I→

It must be remarked that the tautological character of formulas like this one, for which the rule of repetition is used, is often somewhat counterintuitive. This same formula p → (q → p) was one of the tautologies which C. I. Lewis referred to as the *paradoxes of material implication*.

4.3.4 *Disjunction*

We now turn to the rules for the connective ∨. To begin with, we can conclude that $\phi \lor \psi$ on the basis of ϕ. We are dealing with the inclusive disjunction, so that if we are given ϕ, then $\phi \lor \psi$ holds whether ψ does or not. Similarly, we may always conclude $\phi \lor \psi$ on the basis of ψ. Probably we are not much inclined to reason this way in everyday contexts: if we already know that *A*, then in general we are not much inclined to state anything less informative, such as *A or B* (see chap. 6). It must, however, be remembered that we are often dealing with preliminary or auxiliary conclusions here. The *introduction rule* I∨ for the disjunction is as follows:

(i)   1. .
          .
          .
          .
       m. ϕ
          .
          .
          .
       n. $\phi \lor \psi$ I∨, m

(ii)   1. .

        .

        .

        .

    m. ψ

        .

        .

        .

    n. $\phi \vee \psi$ I$\vee$, m

How may $\phi \vee \psi$ be *applied* in drawing some conclusion χ? To know $\phi \vee \psi$ and no more than this is neither to know that ϕ nor to know that ψ, but only to know that at least one of the two holds. So if χ is to follow in either way, it will have to follow in both ways. That is, χ follows from $\phi \vee \psi$ just in case it can be derived from ϕ and also from ψ. In other words: a conclusion χ may be drawn from $\phi \vee \psi$, $\phi \to \chi$ and $\psi \to \chi$. It is then clear what the *elimination rule* E$\vee$ will be:

  1.   .

             .

             .

             .

m_1. $\phi \vee \psi$

             .

             .

             .

m_2. $\phi \to \chi$

             .

             .

             .

m_3. $\psi \to \chi$

             .

             .

             .

  n. χ E$\vee$, m_1, m_2, m_3

One simple derivation which uses both rules is the derivation of $q \vee p$ from $p \vee q$:

1.	$p \vee q$	assumption
2.	p	assumption
3.	$q \vee p$	I$\vee$, 2
4.	$p \to (q \vee p)$	I$\to$
5.	q	assumption
6.	$q \vee p$	I$\vee$, 5
7.	$q \to (q \vee p)$	I$\to$
8.	$q \vee p$	E$\vee$, 1, 4, 7

The application of introduction rule I∨ in steps 3 and 6 of this derivation, in which the conclusion is less informative than the premise, may be considered a *reculer pour mieux sauter*.

We gave a rule of thumb for →; this can also be done for ∧ and ∨. A summary of these heuristic rules is given in (10)

(10)   *Objective*

To derive $\phi \rightarrow \psi$

To derive $\phi \wedge \psi$

To derive $\phi \vee \psi$

To derive χ from $\phi \vee \psi$

Approach

take ϕ as an assumption and attempt to derive ψ.

attempt to derive both ϕ and ψ.

attempt to derive ϕ or attempt to derive ψ.

attempt to derive χ under the assumption ϕ; if this succeeds, draw the conclusion that $\phi \rightarrow \chi$. Now attempt to derive χ under the assumption ψ; if this succeeds, draw the conclusion that $\psi \rightarrow \chi$.

Exercise 7

Show that
(a) $p \vee (p \wedge q) \vdash p$.
(b) $\vdash (p \vee q) \rightarrow ((p \rightarrow q) \rightarrow q)$.
(c) $p \vee (q \vee r) \vdash (p \vee q) \vee r$.

4.3.5 *Negation*

Simple rules for the introduction and the elimination of ¬ are not so obvious as much of the above. To continue along the lines followed so far, under what circumstances may we draw the conclusion that ¬ϕ? When we can show that ϕ cannot be the case; that is, if having assumed ϕ, we can derive a contradiction. And what would we call a contradiction? A pair of formulas ψ, ¬ψ? Or perhaps a single formula of the form $\psi \wedge \neg\psi$? Either would do, but it is more elegant to introduce a new, special-purpose atomic formula ⊥ into the formal language at this stage. We shall refer to it as *the falsum*. This may be seen as the favorite contradiction or undisputably false sentence, like $0 = 1$, for example, or *I do not exist*. We may draw the conclusion that ⊥ if we have both ϕ and ¬ϕ. And that can only occur if we have made certain contradictory assumptions. The following derivation of ⊥ can be considered the *elimination rule* E¬:

1.

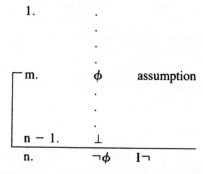

m_1. $\neg\phi$

m_2. ϕ

n. $\bot$ E$\neg$, m_1, m_2

If $\bot$ can be derived from ϕ, then we may draw the conclusion that $\neg\phi$. This is reflected in the *introduction rule* I$\neg$:

1.
.
.
.

m. ϕ assumption
.
.
.
n − 1. $\bot$
n. $\neg\phi$ I$\neg$

What these rules do is interpret $\neg\phi$ as $\phi \rightarrow \bot$. The rule of thumb for deriving $\neg\phi$ follows immediately from this and is found in (11):

(11) *Objective*   *Approach*

     To derive $\neg\phi$ take ϕ as an assumption and try to derive a
                          pair of formulas of the form ψ, $\neg\psi$.

An example is the following derivation without premises of $\neg(p \wedge \neg p)$:

1. $p \wedge \neg p$ assumption
2. p E$\wedge$, 1
3. $\neg p$ E$\wedge$, 1
4. $\bot$ E$\neg$, 3, 2
5. $\neg(p \wedge \neg p)$ I$\neg$

Exercise 8

Show that
(a) $\vdash p \rightarrow \neg\neg p$.
(b) $\vdash (p \wedge \neg q) \rightarrow \neg(p \rightarrow q)$.
(c) $\vdash (p \rightarrow q) \rightarrow (\neg q \rightarrow \neg p)$.
(d) $p \rightarrow \neg q \vdash q \rightarrow \neg p$.

The derivation system for propositional logic which we have now given in the form of the rules for the introduction and elimination of the connectives is not complete in the technical sense to be introduced in §4.4. This is because tautologies remain which cannot be derived without premises. But this system of introduction and elimination has a certain internal coherence; it is known as *minimal logic*. Two important tautologies which cannot be derived within minimal logic are ¬p → (p → q), the *ex falso sequitur quodlibet*, and p ∨ ¬p, the *law of the excluded middle*. We shall now add the *EFSQ rule*, which will enable us to derive the *ex falso sequitur quodlibet*. We simply say that an arbitrary formula may be derived from ⊥:

1.   .
                      .
                      .
                      .

n − 1.   ⊥
n.   φ   EFSQ, n − 1.

Given this rule, ¬p → (p → q) can easily be derived without premises:

1.	¬p	assumption
2.	p	assumption
3.	⊥	E¬, 1, 2
4.	q	EFSQ, 3
5.	p → q	I→
6.	¬p → (p → q)	I→

It should be noted that the *ex falso sequitur quodlibet* is another tautology which C. I. Lewis reckoned to the paradoxes of material implication. That the EFSQ rule is needed for a derivation is, however, not always as obvious as it is in the case of ¬p → (p → q). This is apparent from the following example, which demonstrates that p ∨ q, ¬p ⊢ q. In our system, it is impossible to derive q from p ∨ q and ¬p without the EFSQ rule.

1.	p ∨ q	assumption
2.	¬p	assumption
3.	p	assumption
4.	⊥	E¬, 2, 3
5.	q	EFSQ, 4
6.	p → q	I→
7.	q	assumption
8.	q	Rep, 7
9.	q → q	I→
10.	q	E∨, 1, 6, 9

Adding the EFSQ rule to minimal logic, we obtain a logical system in which
p ∨ ¬p is still not derivable without premises. This system is known as *intuitionistic logic,* since it describes the reasoning done in what is known as
intuitionistic mathematics. This school of mathematical thought was originated by the Dutch mathematician L. E. J. Brouwer at the beginning of the
twentieth century. It was his intention to rid mathematics of what he saw as
metaphysical presuppositions concerning the nature of mathematical objects
and to ground the discipline in our intuitions about natural numbers. If, with
Brouwer, one is of the opinion that all mathematical objects are the creations
of the human mind, then one will not accept a proof that it is impossible that
there is no object with some property A as a proof that there is some object
with the property A. From this perspective, then, the style of reasoning known
as a reductio ad absurdum is unacceptable, and more generally, one is not
justified in drawing the conclusion ϕ from $\neg\neg\phi$. (It is precisely this principle
that we shall soon add to the rest as the ¬¬-rule.) According to more modern
terminology, it is *constructive* reasoning (in mathematics) which is formalized
in intuitionistic logic. According to this, a disjunction may only be asserted
if one of the disjuncts may be asserted. So p ∨ q is true only if p may be
asserted or q may be asserted. Similarly, an existential formula $\exists x\phi$ may
be asserted only if one can give an example: some specific substitution t such
that one may assert $[t/x]\phi$.

Adding the ¬¬-rule to intuitionistic logic, we obtain classical logic, which
is none other than the logical system that we discussed in the preceding chapters. The ¬¬-rule is as follows:

1.   .
             .
             .
             .

m. $\neg\neg\phi$
             .
             .
             .

n. ϕ ¬¬, m

Using the ¬¬-rule, we can derive p ∨ ¬p without premises:

1.	¬(p ∨ ¬p)	assumption
2.	p	assumption
3.	p ∨ ¬p	I∨, 2
4.	⊥	E¬, 1, 3
5.	¬p	I¬
6.	p ∨ ¬p	I∨, 5
7.	⊥	E¬, 1, 6
8.	¬¬(p ∨ ¬p)	I¬
9.	p ∨ ¬p	¬¬, 8

This derivation may need some comment. It should be realized that p ∨ ¬p cannot be derived more directly than this. The rule of thumb for ∨ is of no use here, since neither p nor ¬p can be derived without premises. We therefore attempt a detour with the help of the ¬¬-rule, by trying to derive ¬¬(p ∨ ¬p) first. According to the rule of thumb for ¬, we must first take ¬(p ∨ ¬p) as assumption (1) and then try to obtain a contradiction. Given that ¬(p ∨ ¬p) is the only formula we have at our disposal, it is not surprising that we try to obtain ¬(p ∨ ¬p) and p ∨ ¬p as our two contradictory formulas. To do this, we must derive p ∨ ¬p. According to the rule of thumb for ∨, this means deriving either p or ¬p. Since p doesn't seem to be a very promising starter, we try ¬p first. According to the rule of thumb for ¬, we must then take p as an assumption and try to derive a contradiction from it. Now that we have come this far, everything starts to fall into place. With (3), we obtain p ∨ ¬p, which contradicts ¬(p ∨ ¬p) and thus enables us to conclude first (4) ⊥ and then, with I¬, we have (5) ¬p. Now (6), p ∨ ¬p, follows according to our plan, and (7) ⊥. We can thus derive the falsum from ¬(p ∨ ¬p) and can draw the conclusion, (8) ¬¬(p ∨ ¬p), with I¬; a single application of the ¬¬-rule to (8) results in (9) p ∨ ¬p.

Exercise 9

Show that
(a) ⊢ ((p → q) → p) → p (Hint: try to derive ¬¬p from (p → q) → p)).
(b) ⊢ ¬(p ∧ q) → (¬p ∨ ¬q).
(c) ⊢ ¬(p → q) → (p ∧ ¬q).

Rules can be given for ↔, but they do not bring any new insights and will therefore be omitted.

Exercise 10

Show that
(a) p ∧ (q ∨ r) ⊢ (p ∧ q) ∨ (p ∧ r).
(b) (p ∧ q) ∨ (p ∧ r) ⊢ p ∧ (q ∨ r).
(c) ⊢ (p → (q → r)) → ((p → q) → (p → r)).
(d) p → q, r → s ⊢ (p ∨ r) → (q ∨ s).
(e) p → ¬p, ¬p → p ⊢ ⊥ (this is the 'propositional skeleton' of the liar's paradox).

Exercise 11

Giving introduction and elimination rules for a linguistic expression may be viewed as stating the logical essentials for its use. That is why certain modern theories of meaning (M. Dummett, D. Prawitz) rest on a natural deduction analysis in preference to a truth-conditional one. Nevertheless, merely introducing such proof-theoretic rules may be dangerous, as was pointed out by A. Prior. What is wrong with having a new connective ∘ which has the introduction rules for ∨ and the elimination rules for ∧?

4.3.6 *Quantifiers*

All of the above rules apply equally in predicate logic, so that it will suffice to give introduction and elimination rules for the existential and universal quantifiers. We shall presently see that we can just as well restrict the formulas in our derivations to sentences (these being formulas lacking free variables) as long as we have an unlimited supply of constants at our disposal. We shall proceed on this assumption. The *introduction rule* I∃ for the existential quantifier is obvious enough; we may always draw the conclusion that ∃xφ if we have [a/x]φ for some constant a (it does not matter which one):

1.   .
                  .
                  .

m.   [a/x]φ
                  .
                  .
                  .

n.   ∃xφ   I∃, m

Our example of an application of I∃ is the following derivation of ∃xAxx from Aaa:

1.   Aaa   assumption
2.   ∃xAxx   I∃, 1

In this derivation, the formula φ to which I∃ was applied was Axx: [a/x]Axx = Aaa. As a second example, we have a derivation of ∃x∃yAxy from Aaa:

1.   Aaa   assumption
2.   ∃yAay   I∃, 1
3.   ∃x∃yAxy   I∃, 2

Here I∃ is applied to Aay at step 2: [a/y]Aay = Aaa; it is applied to ∃yAxy at step 3: [a/x]∃yAxy = ∃yAay.

Exercise 12

Show that Aa → Bb ⊢ ∃x∃y(Ax → By). Give for each application of I∃ the formula to which it is applied.

The *elimination rule* E∀ does not present many difficulties either; from ∀xφ we may conclude [a/x]φ; this for any constant a.

1.   .
                  .
                  .
                  .

m. $\forall x\phi$

            .
            .
            .

n. $[a/x]\phi$ E$\forall$, m

Using this rule we can now derive $\exists xAx$ from $\forall xAx$, for example.

1.	$\forall xAx$	assumption
2.	Aa	E$\forall$, 1
3.	$\exists xAx$	I$\exists$, 2

Here E$\forall$ is applied to the formula Ax.

Exercise 13

Show that (a), (b), (c); give for each application of E$\forall$ the formula to which it is applied.

(a) $\forall xAxx \vdash Aaa$.
(b) $\forall x\forall yAxy \vdash Aab$.
(c) $\forall x\forall yAxy \vdash Aaa$.

The *introduction rule* I$\forall$ for the universal quantifier is a little more difficult to formulate. As a first attempt we could say that the conclusion $\forall x\phi$ may be drawn if $[a/x]\phi$ has been derived for every constant a. The problem is that there are infinitely many constants, but we want to keep derivations finite. What we can do is say that we may conclude $\forall x\phi$ if it is certain that all of these derivations could in principle be made. This is the case if $\forall x\phi$ is derivable for some constant a which may be considered arbitrary, a constant whose identity is unknown in the derivation. Now a may be considered arbitrary at any stage in a derivation if a does not appear in any assumptions which have been made previously and which have not been dropped at that stage in the derivation, and if a does not appear in the formula ϕ itself. It turns out that these two conditions are the right restrictions on the applicability of the following rule I$\forall$:

1.   .
            .
            .
            .

m. $[a/x]\phi$
            .
            .
            .

n. $\forall x\phi$ I$\forall$, m

As an example we have the following derivation, which shows that $\forall x\forall yAxy \vdash \forall xAxx$.

1.	∀x∀yAxy	assumption
2.	∀yAay	E∀, 1
3.	Aaa	E∀, 2
4.	∀xAxx	I∀, 3

In 2, 3, and 4, the rules are applied to ∀yAxy ([a/x]∀yAxy = ∀yAay), Aay ([a/y]Aay = Aaa), and Axx ([a/x]Axx = Aaa), respectively. This cannot be reversed. Any attempt to derive ∀x∀yAxy from ∀xAxx is doomed to failure (and this ought to be the case, for everyone can love him- or herself, for example, without everyone loving everyone):

1.	∀xAxx	assumption
2.	Aaa	E∀, 1
3.	∀yAay	: not allowed, because a occurs in Aay ([a/y]Aay = Aaa)

This shows how an undesirable result is prevented by the restrictions given above.

Table (12) gives some rules of thumb for finding derivations with quantifiers.

(12) *Objective*   *Approach*

To derive ∃xφ   try to derive [a/x]φ for any constant a (any a will do).

To derive ∀xφ   try to derive [a/x]φ for some constant a which at that stage in the derivation may be considered arbitrary.

Another illustration involving both E∀ and I∀ is the following example, which shows that ∀x∀yAxy ⊢ ∀x∀yAyx:

1.	∀x∀yAxy	assumption
2.	∀yAay	E∀, 1
3.	Aab	E∀, 2
4.	∀yAyb	I∀, 3
5.	∀x∀yAyx	I∀, 4

Exercise 14

Show that:
(a) ∀x(Ax ∧ Bx) ⊢ ∀xAx ∧ ∀xBx.
(b) ∀xAx ∧ ∀xBx ⊢ ∀x(Ax ∧ Bx).
(c) ∀x∀yAxy ⊢ ∀x∀y(Axy ∧ Ayx).
(d) ∀x(Ax → Bx), ∀xAx ⊢ ∀xBx.
(e) ¬∃xAx ⊢ ∀x¬Ax.
(f) ¬∃x¬Ax ⊢ ∀xAx (Hint: try to derive ¬¬Aa).

We shall now turn to the elimination rule for the existential quantifier. Much the same problems arise in formulating this rule as with I∀. When may a conclusion ψ be drawn from $\exists x\phi$? The only thing we know is that there is something somewhere which satisfies ϕ; about the something we have no right to assume anything at all. In other words, $[a/x]\phi$ may be used to derive ψ provided a may be considered arbitrary in the context formed by this particular derivation. More precisely: a conclusion ψ may be drawn from $\exists x\phi$ and $[a/x]\phi \rightarrow \psi$ if a is 'arbitrary'. Again, an arbitrary constant a is one which appears in neither the premises nor in ϕ; but here we must place the additional requirement that a does not appear in ψ. These, then, are the three restrictions on the applicability of the following rule E∃:

1.   .
                      .
                      .

                      .

m_1. $\exists x\phi$

                      .
                      .

                      .

m_2. $[a/x]\phi \rightarrow \psi$
                      .

                      .

                      .

n. ψ E∃, m_1, m_2

As an example of how this works, we have the following derivation, which shows that $\exists xAxx \vdash \exists x\exists yAxy$:

1.	$\exists xAxx$	assumption
2.	Aaa	assumption
3.	$\exists yAay$	I∃, 2
4.	$\exists x\exists yAxy$	I∃, 3
5.	Aaa $\rightarrow \exists x\exists yAxy$	I→
6.	$\exists x\exists yAxy$	E∃, 1, 5

That the constant may not appear in the conclusion when E∃ is applied is apparent from the following *incorrect*, and of course undesirable, derivation of $\forall x\exists yAay$ from $\exists xAxx$:

1.	$\exists xAxx$	assumption
2.	Aaa	assumption
3.	$\exists yAay$	I∃, 2
4.	Aaa $\rightarrow \exists yAay$	I→
5.	$\exists yAay$	E∃, 1, 4
		faulty, because the constant a occurs in the conclusion $\exists yAay$
6.	$\forall x\exists yAxy$	I∀, 5

This rule gives rise to the rule of thumb for deriving things from existential quantifiers, which is stated in (13):

(13) *Objective*   *Approach*

   To derive ψ from $\exists x\phi$ take $[a/x]\phi$ as an assumption for some constant a which may be considered arbitrary at that stage in the derivation and with respect to ψ, and try to derive ψ. If you can, then draw the conclusion $[a/x]\phi \rightarrow \psi$.

By way of illustration, we give some examples. We begin with a derivation which shows that $\exists x\exists y Axy \vdash \exists x\exists y Ayx$:

1.	$\exists x\exists y Axy$	assumption
2.	$\exists y Aay$	assumption
3.	Aab	assumption
4.	$\exists y Ayb$	I$\exists$, 3
5.	$\exists x\exists y Ayx$	I$\exists$, 4
6.	Aab $\rightarrow \exists x\exists y Ayx$	I$\rightarrow$
7.	$\exists x\exists y Ayx$	E$\exists$, 2, 6
8.	$\exists y Aay \rightarrow \exists x\exists y Ayx$	I$\rightarrow$
9.	$\exists x\exists y Ayx$	E$\exists$, 1, 8

And here we show that $\exists x\forall y Axy \vdash \forall y\exists x Axy$:

1.	$\exists x\forall y Axy$	assumption
2.	$\forall y Aay$	assumption
3.	Aab	E$\forall$, 2
4.	$\exists x Axb$	I$\exists$, 3
5.	$\forall y Aay \rightarrow \exists x Axb$	I$\rightarrow$
6.	$\exists x Axb$	E$\exists$, 1, 5
7.	$\forall y\exists x Axy$	I$\forall$, 6

A few comments may help to clarify how this derivation was found. In step 2, we simply followed the rule of thumb for the elimination of $\exists$. The formula we wanted to derive at that stage was $\forall y\exists x Axy$, and the rule of thumb for deriving universal formulas recommends substituting an 'arbitrary' constant for the y in $\exists x Axy$ and then trying to derive the result. The constant a will not do, since a appears in the assumption $\forall y Aay$, but b will be all right. So we try to derive $\exists x Axb$. This is not too difficult, since Aab can be derived from $\forall y Aay$. The rest follows automatically.

We conclude by deriving $\exists x Ax$ from $\neg\forall x\neg Ax$. We will most certainly need the $\neg\neg$-rule for this, since, as we mentioned in our discussion of intuitionistic logic, this is the nonconstructive argument par excellence.

1.	¬∀x¬Ax	assumption
2.	¬∃xAx	assumption
3.	Aa	assumption
4.	∃xAx	I∃, 3
5.	⊥	E¬, 2, 4
6.	¬Aa	I¬
7.	∀x¬Ax	I∀, 6
8.	⊥	E¬, 1, 7
9.	¬¬∃xAx	I¬
10.	∃xAx	¬¬, 9

Given the ¬¬-rule, this derivation presents no real difficulties. We assume ¬∀x¬Ax as assumption (1) and attempt to derive ¬¬∃xAx. Following the rule of thumb for ¬, we take ¬∃xAx as assumption (2) and attempt to derive a contradiction. It looks promising to try to derive ∀x¬Ax, in contradiction to ¬∀x¬Ax, so we follow the rule of thumb for ∀ and attempt to derive ¬Aa. The rule of thumb for ¬ then leads us to take Aa as assumption (3) and to try to derive a contradiction. This is easy enough: ∃xAx is in contradiction to ¬∃xAx. The rest of the derivation goes according to the plan behind all of the assumptions made above.

Exercise 15

Show that:

(a) ∃x(Ax ∧ Bx) ⊢ ∃xAx ∧ ∃xBx.
(b) ∀x(Ax → Bx), ∃xAx ⊢ ∃xBx.
(c) ∃x¬Ax ⊢ ¬∀xAx.
(d) ∀x¬Ax ⊢ ¬∃xAx.
(e) ¬∀xAx ⊢ ∃x¬Ax.
(f) ∀x(Ax → Bx), ∃x¬Bx ⊢ ∃x¬Ax.
(g) ∀x(Ax ∨ Bx), ∃x¬Bx ⊢ ∃xAx.
(h) ∀x(Ax → Bx), ∃x(Ax ∧ Cx) ⊢ ∃x(Bx ∧ Cx).

4.3.7 *Rules*

We conclude §4.3 by briefly returning to rules (i)–(vii), which we encountered in §3.6.5. Replacing ⊨ by ⊢ in all of them, we obtain corresponding rules (i*)–(vii*), which can be proved without any difficulty. As an example, we shall take (i*), or modus ponens:

(i*) If ⊢ φ and ⊢ φ → ψ, then ⊢ ψ.

This can be proved as follows. Suppose ⊢ φ and ⊢ φ → ψ. This means that there is some derivation of φ without premises (in, say, m lines), and another derivation, also without premises, of φ → ψ (and in, say, n lines). We now write the one derivation above the other, beginning with the derivation of φ, and renumber all of the lines in the derivation of $\phi \to \psi$: all numbers (don't forget those after the formulas) are raised by m. And then we add an application of E$\to$ at the bottom, deriving the conclusion ψ:

1.   .

                         .

                         .

m. ϕ
m + 1.   .

                .

                .

m + n. $\phi \to \psi$
m + n + 1. ψ E$\to$, m + n, m

The end result is a derivation of ψ.

All of the rules apply equally with premises. As an example, we shall prove (vi*) in the following form:

(vi*) $\psi_1, \ldots, \psi_n \vdash \neg\neg\phi$ iff $\psi_1, \ldots, \psi_n \vdash \phi$

Proof $\Rightarrow$: Suppose we have a derivation of $\neg\neg\phi$ from $\psi_1, \ldots, \psi_n$. This can very easily be turned into a derivation of ϕ from $\psi_1, \ldots, \psi_n$ by adding one new line in which the conclusion ϕ is drawn from $\neg\neg\phi$ by means of the $\neg\neg$-rule.

$\Leftarrow$: The required alterations can be read from the following schema:

1. ψ_1

                .

                .

                .

n. ψ_n

                .

                .

                .

m. ϕ
⌐m + 1. $\neg\phi$ assumption
∟ m + 2. $\bot$ E$\neg$, m + 1, m
m + 3. $\neg\neg\phi$ I$\neg$ □

Exercise 16

Show that $\vdash \phi \wedge \psi$ iff $\vdash \phi$ and $\vdash \psi$.

4.4 Soundness and Completeness

In this section we shall (without giving rigorous proofs) go into the connections between the semantic and syntactic approaches to logical inference, that is, between ⊨ and ⊢. As we have said, these amount to the same thing. Or to put it more precisely, for any sentences $\phi_1, \ldots, \phi_n, \psi$ in any language L of predicate logic, we have $\phi_1, \ldots, \phi_n \vDash \psi$ if and only if $\phi_1, \ldots, \phi_n \vdash \psi$. This can be divided into two implications, one in each direction. We shall treat them separately, formulating them as two theorems.

Theorem 14 (*Soundness Theorem for Predicate Logic*)

For all sentences $\phi_1, \ldots, \phi_n, \psi$ (in some language L of predicate logic), if $\phi_1, \ldots, \phi_n \vdash \psi$, then $\phi_1, \ldots, \phi_n \vDash \psi$ too.

Theorem 15 (*Completeness Theorem for Predicate Logic*)

For all sentences $\phi_1, \ldots, \phi_n, \psi$ (in some language L of predicate logic), if $\phi_1, \ldots, \phi_n \vDash \psi$, then $\phi_1, \ldots, \phi_n \vdash \psi$ too.

These theorems are primarily statements about the rules we have given for the system of natural deduction. The soundness theorem establishes that the rules are sound: applying them to some premises $\phi_1, \ldots, \phi_n$, all of which are true in some model **M,** can only give rise to conclusions which are themselves true in **M.** In order to prove this theorem (which we shall not do), it is sufficient to check the above for each of the rules in turn. The introduction rule for $\wedge$ is sound, for example, since if both $V_M(\phi) = 1$ and $V_M(\psi) = 1$, then we can be sure that $V_M(\phi \wedge \psi) = 1$ too. The proof for the other rules poses no real problems, although there are a few complications in the rules for the quantifiers, which we encountered in connection with the restrictions to the rules. The soundness theorem assures us that the restrictions are sufficient to block all undesirable conclusions which might otherwise be drawn. In the special case of $n = 0$, it can be seen that the soundness theorem reduces to: if ϕ can be derived without premises, then ϕ is universally valid.

The completeness theorem assures us that the rules are complete in the sense that if $\phi_1, \ldots, \phi_n/\psi$ is valid, i.e., if $\phi_1, \ldots, \phi_n \vDash \psi$, then there are enough rules to enable us to derive ψ from $\phi_1, \ldots, \phi_n$. In other words, the rules are in themselves sufficient to generate all valid argument schemata; nothing has been forgotten. It is clear that this result is much less obvious than the soundness theorem, even if we thought we could obtain all valid argument schemata while forming the rules, and in particular, that we could derive all tautologies and other universally valid formulas without premises (see the discussion on the EFSQ and ¬¬-rules). And this result is not only less obvious, it is also less easily proved.

But the soundness and completeness theorems are not only statements about the derivation rules. They also say something about semantics, about the concept of semantic validity. What is characteristic of derivation rules is that they leave absolutely no room for doubt about what combinations of symbols are proper derivations and what combinations are not. This is true of natural deduction, but it is equally essential to other existing formal proof systems. What soundness and completeness theorems say is that valid argument schemata are precisely those which can be obtained as derivations in the formal system in question. This is by no means always the case: it holds for predicate logic, but it does not hold for second-order logic or for mathematics in general (for more on this, see below).

It should be noted that the completeness theorem in no way contradicts Church's Theorem on the undecidability of predicate logic, which was briefly mentioned in §4.2. If a given argument schema happens to be valid, then we are assured that there is some finite derivation of its conclusion from its premises. So we have a method at our disposal which is guaranteed to show sooner or later that the schema is valid: we just start generating derivations and wait until the right one turns up. The problem is with the schemata which are not valid; we have no method which is guaranteed to discover this for us. Generating derivations will not help us here, since in that case we would have to wait to make sure that the argument schema does *not* turn up. And since there are infinitely many possible derivations, we could never be sure.

The completeness theorem can also be presented in another form which is of some interest. But first we will introduce the concept of consistency and prove a few simple things about it.

Definition 4

$\phi_1, \ldots, \phi_n$ is said to be *inconsistent* if $\phi_1, \ldots, \phi_n \vdash \bot$; $\phi_1, \ldots, \phi_n$ is said to be *consistent* if it is not inconsistent, that is, if $\phi_1, \ldots, \phi_n \nvdash \bot$.

Theorem 16

(a) $\phi_1, \ldots, \phi_n, \psi$ is inconsistent iff $\phi_1, \ldots, \phi_n \vdash \neg\psi$.
(b) $\phi_1, \ldots, \phi_n, \psi$ is consistent iff $\phi_1, \ldots, \phi_n \nvdash \neg\psi$.
(c) $\phi_1, \ldots, \phi_n, \neg\psi$ is consistent iff $\phi_1, \ldots, \phi_n \nvdash \psi$.

Proof (a) $\Rightarrow$: Suppose $\phi_1, \ldots, \phi_n, \psi$ is inconsistent, that is, suppose $\phi_1, \ldots, \phi_n, \psi \vdash \bot$. Then there is a derivation of $\bot$ from $\phi_1, \ldots, \phi_n, \psi$. This derivation can be converted into a derivation of $\neg\psi$ from $\phi_1, \ldots, \phi_n$ by adding I$\neg$ as a last step:

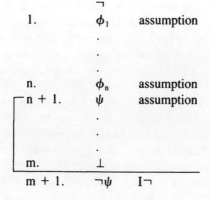

$\Leftarrow$: Suppose $\phi_1, \ldots, \phi_n \vdash \neg\psi$. Then a derivation of $\neg\psi$ from $\phi_1, \ldots, \phi_n$ is given. Now form a derivation starting with the assumptions $\phi_1, \ldots, \phi_n, \psi$, followed by the remainder of the given derivation (some of the numbers will have to be adapted). This will result in a derivation of $\neg\psi$ from $\phi_1, \ldots, \phi_n, \psi$ (in which no real use is made of ψ). This derivation can now be turned into a derivation of $\perp$ from $\phi_1, \ldots, \phi_n, \psi$ by adding $E\neg$ as a last step:

1.	ϕ_1	assumption
.		
.		
.		
n.	ϕ_n	assumption
n + 1.	ψ	assumption
.		
.		
.		
m + 1.	$\neg\psi$	
m + 2.	$\perp$	$E\neg$, n + 1, m + 1

$\square$

(b) is an immediate consequence of (a).

(c) $\phi_1, \ldots, \phi_n, \neg\psi$ is consistent iff (according to (b)) $\phi_1, \ldots, \phi_n$ $\nvdash \neg\neg\psi$ iff (according to (vi*) given in §4.3.7) $\phi_1, \ldots, \phi_n$ $\nvdash \psi$. $\square$

Before we present the completeness theorem in its alternative form, consider first its contraposition: if $\phi_1, \ldots, \phi_n \nvdash \psi$, then $\phi_1, \ldots, \phi_n \nvDash \psi$. Now if the antecedent of this is replaced by means of theorem 16c, then we obtain: if $\phi_1, \ldots, \phi_n, \neg\psi$ is consistent, then $\phi_1, \ldots, \phi_n \nvDash \psi$. Reformulating the consequent of this, we obtain: if $\phi_1, \ldots, \phi_n, \neg\psi$ is consistent, then there is a model **M** suitable for $\phi_1, \ldots, \phi_n, \psi$ and such that $V_{\mathbf{M}}(\phi_1) = \ldots = V_{\mathbf{M}}(\phi_n) = 1$ and $V_{\mathbf{M}}(\psi) = 0$. Or in other words, if $\phi_1, \ldots, \phi_n, \neg\psi$ is consistent, then there is some suitable model **M** such that $V_{\mathbf{M}}(\phi_1) = \ldots = V_{\mathbf{M}}(\phi_n) = V_{\mathbf{M}}(\neg\psi) = 1$. If in order to keep things short we just say that **M** is a *model* for the string of formulas $\chi_1, \ldots, \chi_m$ just in case $V_{\mathbf{M}}(\chi_1) = \ldots = V_{\mathbf{M}}(\chi_m) = 1$, then we see that the completeness theorem is equivalent to the following result.

Theorem 17 (*Consistency Theorem*)

If the string of sentences $\chi_1, \ldots, \chi_m$ is consistent, then there is a model for $\chi_1, \ldots, \chi_m$.

And the soundness theorem can be shown to be the reverse of theorem 17 in exactly the same manner:

Theorem 18

If the string of sentences $\chi_1, \ldots, \chi_m$ has a model, then $\chi_1, \ldots, \chi_m$ is consistent.

Nowadays it is usual to prove theorem 17 instead of proving the completeness theorem directly. One assumes that a set of sentences is consistent and then tries to provide it with a model. This idea was initiated by Henkin (1949). The original proof of the completeness theorem, the one given by Gödel (1930), was more direct.

All these theorems demonstrate a striking peculiarity of modern logic: its ability to theorize about its own systems and prove significant results about them. This 'self-reflecting' activity is sometimes called *metalogic*. In modern metalogic there are many more concerns than those touched upon so far. For instance, one can inquire into soundness and completeness for systems other than standard predicate logic, such as intuitionistic logic or higher-order logic (see chap. 5). But there are also other important metalogical theorems about predicate logic itself; we will survey a few, taking our first cue from an earlier theme.

We said before that the validity of an inference may be described as the absence of any counterexamples. And we also noted what a staggering task is involved in determining the latter state of affairs, since all interpretations in all models might be eligible in principle. But perhaps our apprehension in the face of 'the immense totality of all interpretations' seems a little exaggerated. After all, in propositional logic one can manage by checking the finite list of interpretations which are relevant to the validity of any given schema. In this, as in so many other respects, however, propositional logic is hardly representative of logical theories. Thus, all structures with arbitrary domains D have to be taken into account when evaluating schemata in predicate logic. And there is indeed an 'immense' number of these. The domain D may be finite or infinite, and within the latter type there are different varieties: among these some are countably infinite (like the natural numbers) and some are uncountably infinite (like the real numbers, or even bigger). In 1916, L. Löwenheim proved that predicate logic is at least insensitive to the latter difference between infinite sizes:

> If an inference has a counterexample with an infinite domain, then it has a counterexample with a *countably infinite* domain.

The true force of this result can probably only be appreciated against the background of a working knowledge of Cantor's set theory. But the following stronger formulation, which it received in the hands of D. Hilbert and P. Bernays in 1939, must still be quite surprising:

> If an inference has a counterexample, then it has a counterexample in *arithmetic* gotten by exchanging the predicate letters for suitable

predicates of arithmetic, the formulas thus being seen as propositions
about natural numbers.

This theorem led W. V. O. Quine (1970) to an interesting insight. In good
nominalistic style, he compares the notions of validity that we have considered, $\vdash$ and $\vDash$, to the 'substitutional account' of validity: every substitution
of suitable linguistic expressions in $\phi_1, \ldots , \phi_n, \psi$ which renders all of the
premises true also renders the conclusion true.

It can easily be checked that syntactic derivability implies this form of
validity. But conversely, nonderivability also implies (according to the Completeness Theorem) the existence of a counterexample, which in turn (according to the Hilbert-Bernays result) provides a counterexample in arithmetic
which can serve as a nominalistic counterexample. Now nominalists do not
believe in abstract structures like those involved in the definition of $\vDash$. The
effect of Quine's idea is that the nominalists can nevertheless be reconciled to
the notion: at least with regard to predicate logic, there is nothing wrong with
$\vDash$. So metalogical theorems can sometimes be used to make philosophical
points.

We have now seen how we can use finite and countably infinite structures to
determine validity in predicate logic. If there are counterexamples to be found,
then they are to be found among these structures. Can this be improved upon?
Can we perhaps use just the *finite* structures? The answer is that we cannot.
Every finite model of $\forall x \neg Rxx$ (the irreflexivity of R) and $\forall x \forall y \forall z((Rxy \land
Ryz) \to Rxz)$ (the transitivity of R), for example, has an R-maximal element
$(\exists x \forall y \neg Rxy)$. But the derivation of the last of these formulas from the first
two is nevertheless invalid. As a counterexample we have, for example, the
natural numbers with R interpreted as *less than* (compare this with what is
promised by Hilbert and Bernays's Completeness Theorem). Even worse, as
was proved by B. Trahtenbrot in 1950, there can be no completeness theorem
for the class of predicate-logical inferences which are valid on finite structures. These insights are also of at least some importance for the semantics of
natural language. Given that the structures which natural language sentences
are intended to pertain to are generally finite, the above shows that the infinite
structures are not just a theoretical nicety: they are indispensable if we are to
have a syntactically characterizable notion of validity.

In 1969, P. Lindström proved that the metaproperties which we have discussed are essentially characteristic of predicate logic. (We are now concerned only with languages with the same nonlogical vocabulary as predicate
logic.)

> Any logical system plus semantics which includes predicate logic
> and such that a completeness theorem and Löwenheim's theorem
> hold, must coincide with predicate logic.

This is not put very precisely: finding an exact *formulation* for this metalogical theorem was actually a nontrivial part of Lindström's achievement.

But the idea amounts to the following. Extending predicate logic means losing at least one of the metaproperties of completeness, or the Löwenheim result.

In particular, the stronger system of *second-order logic* is *incomplete,* as will appear in more detail in §5.4. There is no analogue of the completeness theorem for it, because its class of universally valid statements is too complex to admit of effective axiomatization. (Similar Lindström effects appear in connection with the *generalized quantifiers* which will be considered in vol. 2, like 'most' and 'for infinitely many'.) This is the phenomenon which, on the one hand, makes predicate logic so felicitous, and on the other, makes all of its extensions so mysterious and such a challenge to investigate.

Another aspect of inferences which has been studied quite extensively is their *decidability.* Is there, for some logical system, an effective method for deciding whether a given inference is valid or not? For propositional logic, there is. As we have seen, for instance, using the truth table test:

> Being a valid argument schema in propositional logic is a decidable notion.

and a fortiori

> Being a tautology of propositional logic is a decidable notion.

Moreover, by somewhat more complicated methods, one can also establish decidability for *monadic* predicate logic: that part of predicate logic which uses unary predicate symbols. Predicate logic taken as a whole, however, is *undecidable.* In 1936, A. Church proved his previously mentioned negative result (*Church's theorem*):

> Being a universally valid formula of predicate logic is not a decidable notion.

So the same must apply to predicate logic's set of valid argument schemata. The following *is* true, however, in the light of our earlier discussion:

> The set of argument schemata valid in predicate logic has an effective syntactic axiomatization.

For this assertion is always true of a system with a syntactic proof calculus which is complete with respect to its notion of inference. And predicate logic is such a system. For incomplete logical systems, however, like the previously mentioned second-order logic (or the theory of types to be presented in vol. 2), there isn't even an analogue of the last-mentioned result. The set of argument schemata which are valid in these systems has no effective syntactic characterization. This does not mean that one cannot use calculi of natural deduction in such cases: in fact, there exist interesting sound syntactic proof calculi for second-order logic too. But in view of the inescapable incompleteness of the system, they can never produce all of its universally valid formulas.

All of these metaresults give insights into the powers and limitations of the logical apparatus of deduction. But concrete reasoning always involves two distinct factors: there is inference and there are the initial *knowledge* structures from which inference must follow. The second formal aspect has also been studied extensively by logicians from a mathematical perspective, in a long tradition of research into the foundations of mathematics (and occasionally also other sciences). This involves investigations into the logical structure of axiomatized mathematical theories, the various metalogical properties which the theories can have, and the logical relationships they can have to each other in the web of scientific knowledge. Many different facets of our logical apparatus become relevant to the study of such issues as efficient representation and communication of knowledge. They range from the choice of an optimal vocabulary in which to formulate it to the choice of a suitable system of inference by which to develop and transmit it. For example, illuminating results have been achieved about the role of *definitions* in scientific theories (Beth's Theorem). Although foundational research tends to take place within an environment which is more concerned with scientific language than natural language, it is a source of inspiration for general logical and semantic studies too. (See Barwise 1977 for a comprehensive survey).

Exercise 17 ◇

Some logic textbooks are based on *maintaining consistency* rather than drawing inferences as the basic logical skill. So it is interesting to study the basic properties of consistency. Prove or refute the following assertions for sets of formulas X, Y and formulas ϕ:
(i)   If X and Y are consistent, then so is their union X ∪ Y.
(ii)   If X is consistent, then so is X ∪ {ϕ} or X ∪ {¬ϕ}.
(iii)   If X is inconsistent and ϕ is not universally valid, then there is a maximal consistent Y ⊆ X which does not imply ϕ. Is this Y unique?

Exercise 18 ◇

Although full predicate logic is undecidable, many of its *fragments* are better behaved. As was observed in the text, for example, *monadic* predicate logic with only unary predicates is decidable. Another useful instance is the fragment consisting of *universal formulas*, i.e., formulas with arbitrary predicates but only universal quantifiers restricted to occurrences in front of quantifier-free formulas.
(i)   Which of the earlier requirements on binary relations (see §3.3.8) are universal?
(ii)   Prove that valid consequence among universal formulas is decidable, by showing that only certain finite models need be considered for its assessment.

5   Beyond Standard Logic

5.1 Introduction

As we remarked in chapter 1, there is no such thing as *one* general-purpose
logic characterizing *all* valid arguments or the relations between the meanings
of *all* expressions in a language. There is a whole range of logical systems,
each investigating arguments whose validity is dependent on certain expressions, namely, the logical constants occurring in that system. But propositional and predicate logic, the two logical systems discussed in previous
chapters, can nevertheless be regarded as *standard logic*, since just about all
other systems can be seen as extensions of, deviations from, or variations on
them. Two large and important extensions, *intensional logic* and *the logic of
types*, will be discussed at some length in volume 2. In this chapter we will go
into a few smaller and less important extensions, deviations, and variations.
There are two reasons for doing this. First, in order to emphasize that the tool
box which logic offers to other disciplines is quite extensive. A wide range of
different logical systems is available for various purposes, and if the right tool
is not available, it is often possible to adapt another one to the job. And second, especially in the case of second-order logic, which we shall encounter in
§5.4, to prepare the ground for the richer logical systems to be discussed
in volume 2.

A logical system is characterized by its set of *logical constants* and by the
interpretation which is given to them. Or to put it differently, a logical system
is characterized by the *argument schemata* which it renders valid. Now the
main reason for departing from standard logic is to obtain more valid argument schemata, or other ones. An *extension* of a logical system has a larger
set of logical constants, so that it can treat argument schemata on the basis of
the new constants in addition to all of the original argument schemata. It is
said to be an extension of the original system because it expands the set of
valid argument schemata.

A *deviation* from a logical system uses the same logical constants but interprets them differently. So the set of valid argument schemata does not grow
larger; it is changed in some other way. A deviation has the same syntax as the
original system, so it looks the same on paper. What has changed is the content.

A *variation* on (or *variant* of) a logical system is the opposite of a deviation. The content is left the same and the syntax is altered. It characterizes the same set of valid argument schemata. We have already seen one variant of propositional logic, namely, the logical system obtained in §2.7 by replacing the coordinative connective → with the subordinating connective ↦ and then interpreting them directly, by means of truth functions. In §5.6 we will run across a variant of standard predicate logic in which no use is made of variables, their role being played by certain kinds of operations. This means a drastic modification of the syntax, but the content of standard predicate logic is left untouched. One more useful/practicable/common variation on predicate logic is *many-sorted predicate logic*, to which §5.3 is devoted. In many-sorted logic the domain is divided into a number of subdomains, each of which contains some particular kind of entity.

Intuitionistic logic, which was mentioned briefly in §4.3, is one obvious example of a deviation from standard propositional logic. And the various many-valued logics to be discussed in §5.5 are some more. They depart from standard logic in attributing more different truth values to sentences than the two we have been using so far, *true* and *false*. The propositional-logical syntax remains at least initially unchanged, but the logical constants are given another interpretation. One characteristic result of this is that in many-valued logic, as in intuitionistic logic, the law of the excluded middle no longer holds. The formula $\phi \vee \neg\phi$ is no longer universally valid.

The simplest sort of *expansion* is obtained simply by adding one or more logical constants, without changing the system's interpretations in any way. We saw this in §3.7, where *standard predicate logic with identity* was discussed. Having added = as an additional logical constant, we ended up with more valid argument schemata and were, for example, in a position to define the numerals by means of the quantifiers and identity. In §5.2 we shall turn to expansions of standard predicate-logical languages obtained by adding *descriptions*. Descriptions are composite logical expressions by means of which we can refer to individuals. They can, for example, serve as representations for *definite descriptions* like *the present queen of the Netherlands*. Expanding the logical language by adding descriptions, which involves adding the *iota operator* as a new logical constant, in a sense does not bring about any essential changes, since formulas with descriptions in them can under certain circumstances by replaced by formulas containing just the familiar quantifiers and identity.

But expanding standard predicate logic to *second-order logic*, which we will discuss in §5.4, involves essential changes. To put it briefly, it amounts to introducing predicate variables which do the same thing for properties as the familiar individual variables do for individual entities. Quantifiers can be placed before predicate variables, just as they can be placed before individual variables, and this enables quantification over properties. The result is a genuinely richer logical system. The interpretations, on the other hand, remain unchanged: models for standard predicate logic are included in models for second-order logic. The expressions of a language for second-order logic are still interpreted in terms of the two truth values and a set of entities, and the same applies to the *logic of types*, an expansion of second-order logic, and thus of standard predicate logic, which we will investigate in volume 2. The same, however, does *not* apply to another expansion of standard logic which we will discuss in volume 2, *intensional logic*. Not only is intensional logic a richer system, but the models in terms of which the language is interpreted are richer too. In this respect, you could say that intensional logic is to predicate logic as predicate logic is to propositional logic. The models for predicate logic involve something which the models for propositional logic don't have: a set of entities. And the models for intensional logic involve a set of *contexts*, which the models for predicate logic do not have.

So much for the relations between standard logic and the nonstandard logical systems to be developed here and in volume 2. The large variety of logical systems may seem a bit overwhelming at this stage, but as we shall see, their similarities are more numerous and more significant than their differences. The various systems, for example, render different argument schemata valid, but the notion of logical validity is in essence common to them all, as is the concept of meaning in a few important respects. (The concept of meaning used in logic is discussed in chap. 1, vol. 2.) And as far as the relationship between language and meaning is concerned, the principle of compositionality plays a central part in all of the systems. There is a considerable consensus on what logic, language, and meaning are and on their relationships to each other.

5.2 Definite Descriptions

In standard predicate logic there is just one kind of expression which can be used to refer to some entity or individual in particular, and that is the individual constant. The whole idea behind individual variables is that they do not refer to particular individuals but can be used to refer to various different things. In just about all of the examples of translations from natural language into predicate logic which we have seen so far, individual constants have served as translations of proper names. Proper names are expressions which refer to particular individual things, but fortunately they are not the only expressions which can be used for this purpose. If they were, it would be impossible to talk about people without knowing their names. Another way of referring to a particular individual or thing is by means of a description, as in (1)–(4).

(1)   The queen of the Netherlands

(2)   The first man on the moon

(3)   Elvis Presley's mother

(4)   Ronald Reagan's ranch

Expressions like these are called *definite descriptions*. With the exception of
(4), each of the examples comprises a predicate expression, which may be
composite, and a definite article. And the possessive *Ronald Reagan's* in (4)
can be seen as a composite definite article. The predicates in the examples
have been chosen so that we can be reasonably sure that there is just one individual who satisfies them, and these are then the unique individuals to whom
the definite descriptions refer.

So far we have just used individual constants as the formal translations of
definite descriptions. But the translations become more true if we introduce
a special notation for them which does justice to the fact that they are composite expressions. For this purpose we now introduce the *iota operator* ⅂(an
upside-down Greek iota) which, like the existential and universal quantifiers,
always comes with a variable and is always followed by a propositional function which is its scope. Thus it appears in expressions like ⅂xFx, ⅂xGxy, and
⅂x(Fx ∧ Gxa). We call such expressions *descriptions*. Descriptions are complex terms, since while a quantifier followed by a propositional function is
a sentence or another propositional function, the iota operator followed by
a propositional function is always a term, an expression which can appear
among the arguments of an *n*-ary predicate just like an individual constant or
variable. So we obtain formulas like:

(5)	R(⅂xQx)	The queen of the Netherlands is riding a bicycle.
(6)	b = ⅂xQx	Beatrix is the queen of the Netherlands.
(7)	⅂xQx = ⅂xHx	The queen is the head of state.
(8)	∀x(Dx → L(x, ⅂yQy))	Every Dutchman loves the queen.
(9)	w = ⅂xS(x, ⅂yQy)	Willem-Alexander is the queen's son.

Although it is strictly speaking unnecessary, we shall on occasion add extra
brackets and separate the arguments of relations by means of commas, thus
making the formulas more readable. Note also that in these examples the expression *queen of the Netherlands,* among others, has been rendered as a
unary predicate. We could, of course, preserve more structure by translating
(5), for example, as R(⅂xQ(x, n)).

In order to incorporate the descriptions formed with the iota operator into
the language of predicate logic, we must expand the definition of the formulas
of predicate logic (definition 1 in §3.3) to a *simultaneous inductive definition*
of both terms and formulas. We have to define both together because formulas

can now be among the parts from which a term is built up, and vice versa. Here are the clauses which must be added in order to achieve this:

(a) If α is an individual constant or variable in L, then α is a term in L.

(b) If ϕ is a formula in L and x is a variable, then $\imath x \phi$ is a term in L.

The clause giving the atomic formulas is then:

(i)   if A is an n-ary predicate letter ($n \geqslant 1$) and $t_1 \ldots t_n$ are terms in L, then $A t_1 \ldots t_n$ is a formula in L.

Clauses (ii)–(iv) for connectives and quantifiers do not need modification. Only the final clause still needs to be adapted:

(v)   Only that which can be generated by clauses (i)–(iv) in a finite number of steps is a formula or term in L.

The syntactic innovation obtained by introducing the iota operator into the language of predicate logic is not sufficient. We also have to adjust the semantics to fit, saying how the new descriptions are to be interpreted. Here we use the approach to interpretation given as B in §3.6.3, which makes use of assignments. We now join definition 8, which interprets terms, with definition 9, the truth definition, thus obtaining a new definition that simultaneously interprets both terms and formulas of the language for predicate logic with descriptions. In order to interpret descriptions we add the following new clause:

(10) $[\![\imath x \phi]\!]_{M,g}$ is the unique individual d $\in$ D such that $V_{M,g[x/d]}(\phi) = 1$.

We must link the definitions interpreting terms with those interpreting formulas in this way because the interpretation of any term is now dependent on the interpretations of the formulas appearing in it (and vice versa). The problem with (10), however, is that $[\![\imath x \phi]\!]_{M,g}$ is not defined if there isn't exactly one individual satisfying ϕ. If there is no such individual, or if there are too many, then (10) does not say how $\imath x \phi$ should be interpreted. As examples of descriptions where this goes wrong in the real world, we have (11) and (12). Example (13) is a well-known example due to Russell.

(11)   Queen Beatrix's brother

(12)   Queen Beatrix's daughter

(13)   the king of France

The fact that these descriptions are undefined also transfers to some sentences in which they appear. Sentence (14), for example, is neither true nor false:

(14)   The king of France is bald.

To put this formally, if there is no unique individual that satisfies ϕ, then not only $[\![\imath x \phi]\!]_{M,g}$ but also $V_{M,g}(F(\imath x \phi))$ is undefined, which means that the formula $F(\imath x\phi)$ is neither true nor false. But this is not allowed by the fundamental principle of bivalence, which requires every formula to be either true or false. There are various ways this problem can be dealt with, and we shall only discuss here the solutions given by Frege and Russell. They have in common that they both strive to maintain the principle of bivalence. In this their approach differs from that taken in many-valued logic, where more truth values are considered than just *true* and *false*. We shall return to this approach later in this section, and at greater length in §5.5, which is devoted to many-valued logic.

Frege saw as a shortcoming of natural language the occurrence of definite descriptions which do not denote some unique thing. A properly constructed logical language, he thought, should always provide some unique descriptum. One way of doing this is to include a special *nil entity* in the domain, which is then by convention taken to be the entity denoted by descriptions which fail to satisfy the existential requirement or the requirement of unicity. The same thing is done in mathematics, where, for example, 0 is taken as the value of $x/0$ if it is desired that x/y always be defined. It is clear that Frege's solution is purely formal and not very intuitive. But it does solve the technical difficulties.

If d_0 is the special nil individual, then the clause-interpreting descriptions can be as follows:

(15) $[\![\imath x\phi]\!]_{M,g}$ is the unique individual $d \in D$ such that $V_{M,g[x/d]}(\phi) = 1$
       if there is any such thing; otherwise it is the nil individual d_0.

Given (15), the interpretation of descriptions is defined under all circumstances. And if we make sure that d_0 does not belong to the interpretation of any normal predicates such as *bald,* then sentence (14) is false.

The solution given by Russell has in common with that proposed by Frege not only that the principle of bivalence is maintained but also that a shortcoming of natural language is seen as the root of the problem. Russell's solution is known as his *theory of descriptions* and was first presented in his article "On Denoting" (1905). The approach is in line with the *misleading form thesis,* according to which the grammatical form of sentences sometimes does not reflect their 'real' logical form and is as a result misleading (see also §1.5.1). This thesis has played a prominent role in analytic philosophy. To get past the superficial grammatical form of sentences and reveal their underlying logical form was taken to be an important task for philosophy, and Russell's theory of descriptions is a textbook example of an attempt to do this.

In analyzing definite descriptions as descriptions formed by means of the iota operator, we have assumed that definite descriptions and proper names have the same syntactic function. Sentences like (16) and (17) would seem to suggest that this is reasonable enough:

(16)   Beatrix is riding a bicycle.

(17)   The queen of the Netherlands is riding a bicycle.

Both the proper name *Beatrix* and the definite description *the queen of the Netherlands* seem to fit the role of the subject of the predicate *is riding a bicycle*. This is where Russell would interrupt, saying that the grammatical form of these two sentences is misleading. Definite descriptions should not be considered normal subjects any more than quantified expressions like *everyone* and *no one*. The problems with definite descriptions result from our mistaking their misleading grammatical form for their logical form.

Russell's theory of descriptions provides us with a method for translating formulas containing the iota operator into formulas containing only the familiar quantifiers of standard predicate logic. This method uses *contextual definitions*. We cannot give a general definition of the iota operator and the descriptions formed with it (which would be an *explicit definition*). But for any given formula containing a description, that is, in any particular context, we can give an equivalent formula in which the iota operator is replaced by the normal quantifiers. The elimination of the iota operator means that the principle of bivalence can be maintained. According to Russell, a sentence like (17) says that there is an individual x who has the following three properties:

(i)   x is queen of the Netherlands: Qx;
(ii)   there is no individual y besides x that has the property of being queen of the Netherlands: $\forall y(Qy \rightarrow y = x)$; and
(iii)   x is riding a bicycle: Rx.

This means that sentence (17) can be translated as the following formula; it may seem a bit complicated but is in standard predicate logic:

(18) $\exists x(Qx \wedge \forall y(Qy \rightarrow y = x) \wedge Rx)$

Or equivalently and a little more simply:

(19) $\exists x(\forall y(Qy \leftrightarrow y = x) \wedge Rx)$

In general, the above means that every formula of the form $G(\imath xFx)$ can be reduced to a formula in standard predicate logic by means of the following definition:

Definition 1

$G(\imath xFx) =_{def} \exists x(\forall y(Fy \leftrightarrow y = x) \wedge Gx)$

As we have said, this is a contextual definition of descriptions. The iota operator cannot be given an explicit definition in predicate logic. Note also that definition 1 can be made more general, since as it stands it can only be used if the propositional function in the description is an atomic formula with a unary predicate and if the context is such that description itself appears as the argument of a unary predicate. The obvious general formulation of definition 1 will be omitted here.

Sentences like (14), with descriptions which fail to satisfy the existential requirement or which fail to satisfy the requirement of unicity, are simply false, as was the case in Frege's analysis. If the Netherlands were not a monarchy or simply did not have a monarch, then (19), the translation of (17), would be false. This is the strength of Russell's theory, but according to some, like Strawson (1950), it is also its weakness. According to Strawson's analysis, the existence of exactly one individual having the property of being queen of the Netherlands is not *stated* when sentence (17) is uttered; it is *presupposed*. And if this *presupposition* is not satisfied, then we cannot say that a proposition is being expressed which is either true or false. We shall not attempt to say who was right, Strawson or Russell. More important for our purposes here are some of the implications of Strawson's position from a logical point of view. Russell's treatment of definite descriptions leaves standard predicate logic untouched, but Strawson's approach would seem to challenge the principle of bivalence. In §5.5 we shall see some of the attempts to give Strawson's position a logical basis by means of a system of many-valued logic.

Any theory of definite descriptions has to give some account of negative expressions containing definite descriptions like the following:

(20)   The queen of the Netherlands is not riding a bicycle.

(21)   The king of France is not bald.

For Strawson, the question is quite simple: these sentences presuppose the existence of a unique queen of the Netherlands and a unique king of France, just as do the positive sentences we started with, and state that the former is not riding a bicycle and the latter is not bald.

Russell's theory is a little more subtle. Superficially one might think that sentence (21) is just the negation of sentence (14), so that it must be true under any circumstances under which (14) is false. According to Russell, it is not so simple. He takes a sentence like (21) as ambiguous, with one reading in which it is true and another in which, like (14), it is false. The reading in which it is true can be paraphrased as: it is not the case that there is a unique individual who is king of France and who is bald. Formula (22) corresponds to this reading. The reading in which (21) is false can be paraphrased as: there is a unique individual who is king of France and is not bald. Corresponding to this reading we have formula (23) (Kx: x is king of France; Bx: x is bald).

(22) $\neg \exists x (\forall y (Ky \leftrightarrow y = x) \land Bx)$

(23) $\exists x (\forall y (Ky \leftrightarrow y = x) \land \neg Bx)$

Both of these standard predicate-logical formulas can be obtained from the representation of (21) by means of the iota operator: $\neg B(\imath x Kx)$. The first is obtained by applying definition 1 to $B(\imath x Kx)$ in the formula $\neg B(\imath x Kx)$. This gives the negation operator $\neg$ wide scope over the quantifiers, as is apparent from (22). Formula (23) is obtained by applying definition 1 to the formula

¬B(ɿxKx) itself. In this case the quantifiers have wide scope. In Russell's own terminology, (23) represents the reading of (21) in which the definite description has a *primary* occurrence, and (22) represents the reading in which the definite description has a *secondary* occurrence.

In Frege's approach, a sentence like (21) is most naturally given just the reading in which it is untrue. But even if descriptions are given a Fregean interpretation, it is still possible to translate them into the normal quantifiers by means of a contextual definition. And if this is done, then an ambiguity arises which is similar to the one we saw with Russell. The advantage which Russell's theory has over Frege's theory is that it does not need any nil entity. Frege's theory, on the other hand, enables definite descriptions to be interpreted as such. We have mentioned that Russell's theory of descriptions is inspired by the idea that grammatical form is often misleading. From a syntactic point of view, definite descriptions would seem to be able to play the same role as proper names; they would seem to be independent entities. But apparently this is not true from a logical point of view. The fact that descriptions only admit of a contextual definition shows that, at least as far as their logical form is concerned, definite descriptions are not independent entities. There is no logical expression corresponding to the description *the queen of the Netherlands*. In this way, descriptions resemble (other) quantified terms like *every man, some men,* and *all men.* The logical form of expressions like this can only be given relative to the contexts, the whole sentences, in which they appear. Like the logical analysis of universally and existentially quantified sentences, Russell's theory of descriptions would seem to support the idea that there is a fundamental difference between the grammatical, that is, the surface syntactic form of sentences, and their logical form. It is an idea which has been extremely influential.

Note that all the talk here about 'logical expressions' and 'logical form' is really just about expressions in standard predicate logic and standard predicate-logical form. And our conclusion that there is an essential difference between grammatical form and logical form must be read with this restriction in mind. Descriptions and quantifiers may not be independent units from the perspective of predicate logic, but that is not to say that there are no logical systems in which they are independent units. We shall show in volume 2 that both definite descriptions and (other) quantified expressions can be translated into the formal language if we consider a richer logical language than that of standard predicate logic (namely, higher-order logic with lambda abstraction), so that they can be interpreted as independent units. And in that way descriptions and quantified expressions can also be placed in the same logical category, so that the grammatical form which Russell considered so misleading can, as far as logical form is concerned, be rehabilitated. These results have argued against the influential idea that there is a fundamental distinction between grammatical and logical form.

5.3 Restricted Quantification: Many-Sorted Predicate Logic

In §3.3 formulas (26) and (27) were given as translations of sentences (25) and (26), respectively:

(24) All teachers are friendly.

(25) Some teachers are friendly.

(26) $\forall x(Tx \rightarrow Fx)$

(27) $\exists x(Tx \wedge Fx)$

We say that the quantifier $\forall x$ is *restricted to* Tx in (26) and that the quantifier $\exists x$ is *restricted to* Tx in (27). More generally: if ϕ is a formula with x as a free variable, then $\forall x$ is said to be restricted to ϕ in $\forall x(\phi \rightarrow \ldots)$ and $\exists x$ is said to be restricted to ϕ in $\exists x(\phi \wedge \ldots)$. The same applies if the whole formula is a subformula of some other formula. If you examine the translation examples we have given so far, you will see that quantifiers are nearly always restricted. Expressions like *everyone* and *someone* are among the few which can be rendered as unrestricted quantifiers, and even then only if the sentence doesn't say anything about any entities other than people, since that is the condition under which we can restrict the domain to people. If it mentions things other than people, then restricted quantifiers are needed—two in formula (29), which is a translation of (28):

(28) Everyone gave Danny something.

(29) $\forall x(Px \rightarrow \exists y(Ty \wedge Gxyd))$

The quantifier $\forall x$ has been restricted to P (for people), and the quantifier $\exists y$ has been restricted to T (for things). So the domain includes both people and things.

It would perhaps be more natural to split the domain into different subdomains, thus distinguishing among people, other living things, and all other things, for example. Typographically different variables could be used, these being interpreted within the different subdomains. So, for example, we could have x, y, and z as variables for the subdomain containing just people; k, l, and m as variables for other living things; and u, v, and w as variables referring to anything else (subscripts being added to any of these variables in case they threaten to run out). It will then also be necessary to say in what subdomains the various constants have their interpretations. In this way, sentence (28) can be translated as (30):

(30) $\forall x\exists uGxud$

Note that (30) has the unrestricted quantifiers $\forall x$ and $\exists u$ instead of the restricted quantifiers $\forall x(Px\rightarrow$ and $\exists y(Ty\wedge$ of (29). The price to be paid for this simplification is that defining the language and the syntax becomes more complicated.

The logic resulting from the above modifications is called *many-sorted predicate logic*. In defining a language for many-sorted predicate logic, we have to specify what sorts there are, what their respective variables are, and to what sort each of the constants belongs. In formulating the semantics, we must divide all the domains into different subdomains too, one for each sort. It is then not too difficult to give a truth definition, so it is left to the reader.

It is doubtful that much is to be gained by introducing new languages for the above purpose. Any many-sorted language for predicate logic can be turned into a language for standard predicate logic by adding a number of unary predicate letters, one for each sort. The variables can then be interpreted over the whole domain, the predicates taking over the job of referring to the different sorts. Taking (30) as a formula in many-sorted logic, for example, and introducing P and T to refer to the sorts corresponding to x and u, respectively, (29) can be recovered (or at least some variant which, in spite of having different variables from those of (29), has the same interpretation). Similarly, any model for many-sorted predicate logic can easily be turned into a model for standard predicate logic.

But many-sorted predicate logic has some advantages. Consider sentences (31) and (32), for instance.

(31)   Mont Blanc gave Danny something.

(32)   Everyone gave Mont Blanc something.

Translating these into standard predicate logic we obtain the following two sentences:

(33) $\exists y(Ty \wedge Gmyd)$

(34) $\forall x(Px \rightarrow \exists y(Ty \wedge Gxym))$

But in many-sorted logic, we can also choose to block the translation of (31) and (32). We may choose to require that things only be given to or by people, for example, by accepting Ghst as a formula only if h and t are the right kinds of constants or variables—those which refer to people. But this approach raises a great many problems, beginning with giving exact specifications for the sort or sorts of variables which each of the predicates may accept as its arguments. For this reason, it seems not very satisfactory as an approach to such sentences. But it returns in a somewhat more satisfactory form (in vol. 2) in the *logic of types*, where the different sorts (*types*) distinguish between expressions which have wholly different *functions*. Something similar is also to be found in second-order logic (see §5.4). Another way of dealing with some people's uneasiness with (31) and (32) is not to bar them from being translated into formulas but to arrange for the formulas to receive neither *true* nor *false* as a truth value in the semantics. The logical system which then arises, many-valued logic (see §5.5), is not a variant of standard predicate logic but a true deviation from it. These kinds of problems have incidentally also been the subject of lively debate in linguistics, centering on examples like the well-known (35):

(35)   Colorless green ideas sleep furiously.

Sentence (35) violates *selection restrictions*. If one thinks selection restrictions are a syntactic matter, one takes the first alternative outlined above, deeming sentences like (31), (32), and (35) syntactically ill-formed. If one thinks they belong to semantics, one will take the second. There are also those who think that an explanation for what is unsatisfactory about sentences like (31), (32), and (35) is to be sought outside of grammar altogether.

A many-sorted predicate logic offers only a minimal solution to what some people feel is unnatural about the way quantifiers are handled in translating (25) as (26), (25) as (27), and (28) as (29). What about sentences like (36)?

(36)   All wealthy people gave Danny something.

This translates into standard logic as (37), or, equivalently, as (38):

(37) $\forall x((Px \wedge Wx) \to \exists y(Ty \wedge Gxyd))$

(38) $\forall x(Px \to (Wx \to \exists y(Ty \wedge Gxyd)))$

The quantifier $\forall x$ is restricted to $Px \wedge Wx$ in (37), and it is restricted twice in (38), first to Px and then to Wx, which amounts to the same thing. So in order to 'cover up' these restrictions in a many-sorted logic we would have to introduce some more sorts, for Wx and $Px \wedge Wx$. Besides not being very elegant, distinguishing between people and wealthy people by introducing special sorts for them is a bad precedent. It is not clear where the division into increasingly more special sorts should stop. Perhaps whatever is considered unnatural about translations like (37) and (38) is more easily removed if it is remembered that what matters about translations is not the formulas themselves but their meanings. Translation is actually indirect interpretation, in which formulas function as intermediates between sentences and their meanings. Formulas are *notations* for meanings. And notations are neither natural nor unnatural, they are just more or less useful. In this case it might be better to introduce a notation by writing $\forall x^\phi(\psi)$ instead of $\forall x(\phi \to \psi)$, and $\exists x^\phi(\psi)$ instead of $\exists x(\phi \wedge \psi)$. Then (26), (27), (29), (33), and (37) can be rewritten as (39), (40), (41), (42), and (43), respectively:

(39) $\forall x^{Tx}(Fx)$

(40) $\exists x^{Tx}(Fx)$

(41) $\forall x^{Px}\exists y^{Ty}(Gxyd)$

(42) $\exists y^{Ty}(Gmyd)$

(43) $\forall x^{Px \wedge Wx} \exists y^{Ty}(Gxyd)$

A formula like (38) retains a restricted quantifier in this notation, as is apparent from (44):

(44) $\forall x^{Px}(Wx \rightarrow \exists y^{Ty}(Gxyd))$

One solution for this would be to shorten such formulas even more. One could, for example, shorten (44) to (45):

(45) $\forall x^{Px, Wx} \exists y^{Ty}(Gxyd)$

In formulating such shorthands, one must make sure that the original formula can always be recovered from its abbreviation. For this reason, (37) is abbreviated to (43) and (38) is abbreviated to (45). With more complicated sentences such as (46), it is questionable which of the two is more readable, the standard translation (47) or its abbreviation, (48):

(46)   He who has a dog that bites someone, is sad.

(47) $\forall x(Px \rightarrow (\exists y(Dy \wedge Hxy \wedge \exists z(Pz \wedge Byz)) \rightarrow Sx))$

(48) $\forall x^{Px, \exists y^{Dy \wedge Hxy}(\exists z^{Pz}(Byz))}(Sx)$

By way of conclusion, a word on inference relations. Since its models hardly differ from the standard ones, many-sorted logic is not very new as far as its semantics is concerned. As for syntax, the system of natural deduction can easily be modified for our purposes by introducing separate introduction and elimination rules for the quantifiers of each sort. The soundness and completeness theorems for standard predicate logic are then inherited by many-sorted logic.

5.4 Second-Order Logic

Second-order logic works with two different kinds of variables: x, y, z (the individual variables) and X, Y, Z (the predicate variables), and for now, two kinds of constants corresponding to these. Superficially, second-order logic would seem to be a special case of many-sorted logic. But as we shall see, the particular way in which the two sorts are interpreted results in second-order logic being very different from many-sorted logic. The individual variables have the same range as in standard logic: a set of entities which the formulas say things about. The predicate variables have as their range the set of properties which these entities have. In second-order logic, sentences like (50) and (51) can be translated, and it can be shown why (51) follows from (49) and (50):

(49)   Mars is red.

(50)   Red is a color.

(51)   Mars has a color.

Perhaps (50) seems much like many other sentences we've run across before. If *Socrates is a man* can be translated as Ms, why not just translate (50) as Cr? We could, but not if we also wanted to translate (49) as Rm. We can't treat red as a property one time (in Rm) and as an entity the next (in Cr). So *x is a color* must be seen not as a property of entities but as a property of properties of entities. Any such property is called a *second-order property.* In second-order logic, special symbols are reserved for second-order properties. Standard predicate logic is sometimes called *first-order predicate logic* in order to distinguish it from second-order logic, since it only treats properties of and relations between entities, the *first-order* properties and relations.

Second-order logic is then an extension of first-order logic in that it also contains variables and quantifiers over properties (and if desired) relations. Now (49)–(51) can be translated as (52)–(54):

(52)   Rm

(53) CR

(54) $\exists X(CX \wedge Xm)$

It is apparent from (52) and (53) that what we have called predicate letters in first-order logic are now first-order predicate constants. A first-order predicate constant can be applied to an individual constant, like the R in (52), but it can also itself appear as the argument of a second-order predicate constant, like the R in (53). As is apparent from (54), (51) is interpreted as the proposition that Mars has a property (namely, the property of being red) which has the property of being a color. There is, it states, a color which is a property of Mars. Expressing this involves quantifying over first-order properties. The variable X is a variable over properties. Here we shall disregard variables over relations between entities, since they complicate everything without introducing anything really new. (In the logic of types with lambda abstraction there is another and better approach; see vol. 2.) Similarly, we will restrict ourselves to second-order predicate constants which express the properties of and relations between properties. Thus we shall not consider properties of relations or relations between relations.

From (52)–(54) it is immediately apparent that second-order logic is not just a particular kind of many-sorted logic, as described in §5.3. The distinction between individual variables x, y, z and predicate variables X, Y, Z is, for example, not one between variables over different subdomains of one and the same domain. It is more a distinction between different functions: the first refer to entities and the second refer to the properties of those entities (the sets they form). Much the same applies to the distinction between first- and second-order predicate constants.

The vocabulary of a *second-order language for predicate logic* L consists of a set of *individual constants,* a set of *first-order predicate constants,* and a set of *second-order predicate constants.* The set of first-order predicate constants contains things like the R in (52); the set of second-order predicate constants contains things like the *C* in (53). As with the predicate letters in first-order predicate logic, a number is associated with each predicate constant which gives its arity. Besides these constants, all second-order languages contain the same set of individual variables x, y, z and predicate variables X, Y, Z, the quantifiers, the connectives, and brackets. We can now define the formulas of a second-order language L for predicate logic:

Definition 2

If L is a language for second-order predicate logic, then:

(i)   If A is an *n*-ary first-order predicate constant in L and $t_1, \ldots, t_n$ are individual terms in L, then $At_1 \ldots t_n$ is an (atomic) formula in L;

(ii)   if X is a predicate variable and t is an individual term in L, then Xt is an atomic formula in L;

(iii)   if *A* is an *n*-ary second-order predicate constant in L and $T_1, \ldots, T_n$ are first-order unary predicate constants in L, or predicate variables, then $AT_1 \ldots T_n$ is an (atomic) formula in L;

(iv)   if ϕ is a formula in L, then $\neg\phi$ is a formula in L;

(v)   if ϕ and ψ are formulas in L, then $(\phi \wedge \psi)$, $(\phi \vee \psi)$, $(\phi \rightarrow \psi)$, and $(\phi \leftrightarrow \psi)$ are also formulas in L;

(vi)   if x is an individual variable and ϕ is a formula in L, then $\forall x\phi$ and $\exists x\phi$ are also formulas in L;

(vii)   if X is a predicate variable and ϕ is a formula in L, then $\forall X\phi$ and $\exists X\phi$ are also formulas in L;

(viii) Only that which can be generated by the clauses (i)–(vii) in a finite number of steps is a formula in L.

As in first-order predicate logic, a definition can be given for free and bound occurrences of variables in formulas.

A model for a second-order language always includes a model for the first-order part of that language. As usual, this consists of some domain D and an interpretation function I which maps all the individual constants onto elements of D and maps *n*-ary first-order predicate constants onto subsets of D^n. But how is quantification over properties to be interpreted? Given that properties are to be interpreted as subsets of the domain, and that the quantifiers are supposed to apply to all properties, presumably quantifiers must apply to *all subsets of the domain D.* The set of all subsets of a set A is called A's *power set,* which has the notation POW(A). It can be defined as follows: POW(A) = $\{B | B \subseteq A\}$. For example, if A = $\{1, 2, 3\}$, then POW(A) = $\{\varnothing, \{1\}, \{2\}, \{3\}, \{1, 2\}, \{1, 3\}, \{2, 3\}, \{1, 2, 3\}\}$. So now an assignment g will assign elements of the domain D to individual variables and subsets of D, that is, elements of POW(D), to predicate variables. And how should second-order predicate constants be interpreted? They express properties of, or relations between, properties of entities. So just as a unary first-order predicate is interpreted as a set of entities, a unary second-order predicate is interpreted as a set of sets of entities, that is, a subset of POW(D). I(C), the interpretation of the second-order predicate constant *is a color,* is then {I(R), I(G), . . .}, in which R is the first-order predicate constant *is red,* G is *is green,* and so on. Generally, the interpretation I(F) of an n-ary second-order predicate constant F is a subset of (POW(D))^n. The truth definition for a second-order language L for predicate logic then consists in the usual truth definition for its first-order part, which we shall not repeat here (see definition 9 in §3.6.3), together with the following clauses:

(ii') $V_{M,g}(Xt) = 1$ iff $[\![t]\!]_{M,g} \in g(X)$;
(iii') $V_{M,g}(AT_1 \ldots T_n) = 1$ iff $\langle [\![T_1]\!]_{M,g}, \ldots, [\![T_n]\!]_{M,g} \rangle \in I(A)$;
(vii') $V_{M,g}(\forall X\phi) = 1$ iff for all $E \subseteq D$, $V_{M,g[X/E]}(\phi) = 1$;
    $V_{M,g}(\exists X\phi) = 1$ iff there is at least one $E \subseteq D$ such that $V_{M,g[X/E]}(\phi) = 1$.

In extending the system of natural deduction dealt with in §4.3 to second-order logic, we can begin by adding rules $I\forall_2$, $E\forall_2$, $I\exists_2$, and $E\exists_2$ for the new quantifiers. They are analogous to the ones we already have; here $I\forall_2$ is given as an example.

1.   .
.   .
.   .
.   .
m. $[A/X]\phi$
.   .
.   .
.   .
n. $\forall X\phi$ $I\forall_2$, m

This rule can be illustrated as follows. It can be shown that $\vdash \forall z((Ay \wedge Az) \rightarrow Ay)$ solely by means of first-order rules. Adding an application of $I\forall_2$ as a last step to the derivation of this formula, we obtain a derivation of $\forall X\forall y\forall z ((Xy \wedge Xz) \rightarrow Xy)$. Just as in first-order logic, A must be such that it can be considered arbitrary, which means that it may occur in neither the assumptions nor ϕ. And since we are restricting the quantification to properties, A must furthermore always be a unary predicate constant.

The following may be a surprise. There can be no completeness theorem for second-order logic. There is a soundness theorem, but that just means that none of the derivation rules are faulty. Second-order logic is much more powerful than first-order logic, with a perhaps unexpected expressive power. For example, identity is definable in second-order logic, since Leibniz's Law holds: $\forall y\forall z(y = z \leftrightarrow \forall X(Xy \leftrightarrow Xz))$. Even the set of natural numbers with the operations + and × is definable, which means that Gödel's incompleteness result is applicable and thus that a complete syntactic proof system is not available. That is, there are inferences which are semantically valid but which cannot be verified syntactically by a proof system, either by the system of natural deduction we have given or by any extension of it. In applications in linguistics this does not seem to pose much of a problem. To begin with, the given system can be strengthened such that it yields all obvious inferences (or in any case, all those that seem to play a part in natural language). This can be achieved by strengthening rules $I\exists_2$ and $E\forall_2$ to $I\exists_2^*$ and $E\forall_2^*$. $I\exists_2$ was introduced as an analogy to $I\exists$ and therefore has the form given here.

1.   .
.   .
.   .
.   .
m. $[A/X]\phi$
.   .
.   .
.   .
n. $\exists X\phi$ $I\exists_2$, m

But it would seem reasonable that we could infer $\exists X\phi$ not only from $[A/X]\phi$ but also from $[\psi/X]\phi$, if ψ is a formula with just one free variable. For any such formula also expresses a property. The new rule $I\exists_2^*$ is the strengthened rule which allows this. As an application of this rule we have, for example, the following. A first-order derivation of $\forall y((Ay \wedge By) \leftrightarrow (Ay \wedge By))$ can be given. If we treat this formula as $[Ay \wedge By/X]\forall y(Xy \leftrightarrow (Ay \wedge By))$ we obtain a derivation of $\exists X\forall y(Xy \leftrightarrow (Ay \wedge By))$ by adding a single application of $I\exists_2^*$. In concrete terms, what this means is that if *angry* and *beautiful* are both properties, then *angry and beautiful* is also a property. It can be shown that any given formula ϕ with just one free variable has some corresponding property in exactly the same way. It is, however, only the *existence* of the new properties which is guaranteed. Except in the logic of types (see vol. 2), where the lambda operator is used for this purpose, we do not create any new *notation* for this property. The quantifier rule $E\forall_2$ is strengthened to $E\forall_2^*$ in the same way as $E\exists_2$ is strengthened to $E\exists_2^*$.

A second comment which can be made in view of the incompleteness of second-order logic concerns the connection with many-sorted logic. To a certain extent, second-order logic can be considered a special many-sorted logical system of the type we saw in §5.3. This can be done as follows. The predicate variables X, Y, Z are replaced by variables u, v, w, and a sort of 'applicability' relation A is introduced. The idea is that Aux means that u is applicable to x (or that u is true of x). Then all formulas of the form Xt can be replaced by formulas of the form Aut. In view of the restrictions in §5.3, formulas like Auv and Axu can be excluded. What we have then is just a normal many-sorted logic. There is a completeness theorem for this many-sorted logic which is inherited by second-order logic, with the restriction that this second-order logic is not complete with respect to the semantics defined above, but with respect to the part of that semantics which can be expressed by means of the applicability relation A. In the models for this many-sorted logic, we don't really have entities and their properties but their simulation by means of two sorts of entities and the applicability relation A from one to the other. We shall not discuss this further now. But the simulation is not perfect, since the intuitive meaning of A cannot be fully captured by axioms, and only those inferences can be justified which depend on requirements which can explicitly be placed on A.

Translation into many-sorted logic leaves the rules $I\forall_2$, $E\forall_2$, $I\exists_2$, and $E\exists_2$ valid, but not $I\exists_2^*$ and $E\forall_2^*$. To save these two, it is necessary to add axioms in which more of the intuitive meaning of A is given. This can, for example, be achieved by adding the following axiom schema, the *comprehension principle* (55):

(55) $\exists u \forall x (Aux \leftrightarrow \psi)$

If (55) is added for each formula ψ with a single free variable x, then the resulting system amounts to the system of natural deduction with the rules $I\forall_2$, $E\forall_2^*$, $I\exists_2^*$, and $E\exists_2$. But since, as we have mentioned, not all aspects of the meaning of A can be given in this manner, second-order logic can never be treated entirely as a special case of many-sorted logic.

5.5 Many-Valued Logic

5.5.1 *Introduction*

In standard propositional logic (and of course in standard predicate logic), formulas all end up with either 1 or 0 as their truth value. We say that classical logic is *two-valued*. In a two-valued logic, the formula known as the *principle of the excluded middle*, $\phi \vee \neg \phi$, is valid. But other systems with three or even an infinity of truth values have been developed for various reasons and for a variety of applications. Logical systems with more than two values are called many-valued logical systems, or many-valued logics.

In this section we will discuss several many-valued propositional logics, their intuitive bases, and their applications. Most attention will be paid to those aspects which are relevant to research into natural language. In particular, we will consider possible applications of many-valued logic in the analysis of the semantic concept of presupposition.

Many-valued propositional logics are not, in the sense introduced in §5.1, *extensions* of standard logic. They are what we have called *deviations* from standard propositional logic. Many-valued logical systems are not conceived in order to interpret more kinds of expressions but to rectify what is seen as a shortcoming in the existing interpretations of formulas. Once a new logical system has been developed, it often proves desirable and possible to introduce new kinds of expressions, and then the deviation becomes, in addition, an extension. But we shall begin with the familiar languages of standard propositional logic and show how a semantics with more than two truth values can be given for these.

5.5.2 *Three-Valued Logical Systems*

Since as far back as Aristotle, criticism of the principle of the excluded middle has been intimately linked to the status of propositions about contingent events in the future, and thus to the philosophical problem of determinism. This also applies to the three-valued system originated by the Polish logician Łukasiewicz, whose argument against bivalence derives from Aristotle's *sea battle argument*. Consider the sentence *A sea battle will be fought tomorrow*. This sentence states that a contingent event will take place in the future: it is possible that the sea battle will take place, but it is also possible that it will not. From this we can conclude that today the sentence is neither true nor false. For if the sentence were already true, then the sea battle would necessarily take place, and if it were already false, then it would be impossible for the sea battle to take place. Either way, this does not conform to the contingency of the sea battle. Accepting that propositions about future contingent events are now true or false amounts to accepting determinism and fatalism.

The validity of this argument is debatable. Its form can be represented as follows:

(56) $\phi \rightarrow$ necessary ϕ

(57) $\neg\phi \rightarrow$ impossible ϕ ($= \neg\phi \rightarrow$ necessary $\neg\phi$)

(58) $\phi \lor \neg\phi$

(59) necessary $\phi \lor$ necessary $\neg\phi$

In order to escape the deterministic conclusion (59), Aristotle rejected (58), the law of the excluded middle. These days, though, one would be much more inclined to think that something is wrong with premises (56) and (57) than with (58). From the truth of ϕ we cannot infer that *necessary* ϕ, and the same applies to falsity. From the falsity of ϕ we cannot conclude that *necessary* $\neg\phi$. In order to defend this conception properly, a logical analysis of the notion of necessity is required. One such analysis is given in modal logic, which is discussed in volume 2. There the (in)validity of arguments like the above is discussed in §2.3.5.

Although the original motivation for Łukasiewicz's many-valued logic is not watertight, it is interesting enough in its own right, since motivations other than the original one can be (and have been) given. Łukasiewicz's system can be given by means of the truth tables in (60):

(60)

ϕ	$\neg\phi$
1	0
#	#
0	1

$\phi \wedge \psi$

ϕ \ ψ	1	#	0
1	1	#	0
#	#	#	0
0	0	0	0

$\phi \vee \psi$

ϕ \ ψ	1	#	0
1	1	1	1
#	1	#	#
0	1	#	0

$\phi \rightarrow \psi$

ϕ \ ψ	1	#	0
1	1	#	0
#	1	1	#
0	1	1	1

The third value (#) stands for *indefinite* or *possible*. It should be clear how these tables should be read. They are slightly different in form from the truth tables we have dealt with so far. Figure (61a) shows how the two-valued truth table for the conjunction can be written in this manner. And figure (61b) shows how the three-valued conjunction can be written in the original way.

(61) a.

$\phi \wedge \psi$

ϕ \ ψ	1	0
1	1	0
0	0	0

b.

ϕ	ψ	$\phi \wedge \psi$
1	1	1
1	#	#
1	0	0
#	1	#
#	#	#
#	0	0
0	1	0
0	#	0
0	0	0

Tables like those in (61) are useful if we only want to say how the connectives should be interpreted, but we have to stick with the original way of writing truth tables if we want to use them for calculating the truth values of composite formulas from the truth values of the proposition letters in them.

According to the table for negation in (60), the value of ϕ is always indeterminate if the value of $\neg\phi$ is. And from the table for disjunction it follows that *the law of the excluded middle* does not hold. As can be seen from (62), $\phi \vee \neg\phi$ never has the truth value 0, but it doesn't always have the value 1 either. If ϕ has # as its truth value, then $\neg\phi$ has value # too.

(62)

ϕ	$\neg\phi$	$\phi \vee \neg\phi$
1	0	1
#	#	#
0	1	1

It follows similarly from the table for conjunction that *the law of noncontradiction* $\neg(\phi \wedge \neg\phi)$ does not hold. The *law of identity,* on the other hand, does hold: $\phi \to \phi$ is valid, since according to (63) it always has 1 as its truth value.

(63)

ϕ	$\phi \to \phi$
1	1
#	1
0	1

This is because according to the table for implication in (60), if ϕ has # as its truth value, then $\phi \to \phi$ has, not #, but 1 as its truth value. Related to this is the fact that while the interdefinability of $\vee$ and $\wedge$ by means of $\neg$ still holds, the interdefinability of $\vee$ and $\to$, or that of $\wedge$ and $\to$, does not. The reason for this is that both $\phi \vee \psi$ and $\phi \wedge \psi$ have truth value # if both ϕ and ψ have value #, while $\phi \to \psi$ has 1 as its truth value in that case.

Kleene has proposed a three-valued system which differs from Łukasiewicz's on exactly this point. His interpretation for $\to$ is given in (64):

(64) a.

ϕ	$\neg\phi$
1	0
#	#
0	1

b. $\phi \wedge \psi$

ϕ \ ψ	1	#	0
1	1	#	0
#	#	#	0
0	0	0	0

c. $\phi \vee \psi$

ϕ \ ψ	1	#	0
1	1	1	1
#	1	#	#
0	1	#	0

d. $\phi \to \psi$

ϕ \ ψ	1	#	0
1	1	#	0
#	1	#	#
0	1	1	1

Although Kleene's system only differs from Łukasiewicz's system in the implication, we have listed it completely in (64), since we will often want to refer to it in what is to come. According to Kleene's table for implication, $\phi \to \phi$ is no longer a valid formula. On the other hand, the interdefinability of $\vee$ and $\to$ via negation, as well as that of $\wedge$ and $\to$, has been regained. Kleene interprets the third value not as 'indefinite' but as 'undefined'. The value of a composite formula can be definite or defined even if the value of one or more of its parts is not. This is the case if the known value of some part is enough to decide the value of the whole formula. We know, for example, that $\phi \to \psi$ is always true if its antecedent is false, whatever the value of the consequent is. So if ϕ has the value 0, then $\phi \to \psi$ has the value 1, whether or not ψ is #.

One undesirable result of the interpretation of the third value as 'undefined' is that the truth value of $\phi \lor \neg\phi$ is undefined if that of ϕ is. This is not very satisfactory, since even if it is not known yet what the value of ϕ is, it certainly is clear that the value of ϕ depends on that of $\neg\phi$. We don't know what value ϕ has, but we do know that $\neg\phi$ has the value 1 if ϕ has value 0, and vice versa. So one could argue that we know that $\phi \lor \neg\phi$ has 1 as its truth value, even if we do not know yet what truth value ϕ has.

Van Fraasen's method of *supervaluations* was developed in order to meet this difficulty. This method gives all formulas which have the same value under all valuations in standard logic (that is, the tautologies and contradictions of standard logic) that same value. But the same does not apply to contingent formulas. We shall not further discuss supervaluations here.

Another sort of three-valued system originates when the third value is interpreted as *meaningless* or *nonsense,* and Bochvar proposed the three-valued system presented in (65) with this interpretation in mind

(65) a.

ϕ	$\neg\phi$
1	0
#	#
0	1

b.

$\phi \land \psi$	ψ = 1	#	0
ϕ = 1	1	#	0
#	#	#	#
0	0	#	0

c.

$\phi \lor \psi$	ψ = 1	#	0
ϕ = 1	1	#	1
#	#	#	#
0	1	#	0

d.

$\phi \to \psi$	ψ = 1	#	0
ϕ = 1	1	#	0
#	#	#	#
0	1	#	1

The third value in (65) is dominant in the sense that a composite formula receives # as its value whenever any of its composite parts does. If any part of a sentence is nonsense, then the sentence as a whole is nonsense. This interpretation of the connectives is known as the *weak interpretation,* this in contradistinction to Kleene's *strong interpretation.* Łukasiewicz's, Kleene's, and Bochvar's systems all agree in giving the same truth value as classical logic to any formula whose subformulas all have classical truth values. Bochvar's system differs from the other two in that if a formula has a classical truth value in his system, then all of its subformulas must too. As we have just seen, in Łukasiewicz's and Kleene's system, a formula can have a classical truth value even if some of its subformulas do not.

5.5.3 *Three-Valued Logics and the Semantic Notion of Presupposition*

One important if much-debated application of three-valued logic in linguistics is in dealing with *presupposition*. In §5.2 we saw how Russell's theory of descriptions analyzes sentences with definite descriptions, like (66) and (67):

(66)   The king of France is bald.

(67)   The queen of the Netherlands is riding a bicycle.

His theory analyzes the sentences in such a way that the existence of a king of France and a queen of the Netherlands are among the things which these sentences state. A sentence like (66) is then, according to Russell, false. Russell's analysis of definite descriptions was criticized by Strawson in 'On Referring' (1950). According to Strawson, Russell's theory gives a distorted picture of the way definite descriptions are used. That there is a king of France is not something which is being stated when sentence (66) is stated; it is something which is assumed by (66), a *presupposition*. And if there is no king of France, then sentence (66) is not false, since then there is no proposition of which it can be said that it is true or false.

It has always been a moot point what field the concept of presupposition belongs to, semantics or pragmatics. If it belongs to semantics, then the falsity of a presupposition affects the truth value of a sentence. And if it belongs to pragmatics, then the concept of presupposition must be described in terms of the ways we use language. In order to utter a sentence correctly, a speaker, for example, must believe all of its presuppositions. We shall not attempt to decide the issue here. But in chapter 6 we return to the distinction between semantic and pragmatic aspects of meaning.

In the following, we shall restrict ourselves in the examples to the *existential presuppositions* of definite descriptions. The *existential presupposition* of a definite description is the assumption that there is some individual answering to it. There is also the *presupposition of uniqueness*, which is the presupposition that no more than a single individual answers to it. And other kinds of expressions have their own special kinds of presuppositions. Verbs and verb phrases like *to know* and *to be furious* have *factive presuppositions*, for example. Sentences (68) and (69) both presuppose that John kissed Mary:

(68)   Peter knows that John kissed Mary.

(69)   Peter is furious that John kissed Mary.

Verbs like *to believe* and *to say*, on the other hand, do not carry factive presuppositions. One last example.

(70)   All of John's children are bald.

A sentence like (70) also has an existential presupposition, namely, that John has children.

Proponents of many-valued logic in the analysis of presupposition see it as a *semantic* concept. Strawson's position is then presented as follows. If one of a sentence's presuppositions is not true, then the sentence is neither true nor false, but has a third truth value. A mistaken presupposition would thus affect the truth value of a sentence. This approach leads to the following definition for presuppositions:

Definition 3

ψ is a *presupposition* of ϕ iff for all valuations V: if $V(\psi) \neq 1$, then $V(\phi) \neq 1$ and $V(\phi) \neq 0$.

In a three-valued system, this means that if $V(\phi) \neq 1$ and $V(\phi) \neq 0$, then $V(\phi) = \#$. So definition 3 is equivalent to the more usual formulation:

    (71) ψ is a presupposition of ϕ iff for all valuations V: if $V(\psi) \neq 1$, then $V(\phi) = \#$.

Negation has been the same in all three-valued systems we have seen so far. In particular, in all cases, $V(\phi) = \#$ iff $V(\neg\phi) = \#$. Together with (71), this gives us (72):

    (72) ψ is a presupposition of ϕ just in case ψ is a presupposition of $\neg\phi$.

This property is considered characteristic of presuppositions. Not only sentences (66) and (67) but also their negations, (73) and (74), respectively, presuppose the existence of a French king and a Dutch queen:

    (73)   The king of France is not bald.

    (74)   The queen of the Netherlands is not riding a bicycle.

We could also have taken the fact that presuppositions are retained under negation as our starting point and used it as an argument in favor of many-valued logic in the analysis of semantic presuppositions. We could then reason as follows: Both the truth of (67) and that of its negation (74) 'imply' the truth of (75):

    (75)   There is a queen of the Netherlands.

But then the implicational relation between (67) and (75) and that between (74) and (75) cannot be a normal notion of logical inference in a two-valued system, since in any such logical system, tautologies are the only formulas implied by both a formula and its negation, while (75) is clearly a contingent proposition. This can be seen as follows. That both ϕ and $\neg\phi$ 'imply' the formula ψ means:

    (76)   For all valuations V: if $V(\phi) = 1$, then $V(\psi) = 1$; and if $V(\neg\phi) = 1$, then $V(\psi) = 1$.

This is equivalent to:

(77)   For all valuations V: if $V(\phi) = 1$ or $V(\neg\phi) = 1$, then
$V(\psi) = 1$.

But the antecedent of (77), $V(\phi) = 1$ or $V(\neg\phi) = 1$, is always true in a two-valued system, so (77) amounts to:

(78)   For all valuations V: $V(\psi) = 1$.

That is, ψ is a tautology. The remedy is to abandon bivalence, that is, the requirement that for any sentence ϕ, either $V(\phi) = 1$ or $V(\neg\phi) = 1$. (Russell had a different remedy: withdraw the assumption that (74) is the direct negation of (67).) In a three-valued system with $\neg$ defined as in the tables in §5.5.2, (77) is equivalent to the definiendum of definition 3, the definition of presupposition. So a preference for a semantic treatment of the concept of presupposition gives us an argument in favor of three-valued logic.

In §5.2.2 we presented a number of different three-valued systems. The question arises at this point as to which of these systems is best suited for a treatment of presupposition. This question is related to the way the presuppositions of a composite sentence depend on the presuppositions of its composite parts, which is known as the *projection problem for presuppositions*. As we shall see, the different many-valued systems with their different truth tables for the connectives give different answers.

If we choose Bochvar's system, in which composite sentences receive # as their value whenever any of their composite parts does, presupposition becomes *cumulative*. The presuppositions of a composite sentence are just all the presuppositions of its composite parts. If any presupposition of any of the composite parts fails, then a presupposition of the sentence as a whole likewise fails. If a presupposition of any of the composite parts does not have 1 as its truth value, then the whole formula has # as its truth value. This follows directly from the truth tables given for the connectives in (65) and definition 3.

If we add a new operator P to our propositional languages, then $P\phi$ can stand for the presuppositions of ϕ. We define this operator as in (79):

(79)

ϕ	$P\phi$
1	1
#	0
0	1

The formula $P\phi$ is equivalent to the necessary and sufficient conditions for the satisfaction of ϕ's presuppositions. The formula $P\phi$ receives value 1 if all ϕ's presuppositions are satisfied, and otherwise it receives 0. $P\phi$ itself does not have any presupposition, since it never receives # as its value. $PP\phi$ is always a tautology. The logical consequences of $P\phi$ are precisely the presuppositions of ϕ. It can easily be checked that the following equivalences hold by constructing truth tables:

(80) $P\phi$ and $P\neg\phi$ are equivalent.

(81) $P(\phi \vee \psi)$, $P(\phi \wedge \psi)$, and $P(\phi \rightarrow \psi)$ are equivalent to
       $P\phi \wedge P\psi$.

Here (80) is just a reformulation of the characteristic property of presupposition already given as (72), namely, that ϕ and $\neg\phi$ have the same presuppositions. What (81) says is that if presuppositions are cumulative, then the presuppositions of a conjunction and a disjunction can be written as the conjunction of the presuppositions of its conjuncts and disjuncts, respectively, and the presupposition of an implication can be written as the conjunction of the presupposition of its antecedent and its consequent. This is because # appears in the same places in the truth tables of all three connectives in Bochvar's system. The value # appears whenever any of the formulas joined by the connective has # as its value. (See (65).)

So by using Bochvar's system, we obtain a cumulative notion of presupposition. But presupposition is generally thought not to be cumulative. There are cases in which presuppositions are, as we say, *canceled* in the formation of composite formulas, and this makes the projection problem much more interesting. Sentences (82)–(84) are clear examples of the fact that a formula does not need to inherit all the presuppositions of its subformulas:

(82)   If there is a king of France, then the king of France is bald.

(83)   Either there is no king of France or the king of France is bald.

(84)   There is a king of France and the king of France is bald.

Sentence (85):

(85)   The king of France is bald.

is a part of (82), (83), and (84). Sentence (86):

(86)   There is a king of France.

is a presupposition of (85), but not of (82)–(84). If sentence (86) is false, then (82) and (83) are true, and (84) is false. This can be explained if we choose, not Bochvar's system, but Kleene's. A sentence like (82) is of the form $p \rightarrow q$, in which p is a presupposition of q. That p is not a presupposition of $p \rightarrow q$ in Kleene's system can now be seen as follows. Suppose p has value 0; then q has #, since p is one of its presuppositions. But according to Kleene's truth table for implication, the whole implication still has 1 as its value, since its antecedent has value 0. So according to definition 3, p is not a presupposition of $p \rightarrow q$, since although in this case, p does not have 1 as its value, $p \rightarrow q$ still doesn't have # as its value. Something similar holds for sentence (83), which is of the form $\neg p \vee q$, in which p is once again a presupposition of q. If p has value 0 (in which case q has #), then Kleene's table for $\vee$ still results in $\neg p \vee q$ having 1 as its truth value. Sentence (84), finally, has the form $p \wedge q$, with p again a presupposition of q. Now if p has truth value 0, then so does the whole conjunction, in spite of the fact that q has $\neq$ as its truth value. So Kleene's three-valued system explains why (86), a presupposition of formula (85), is canceled when the latter is incorporated into composite sentences (82)–(84). In §5.5.6 we will see, however, that Kleene's system is not the last word in the analysis of presuppositions.

As in Bochvar's system, ϕ's presuppositions can be represented by means of Pϕ in Kleene's system. Since negation is the same in both, equivalence (80) still holds. But since the other connectives are different, the equivalences in (81) no longer hold. Instead we have the somewhat more complicated equivalences in (87)–(89).

(87)   P($\phi \vee \psi$) is equivalent to (($\phi \wedge$ Pϕ) $\vee$ Pψ) $\wedge$ (($\psi \wedge$ Pψ) $\vee$ Pϕ).

(88)   P($\phi \wedge \psi$) is equivalent to (($\neg\phi \wedge$ Pϕ) $\vee$ Pψ) $\wedge$ (($\neg\psi \wedge$ Pψ) $\vee$ Pϕ).

(89)   P($\phi \rightarrow \psi$) is equivalent to (($\neg\phi \wedge$ Pϕ) $\vee$ Pψ) $\wedge$ (($\psi \wedge$ Pψ) $\vee$ Pϕ).

We now introduce a second operator A, to be interpreted according to (90):

(90)

ϕ	Aϕ
1	1
#	0
0	0

Then as a result of the equivalence of Aϕ and $\phi \wedge$ Pϕ, (87)–(89) amount to (91)–(93):

(91)   P($\phi \vee \psi$) is equivalent to (A$\phi \vee$ Pψ) $\wedge$ (A$\psi \vee$ Pϕ).

(92)   P($\phi \wedge \psi$) is equivalent to (A$\neg\phi \vee$ Pψ) $\wedge$ (A$\neg\psi \vee$ Pϕ).

(93)   P($\phi \rightarrow \psi$) is equivalent to (A$\neg\phi \vee$ Pψ) $\wedge$ (A$\psi \vee$ Pϕ).

A third way of writing P($\phi \vee \psi$), which avoids A, is:

(94)   P($\phi \vee \psi$) is equivalent to ($\phi \vee$ Pψ) $\wedge$ ($\psi \vee$ Pϕ) $\wedge$ (P$\phi \vee$ Pψ).

Equations resembling (94) can of course also be given for the other two connectives.

The P-operator can also be used to clarify the cancellation of presuppositions in Kleene's system. If (86) is the only presupposition of (85) then writing q for (85) (and thus Pq for (86)), sentences (82)–(84) can be represented as follows:

(95)   Pq $\rightarrow$ q

(96) $\neg Pq \vee q$

(97) $Pq \wedge q$

That q's presupposition Pq is canceled in the formation of (95)–(97) is apparent from the fact that (95)–(97) themselves have no presuppositions at all, or more precisely, that they only have tautologies as their presuppositions. The formulas $P(Pq \rightarrow q)$, $P(\neg Pq \vee q)$, and $P(Pq \wedge q)$ are tautologies; they always have 1 as their truth value. This explains why the contingent sentence (86) is not a presupposition of (82)–(84).

Equivalences like those in (87)–(89) and (91)–(94) are interesting on more than one account. First, they shed some light on how the projection problem for presupposition is approached in a three-valued system like Kleene's. For example, (87) says directly that the presuppositions of $(\phi \vee \psi)$ are satisfied in each of the following three cases: if the presuppositions of both ϕ and ψ are satisfied (compare this with cumulative presupposition); if ϕ's presuppositions are not satisfied, but ψ is true; and last, if ψ's presuppositions are not satisfied, but ϕ is true. That this concept of presupposition is weaker than the cumulative one is because of the last two cases. They correspond to the two places in Kleene's table for $\vee$ (see (64)) in which there is a 1 instead of the $\#$ in Bochvar's system (see (65)).

A second reason why these equivalences are interesting is that they have much in common with the inductive definitions of the concept of a presupposition which have been published as an alternative to three-valued approaches. These definitions inductively define a formula ϕ^{Pr} which amounts to the set of ϕ's presuppositions. They begin by stipulating what the presuppositions of atomic formulas are. The inductive clauses are then, for example:

(98) $(\neg\phi)^{\text{Pr}} = \phi^{\text{Pr}}$

(99) $(\phi \vee \psi)^{\text{Pr}} = ((\phi \wedge \phi^{\text{Pr}}) \vee \psi^{\text{Pr}}) \wedge ((\psi \wedge \psi^{\text{Pr}}) \vee \phi^{\text{Pr}})$

The remaining connectives have something similar. In the literature it is common to speak in terms of the set of a formula's presuppositions. The approach sketched here amounts to forming the conjunction of all formulas in such a set. It has been suggested that this kind of inductive definition is more adequate than a treatment in terms of a three-valued semantics. But in view of the similarity of (87) and (99) it seems likely that both approaches give the same results.

Although a three-valued system like Kleene's deals satisfactorily with certain aspects of the projection problem for presuppositions, it leaves certain problems open. These will be discussed to some extent in §5.5.6. But first we shall describe many-valued logical systems with more than three values (§5.5.4) and their applications in the analysis of the semantic notion of presupposition (§5.5.5).

5.5.4 *Logical systems with more than three values*

So far the discussion of many-valued logical systems has gone no further than three-valued systems. But logics with more than three values have also been developed. A system like Kleene's, for example, can easily be generalized to systems with any finite number n ($n \geqslant 2$) of truth values. One convenient notation for the truth values of such a system uses fractions, with the number $n - 1$ as their denominator and the numbers $0, 1, \ldots, n - 1$ as their numerators. The three-valued system ($n = 3$) then has the truth values $\frac{0}{2}$, $\frac{1}{2}$, and $\frac{2}{2}$, or 0, $\frac{1}{2}$, and 1. So the third value of the Kleene system is written as $\frac{1}{2}$ instead of as $\#$. A four-valued system ($n = 4$) then has the truth values $\frac{0}{3}$, $\frac{1}{3}$, $\frac{2}{3}$, and $\frac{3}{3}$, or 0, $\frac{1}{3}$, $\frac{2}{3}$, and 1. The truth values of composite formulas in a Kleene system with n truth values can now be calculated as follows:

Definition 4

$$
\begin{aligned}
V(\neg\phi) \quad &= 1 - V(\phi) \\
V(\phi \wedge \psi) \quad &= V(\phi) \text{ if } V(\phi) \leqslant V(\psi) \\
&= V(\psi) \text{ otherwise} \\
V(\phi \vee \psi) \quad &= V(\phi) \text{ if } V(\phi) \geqslant V(\psi) \\
&= V(\psi) \text{ otherwise} \\
V(\phi \rightarrow \psi) \quad &= V(\psi) \text{ if } V(\psi) \geqslant (1 - V(\phi)) \\
&= 1 - V(\phi) \text{ otherwise}
\end{aligned}
$$

So a conjunction is given the truth value of whichever of its conjuncts has the lowest truth value; a disjunction is given the truth value of whichever of its disjuncts has the highest truth value. The truth value of the implication $\phi \rightarrow \psi$ is equal to that of the disjunction $\neg\phi \vee \psi$. For a three-valued system, the truth tables are the same as those in (64), but with $\frac{1}{2}$ instead of $\#$. For $n = 2$ this reduces to standard propositional logic. A four-valued Kleene system has the truth tables given in (100):

(100)

ϕ	$\neg\phi$
1	0
$\frac{2}{3}$	$\frac{1}{3}$
$\frac{1}{3}$	$\frac{2}{3}$
0	1

$\phi \wedge \psi$

ϕ \ ψ	1	$\frac{2}{3}$	$\frac{1}{3}$	0
1	1	$\frac{2}{3}$	$\frac{1}{3}$	0
$\frac{2}{3}$	$\frac{2}{3}$	$\frac{2}{3}$	$\frac{1}{3}$	0
$\frac{1}{3}$	$\frac{1}{3}$	$\frac{1}{3}$	$\frac{1}{3}$	0
0	0	0	0	0

$\phi \vee \psi$

ϕ \ ψ	1	$\frac{2}{3}$	$\frac{1}{3}$	0
1	1	1	1	1
$\frac{2}{3}$	1	$\frac{2}{3}$	$\frac{2}{3}$	$\frac{2}{3}$
$\frac{1}{3}$	1	$\frac{2}{3}$	$\frac{1}{3}$	$\frac{1}{3}$
0	1	$\frac{2}{3}$	$\frac{1}{3}$	0

$\phi \rightarrow \psi$

ϕ \ ψ	1	$\frac{2}{3}$	$\frac{1}{3}$	0
1	1	$\frac{2}{3}$	$\frac{1}{3}$	0
$\frac{2}{3}$	1	$\frac{2}{3}$	$\frac{1}{3}$	$\frac{1}{3}$
$\frac{1}{3}$	1	$\frac{2}{3}$	$\frac{2}{3}$	$\frac{2}{3}$
0	1	1	1	1

Similarly, a Kleene system can have infinitely many truth values, for example, by taking all fractions between 0 and 1 as truth values.

The above systems with more than three values are all obtained by generalizing a system with three values. Other systems with more than three values can be obtained, for example, by 'multiplying' systems by each other. These are called *product systems*. In such a product of two systems S_1 and S_2, formulas are given truth values $\langle v_1, v_2 \rangle$, in which v_1 derives from S_1, and v_2 from S_2. A product system can be applied if we want to evaluate formulas under two different and independent aspects and to represent the evaluations in combination. We can, for example, multiply the standard two-valued system by itself. We then obtain a four-valued system with the pairs $\langle 1, 1 \rangle$, $\langle 1, 0 \rangle$, $\langle 0, 1 \rangle$, and $\langle 0, 0 \rangle$ as its truth values. In order to calculate the truth value of a formula in the product system, we must first calculate its truth value in each of the two systems of which it is a product. The value in the first system becomes the first member of the ordered pair, and the value in the second system is the second member. The truth tables for the connectives for this four-valued system are as in (101) (we write 11 instead of $\langle 1, 1 \rangle$, etc.).

(101)

ϕ	$\neg\phi$
11	00
10	01
01	10
00	11

$\phi \wedge \psi$	11	10	01	00
ϕ				
11	11	10	01	00
10	10	10	00	00
01	01	00	01	00
00	00	00	00	00

$\phi \vee \psi$	11	10	01	00
ϕ				
11	11	11	11	11
10	11	10	11	10
01	11	11	01	01
00	11	10	01	00

$\phi \rightarrow \psi$	11	10	01	00
ϕ				
11	11	10	01	00
10	11	11	01	01
01	11	10	11	10
00	11	11	11	11

Systems with different kinds and numbers of truth values can, of course, just as easily be multiplied by each other. If one system has m truth values and the other n, then the product system will have $m \times n$ truth values.

5.5.5 *Four-valued logics and the Semantic Notion of Presupposition*

The four-valued Kleene system can also be applied in the analysis of the semantic notion of presupposition. Using four values has the advantage that the truth of a formula can be distinguished from the satisfaction of its presuppositions. The four truth values are thus associated with the following four situations:

> *true* and the presuppositions are *satisfied*
> *true* and the presuppositions are *not satisfied*
> *false* and the presuppositions are *satisfied*
> *false* and the presuppositions are *not satisfied*

Now instead of saying that *The king of France is bald* is neither true nor false, we will say that it is false, and one of its presuppositions has failed. And of the negation of this sentence, we will say that it is true, and one of its presuppositions has failed. It is then convenient to represent the four different truth values as 11, 10, 01, 00. In spite of the notation, we are not dealing with a product system here, as is apparent from the truth tables in (102). Rewriting the truth tables for the four-valued Kleene system with the new truth values, with 11 instead of 1, 10 instead of ⅔, 00 instead of ⅓, and 01 instead of 0, we obtain (102):

(102)

ϕ	$\neg\phi$
11	01
10	00
00	10
01	11

$\phi \wedge \psi$

ϕ \ ψ	11	10	00	01
11	11	10	00	01
10	10	10	00	01
00	00	00	00	01
01	01	01	01	01

$\phi \vee \psi$

ϕ \ ψ	11	10	00	01
11	11	11	11	11
10	11	10	10	10
00	11	10	00	00
01	11	10	00	01

$\phi \rightarrow \psi$

ϕ \ ψ	11	10	00	01
11	11	10	00	01
10	11	10	00	00
00	11	10	10	10
01	11	11	11	11

Definition 3 of the notion of presupposition given in §5.5.3 can be left as it is (with 11 instead of 1, and 01 instead of 0). The four-valued Kleene system then gives exactly the same results as the three-valued system. The following should be said of the truth tables in (102). Under the interpretation we have given to the values 11, 10, 00, and 01, the first element of the values refers to the truth value of the sentence in question. A glance at the tables shows that these truth values agree with standard two-valued logic, and that they are assigned independently of the second element in the values, which we shall call the *presupposition values*. The presupposition value of a sentence is to some extent dependent on its truth value, as is apparent from the following example: If V(ϕ) = 11 and V(ψ) = 10, then V($\phi \vee \psi$) = 11. But if V(ϕ) = 01 and V(ψ) = 10, then V($\phi \vee \psi$) = 10. The presupposition values of ϕ and ψ are in both cases the same: ϕ has 1, and ψ has 0. But the presupposition values for the disjunction as a whole differ. The reason for this is that the satisfaction of the presuppositions of one of its disjuncts is not enough to guarantee the satisfaction of the presuppositions of a disjunction as a whole. If only one member of a disjunction is true, then the presuppositions of that disjunct have to be satisfied if the presuppositions of the disjunction are to be satisfied. This is the difference between the four-valued Kleene system and a product system. In a product system, the two values are independent of each other. In the above example, the value 11 would have resulted in both cases. It is precisely this dependence of presupposition values on truth values which is responsible for the degree of success which the Kleene system has had in solving the projection problem.

Let us define the operators A and P which we encountered in §5.5.3 as in (103):

(103) ϕ	Aϕ	Pϕ
11	11	11
10	01	01
00	01	01
01	01	11

The equivalences (87)–(89) and (91)–(94) still hold. As in the three-valued system, Aϕ has the maximum value just in case ϕ does, and otherwise it has the minimum value. And Pϕ has the maximal value just in case all of ϕ's presuppositions have been satisfied, that is, just in case its presupposition value is 1, and otherwise the minimal value.

An operator T which only takes truth values into account can be defined analogously to P, as in (104).

(104) ϕ	Tϕ
11	11
10	11
00	01
01	01

Tϕ has the maximal value just in case ϕ has truth value 1, and otherwise the minimal value, just as P only has the maximal value if the presupposition value is 1. Now the following equivalences can be proved:

(105) P($\phi \lor \psi$) is equivalent to (T$\phi \lor$ Pψ) $\land$ (T$\psi \lor$ Pϕ) $\land$ (P$\phi \lor$ Pψ).

(106) P($\phi \land \psi$) is equivalent to (T$\neg\phi \lor$ Pψ) $\land$ (T$\neg\psi \lor$ Pψ) $\land$ (P$\phi \lor$ Pψ).

(107) P($\phi \rightarrow \psi$) is equivalent to (T$\neg\phi \lor$ Pψ) $\land$ (T$\psi \lor$ Pψ) $\land$ (P$\phi \lor$ Pψ).

Let us compare these equivalences with those in (108)–(111):

(108) $T(\phi \vee \psi)$ is equivalent to $T\phi \vee T\psi$.

(109) $T(\phi \wedge \psi)$ is equivalent to $T\phi \wedge T\psi$.

(110) $T(\phi \rightarrow \psi)$ is equivalent to $T\phi \rightarrow T\psi$.

(111) $T\neg\phi$ is equivalent to $\neg T\phi$.

We see that, unlike the presupposition value, the truth value of a sentence is wholly determined by the truth values of its parts.

In their article "Conventional Implicature," (1979) Karttunen and Peters (working within the framework of Montague grammar, which will be discussed in volume 2) proposed translating natural language sentences ϕ as pairs of formulas $\langle \phi^t, \phi^p \rangle$, in which ϕ^t represents ϕ's truth conditions and ϕ^p represents its presuppositions (or what they call *conventional implicatures*) (see chap. 6). The translation of a disjunction A or B can then be given the following inductive definition:

(112) If A translates as $\langle A^t, A^p \rangle$ and B as $\langle B^t, B^p \rangle$, then A *or* B translates as $\langle (A \ or \ B)^t, (A \ or \ B)^p \rangle$, in which $(A \ or \ B)^t = A^t \vee B^t$ and $(A \ or \ B)^p = (A^t \vee B^p) \wedge (B^t \vee A^p) \wedge (A^p \vee B^p)$.

(Our (112) differs slightly from Karttunen and Peter's original definition, but the differences all concern details which are not relevant here.) The parallel between (112) and the equivalences (105) and (108) should be clear. Just as with the inductive definitions we encountered when we discussed presuppositions in a three-valued system in §5.5.3, it would seem that these inductive syntactic definitions yield the same results as four-valued semantics. There are exact logical connections between the two approaches, but we can't go into that here.

5.5.6 *The Limits of Many-Valued Logics in the Analysis of Presupposition*

There are a few ways that a three- or four-valued Kleene system can furnish a good explanation for the cancellation of presuppositions in the composition of sentences. But there are also certain problems. The first problem is displayed very clearly in sentences like (113) and (114).

(113) The king of France is not bald, since there is no king of France.

(114) There is no king of France; thus the king of France is not bald.

If (113) is true, then both (115) and (116) must be true (and the same applies for (114)):

(115) The king of France is not bald.

(116) There is no king of France.

But the problem is that (115) and (116) cannot both be true at the same time, because (116) is the negation of one of the presuppositions of (115). What we seem to need here is for (115) to be true even if there isn't any king of France. This does not present any problem for Russell's theory of descriptions, since according to Russell, sentence (115) is ambiguous (see §5.2). A similar solution can be found within a many-valued system. We distinguish two readings of (115), introducing for this purpose a new kind of negation, $\sim$. This negation is defined by the table in (117):

(117)

ϕ	$\sim\phi$
1	0
#	1
0	1

If p is a presupposition of q, then $\sim$q is true according to the table for $\sim$ if p is not true. The negation $\sim$ is called *internal negation* and $\neg$ *external negation*. Interpreting the negation in (115) as external negation, (115) and (116) can both be true at the same time, so (113) and (114) can both be true.

Note that the operators A and $\sim$ are interdefinable via $\neg$: $\sim\phi$ is equivalent to $\neg$Aϕ (and thus Aϕ is equivalent to $\neg\sim\phi$). By introducing operators like $\sim$, A, and P we have extended standard propositional logic by adding new logical constants. But the introduction of these operators only makes sense if we choose a many-valued interpretation. This is what we meant in §5.5.1 when we said that deviations from standard interpretations often give rise to extensions.

The problem with sentences like (113) and (114) can then be solved by distinguishing two different kinds of negation. This seems a bit ad hoc, since we have not given any systematic way to determine whether a negation should be given the internal or the external reading. There is, however, an even more serious problem than that with (113) and (114). It can be illustrated by means of a sentence like:

(118) If baldness is hereditary, then the king of France is bald.

Now intuitively it is clear enough that one presupposition of (118) is (119) (= (86)):

(119) There is a king of France.

According to definition 3, then, no valuation which renders (119) false may render (118) true. But consider (120):

(120) Baldness is hereditary.

Even though (120) is the antecedent of (118), it can be false without there being a king of France, since sentences (119) and (120) are logically independent of each other. So let V be any valuation which renders both sentences false. Then V renders (118) true, since it renders its antecedent (120) false. So

V renders (119) false and (118) true, in contradiction with the above remark that (119) is a presupposition of (118). In general the problem is this: implications with contingent antecedents which are logically independent of certain presuppositions of their consequents have too many of their presuppositions canceled. Similar complications arise with the other connectives.

At this point various lines of action could be taken. One idea would be to try to find better many-valued definitions for the connectives. Bochvar's system would do very well for sentences like (118), but it has its own problems with sentences like (82)–(84). So far no single system has been found which deals with both (82)–(84) and (118) in a satisfactory manner, and it is questionable if there is any such system to be found. A second possibility might be to adapt definition 3. This has been tried a couple of times, and the results have not been satisfactory.

A third idea, which has so far been the most successful, is to stick to both a three- or four-valued Kleene system and definition 3, but to drop the idea that the presupposition of (118) that there is a king of France is a *semantic* presupposition. We then give a *pragmatic* explanation for the fact that anyone who asserts (118) or its negation must believe that France has a king. This means that we must introduce the notion of *pragmatic presuppositions* as a complement to the semantic notion. Any such pragmatic explanation must lean heavily on Grice's theory of *conversational maxims*. We shall return to these maxims at length in chapter 6, where we shall also briefly consider the possibility that presupposition is not a semantic notion at all but must be wholly explained in pragmatic terms.

5.6 Elimination of Variables

Readers who have worked through the chapter on predicate logic have probably received the impression that variables play an essential role in predicate logic. In this section we shall see that this is not the case. Predicate logic can be formulated without using variables. A number of lessons can be learned from this section. First, the way a logical language is formulated, what it looks like on paper, is not always essential. This may be of some comfort to those who worry about the fact that formal languages are constructed very differently from natural ones. If logical systems are applied to natural language, then logical languages are instruments for the representation of meaning. Only the choice of logical system matters in this connection; the particular syntactic variant is irrelevant. The choice of logical language is merely the choice of a notation. It involves no commitment to any particular interpretation and is as such only subject to considerations like simplicity and convenience. Having seen how variables can be avoided, the reader may have a better idea of why variables are so useful technically. This is the second thing to be learned from this section. Seeing what you have to do to eliminate them gives you a better picture of what they were doing. A third point which is being made here is one we have been trying to make throughout this chapter: that logic provides us with a set of tools which can be applied to a wide range of questions.

The method of eliminating variables to be discussed here was originally explained by Quine in his article "Variables Explained Away" (1966). It makes use of a fact which we have seen a number of times: propositional functions, formulas with free variables, can be interpreted as predicates. Composite formulas with free variables, like $Px \wedge Qx$ and $Py \vee Rxy$, for instance, can be interpreted as composite predicates. Their arity depends on how many free variables the propositional function has. Binding a variable x in a propositional function by prefixing a quantifier $\exists x$ or $\forall x$ to it can be seen as a way of reducing the arity of a predicate.

In what follows, alternatives to the standard languages for predicate logic will be defined. The formulas in these new languages do not have any variables. The set of formulas is divided into n-ary predicate expressions, this for each $n \geq 0$. The predicate expressions with arity 0 correspond to the sentences familiar from standard predicate logic, that is, to formulas lacking free variables. And corresponding to the n-ary predicate letters of standard predicate logic, the new languages have noncomposite n-ary predicate expressions.

The semantic interpretation of the formulas will be given together with their recursive definition. As usual, a model will consist of a domain D and an interpretation function I. The interpretation function interprets the individual constants and the noncomposite n-ary predicate expressions. I is then expanded to a function which interprets all the formulas and thus does the same work as the valuation function V familiar from standard predicate logic. If ϕ is an n-ary predicate expression, then $I(\phi)$ is a set of rows of elements derived from D, each being of length n. That is, $I(\phi) \subseteq D^n$. We shall describe how this is done for predicate expressions with arity 0, that is, sentences, shortly.

In standard predicate logic, variables indicate what arguments of propositional functions are bound by what quantifiers. So as long as we are only dealing with unary propositional functions, variables are obviously dispensable. We could just as well write $\exists P$ and $\forall P$ instead of $\exists x Px$ and $\forall x Px$. The corresponding syntactic rule and interpretation of such an expression could be formulated as:

(i)   If ϕ is a unary predicate expression, then $\exists(\phi)$ and $\forall(\phi)$ are sentences;
   $I(\exists(\phi)) = 1$ iff there is a $d \in D$ such that $d \in I(\phi)$;
   $I(\forall(\phi)) = 1$ iff for all $d \in D$ we have $d \in I(\phi)$.

So with unary predicates we simply discard the variables from the formula. In order to interpret the formulas obtained in this manner, we only have to take the interpretation of the predicate expression into consideration. The existential expression will be true just in case there is at least one domain element in the interpretation of the predicate expression, and the universally quantified expression will be true just in case they are all in it.

This becomes less straightforward when it comes to predicate expressions with more argument positions. If we were simply to discard the variables from such propositional functions, then both $\exists x \forall y Rxy$ and $\exists y \forall x Rxy$ would reduce to $\exists \forall R$. But these two formulas with variables mean quite different things. Clearly we must find a way to indicate what quantifiers concern what argument positions. We could, for example, associate a numerical parameter to each quantifier, which would tell us what position the quantifier applies to. Another and more elegant solution would be to assign some fixed position to the quantifiers, for example, the last position in the formula in question. We would then have to introduce a permutation which would enable us to turn any given position into the last one, for example, by having the positions rotate. An operator ROT which does just this, and its interpretation, are defined in (ii):

(ii)   If ϕ is an n-ary predicate expression ($n > 1$), then $\text{ROT}(\phi)$ is another predicate expression;
$\langle d_1, \ldots, d_n \rangle \in I(\text{ROT}(\phi))$ iff $\langle d_n, d_1, \ldots, d_{n-1} \rangle \in I(\phi)$.

The idea is that a sentence like $\exists x \forall y Rxy$ can be written as $\exists \forall R$, while a sentence like $\exists y \forall x Rxy$ is written as $\exists \forall \text{ROT}(R)$. But these formulas cannot be formed with the rules we have given so far. Rule (i) only says what to do with unary predicate expressions, and in order to form the above formulas we must say how a unary predicate expression can be obtained from a binary one by associating a quantifier to it. The rule which does this, not only for the special case of binary, but also for the general case of n-ary predicate expressions is given below, together with its interpretation:

(iii)   If ϕ is an n-ary predicate expression ($n \geq 1$), then $\exists(\phi)$ and $\forall(\phi)$ are $(n - 1)$-ary predicate expressions;
$\langle d_1, \ldots, d_{n-1} \rangle \in I(\exists(\phi))$ iff there is a $d \in D$ such that $\langle d_1, \ldots, d_{n-1}, d \rangle \in I(\phi)$;
$\langle d_1, \ldots, d_{n-1} \rangle \in I(\forall(\phi))$ iff for all $d \in D$ we have $\langle d_1, \ldots, d_{n-1}, d \rangle \in I(\phi)$.

Note that rule (i) is in fact a special case of (iii). We shall return to this soon.
    Besides adding quantifiers, applying a predicate expression to an individual constant is another way to reduce its number of arguments.

(iv)   If ϕ is an n-ary predicate expression ($n \geq 1$) and c is an individual constant, then $\phi(c)$ is an $(n - 1)$-ary predicate expression;
$\langle d_1, \ldots, d_{n-1} \rangle \in I(\phi(c))$ iff $\langle d_1, \ldots, d_{n-1}, I(c) \rangle \in I(\phi)$.

Now we are in a position to simulate the effect of a quantifier working on any single variable in a formula. An example: $\exists y Gxyz$ becomes $\text{ROT}(\exists(\text{ROT}(G)))$ (by applying ROT, we bring the variable y to the last position, and by applying ROT once more after the existential quantification we restore the variables x and z to their original positions); $\forall z \exists y Gxyz$ becomes $\forall(\text{ROT}(\exists(\text{ROT}(G))))$; $\forall z \exists y Gayz$ becomes $\forall(\text{ROT}(\exists(\text{ROT}(G))))(a)$, or $\forall(\exists(\text{ROT}(G))(a))$ (the second alternative being obtained by substituting a for x before applying the universal quantifier; another possibility would be to have the substitution of a for x also precede the existential quantification).

We still have to show how formulas with quantifiers binding different occurrences of one and the same variable can be translated into formulas lacking variables. In order to do this, we now introduce an operation ID which turns any n-ary predicate expression into an $(n - 1)$-ary one. If R is a binary predicate expression, for example, then ID(R) is interpreted as the set of domain elements d which bear the interpretation of R, a relation, to themselves. In symbols: $d \in I(ID(R))$ iff $\langle d, d \rangle \in I(R)$.

For predicate expressions with more than two positions we must indicate what two positions are identified by ID. We could, for example, attach a numerical parameter to the ID operator, which would indicate that the position given in the parameter should be identified with the last position, say. But once again, a more elegant solution would be to assign fixed positions to ID, for example, the last two. We then need a way to regroup the positions in any predicate expression such that any two given positions can be turned into the last two positions. The operation ROT is not sufficient to achieve this. But introducing an operation PERM, which interchanges the last two positions, makes it possible. This operation can be introduced as follows:

(v)   If ϕ is an n-ary predicate expression ($n > 1$), then PERM(ϕ) is too; $\langle d_1, \ldots, d_n \rangle \in I(PERM(\phi))$ iff $\langle d_1, \ldots, d_{n-2}, d_n, d_{n-1} \rangle \in I(\phi)$.

The operation ID can now be defined as follows:

(vi)   If ϕ is an n-ary predicate expression ($n > 1$), then ID(ϕ) is an $(n - 1)$-ary predicate expression; $\langle d_1, \ldots, d_{n-1} \rangle \in I(ID(\phi))$ iff $\langle d_1, \ldots, d_{n-1}, d_{n-1} \rangle \in I(\phi)$.

A formula like ∀xRxx can now be written as ∀(ID(R)). And the formula ∃y∀xRxyxy can now be written as:

∃(ID(∀(ID(ROT(PERM(ROT(R)))))))).

Changes must also be made in order to deal with connectives. Leaving out variables, ∃x¬Px and ¬∃xPx are to be written as ∃¬P and ¬∃P. This indicates that it must be possible to apply ¬ to any n-ary predicate expression for arbitrary $n \geq 0$:

(vii)   If ϕ is an n-ary predicate expression, then ¬(ϕ) is too; $\langle d_1, \ldots, d_n \rangle \in I(¬(\phi))$ iff $\langle d_1, \ldots, d_n \rangle \notin I(\phi)$.

So in the particular case of a unary expression P, ¬(P) is interpreted as the set of all domain entities which fall outside of the interpretation of P. And for a binary predicate expression R, ¬(P) is interpreted as the set of all ordered pairs which do not fall within the relation which R is interpreted as.

The other connectives must also be able to work on n-ary predicate expressions. It is easiest to arrange for this as follows:

(viii) If ϕ is an m-ary predicate expression and ψ is an n-ary predicate expression, then $(\phi \wedge \psi)$, $(\phi \vee \psi)$, and $(\phi \to \psi)$ are $(m + n)$-ary predicate expressions; $\langle d_1, \ldots, d_m, d_{m+1}, \ldots, d_{m+n} \rangle \in I(\phi \wedge \psi)$ iff $\langle d_1, \ldots, d_m \rangle \in I(\phi)$ and $\langle d_{m+1}, \ldots, d_{m+n} \rangle \in I(\psi)$ (and analogously for the other connectives).

A formula like $\exists x(Px \vee Qx)$ can now be written without variables as $\exists(ID(P \wedge Q))$; and $\exists x \forall y(Py \to Rxy)$ as $\exists(\forall(ID(ROT(PERM(P \to R)))))$. Note that clauses (vii) and (viii) are also defined for 0-ary predicate expressions, which are the sentences in this system. That I does for these just what the valuation function V familiar from standard predicate logic does for formulas can be seen as follows. The interpretation of an n-ary predicate expression is a subset of D^n, a set of rows of elements of D each having n elements. D^0 is the set of rows without any elements at all. There is, of course, just one of these: the empty row $\langle \rangle$. So D^0 is the set $\{\varnothing\}$. This set has exactly two subsets; $\{\varnothing\}$ itself and the empty set $\varnothing$. These two objects can now be associated with the truth values 1 and 0: $\{\varnothing\}$ with 1, and $\varnothing$ with 0. In this way, clauses (iii), (iv), (vii), and (viii) give the right results for all values of $n \geqslant 0$.

We have now created some languages for predicate logic which at least superficially differ considerably from the standard languages. But they mean the same thing; the interpretations have not changed. This system renders the same argument schemata valid as standard predicate logic, so the choice between languages with and without variables is purely one of notation. It is clear that of the two notations, predicate logic with variables is much to be preferred, since it is much easier to understand what the formulas mean. By showing how variables can in principle be eliminated, we have at the same time shown why it is better not to eliminate them.

6   Pragmatics: Meaning and Usage

6.1 Non-Truth-Conditional Aspects of Meaning

One theme of this book is the application, in research on natural language, of semantic methods and techniques developed in the field of logic. And logical semantics has indeed made important contributions to the study of meaning in natural language. But as we have emphasized (among other places, in §1.2), logical semantics is not the last word in meaning. We saw this, for example, in §2.2, where certain usages of the natural language conjunctions *and, or,* and *if* (. . . *then*) were mentioned which are not explained by the truth tables for the corresponding logical connectives ∧, ∨, and →.

Those aspects of meaning which logical semantics accounts for are most simply characterized as the *truth-conditional aspects of meaning*. Logical semantics is primarily concerned with the truth values of sentences, and the meaning of expressions other than sentences is analyzed purely in terms of the contribution they make to the truth conditions of sentences in which they occur.

That logical semantics does not account for all aspects of meaning can mean either or both of two things. It may mean that the logical and semantic analyses which are now available need *improvement*. But it may also mean that there are aspects of meaning which lie beyond the reach of logical semantics, aspects which are ultimately not truth-conditional. Since not all presently available analyses are perfect, logical semantics is undoubtedly limited in this first sense, but that is not an essential shortcoming. The second kind of shortcoming, however, is essential, since logical semantics forms no more than a part of the theory of meaning if there are aspects of meaning which lie beyond it.

In this section we shall argue with reference to the conjunctions *and, or,* and *if* (. . . *then*) that logical semantics is indeed limited in this second and rather essential way. We shall see that certain aspects of the meanings of natural language conjunctions are not in any way expressed in the truth tables of the corresponding logical connectives. And we shall give reasons why these aspects cannot be captured in truth tables but are better explained in terms of conditions under which expressions can properly be used. This is a mode of explanation which makes use of general principles of language usage, but which nevertheless depends largely on the semantics provided by propositional logic.

With the introduction of the concept of language use we have entered the field of pragmatics, the third vertex of the traditional semiotic triangle consisting of *syntax, semantics,* and *pragmatics.* If syntax is concerned with the relations between expressions of a language, and semantics with the relations of the expressions to entities outside of language, then pragmatics is primarily concerned with the relationship between expressions and their usage. But the borders between these regions are far from clear. This applies especially to pragmatics, which, as Bar-Hillel once said, functions as the wastepaper basket of linguistics, a place where recalcitrant phenomena can be deposited after they have been declared irrelevant. The borders of regions become clearer once the borders of the surrounding regions are clarified. This is one reason why the advent of Montague grammar, which gives a clear picture of semantics and its relation to syntax (see vol. 2), has given rise to a consensus on what belongs to pragmatics and what does not.

As we have said, semantics is not the last word in the theory of meaning. Semantics is a part of the theory of meaning and no more than that. We are of the opinion that the remaining part belongs to pragmatics, so for us pragmatics is concerned with all those aspects of meaning which are not truth-conditional. We shall argue that the study of conditions for proper usage is a promising approach to pragmatics in this sense (we will not go into the possibility that there are other fields which properly belong to pragmatics). For us, then, the theory of meaning has just two subdivisions: semantics and pragmatics.

The logical and semantic background to the above perspective on pragmatics also results in a particular methodological approach. Chomsky opened the possibility of a *formal syntax* and Montague the possibility of a *formal semantics* (see vol. 2), and with these precedents, proponents of this style of pragmatics should not be satisfied with anything less in the way of rigor. This, however, is a delicate point, since the two most influential representatives of pragmatics, Searle and Grice, are both convinced opponents of formalism. In any case, making precise the kind of informal work which they and others have done remains an important task for a pragmatics which draws from a logical grammar.

In the coming sections we will discuss several phenomena concerning the fact that the meanings of the conjunctions *and, or,* and *if* (. . . *then*) are not in all respects truth-conditional. The discussion alternates with a presentation of Grice's theory, which centers on his Principle of Cooperation in Conversation. Then we will see how this theory can be applied to explain the pragmatic aspects of meaning. We will end this chapter with a few comments on the relationship between the phenomena we discuss here and presuppositions, which were discussed in §5.5.

6.2 Logical Conjunction and Word Order

As can be seen from its truth table, a logical conjunction $\phi \wedge \psi$ is true just in case both of its conjuncts ϕ and ψ are true. This means that any difference between the meanings of sentences (1) and (2) cannot be expressed if they are analyzed in terms of the logical conjunction of propositional logic.

(1)   Annie took off her socks and jumped into bed.

(2)   Annie jumped into bed and took off her socks.

The formulas which correspond to (1) and (2), $p \wedge q$ and $q \wedge p$, are logically equivalent. Their equivalence is known as the commutativity of $\wedge$ (see exercise 2 in chap. 2).

This problem can be approached in different ways. One approach which might at first seem plausible would be to change the interpretation of the connective $\wedge$ in such a way that a conjunction $\phi \wedge \psi$ is true only if whatever action is described in ϕ takes place *before* whatever is described in ψ. Any such reinterpretation of the logical conjunction would, of course, take us outside of the safe framework of standard propositional logic. We would need a richer, intensional system for the logic of time (see vol. 2). Under such a reinterpretation, sentence (2) would be false if Annie were to take her socks off before jumping into bed. One problem for this approach comes from sentences like (3):

(3)   Annie took off her socks and jumped into bed, but I do not
       know which she did first.

Sentence (3) would be translated into a propositional logic as some formula $(p \wedge q) \wedge \neg r$. The above reinterpretation of $\wedge$ would incorrectly predict that (3) is false if Annie took off her socks while already in bed. For if the event described in p occurred only after the event described in q, the conjunction $p \wedge q$ and thus the conjunction $(p \wedge q) \wedge \neg r$ are both false.

This approach could perhaps be saved if we were to attribute two meanings to *and*. One meaning would be the one that corresponds to the logical connective $\wedge$, and the other would be what we were getting at above by reinterpreting *and* as *and then*. The price we would have to pay is that sentences with *and* would become ambiguous. In a situation in which Annie has taken off her socks while in bed, one reading of sentences (1) and (3) renders them true and the other false (both readings of sentence (2) would be true).

The following would be another and completely different approach. We assume that neither the word *and* nor sentences (1)–(3) are ambiguous. The former has the meaning given to it by propositional logic. This means that (2) is not untrue in a situation in which Annie removed her socks, as usual, before getting into bed. Not untrue, but if the speaker were aware of the order in which the events took place, certainly rather uncooperative. For (2) is under those circumstances rather misleading. We normally assume that speakers are inclined to be orderly. If two events are mentioned one after the other, then we tend to assume—as long as we have not heard the contrary—that the temporal order in which they were described is a reflection of that in which they took place. The qualification "as long as we have not heard the contrary" contains the explanation for sentences like (3). In stating (3), a speaker explicitly underlines the fact that he is unaware of the order in which the events took place so as to avoid misleading the listener.

One advantage of this approach is that a completely analogous explanation can be given for the difference between (4) and (5):

(4)   Annie took off her socks. She jumped into bed.

(5)   Annie jumped into bed. She took off her socks.

The difference in meaning between (4) and (5) is exactly the same as the difference between (1) and (2). But it is difficult to see how the first approach, which localized the difference in the conjunction *and,* could account for it, since the word is absent (especially given that leaving out the conjunction, a stylistic device known as asyndeton, generally only strengthens the suggestion of temporal succession). A uniform explanation such as that given by the second approach is preferable.

We have now distinguished two different approaches. One can assume that the conjunctions have various meanings, only one of which is found in propositional logic. This could be called the *semantic approach,* since an attempt is made to solve problems by adjusting truth conditions. An approach other than the semantic approach is the *pragmatic approach,* in which it is assumed that conjunctions in natural language only have the truth-conditional meaning attributed to them in propositional logic, and that all other aspects of their meaning can be explained in terms of language usage. The second approach will be discussed in the remainder of this chapter.

6.3 Usage and the Cooperation Principle

The pragmatic approach derives from the American philosopher H. P. Grice. We shall now take a closer look at its structure. The notion of *conversational implicature* plays a central part in Grice's theory. A conversational implicature of a sentence is something which follows from it, but not in the strict, logical sense. An implicature is something which is not explicitly stated but is only suggested by a sentence. It is not a logical consequence; it is a consequence in some nonlogical sense. But that is not to say that it is arbitrary. Conversational implicatures are obtained in a systematic manner, and in this the principle of cooperation in conversation plays an important role.

The idea behind this principle is that participants in a conversation assume that their partner is being cooperative. They assume that all are behaving in a manner which is conducive to the common goal, namely, communication. Within the general code of cooperative behavior several more specific rules can be distinguished. Grice calls these rules *conversational maxims.*

One of the maxims, perhaps not the most interesting one, requires participants to present as clearly as possible the information which they wish to communicate. Among other things, this will involve ordering the different items as well as possible. This is the maxim which plays a part in the example described above. Suppose that a language user wants to convey the information that two things, A and B, have happened. If A happened before B, then a speaker who orders this information as well as possible will say *A and B.* And if there are no indications to the contrary, the listener will assume that the speaker is obeying the cooperation principle and ordering the information as well as possible; he will conclude that A happened before B.

We can distill the following general characterization of conversational implicature from this. A conversational implicature is not a (logical) consequence of a sentence, but it is a logical consequence of the assumption that the speaker in uttering the sentence is conforming to the conversational maxims.

Sometimes additional contextual information may play a part in the derivation of implicatures. To the extent that this is not the case, we speak of *generalized conversational implicatures.* Unlike logical consequences, these implicatures are not grounded in the truth-conditional aspects of meaning. They are nevertheless so intimately bound up with the corresponding expressions and constructions that they cannot be left out of an account of the meanings of the latter. In the following, the conversational implicatures we discuss, unless an explicit exception is made, will all be generalized conversational implicatures.

6.4 Inclusive and Exclusive Disjunction

Usually the discussion of the extent to which connectives in propositional logic correspond to the conjunctions of natural language centers not around *and* but around *or* and *if* (. . . *then*). In this section and §6.6, we shall discuss the relationship between *or* and the connective $\vee$. In §6.8 we will turn to the relationship between *if* (. . . *then*) and the connective $\rightarrow$.

The distinction between the exclusive and inclusive disjunctions was made in chapter 2. Both disjunctions are false if both disjuncts are false and true if one disjunct is true. But they differ in that the inclusive disjunction is true whenever both of its disjuncts are, whereas the exclusive disjunction is false in that case. Both disjunctions can be represented by means of a truth-functional connective (see §2.2). In logic we opt for the inclusive disjunction.

But it is often suggested that disjunction in natural language, for example, as it is expressed by the English word *or,* is not inclusive but exclusive, or at least that it is ambiguous between the two. The issue is not whether the English language contains devices by means of which the exclusive disjunction can be expressed. It certainly does, as can be seen in the following examples:

(6)   Either we are going on a hike or we are going to the theater.

(7)   We are going on a hike unless we go to the theater.

(8)   We are going on a hike or we are going to the theater (but not both).

(9)   If we are not going on a hike, we are going to the theater.

The issue is the number of meanings a bare, unassisted *or* carries. Are there examples of sentences which would force us to assume an exclusive *or?* Does sentence (10) have a reading under which it is false if we are going both on a hike and to the theater?

(10)   We are going for a hike or we are going to the theater.

Tarski argues for the ambiguity of *or* on the basis of the following examples, in his *Introduction to Logic* (1939), p. 21):

> Suppose we see the following notice put up in a bookstore: "*Customers who are teachers or college students are entitled to a special reduction.*" Here the word "or" is undoubtedly used in the first [inclusive] sense, since it is not intended to refuse the reduction to a teacher who is at the same time a college student. If, on the other hand, a child asked to be taken on a hike in the morning and to a theater in the afternoon, and we reply: "*No, we are going on a hike or we are going to the theater,*" then our usage of the word "or" is obviously of the second [exclusive] kind since we intend to comply with only one of the two requests.

The second example, which is supposed to be an example of an exclusive *or,* is not very convincing. A child asks to go for a hike and then to the theater, and the answer is: *No* [i.e., *we are not going both on a hike and to the theater*], *we are going on a hike or we are going to the theater.* The disjunction in this answer can quite easily be given an inclusive interpretation. The word *no* which precedes the disjunction serves as an explicit denial of the possibility, suggested by the child, that both disjuncts are realized. The logical form of the sentence *No, we are going on a hike or we are going to the theater* is not a formula like $p \lor q$, but rather one like $\neg(p \land q) \land (p \lor q)$. That a false answer has been given if the child is taken both on a hike and to the theater does not have to be explained by assuming an exclusive *or,* for it follows from the given logical representation of the answer with its inclusive connective $\lor$. For the conjunction $\neg(p \land q) \land (p \lor q)$ is false if both p and q are true.

Let us imagine an analogous situation in which somebody asks if we are going out today, and the answer which is given is this: *Yes, we are going on a hike or we are going to the theater.* And let us suppose that we decide to go to the theater. But it is still quite early on in the day. The first performance at the theater is in the early evening, and since the weather is perfect we decide to go for a hike. Could we say, under these circumstances, that the promise of a hike or the theater has not been kept? Is the original answer false, if we, perhaps contrary to our first intentions, go on a hike first and then to the theater? Obviously not: the answer remains as true as it would have been if we had been on just one of the two excursions. Apparently it does not matter whether the exclusive disjunction was intended or the inclusive disjunction. The intention that just one disjunct will be the case does not affect the truth value when both disjuncts turn out to be the case.

Besides these kinds of examples, in which promises are made using an inclusive disjunction with exclusive intentions, and in which the two promised alternatives do not exclude each other logically or in practice, there are also examples in which the alternatives are mutually exclusive:

(11)   It is raining or it is not raining.

(12)   John is in London or John is in Paris.

Here the two disjuncts can never both be true at the same time. It cannot both rain and not rain at the same time and place, and no one can be in two places at once. Such examples suggest an exclusive disjunction even less. If for any reason the two disjuncts cannot both be true, then the inclusive disjunction gives exactly the same results as the exclusive one, so it is not necessary to assume an exclusive *or* (we made the same argument in §2.2).

We may draw the following conclusions. First, natural languages like English have exclusive disjunctions, but they express them by means other than the bare, unassisted *or*. Furthermore, an exclusive *or* is completely unnecessary for the analysis of disjunctions where the disjuncts rule each other out, logically or in practice. And finally, it is incorrect to assume an exclusive *or* just because a disjunction is intended to be exclusive. If, contrary to the expectations or intentions of the speaker, both disjuncts are true, then this does not render the disjunction false.

6.5 Disjunctions and Informativeness

The distinction between inclusive and exclusive disjunctions does not have much to do with non-truth-conditional aspects of meaning. As we have said, both disjunctions can be represented as truth-functional connectives. But the following two points, often mentioned in connection with the role of disjunction in natural language, involve non-truth-conditional aspects of meaning.

The first point is that we generally use a disjunction in communication only if we believe that one of the disjuncts is true but are not sure which of the two. The second point, which is not entirely independent of the first, is that there is always some connection between the two halves of a disjunction in natural language. The latter point also applies to conjunctions, but for them it is less clear.

The first point would not seem to accord with the truth conditions for disjunctions. A disjunction is true if (at least) one of its disjuncts is, but disjunction (12) would not be expressed under normal circumstances if the speaker knew that John was in fact in London, that is, if he knew which of the disjuncts was true. Another way of putting this is that the truth conditions for disjunctions are not parallel to the conditions under which it is acceptable to express them. While a disjunction is true just in case one or both of its disjuncts is, it is not the case that a disjunction may be expressed under all circumstances in which one of its disjuncts may be expressed. For example, it is acceptable to say *John is in London* if one knows that he is in fact in London. But under these circumstances, it is not acceptable to express the disjunction *John is in London or John is in Paris,* since this sentence suggests that one knows that John is in one of these cities, but does not know which of the two. If someone were to ask where John is and you knew that he was in London, then you would not normally answer that he was either in London or in Paris. That would be a misleading answer, and giving misleading answers is not a cooperative form of behavior. It would be much more informative in such circumstances simply to answer that John is in London. In order to be cooperative, one will in general and within the limits imposed by the subject and the nature of the conversation try to be as informative as possible. And partners in a conversation will each assume that the other is behaving in this manner. If someone were to answer our query as to when he is leaving the city with *today, tomorrow, or maybe the day after that,* then we would feel misled if we were later to discover that when he spoke he had a ticket in his pocket for a plane which was to depart in two hours. Apparently one feels wronged if someone states a disjunction where he could have stated one of its disjuncts. The speaker could have given more (relevant) information, but he chose not to. This is not what one expects from a partner in a conversation; one expects him to behave correctly and cooperatively.

There are, of course, exceptions to these rules. First, being cooperative does not always mean being as informative as possible. In a guessing game, for example, to pass on all the information you have is to be uncooperative. This (partial) characterization of cooperation as being informative applies only to the use of language to give information. Second, other obligations sometimes weigh more heavily than the obligation to be cooperative. Cooperation is not an absolute norm; it must sometimes be overruled.

That a speaker in asserting a disjunction may not be in a position to assert either of its disjuncts is so directly and systematically related to disjunctions that it seems correct to see it as an aspect of their meaning. But clearly it is not an aspect which can be built into their truth conditions. Truth conditions make no mention of speakers and of what they are in a position to assert. Why don't we just change the truth conditions? This would be wrong. The truth or falsity of a disjunction must not depend on what speakers believe. It is not only sensible but also practicable to separate two things, the truth conditions for disjunctions and their conditions for correct usage. Truth conditions belong to semantics, and correctness conditions to pragmatics. The latter is concerned with the relation between language and usage. As is apparent from the example of disjunction, correctness conditions can require language users to believe certain things or not to believe certain things. For disjunction, they say that anyone who expresses a disjunction while convinced that one of the disjuncts is true is speaking incorrectly, independently of whether what he has said is true or not. The truth of a proposition can in principle be evaluated independently of conversational maxims, and we can stick with the semantics of disjunction as given by propositional logic. But we supplement the semantics with correctness conditions for disjunctions; the conditions can be defended in terms of Gricean conversational maxims.

Although truth and correctness are in principle independent of each other, there are cases in which the two seem to be related. One well-known example of this is sentence (13), which is known as *Moore's paradox:*

(13)   The cat is on the mat, but I do not believe it.

The problem with (13) is not that it cannot be true; it can. Sentence (13) is not a contradiction, since it is true if the cat is in fact on the mat and if I for any reason at all do not believe this to be the case (for example, because I believe the cat is outside). The problem with (13) is that there is no way to use this sentence correctly. This can be explained, once again, in terms of the principle of cooperation. If language is being used to give information, then cooperation requires speakers to assert only things they believe to be true. But no speaker could ever be convinced that (13) is true. It would involve his believing that the cat is on the mat, which is exactly what is denied in the second part of (13).

This aspect of cooperation also concerns the second non-truth-conditional aspect of disjunction: the fact that there must always be some relationship between the two disjuncts of a disjunction. As we have seen, using a disjunction correctly involves not having positive beliefs about the truth of either disjunct separately. On the other hand, the speaker must believe that the disjunction is true as a whole. But how could a speaker believe a disjunction to be true without believing either of the disjuncts? This is only possible if the speaker sees some connection between the two. Lacking special beliefs about either of the disjuncts separately, he must nevertheless believe them to be related to the extent that whatever the facts may be, one or the other will always be the case. Correct usage of a disjunction, then, involves the belief that there is some connection between the disjuncts. So we see that these two non-truth-conditional aspects of the meaning of the disjunction can be explained in terms of their conditions for proper usage.

Now we can also explain why connection is much less important with conjunctions. For conjunctions, the aspects of cooperation already considered in connection with disjunctions enable us to say that a speaker, in order to express a conjunction correctly, only has to be convinced that both conjuncts are true. There is nothing to stop him from entertaining beliefs about the truth of two completely separate matters. So it does not follow that he must have any particular opinions about a relationship between the two. For the latter, more is required. What would commit him is, for example, that everything that is said must be relevant to the subject of the conversation in which he is participating. For a conjunction, this means that both conjuncts must be relevant to the subject of the conversation. So the only required connection between the two conjuncts is that they both be concerned with the same subject matter. This is a much looser connection than what disjuncts must have.

We conclude this section with the observation that the semantics of disjunction provided by classical propositional logic is not lacking. It provides an adequate account of all truth-functional aspects of disjunction. The other aspects of its meaning can be explained in terms of conditions for proper usage.

6.6 Conversational Maxims and Conversational Implicatures

In Grice's theory, the non-truth-conditional aspects of meaning are treated with the aid of conversational implicature. In this section, we will examine Grice's theory in more detail. If the conversational maxims are made a little more precise, a notion of conversational implicature arises which we can apply in §6.7, where we will return to the phenomena we have just discussed in connection with disjunction.

In §6.3 we said that the principle of conversational cooperation is at the core of Grice's theory, and that a number of more specific rules can be distinguished within this general principle. These are the conversational maxims. A few of the maxims have been discussed implicitly in the preceding sections. The maxim which plays such an important part in disjunction is called the *Maxim of Quantity,* so named to remind us that it concerns the quantity of information given. The maxim can be divided into two submaxims:

Maxim of Quantity:

(i)   Make your contribution to the conversation as informative as is required.
(ii) Do not make your contribution any more informative than necessary.

The second and very fundamental maxim is the maxim of *Quality:*

Maxim of Quality:

(i)   Do not say what you believe is false.
(ii) Do not say that for which you lack adequate evidence.

The third maxim is the maxim of *Relation:*

Maxim of Relation:

Be relevant.

The fourth and last maxim given by Grice is the maxim of *Manner:*

Maxim of Manner:

(i)   Avoid obscurity of expression.
(ii) Avoid ambiguity.
(iii) Be brief.
(iv) Be orderly.

Not all of the maxims are equally significant, and Grice does not intend the four he gives to be exhaustive. Undoubtedly other (sub)maxims could be formulated. And maybe the (sub)maxims which have been given overlap to some extent. Furthermore, they have been formulated informally, so that many of the concepts appearing in them should be expanded upon. We hope to clarify them to some extent in the following partial reformulation of the maxims. It should be remembered that this reformulation is not the only one which could be given, and that it omits certain aspects of usage. Nor is it intended as a reasoned choice between different interpretations of Grice's maxims; all we want to do here is show how all kinds of pragmatic phenomena can be explained once the maxims are made more explicit.

We will reformulate Grice's maxims as conditions under which statements can be made correctly. So the maxims are explicitly being narrowed down to one particular kind of speech act: making a statement. Other conditions could be given for other speech acts: asking a question, giving an order, making a promise, etc. We shall omit the Maxim of Manner for convenience. We then arrive at the following conditions in which it is correct to make statements:

(14)   A speaker S makes correct use of a sentence A in order to make a statement before a listener L just in case:

(i)   S believes that A is true;

(ii)   S believes that L does not believe that A is true;

(iii) S believes that A is relevant to the subject of the conversation;

(iv)   For all sentences B of which A is a logical consequence (and which are not equivalent to A), (i)–(iii) do not all hold with respect to B.

The clause *L does not believe that A* is being consistently used here in the sense *It is not the case that L believes A*, which is weaker that *L believes that not-A*. Condition (i) corresponds to the Maxim of Quality. The concept of belief which appears here is that of *strict belief*. Not only must the speaker think it more probable that A holds than that A does not hold, he must also be quite convinced that A is indeed true. As are the other conditions, (i) is subjective in the sense that the speaker is all that is subjected to requirements. Sentence A does not need to be true for S to state it correctly; it is only necessary that S believe by it. This corresponds to the fact that correctness and truth are independent.

Condition (ii) corresponds to the second submaxim of the Maxim of Quantity. A speaker who supplies the listener with information which he believes she already has is supplying more information than necessary. Note that condition (ii) allows A to provide not only new information but also things the listener already believes. If L believes that B but does not believe that A, then L will not believe that A *and B* either. The conjunction A *and B* contains some information which is new to L and some information which is not. If speaker S is aware of these facts, then he can state A *and B* in accordance with condition (ii).

Condition (iii) corresponds to the Maxim of Relation. The notion of relevance will not be analyzed here. But it is made explicit here that what counts as relevant is dependent on the subject of the conversation. One simple way of explicating relevance is to consider a question to be the subject of the conversation. Relevant sentences are then those which can intuitively be considered (partial) answers to the question.

Condition (iv), finally, corresponds to the first submaxim of the Maxim of Quantity. This is the maxim that plays such an important part in disjunctions. The condition says that a speaker is being as informative as he should be if he makes the strongest correct statement which he can make. The notion of the 'strength' of a statement is here understood in a logical sense: a sentence B is stronger than a sentence A if A is a logical consequence of B, while B is not a logical consequence of A. If a speaker can in accordance with conditions (i)–(iii) assert a sentence B which is stronger than A, then condition (iv) forbids him to assert A. This condition does not mean that there is some unique strongest sentence which he can assert. There will be different logically equivalent sentences for him to choose between. He will perhaps find the Maxim of Manner useful in making his choice.

No doubt this condition, like the others, is both too strict and too permissive. Condition (iv) forbids us to spread out the information we want to give over a number of installments, for example, which might otherwise be conducive to clarity. Furthermore, as we pointed out, condition (ii) allows the speaker to tell the listener things he has already heard and believed. In combination with condition (iv) it compels the speaker to present all of this old information all over again. Surely this is going a little too far. Note that in view of condition (iii), all of the old information must be relevant to the subject of the discussion. If, as we suggested above, the subject is considered a question, then making a relevant statement amounts to giving as complete an answer as possible to the question, even if part of the answer was already assumed. It is certainly possible to improve the conditions given here and to adapt them better to what happens in conversations. But that would carry us too far beyond the purposes of the present book. Our purpose here is merely to demonstrate how conditions like these can be used to explain non-truth-conditional aspects of meaning in terms of conversational implicatures.

Conversational implicatures can be defined as follows:

> (15) A sentence *B* is a *conversational implicature* of a sentence *A* iff *B* is a logical consequence of the conditions under which *A* can correctly be used.

Note that although it is characteristic of the conversational implicatures of a sentence that they are not logical consequences of that sentence, (15) may still define them in terms of logical consequences. Conversational implicatures do not follow from the sentence itself, but from the assumption that the sentence is being used correctly. So we see that this central notion of pragmatics, which is intended to account for aspects of meaning which cannot be treated satisfactorily in a logico-semantic theory, nevertheless makes essential use of the notion of logical consequence.

6.7 The Conversational Implicatures of Disjunctions

In this section we shall demonstrate how the non-truth-conditional aspects of the meaning of disjunction, which we discussed in §6.5, can be accounted for as conversational implicatures of disjunctions. We shall demonstrate that sentences (17)–(20) are all conversational implicatures of (16):

> (16) *A or B.*

> (17) S does not believe that *A*.

> (18) S does not believe that *B*.

> (19) S does not believe that *not-A*.

> (20) S does not believe that *not-B*.

According to (15), this is done by showing that (17)–(20) are logical consequences of (21):

> (21) S makes correct use of *A or B* in making a statement to L.

And it can be done as follows. Sentences (22)–(24) follow from (21) given conditions (i)–(iii) of definition (14), the definition of correctness:

> (22) S believes that *A or B* is true.

> (23) S believes that L does not believe that *A or B* is true.

> (24) S believes that *A or B* is relevant to the subject of the conversation.

Furthermore, *A or B* is a logical consequence of *A* without being equivalent to it. We assume here that neither *A* nor *B* is a logical consequence of the other (a disjunction for which this is not the case would be ruled out by the Maxim of Manner, in particular by its submaxim: Be brief). Thus, according to condition (iv) in (14), we may also conclude that (25) follows from (21):

(25)   Either S does not believe that *A* is true, or S does not believe
that L does not believe that *A* is true, or S does not believe that
A is relevant to the subject of the conversation.

Only under very special circumstances does it ever occur that a disjunction is relevant while one of its disjuncts is not. Let us now add the extra premise that S believes both *A* and *B* are relevant to the subject of a conversation if he believes the sentence *A or B* is relevant. Then (26) follows from (24):

(26)   S believes that *A* is relevant to the subject of the conversation.

Furthermore, (27) follows from (23):

(27)   S believes that L does not believe that *A* is true.

Otherwise, if L were to believe that *A* is true, then L would also believe that *A or B* is true, since this is a simple logical consequence of *A*. Now (26) and (27) deny two of the three disjuncts of (25), so that we may draw the third disjunct ((17) S does not believe that *A* is true.) as a conclusion. So now we have derived the first of the four implicatures of (16) from assumption (21), the assumption that (16) is being used correctly.

Sentence (18) can be derived as a conversational implicature of (16) in exactly the same manner. But we need a little more in order to derive (19) and (20). Take (20), for example. We have demonstrated that (17) follows from (21), and that (22) does too. Sentence (20) follows from (17) together with (22): A rational S who believes that *A or B* is true and who does not believe that *A* is true will not believe that *not-B* is true, for if he did he would have to believe *A* in order to be able to believe that *A or B*. And sentence (19) can be derived from (18) and (20) in exactly the same manner. So now we have demonstrated that (17)–(20) are conversational implicatures of the disjunction (16).

A comment on relevance seems to be required here. We stated, in defending the assumption on which the derivation of (26) is based, that only under very special circumstances will a disjunction be relevant while neither of its disjuncts is relevant. One example of such a special circumstance is given by a tax form with the following question:

(28)   Are you a widow or a divorcee? Yes/No; please cross out what
is not applicable.

Now if whoever is filling in the form is a widow, she will (if she is being truthful) strike out the word *no*. This amounts to her stating (29); but (30) would also have been a good answer:

(29)   I am a widow or a divorcee.

(30)   I am a widow.

But given the question on the tax form, the (more informative) answer (30) is not relevant. The only thing the tax inspector wants to know is whether she belongs to either of the two categories, for example, because this is what determines how heavily she will be taxed. It is of no importance to which of the two categories she belongs. Under these circumstances, we may not conclude, from the fact that (29) is correct, that the woman filling in the form does not believe that she is a widow. We may only draw the weaker conclusion that either she does not believe she is a widow, or she does not believe the information is relevant. So the assumption on which (26) is based plays an essential role. Strictly speaking, then, (17)–(20) are conversational implicatures only under this assumption.

The same kinds of phenomena as we have seen in connection with disjunctions also appear with other constructions. Consider the following sentences, for example:

(31)   a. All the cookies in the jar taste good.
       b. There are some cookies left.

(32)   a. Some students have passed.
       b. Some students have failed.

Neither (b) sentence is a logical consequence of the corresponding (a) sentence. But the (a) sentences carry a strong suggestion that the (b) sentences are true. This can be explained by showing that (33) and (34) are conversational implicatures of (31a) and (32a):

(33)   S does not believe that the cookies are gone.

(34)   S does not believe that all the students have passed.

The derivations of these implicatures are similar to those of the implicatures we just discussed in connection with disjunctions.

6.8 Implication and Informativeness

The question of the relationship between connectives in propositional logic and conjunctions in natural language is most pressing in the case of material implication. Every introduction to logic points out the lack of analogies between the material implication → and the *if* (. . . *then*) constructions familiar from natural language. We also mentioned in §2.2 some of the difficulties involved in treating *if* (. . . *then*) truth-functionally. We defended the truth table given for → by saying that it was the only acceptable truth table if *if* (. . . *then*) were to be treated as a truth-functional conjunction.

In §6.5 we saw that similar doubts about the analogy between the word *or* in natural language and the connective ∨ can be removed by dealing with it not only in terms of truth values but also in terms of conditions for proper usage. In this section we will see that the same approach is also quite successful in the case of implication. Quite successful, but not completely. As we shall see, this approach still leaves one with the feeling that a number of essential aspects of the meaning of implication are left unaccounted for. The combination of a pragmatic explanation and a semantic analysis borrowed from propositional logic is not completely satisfactory. Apparently there is much more to the semantics of implication than is accounted for by propositional logic.

It may be noted that modal logic has to a large extent been developed as a response to the shortcomings of material implication (see vol. 2). Modal logic can be seen as an attempt to define a stronger, non-truth-functional form of implication. But the strict implication of modal logic has its own shortcomings. New attempts are continually being made to develop a richer semantics of implication which does more justice to our semantic intuitions. These analyses always throw some light on one or another particular aspect of implication, but so far none is generally accepted as the last word. Perhaps this is too much to hope for, and we must manage with a whole range of different analyses, each specialized in its own aspect of implication.

Although we are well aware that the combination of a semantic analysis of implication in terms of material implication and a pragmatic analysis in terms of conditions for correct usage falls short of a full account of the meaning of implication, we shall nevertheless discuss this approach here. We do this not only because we believe that conditions for correct usage play an important part in implication, but also in order to illustrate some of the shortcomings of the semantic approach to implication in propositional logic. Two obvious shortcomings of treating *if* (. . . *then*) as a material implication are the same as those discussed in §6.5 in connection with disjunctions. The truth conditions of the material implication do not require any connection between the antecedent and consequent of an implication, nor do they in any way recognize that we assert an implication only if we do not know whether its antecedent and consequent are true or false.

This last does not apply to all conditional sentences, but it does apply to that archetype of the conditional sentence, the *indicative conditional sentence*. Here (35) is an example:

    (35)   If cod are fish, then they have gills.

Coming from a fisherman, who can be assumed to know that cod is indeed a kind of fish, sentence (35) would be a bit strange. A fisherman would be more likely to say something like (36) or a succession of sentences such as those in (37):

    (36)   Since cod are fish, they have gills.

    (37)   All fish have gills. Cod are fish. Therefore cod have gills.

And anyone who knows much about frogs will not say (38) (even if he also is a fisherman-logician who knows that (38) is true). He is much more likely to say something like (39), or perhaps (40):

(38)   If frogs are fish, then they have gills.

(39)   Frogs do not have gills, so they are not fish. (Since all fish have gills).

(40)   If frogs were fish, they would have gills.

Sentence (40) is not a normal indicative conditional sentence; it is a *counterfactual conditional sentence.*

One last example: a true sentence like (41) would not under normal circumstances be expressed by a speaker who is conversant with biology either. He would prefer a sentence like (42):

(41)   If axolotls are fish, then they have gills.

(42)   Even though axolotls are not fish, they still have gills.

These examples show that for indicative conditionals, correct usage involves the speaker not knowing whether the antecedent and consequent are true or not. For if he does know this, then natural language provides him with all kinds of other devices which enable him to communicate his knowledge about them more effectively.

These conditions for proper usage are quite analogous to those we have given for disjunctions. And our defence of them is also parallel. (The parallels should not surprise us, if we remember that $\phi \rightarrow \psi$ and $\neg\phi \lor \psi$ are logical equivalents in propositional logic.) So here it will suffice to give the general form of the defence, leaving out the details.

Sentence (35) is of the form $p \rightarrow q$. The consequent q (*Cod have gills*) is a stronger proposition than the whole implication $p \rightarrow q$, which is a logical consequence of q. So all other things being equal, the Maxim of Quantity requires the speaker to state the stronger q if he can do so correctly. So from the fact that $p \rightarrow q$ is being used correctly, we may conclude that the speaker does not believe the consequent q to be true.

Sentence (41) is of the same form. The negation of the antecedent, $\neg p$ (*Axolotls are not fish*) is once again a stronger proposition than the implication $p \rightarrow q$ as a whole, and the Maxim of Quantity once again requires the speaker to state $\neg p$ if he can do so correctly, all other things being equal. So from the fact that $p \rightarrow q$ is being used correctly we may conclude that the speaker does not believe the negation of its antecedent to be true.

That the speaker may not believe the antecedent to be true either follows from the combined maxims of quality and quantity. For if he were to believe the antecedent, then, since according to quality he would really believe the implication as a whole, he would also have to believe the consequent. But this, as we have seen, is ruled out by the maxim of quantity. A similar argument is applicable to the negation of the consequent. A speaker who believes the negation of the consequent to be true since according to quality he would really believe that the implication as a whole is true, would also have to believe the negation of the antecedent to be true. And this we have just seen to be ruled out by the maxim of quantity.

That there must be some connection between the antecedent and the consequent of an implication can be explained in the same way as the fact that the disjuncts of a disjunction must be related. If we have no basis for belief in the truth or falsity of either an antecedent or its consequent, then any belief in the truth of an implication must derive from beliefs about a connection between the facts described by the two. Our belief that $p \rightarrow q$ is true must derive from a conviction that a situation in which p is true and q is false cannot arise.

A number of important aspects of the meaning of implication can be explained in this manner. But as we said at the beginning, certain other phenomena cannot be accounted for. One example concerns the negation of a conditional sentence:

(43)   It is not true that if axolotls have gills, then they are fish.

Suppose we are in the middle of a discussion about whether axolotls are fish. And suppose someone states that if investigations were to show that axolotls have gills, then this would mean that they are fish, since only fish have gills. Then (43) could quite properly be used to deny this: we mean to say that having gills does not necessarily involve being a fish. We then mean to deny that there is a connection between having gills and being a fish, but we do not mean to answer the question of whether or not axolotls have gills, or indeed the original question of whether axolotls are fish. Apparently for the negations of conditionals as for the conditionals themselves, correct usage involves not knowing whether the antecedent and consequent are true or not. But the propositional semantics of negation and material implication force us to treat the assertion of the negation of a conditional as the assertion of its antecedent together with the assertion of the negation of its consequent. It has not yet proved possible to bring this fact in line with the non-truth-functional aspects of the meaning of implications discussed so far.

6.9 Presuppositions and Conversational Implicatures

We can now return to a problem which was left unsolved in chapter 5. In §5.5.6 we mentioned the limited extent to which many-valued logical systems account for presupposition. The problem can be illustrated by means of the following sentences:

(44)   If there is a king of France, then he is bald.

(45)   If baldness is hereditary, then the king of France is bald.

(46)   There is a king of France.

(47)   The king of France is bald.

(48)   Baldness is hereditary.

Sentence (46) is not intuitively a presupposition of (44), but it is a presupposition of (47), the consequent of the implication (44). In the many-valued semantic approach to presupposition, this fact was explained as follows. The truth conditions of sentence (47) are such that it is neither true nor false if there is no king of France, but has some third truth value. If a presupposition of a sentence is not true, then that sentence is neither true nor false. That (46) is not a presupposition of (44) is accounted for by choosing a truth table for implication which gives an implication 1 as its truth value if it gives its antecedent 0. Under this many-valued interpretation of implication, sentence (44) is true if France does not have a king. So the falsity of (46) does not result in (44) being neither true nor false: (46) is not a semantic presupposition of (44).

So far so good. A many-valued semantic approach would seem to result in a practicable notion of presupposition. The problem arises with sentences like (45). Intuitively, (46) seems to be a presupposition of (45). And this is not accounted for by the many-valued semantic notion of presupposition. If (48) is false, then (45) must be true, even if (46) is false. So that (46) is not true does not necessarily mean that (45) is neither true nor false: apparently (46) is not a semantic presupposition of (45).

There are, however, certain significant differences between (44) and (45). The antecedent of (44) is a presupposition of its consequent. But the antecedent of (45) is logically independent of the presupposition (46) of its consequent. Both the truth and the falsity of (46) can be reconciled with the truth and falsity of (48). It is this point which can help us find pragmatic grounds for a connection between (46) and (45), without there being the same connection between (46) and (44). So although (46) is not a semantic presupposition of (45), we can show that a speaker who observes the conversational maxims must believe (46) in order to express (45). This does not, however, apply to (44), which a speaker can say in accordance with the conditions of correct usage without having to believe (46).

As in §6.8, we will only give a sketch of the proof. We must show that it follows as a logical consequence of the assumption that a speaker S states (45) correctly that S believes (46) to be true, and that this does not follow as a logical consequence of the assumption that S states (44) correctly. Suppose now that it is not the case that S believes (46) to be true. Then either S believes (46) not to be true, or S simply does not have any beliefs about the truth value of (46). As far as the first of these two alternatives is concerned: if S believes that (46) is not true, then S believes that (47) has the third truth value. Then according to the many-valued truth table for implication, S can only believe (45) to be true if S at the same time believes (48) to be false. But as we saw in

§6.8, belief in the falsity of the antecedent of an implication is incompatible with correct usage. So the first alternative is incompatible with the assumption that S says (45) correctly. As far as the second alternative is concerned: if S does not have any beliefs about the truth value of (46), then S is willing to entertain the possibility that (47) is given the third truth value. But this is compatible with S's belief in (45) only if S believes that the falsity of (48) is a logical consequence of the falsity of (46) (as a result of which (47) obtains the third truth value). But this contradicts the logical independence of (48) and (46). So the second alternative is also incompatible with the assumption that S states (45) correctly. So the original assumption that it is not the case that S believes (46) to be true must be mistaken. We have now shown that it follows as a logical consequence of the assumption that a speaker S uses (45) correctly that S believes (46) to be true.

This chain of reasoning cannot be repeated for (44). For in this case there certainly is a connection between the antecedent and the presupposition of the consequent: they are identical.

We conclude that working in many-valued logic, a pragmatic connection can be made between (45) and (46) by showing that (49) is a pragmatic implicature of (45):

(49)   S believes that there is a king of France.

The difference between (44) and (45) is due to the fact that (49) is not a pragmatic implicature of (44). Such results may be seen as a first step toward an integrated theory of semantic and pragmatic presupposition.

6.10 Conventional Implicatures, Presuppositions, and Implications

We have seen that a number of important non-truth-functional aspects of meaning can be explained in terms of conversational implicatures. Although conversational implicatures are always dependent on, among other things, conventional meaning, they do not themselves form a part of conventional meaning. The conversational implicatures in the preceding sections, for example, do not follow purely on the grounds of conventional meaning. The principle of conversational cooperation plays an essential part in their derivations.

This nonconventional nature of conversational implicatures has to do with one of their characteristic properties namely, that they are not inseparable from the sentences they belong to but can implicitly or explicitly be *canceled* by the context. Sentence (50) ((3) in §6.2) is a clear example of a sentence in which a conversational implicature is explicitly canceled:

(50)   Annie took off her socks and jumped into bed, but I do not know which she did first.

Not all non-truth-conditional aspects of meaning derive in this indirect manner from the principle of cooperation. There are other non-truth-conditional aspects of meaning which are inseparable from certain kinds of expressions and constructions. Unlike conversational implicatures, these therefore belong to the realm of conventional meaning. But like conversational implicatures, they give rise to nonlogical implications. These implicatures are solely based on the conventional meanings of expressions and are therefore called *conventional implicatures*. Unlike conversational implicataures, conventional implicatures cannot be canceled.

A standard example of a conventional implicature arises from the difference between *and* and *but*. The two words have different meanings, but the differences are not reflected in the (identical) truth tables for the sentences *A and B* and *A but B*. So the difference in their meanings is a non-truth-functional aspect of meaning. It is objective in the sense that everyone who is competent in English uses these words in the same way. The aspect of meaning in which *and* and *but* differ can be given a general formulation as follows: there must be some kind of opposition between propositions conjoined by means of *but*. Or more precisely: a speaker must in any case *believe* that there is some such opposition in order to state a sentence of the form *A but B* correctly. Whether there is in fact any such connection does not matter for the truth value of *A but B*. So we have here a non-truth-conditional aspect of conventional meaning. The corresponding implicature, that the speaker believes there is some opposition between the two conjuncts conjoined by *but*, is a conventional implicature.

Words like *still, too,* and *even* in sentences (51)–(53) are other examples which do not seem to affect truth conditions in any way, but which yield conventional implicatures:

(51)   John still got a passing grade.

(52)   John got a passing grade too.

(53)   Even John got a passing grade.

The truth conditions for each of these sentences would seem to be the same as those for (54):

(54)   John got a passing grade.

The word *still* in (51) carries the suggestion that it was not expected that John would pass, but this is not something which enters into the truth conditions of (51); it is rather something which one must believe in order to assert (51) correctly. But it is an aspect which belongs to conventional meaning, so we are dealing with a conventional implicature here. That this cannot be canceled is what makes (55) so peculiar:

(55)   John still got a passing grade, but that was to be expected.

Other than conversational implicatures, then, conventional implicatures cannot be canceled by explicitly denying them. The implicature which (52) carries is that there is someone else besides John who got a passing grade. And the implicature carried by *even* is very much like the conjunction of the implicatures of *still* and *too*.

That we are dealing here with conventional non-truth-functional aspects of meaning becomes even clearer if we consider the negations of sentences (51)–(53):

(56)   It is not the case that John still got a passing grade.

(57)   It is not the case that John got a passing grade too.

(58)   It is not the case that even John got a passing grade.

Assuming these sentences are pronounced with normal intonation, without special emphasis on the *still, too,* or *even,* then these sentences only deny that John has received a passing grade. They have the same implicatures as (51)–(53). This underlines the fact that we are again not dealing with logical consequences but with implicatures. For what follows from (51) and its negation in (56) is a contingent sentence: *It was not to be expected that John would receive a passing grade.* But only tautologies follow as logical consequences of both a sentence and its negation, so apparently this sentence follows not as a logical consequence but as something else: an implicature. The conventional implicature that it was not to be expected that John would receive a passing grade cannot be canceled in (51); this was quite apparent from sentence (55). But (56), the negation of (51), is a little more complicated. When pronounced with emphasis on the *still,* (59) is a perfectly acceptable statement:

(59)   It is not the case that John *still* got a passing grade; it was only to be expected that he would get a passing grade.

If (59) is pronounced in this manner, then it, unlike (56) does not deny that John got a passing grade. What is being denied is the implicature conveyed by *still.* One thing which certainly plays a part in this and which would be worth going into in more depth is the way the negation works. Negation seems to function differently in (59) from in (56), for example (compare this with the discussion of (43) at the end of §6.8, and with the comments on negation in §5.5.6).

That they are difficult to cancel is something which conventional implicatures have in common with logical consequences. If we try to cancel a logical consequence, then a logical contradiction is the result:

(60)   John is coming and Mary is coming, but John is not coming.

Logical consequences are of course not preserved under negation. There is nothing at all wrong with (61):

(61)   It is not true that John is coming and Mary is coming, for John
       is not coming.

Conventional implicatures and logical consequences are both dependent on
conventional aspects of meaning; in the case of implicatures, these are not
truth-conditional, and in the case of logical consequences they are.

Conventional implicatures and presuppositions also have certain characteristics in common, for example, the fact that they are both conventional. In
their article "Conventional Implicatures" (1979), Karttunen and Peters argued that various kinds of things which are usually seen as presuppositions
can more profitably be seen as conventional implicatures. They also show how
an analysis of conventional implicatures can be incorporated into the framework of Montague grammar (see vol. 2). A Montague grammar provides a
sentence derived from natural language with a formal counterpart in the form
of a logical formula which represents its truth conditions. Karttunen and
Peters suggest associating not one but two formulas with every sentence: the
first to represent its truth conditions and the second to represent its conventional implicatures. This composite representational form would do justice not
only to the truth-conditional aspects of meaning but also to its non-truth-
conditional aspects. An example. Sentence (62) has the same truth conditions
as sentence (63), but it also has (64) as a conventional implicature:

(62)   John is coming too.

(63)   John is coming.

(64)   Someone besides John is coming.

Following Karttunen and Peters, the following ordered pair of formulas may
be associated with (62):

(65) $\langle Cj, \exists x(x \neq j \wedge Cx) \rangle$

Each of the two formulas in this pair can be either true or false. So there are four
possible combinations of truth values, which may be represented as follows:

(66) $\langle 1, 1 \rangle$ John is coming and someone else is coming too.
       $\langle 1, 0 \rangle$ John is the only one coming.
       $\langle 0, 0 \rangle$ No one is coming.
       $\langle 0, 1 \rangle$ John is not coming, but someone else is.

Each of these four possibilities can be considered a (composite) value which
the sentence in question can take on. So this form of representation amounts
to a four-valued local system. The system is one we encountered in §§5.5.4
and 5.5.5, where we also showed that such a four-valued system gives the
same results as the three-valued Kleene system. Both systems give the same
predictions about the implicatures as about the presuppositions of composite
sentences. So in this respect no distinction is drawn between conventional im-

plicatures and presuppositions. The difference between using a four- or a three-valued system lies in what happens when the implicature or presupposition is false. In the first case, the sentence in question can still be said to be true or false, while in the second case it must be said to be neither true nor false. So whether any particular aspect of the meaning of a sentence is to be treated as a conventional implicature or as a presupposition depends on whether we think the sentence has a truth value when the implicature or presupposition is false. It would seem unlikely that such things can be decided purely on the basis of our intuitions about language. So empirical arguments for classifying things as conventional implicatures or as presuppositions will be difficult to find. But as we have just seen, from a theoretical standpoint it doesn't make any difference, if conventional implicatures are treated with a four-valued Kleene system and presuppositions are treated with a three-valued Kleene system. So the value of the Karttunen and Peters article is not that it distinguishes conventional implicatures from presuppositions, but that it presents a method which demonstrates how non-truth-conditional aspects of meaning can be dealt with in the same formal recursive manner as truth-conditional ones.

So it is not easy to draw a sharp line between conventional implicatures and presuppositions. And since we have said that the latter are truth-conditional and the former are not, it follows that the border between semantics and pragmatics is not as clear as we might have hoped.

Conventional implicatures, presuppositions, and logical consequences are all essentially conventional. And it is not only the first two which are difficult to distinguish from each other. The border with logical consequences is not without its conflicts either. This can be illustrated by means of example (62). It could be argued that (64) is a logical consequence of (62). This is equivalent to saying that if (64) is false, then (62) is false too. Here too intuitions alone are not enough to decide the issue. Theoretical arguments are required. One important factor in the theoretical discussion is the negation of sentences like (62):

(67)   It is not the case that John is coming too.

If (64) is treated as an implicature or presupposition of (62) then it also has to be accepted as an implicature or presupposition of (67). But it is different if it is treated as a logical consequence. In a two-valued semantics, a contingent sentence and its negation cannot have the same (contingent) logical consequences (see §5.5.3). If one wishes to stick to the idea that (64) is a logical consequence of (62), then one way out would be to deny that (67) is a simple denial of (62). In this approach, (62) is taken to be the following conjunction:

(68) $Cj \land \exists x(x \neq j \land Cx)$

Then (67) can be said to be ambiguous between (69) and (70).

(69) $\neg(Cj \land \exists x(x \neq j \land Cx))$.

(70) $\neg Cj \wedge \exists x(x \neq j \wedge Cx)$.

Formula (69) gives the unlikely reading of (67) in which it is the simple denial of (62). The more plausible reading of (67) is (70), from which (64) still follows. A third reading of (67) can be distinguished and represented as (71):

(71) $Cj \wedge \neg \exists x(x \neq j \wedge Cx)$

This reading arises if extra emphasis is placed on the *too* in (67).

Our approach to *too,* of course, closely resembles Russell's analysis of definite descriptions (see §5.2). In this theory, the existential implications of denials of sentences with definite descriptions, like (72), for example, are explained by assuming that such sentences have both an internal and an external negation:

(72)   It is not the case that the king of France is bald.

Formulas (69) and (70) analogously function as the external and internal negations of (62), respectively.

This approach in which (64) is treated as an implicature (or presupposition) of (62) is more in harmony with Strawson's ideas about definite descriptions. Both approaches encounter their own difficulties. As we saw in §5.5.6, in Strawson's approach (67) can be pronounced ambiguous only under the assumption that negation is lexically ambiguous. In Russell's approach, ambiguity is explained as a scope ambiguity. Both theories, incidentally, must explain why the reading with internal negation is so much more natural than the reading with external negation. (Perhaps the principle of cooperation could again be summoned here. The reading with internal negation is logically stronger than the reading with external negation. A speaker confronted with this ambiguity would then, in accordance with the principle of cooperation, choose the stronger reading, all other things being equal.)

From the above it is clear that no one knows the exact borderline between the truth-conditional and non-truth-conditional aspects of meaning. This gives rise to some lively conflicts in the literature. But whatever is the outcome of the conflicts, it should by now at least be clear that the non-truth-conditional aspects of meaning can usefully be approached from within the framework of logic. And this is the main point we have been trying to make in this chapter.

7   Formal Syntax

In this book the emphasis has been on the logical study of semantic questions. Nevertheless, the pure syntax of natural and formal languages also has an interesting structure which is accessible to treatment by mathematical methods. In this chapter we shall attempt to sketch some central notions and themes in this area, pointing out some connections with the rest of our text. There is no pretense at completeness here: for a more thorough study, the reader is referred to, e.g., Hopcroft and Ullman 1979.

7.1 The Hierarchy of Rewrite Rules

We shall be considering a finite alphabet A of symbols $a_1, \ldots, a_n$. Corresponding to this is the set A^* of all finite sequences of symbols taken from A (including the 'empty sequence' $\langle \rangle$). A *language* L can now be seen as a subset of A^* (the 'grammatical expressions of L'). If this abstract idea is applied to natural language, then, for example, words, or even whole parsed expressions, would correspond to symbols in alphabet A.

Description of a language L now amounts to finding a *grammar* G for L. Grammars are usually thought of as sets of *rewrite rules* of the form:

$X \Rightarrow E$ (Rewrite symbol X as expression E.)

Example: Let G consist of the following two rules (in the alphabet {a, b}):

$S \Rightarrow \langle \rangle$
$S \Rightarrow aSb$

The symbol S is called the 'start symbol' (which often refers to the category 'sentence'). The class of expressions generated by G consists of all sequences of the form:

$a^i b^i$ (i letters a, followed by the same number of letters b)

The sequence aabb, for example, may be obtained by means of the following rewrite steps:

$S, aSb, aaSbb, aa\langle \rangle bb (=aabb)$

Thus, more generally, besides the *terminal symbols* in A, rewrite rules also involve *auxiliary symbols* which can be rewritten as expressions formed out of terminal and auxiliary symbols. We say that the grammar G generates the language L(G) of all strings E composed from terminal symbols only which are *derivable* from G, that is, such that there is a finite sequence of expressions starting with S and ending with E, in which every expression can be obtained from its predecessor by rewriting a single auxiliary symbol with the aid of one of the rules in G. Here is another illustration.

Example: The following grammar describes the formulas of propositional logic, with the alphabet {p, ', ¬, ∧,), (} (where propositional letters are of the form p, p', p", . . .):

$$A \Rightarrow p$$
$$A \Rightarrow A'$$
$$S \Rightarrow A$$
$$S \Rightarrow \neg S$$
$$S \Rightarrow (S \land S)$$

Here the auxiliary symbol A stands for propositional letters or 'atomic formulas'. In fact, auxiliary symbols often correspond to grammatical categories which are also useful by themselves.

Rewrite grammars can be classified according to the kinds of rules used in them. Notably, the grammars which we have introduced so far are said to be *context-free,* which means that their rules allow the rewriting of single auxiliary symbols independently of the context in which they occur. Context-free grammars are very common and are very important.

A simpler, but still useful subspecies of this class is formed by the *regular* grammars, in which an additional requirement is placed on the expression E to the right of the arrow: it must consist of either (i) a single terminal symbol (or the empty sequence ⟨⟩) or (ii) a single terminal symbol and a single auxiliary symbol. In the latter case, all of the rules in G must have the same order: the terminal symbol must be in front (the grammar is 'left-regular') or at the end ('right-regular').

Example: Consider the alphabet {a, b} and the grammar G with the rules:

$$S \Rightarrow aX$$
$$X \Rightarrow b$$
$$X \Rightarrow bS$$

L(G) consists of all sequences of the form ab . . . ab.

A more realistic example of a 'language' with a regular description would be the decimal notation of numerals, like 123.654.

On the other hand there are also more complex kinds of grammars, with 'conditional' rewrite rules of the form:

$(E_1)X(E_2) \Rightarrow E$ (Rewrite X as E if it appears in the context E_1XE_2.)

One well-known example of such a *context-sensitive* grammar is the following:

S ⇒ aSBC
S ⇒ abC
(C)B ⇒ D
C(D) ⇒ B
(B)D ⇒ C
(b)B ⇒ b
C ⇒ c

The language L(G) produced by this grammar consists of all sequences of terminal symbols with equal numbers of a's, b's and c's (in that order). A derivation of aabbcc, for example, goes like this:

S, aSBC, aabCBC, aabCDC, aabBDC, aabBCC, aabbCC, aabbcC, aabbcc.

Finally, the most complex variety, *type-0* grammars, admits rules in which any expression formed out of auxiliary and terminal symbols may be rewritten as any other:

$E_1 \Rightarrow E_2$

A gradient of grammar models results for linguistic description:

regular, context-free, context-sensitive, type-0.

This is often called the *Chomsky hierarchy* after the originator of this fundamental categorization.

7.2 Grammars and Automata

Intuitively, a grammar is a system of rules by means of which a language can be produced. But besides the 'generative' aspect of language, there is also the question of recognition: i.e., deciding whether a given sequence of symbols is an expression in the language in question or not. The latter function is often given a mathematical description in terms of machine models. Parallel to the above hierarchy of grammars, then, we have a hierarchy of recognizing machines ordered according to their 'engine power'.

The simplest recognizing machines are the *finite state automata*. These can read expressions, symbol by symbol (say, encoded on a linear tape), while always being in one of a finite number of internal states. So the behavior of such a machine is wholly determined by the following features:

(i)   its 'initial state'
(ii)   its 'transition function', which says which state the machine will go into, given any present state and the symbol last read

(iii) a classification of all the states as 'recognizing' or 'rejecting' (for the string read so far)

Example: The regular language consisting of all sequences of pairs ab is recognized by the following finite-state automaton:

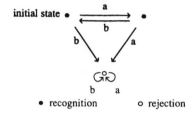

initial state

• recognition   o rejection

Here exactly those strings count as 'recognized' whose processing brings the machine to an accepting state.

The correlation exhibited in this example is not a fluke. It can be proved that, given any language with a regular grammar, there is some finite-state automaton which precisely recognizes that language. And the converse also holds: for any such machine a regular grammar can be constructed generating precisely the language consisting of the expressions recognized by that machine. (For detailed definitions and arguments, the reader is referred to the literature.)

Now it could be argued that any physically realizable machine must be a (perhaps rather large) finite-state automaton. But there are other natural notions of computation too. In particular, if we are prepared to idealize away all restrictions of memory or computational cost, considering only what a human of mechanical computer could do *in principle,* then we arrive at the notion of a *Turing machine,* which realizes the most general idea of an effective procedure, or *algorithm.* Compared to a finite-state machine, a Turing machine has two extra capacities: it has a memory which is in principle unlimited, and it can apply transformations to the memory. A more concrete description is the following. The machine works on an infinitely long tape with symbols on it (initially just the string which is to be investigated). It scans this tape with its read/write head, and depending on its internal state and the symbol it has just read, it may:

(i)   replace that symbol with another
(ii)   shift its read/write head one position to the left or to the right
(iii) assume a different state.

Turing machines provide a very powerful and elegant analysis of effective computability in the foundations of mathematics and computer science. Even so, it is generally assumed that they are too powerful for the description of natural languages. This is connected with the following fact: the languages recognized by Turing machines are precisely those for which a type-0 grammar can be written.

There is also an intermediate kind of machine which corresponds to the above-mentioned context-free grammars between these two extremes, namely, the *push-down automaton*. This is a finite-state machine which is also capable of maintaining and using a 'stack' containing information about symbols already read in. While it is reading in symbols, and depending on its present state and whatever symbol has just been read in, a push-down automaton has the following options: it can remove the top symbol in its memory stack, it can leave this symbol untouched, or it can replace it with a new combination of symbols. The result is that linguistically relevant information can be stored in the memory and later retrieved. The following may serve as an illustration.

The language $a^i b^i$ of strings of symbols a followed by an equal number of symbols b was generated earlier on by a context-free grammar. And in fact it cannot be recognized by a finite-state automaton, since any such machine has only a finite number of states in which it can encode the symbol patterns encountered so far. Consequently, there are always sequences whose initial segment a^i gets too long to remember, as a result of which no sufficient comparison can be made with the number of b's which are to come. A push-down automaton, however, solves the problem by storing in its stack all of the a's it reads in and then simply checking these off with the b's it reads in.

Again, a string counts as recognized by some push-down automaton if its processing drives the machine into an accepting state. There is a subtlety here, however. In general, context-free languages may need *nondeterministic* push-down automata for their recognition, which have several options for possible moves at each stage. In the latter case, a string counts as being recognizable if there exists at least one successful sequence of choices on the part of the machine leading to an accepting state after its perusal.

In more linguistic terms, a push-down automaton can deal with one 'coordination' at a distance. More than one coordination, however, cannot be performed: the earlier example of $a^i b^i c^i$ cannot be given a context-free description. It must be described by context-sensitive means. The question of whether the syntax of natural language really has such multiple coordination patterns is still a matter of continuing debate in linguistics.

7.3 The Theory of Formal Languages

The concepts discussed above have given rise to a rich general theory of languages. Once again, the reader is referred to Hopcroft and Ullman (1979), which also contains exact formulations and proofs of the results discussed in this chapter. An interesting up-to-date survey of current discussions is Savitch et al. (1987).

One important question is how specific natural languages (but also, e.g., programming languages) should be fitted into the above hierarchies. An explicit generating grammar or recognizing machine indicates a highest level of complexity at which the language must be placed, but in order to show that it could not be placed farther down we need a way to demonstrate that it cannot be described by means of some simpler kind of grammar or automaton. We have already briefly indicated one refutation method to this effect in §7.2, for regular languages as recognized by finite-state machines. The restriction to a fixed finite number of states gives rise to a result which is called the 'Pumping Lemma':

Lemma: For every regular language L there is a constant N such that if $E_1E_2E_3$ is any expression in L in which the length of E_2 is larger than N, then there are x, y, z such that E_2 is of the form xyz, and every expression of the form $E_1xy^kzE_2$ is also an expression in L (for any number k of repetitions of y).

That the earlier language a^ib^i is not regular is a direct consequence of this lemma ('pump the initial segment a^i', for i > N). Subtler pumping results, involving more complex duplication patterns, hold for context-free and higher languages.

A second important matter concerns the complexity of various languages. Just as we can consider the effective decidability of the laws of reasoning valid in logical systems (cf. chap. 4 above), we can also consider the decidability of the grammatical forms of expression of a language. This question can be approached by associating algorithms with the system of rewrite rules; the algorithm will check to see if any given string can be produced by means of some combination of the rules. It turns out that the membership of L(G) is decidable for grammars G up to and including context-sensitive grammars. But the languages produced by type-0 grammars are not necessarily decidable. They are in general only 'effectively enumerable': that is, we have an effective procedure for successively generating all strings belonging to the language. (Essentially one merely traces all possible derivations according to some sensible schema.) Since this will generally be an infinite process, however, it does not allow us to reject any given expression at some finite stage of the procedure: its turn might come later. This situation is analogous to one we encountered before when discussing the complexity of the valid laws in predicate logic (see §4.2). The full class of decidable languages must lie somewhere between that described by context-sensitive grammars and the full type-0 level in the Chomsky hierarchy.

This whole topic has direct practical ramifications in the parsing of linguistic expressions, with an added concern as to the efficiency with which our decision procedures can be implemented. For context-free languages, at least, parsing algorithms can be efficient: these languages can be parsed by means of an algorithm which requires no more than k^3 successive computational steps to parse an expression with k symbols. (In this connection, an independent, more finely structured hierarchy of languages ordered according to their parsing complexity can be drawn up too. The theory of the latter hierarchy is as yet fairly undeveloped.)

A third and last matter concerns investigations into families of languages which are associated with different kinds of grammars. Certain operations on the universe of all expressions in the relevant alphabet are of particular importance in this field of study. The family of regular languages is, for example, closed under all Boolean operations (corresponding to the connectives of propositional logic): intersections, unions, and complements of regular languages are regular languages. But this does not hold for context-free languages, where only closure under unions is guaranteed. One useful 'mixed' result, however, is that the intersection of a context-free and a regular language must always be a context-free language. We shall have an opportunity to apply it in §7.5.

In addition to Boolean operations, which are familiar from logic, there are many other important operations on languages with a more intrinsic syntactic flavor. For instance, given any two languages L_1, L_2, one may form their 'product' consisting of all sequences formed by concatenating a string from L_1 and one from L_2, in that order. Both regular languages and context-free languages are also closed under products of this kind.

7.4 Grammatical Complexity of Natural Languages

One of the most convincing aspects of Chomsky's classical work *Syntactic Structures* (1957) was its discussion of the complexity of natural languages. Regular and context-free grammars were successively considered as grammatical paradigms and then rejected as such. The eventually resulting model of linguistic description was the well-known proposal to make use of a context-free *phrase structure* component generating a relatively perspicuous linguistic base, with another set of rules, *transformations*, which would operate on the latter to get the details of syntax right. But around 1970, Peters and Ritchie proved that the two-stage approach has the same descriptive power as type-0 grammars, or Turing machines: something which was generally seen as combinatorial overkill. Even so, the prevalent linguistic opinion on the matter remained that the complexity of natural languages is higher than that of context-free languages.

The discussion has been revived in the last few years (for a survey, see Gazdar and Pullum 1987). It turns out, for example, that various traditional arguments for non–context freedom are formally incorrect. One favorite mathematical fallacy is that if some sublanguage of the target language L is not context-free, for example, because of the occurrence of ternary or higher patterns of coordination, then L cannot be context-free either. Other at least formally correct arguments turned out to be debatable on empirical grounds. At this moment, only a few plausible candidates are known for natural languages which are not context-free (among them Swiss German, Bambara, and Dutch).

But perhaps the more interesting question in any case is a 'local' one: which natural subsystems of a language admit of a context-free or perhaps an even simpler description? Recently, for example, many writers have pointed out the regular character of many important syntactic constructions.

Example: The following context-free grammar generates complex noun phrases with prepositional complements:

NP $\Rightarrow$ Det N
Det $\Rightarrow$ *every*
Det $\Rightarrow$ *a*
N $\Rightarrow$ *boy*
N $\Rightarrow$ *dog*
N $\Rightarrow$ N PP
PP $\Rightarrow$ Prep NP
Prep $\Rightarrow$ *with*
Prep $\Rightarrow$ *without*

This grammar generates complex expressions like *a boy without a dog with every boy.* But it can be 'regularized' to the equivalent set of rewrite rules

NP $\Rightarrow$ *a* N
NP $\Rightarrow$ *every* N
N $\Rightarrow$ *boy*
N $\Rightarrow$ *dog*
N $\Rightarrow$ *boy* PP
N $\Rightarrow$ *dog* PP
PP $\Rightarrow$ *without* NP
PP $\Rightarrow$ *with* NP

Presumably we need a more sensitive formal approach to the complexity of grammatical mechanisms within a single language in order to meaningfully judge the latter's 'complexity'.

In this connection we may also mention the framework of *categorial grammar,* which is discussed in chapter 4 of volume 2. In around 1960 it was shown that categorial grammars in their original form recognize precisely all context-free languages, and no more. At the time this was seen as an important objection to using the categorial paradigm in linguistics. As will be seen in volume 2, however, more flexible and powerful varieties of categorial grammar have been developed in recent years that use logical rules of 'category change'. Again, there is an incipient language theory for the latter framework in terms of the notions developed here. But no conclusive results are yet known concerning its recognizing power.

The very fact that it serves as a kind of accepted norm against which proposed linguistic paradigms may be calibrated is an indication of the success which the formal theory of rewrite grammars has had. Indeed, the calibration does not need to be restricted to natural languages but may also be extended to programming languages. For instance, it turns out that many of the well-known programming languages are context-free. But regular languages also play an important part in computer science, for example, in the construction of compilers.

Finally, we should draw attention to a grammatical question which we have ignored so far. From a linguistic point of view, recognition by means of some grammar of the right class of 'flat' strings is not the only thing which matters. (The term *weak* recognizing power is used in this connection.) The *way* a grammar does this is of equal importance, since the form of its derivation of a string determines a 'constituent structure' for that string. For an adequate linguistic description it matters whether a given grammar attributes the right, or at least plausible, constituent structures to expressions. (The term *strong* recognizing power is used in connection with this more stringent requirement.) For example, the possible reduction of context-free to regular grammars mentioned earlier will only be really successful if it neither introduces parsing trees, and hence constituent structures, which are too artificial, nor fails to produce parsing trees corresponding to natural readings of expressions.

7.5 Grammars, Automata, and Logic

Although initially developed in a more linguistic context, the above perspective can also be transferred to logic itself—and that in several different ways.

To begin with, the complexity of logical formal languages can be investigated. The standard languages turn out to be context-free; witness the above example with propositional formulas. If the disambiguating function of the brackets is removed, however, then the resulting languages are mostly regular.

Example: The following finite-state automaton recognizes precisely all expressions in the language for propositional logic discussed above in §7.1, but with the brackets removed (so the alphabet is $\{p, ', \neg, \wedge\}$):

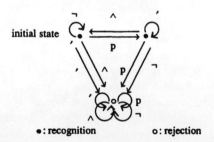

● : recognition   o : rejection

But apparently harmless changes in formal syntax can increase the complexity beyond context-free. Predicate-logical formulas lacking vacuous quantification (see §3.3), for example, form a non-context-free language. (For a proof, as well as further illustrations, see Van Benthem 1987.) This is not an isolated phenomenon. For instance, it is also known that introducing certain reasonable constraints on variable binding conventions for programming languages can lead to loss of context freedom.

But the above notions can also be applied in logical semantics. Automata may, for example, be used as procedures for calculating the semantic values of various kinds of expressions. Thus we could come to terms with the semantic counterpart of the earlier central syntactic concern: the complexity of *denotations* or *meanings*. This has been done for the special case of quantifying expressions in Van Benthem (1986, chap. 8), which introduces a hierarchy of 'semantic automata' that compute quantificational relations. For present purposes, a more accessible example is the earlier calculation of truth values of propositional formulas (see §2.2). It can be shown that no finite-state automaton is able to do this: and that for two reasons. Not only will it evaluate some ungrammatical expressions as if they were well-formed formulas, but worse than that, it will also evaluate some well-formed propositional formulas incorrectly. (For a proof of this assertion, see Van Benthem 1987.) Thus, the notions developed so far may also be used to formulate a semantic moral: truth-table evaluation is at least a context-free process. In other words, there is nothing intrinsically syntactic about the apparatus introduced in this chapter; it can just as well be applied to semantics.

We can go one step further and consider logical patterns of inference in the present perspective. What, for example, is the grammatical complexity of the class of propositional tautologies? Let us assume henceforth that our basic vocabulary has only a fixed finite number of propositional letters. Then the class of propositional tautologies is context-free, as can be shown by means of a simple construction. But with more expressive logics involving further logical constants, the complexity starts increasing; note the following illustration from intensional propositional logic.

Example: The 'minimal modal propositional logic' K introduced in volume 2, §2.3.3, enriches ordinary propositional logic with a so-called necessity operator $\Box$ (read as: 'it is necessary that . . .'). In this calculus of inference, a principle of the form

$$(\Box^i p \land \Box^j q) \to \Box^k (p \land q)$$

is valid if and only if $i = j = k$. Consider the intersection of the class of valid laws of this logic and the regular language consisting of all strings of the form:

$$(\Box^* p \land \Box^* q) \to \Box^* (p \land q),$$

in which $\Box^*$ refers to an arbitrary number of occurrences of the symbol $\Box$. The intersection consists of all strings of the form

$$(\Box^i p \land \Box^i q) \to \Box^i (p \land q).$$

Because of the required ternary coordination in these validities, the latter language is not context-free. But in view of an observation we made at the end of §7.3, it follows that the class of laws of modal propositional logic cannot be context-free either.

We have by no means exhausted the logical aspects of syntax, or for that matter the syntactic aspects of logic. There are many other interesting themes in the current literature, such as the relation between logical proof and syntactic parsing ('parsing as deduction' is a current catchword). Here one exploits the analogy between searching for a parse of an expression given a certain rewrite grammar and searching for a proof of the assertion that the expression belongs to the category of sentences using the information contained in that grammar. This idea is prominent in current models of natural language processing based upon so-called logic programming (see Pereira and Shieber 1987), but it is also central to the categorial grammar of volume 2, chapter 4 (see Moortgat 1988). We cannot pursue these matters here, but hope to have conveyed at least the flavor of the syntactic interface between logic and linguistics.

Solutions to Exercises

Chapter 2

Exercise 1

(i)   Yes.
(ii)   No, but (p ∨ q) is a formula.
(iii)   No, but ¬q is a formula.
(iv)   Yes.
(v)   No, but (p → (p → q)) is a formula.
(vi)   Yes.
(vii)   Yes.
(viii)   No, but (p → ((p → q) → q)) and ((p → (p → q)) → q) are formulas.
(ix)   Yes.
(x)   No.
(xi)   Yes.
(xii)   Yes.

Exercise 2

(a) See figures i–iii
     The subformulas of $(p_1 \leftrightarrow p_2) \vee \neg p_2$ are: p_1, p_2, $p_1 \leftrightarrow p_2$, $\neg p_2$ and
     $(p_1 \leftrightarrow p_2) \vee \neg p_2$.
     The subformulas of $p_1 \leftrightarrow (p_2 \vee \neg p_2)$ are: p_1, p_2, $\neg p_2$, $p_1 \vee \neg p_2$, and
     $p_1 \leftrightarrow (p_2 \vee \neg p_2)$.
     The subformulas of $((p \vee q) \vee \neg r) \leftrightarrow (p \vee (q \vee \neg r))$ are: p, q, r, p ∨ q,
     ¬r, (p ∨ q) ∨ ¬r, q ∨ ¬r, p ∨ (q ∨ ¬r), and $((p \vee q) \vee \neg r) \leftrightarrow (p \vee$
     $(q \vee \neg r))$.

     i.

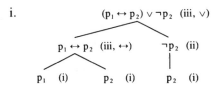

ii.

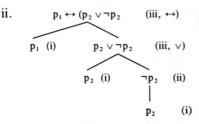

$$p_1 \leftrightarrow (p_2 \vee \neg p_2) \quad \text{(iii, }\leftrightarrow)$$

$$p_1 \text{ (i)} \qquad p_2 \vee \neg p_2 \quad \text{(iii, }\vee)$$

$$p_2 \text{ (i)} \qquad \neg p_2 \quad \text{(ii)}$$

$$p_2 \quad \text{(i)}$$

iii.

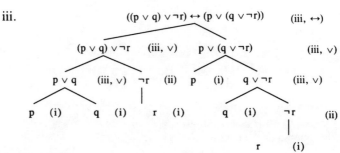

$$((p \vee q) \vee \neg r) \leftrightarrow (p \vee (q \vee \neg r)) \quad \text{(iii, }\leftrightarrow)$$

$$(p \vee q) \vee \neg r \quad \text{(iii, }\vee) \qquad p \vee (q \vee \neg r) \qquad \text{(iii, }\vee)$$

$$p \vee q \quad \text{(iii, }\vee) \quad \neg r \quad \text{(ii)} \quad p \quad \text{(i)} \quad q \vee \neg r \quad \text{(iii, }\vee)$$

$$p \quad \text{(i)} \qquad q \quad \text{(i)} \qquad r \quad \text{(i)} \qquad q \quad \text{(i)} \qquad \neg r \quad \text{(ii)}$$

$$r \quad \text{(i)}$$

(b) $(p \wedge \neg q) \to r$
       $p \wedge (\neg q \to r)$
       $p \wedge \neg (q \to r)$

See figures iv–vi.

iv.

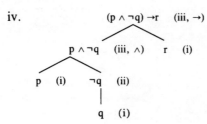

$$(p \wedge \neg q) \to r \quad \text{(iii, }\to)$$

$$p \wedge \neg q \quad \text{(iii, }\wedge) \qquad r \quad \text{(i)}$$

$$p \quad \text{(i)} \qquad \neg q \quad \text{(ii)}$$

$$q \quad \text{(i)}$$

v. $p \wedge (\neg q \to r) \quad \text{(iii, }\wedge)$

$$p \quad \text{(i)} \qquad \neg q \to r \quad \text{(iii, }\to)$$

$$\neg q \quad \text{(ii)} \qquad r \quad \text{(i)}$$

$$q \quad \text{(i)}$$

vi. $p \wedge \neg (q \to r) \quad \text{(iii, }\wedge)$

$$p \quad \text{(i)} \qquad \neg (q \to r) \quad \text{(ii)}$$

$$q \to r \quad \text{(iii, }\to)$$

$$q \quad \text{(i)} \qquad r \quad \text{(i)}$$

(c) (i) $p \rightarrow q$ implication
     (ii) $\neg p$ negation
     (iii) p atomic formula
     (iv) $(p \wedge q) \wedge (q \wedge p)$ conjunction
     (v) $\neg(p \rightarrow q)$ negation
     (vi) $(p \rightarrow q) \vee (q \rightarrow \neg\neg p)$ disjunction
     (vii) p_4 atomic formula
     (viii) $(p_1 \leftrightarrow p_2) \vee \neg p_2$ disjunction
     (ix) $\neg(p_1 \wedge p_2) \wedge \neg p_2$ conjunction
     (x) $(p \wedge (q \wedge r)) \vee p$ disjunction

Exercise 3

(a) Let us write od(ϕ) for the operator depth of ϕ. Then
   (i)   od(p) = 0 for propositional letters p;
   (ii) od($\neg\phi$) = od(ϕ) + 1;
   (iii) od($\phi \circ \psi$) = max(od(ϕ), od(ψ)) + 1 for two-place connectives $\circ$.
(b) A(ϕ) gives the length of the longest branch in the construction tree of ϕ.
   (A branch of a tree is a consecutive sequence of nodes in the tree from the
   root to one of the end points [leaves].) B(ϕ) gives the longest sequence of
   nodes that can be gone through by passing from a node to one connected
   to it without passing through any node twice. (See also Dewndey's column in the June 1985 *Scientific American*.)

Exercise 4

(a) ϕ^+ measures the number of occurrences of propositional letters in ϕ, and
   ϕ^* the number of occurrences of binary connectives.
(b) The inductive proof of the relation between these two numbers rests on
   the following three observations:
   $p^+ = 1 = 0 + 1 = p^* + 1$;
   $(\neg\phi)^+ = \phi^+ = \phi^* + 1$ (by the inductive hypothesis) $= (\neg\phi)^* + 1$;
   $(\phi \circ \psi)^+ = \phi^+ + \psi^+ = \phi^* + 1 + \psi^* + 1$ (by the inductive hypothesis)
   $= (\phi \circ \psi)^* + 1$.

Exercise 5

(1) Translation: $\neg p \wedge q$.
   Key: p: this engine is noisy; q: this engine uses a lot of energy.
(2) Translation: $\neg((p \vee q) \rightarrow r)$.
   Key: p: Peter comes; q: Harry comes; r: Guy comes.
(3) Translation: $\neg(p \wedge \neg q)$.
   Key: p: Cain is guilty; q: Abel is guilty.

(4) Translation: ¬(p ∨ q).
Key: p: this has been written with a pen; q: this has been written with a pencil.

(5) Translation: p ∧ q.
Key: p: John is stupid; q: John is nasty.

(6) Translation: (p ∧ q) ∧ (¬r ∧ ¬s).
Key: p: John wants a train from Santa Claus; q: John wants a bicycle from Santa Claus; r: John will get a train from Santa Claus; s: John will get a bicycle from Santa Claus.

(7) Translation: ¬(p ∨ q).
Key: p: somebody laughed; q: somebody applauded.

(8) Translation: (p ∨ q) ∨ (r ∨ s).
Key: p: I go to the beach on foot; q: I go to the movies on foot; r: I go to the beach by bike; s: I go to the movies by bike.

(9) Translation: p ∨ q.
Key: p: Charles and Elsa are brother and sister; q: Charles and Elsa are nephew and niece.
Alternative translation: (p ∧ q) ∨ (r ∧ s).
Key: p: Charles is Elsa's brother; q: Elsa is Charles's sister; r: Charles is Elsa's nephew; s: Elsa is Charles's niece.

(10) Translation: p ∨ q.
Key: p: Charles goes to work by car; q: Charles goes to work by bike and train.
Note that p ∨ (q ∧ r) is an incorrect translation, because q in the key means that Charles uses both the bike and the train one after the other to go to work.

(11) p → q.
Key: p: God (is) willing; q: peace will come.

(12) Translation: (p ∧ q) → r.
Key: p: it rains; q: the sun shines; r: a rainbow will appear.

(13) Translation: (p ∨ q) → ¬r.
Key: p: the weather is bad; q: too many are sick; r: the party is on.

(14) Translation: p ∧ (q → r).
Key: p: John is going to school; q: it is raining; r: Peter is going to school.

(15) Translation: ¬p → ((r ∨ s) → (q ∧ t))
Key: p: it is summer; q: it is damp; r: it is evening; s: it is night; t: it is cold.

(16) Translation: (p ∧ ¬q) → (s → ¬r) or (p → ¬q) → (s → ¬r).
Key: p: I need you; q: you help me; r: I help you; s: you need me.

(17) Translation: (¬p → q) → ¬p.
Key: p: I drink; q: you stay with me.

(18) Translation: p ↔ q or (p → q) ∧ (q → p).
Key: p: Elsa comes; q: Charles comes.

(19) Translation: p → ¬q.
Key: p: John comes; q: Peter comes.

(20) Translation: $p \leftrightarrow \neg q$.
     Key: p: John comes; q: Peter comes.
(21) Translation: $p \leftrightarrow q$.
     Key: p: John comes; q: Peter stays home.
(22) Translation: $p \leftrightarrow \neg q$ or $p \propto q$.
     Key: p: we are going; q: it is raining.
(23) Translation: $p \rightarrow q$
     Key: p: John comes; q: it is unfortunate if Peter and Jenny come.
(24) Translation: $((p \wedge q) \rightarrow \neg r) \wedge ((p \wedge \neg q) \rightarrow r)$.
     Key: p: father goes; q: mother goes; r: I will go.
(25) Translation: $((p \wedge q) \rightarrow r) \wedge ((\neg p \wedge q) \rightarrow r))$.
     Key: p: Johnny wants to get a bicycle from Santa Claus; q: Johnny is nice; r: Johnny will get a bicycle from Santa Claus.
(26) Translation: $\neg p \wedge (p \rightarrow \neg q)$.
     Key: p: you mean it; q: I believe you.
(27) Translation: $p \rightarrow q$.
     Key: p: John stays out; q: it is mandatory that Peter or Nicholas participates.

Exercise 6 (only the odd parts)

(a) See figures i and ii.   (i) See figure vi.
(c) See figure iii.   (k) See figure vii.
(e) See figure iv.   (m) See figure viii.
(g) See figure v.   (o) See figure ix.

i.

ϕ	$\neg\phi$	$\neg\neg\phi$	$\phi \wedge \phi$	$\phi \vee \phi$
1	0	1	1	1
0	1	0	0	0

ii.

ϕ	ψ	$\phi \vee \psi$	$\phi \wedge (\phi \vee \psi)$	$\phi \wedge \psi$	$\phi \vee (\phi \wedge \psi)$
1	1	1	1	1	1
1	0	1	1	0	1
0	1	1	0	0	0
0	0	0	0	0	0

iii.

ϕ	ψ	$\phi \vee \psi$	$\neg(\phi \vee \psi)$	$\neg\phi$	$\neg\psi$	$\neg\phi \wedge \neg\psi$
1	1	1	0	0	0	0
1	0	1	0	0	1	0
0	1	1	0	1	0	0
0	0	0	1	1	1	1

iv.

ϕ	ψ	$\phi \vee \psi$	$\psi \vee \phi$	$\neg\phi$	$\neg\phi \rightarrow \psi$	$\neg\psi$	$\neg\phi \wedge \neg\psi$	$\neg(\neg\phi \wedge \neg\psi)$	$\phi \rightarrow \psi$	$(\phi \rightarrow \psi) \rightarrow \psi$
1	1	1	1	0	1	0	0	1	1	1
1	0	1	1	0	1	1	0	1	0	1
0	1	1	1	1	1	0	0	1	1	1
0	0	0	0	1	0	1	1	0	1	0

v.

ϕ	ψ	$\phi \rightarrow \psi$	$\neg\phi$	$\neg\phi \vee \psi$	$\neg\psi$	$\phi \wedge \neg\psi$	$\neg(\phi \wedge \neg\psi)$	$\neg\phi \rightarrow \psi$
1	1	1	0	1	0	0	1	1
1	0	0	0	0	1	1	0	0
0	1	1	1	1	0	0	1	1
0	0	1	1	1	1	0	1	1

vi.

ϕ	ψ	$\phi \leftrightarrow \psi$	$\phi \rightarrow \psi$	$\psi \rightarrow \phi$	$(\phi \rightarrow \psi) \wedge (\psi \rightarrow \phi)$	$\phi \wedge \psi$	$\neg\phi$	$\neg\psi$	$\neg\phi \wedge \neg\psi$	$(\phi \wedge \psi) \vee (\neg\phi \wedge \neg\psi)$
1	1	1	1	1	1	1	0	0	0	1
1	0	0	0	1	0	0	0	1	0	0
0	1	0	1	0	0	0	1	0	0	0
0	0	1	1	1	1	0	1	1	1	1

vii.

ϕ	ψ	χ	$\psi \vee \chi$	$\phi \wedge (\psi \vee \chi)$	$\phi \wedge \psi$	$\phi \wedge \chi$	$(\phi \wedge \psi) \vee (\phi \wedge \chi)$
1	1	1	1	1	1	1	1
1	1	0	1	1	1	0	1
1	0	1	1	1	0	1	1
1	0	0	0	0	0	0	0
0	1	1	1	0	0	0	0
0	1	0	1	0	0	0	0
0	0	1	1	0	0	0	0
0	0	0	0	0	0	0	0

viii.

ϕ	ψ	χ	$\phi \vee \psi$	$(\phi \vee \psi) \rightarrow \chi$	$\phi \rightarrow \chi$	$\psi \rightarrow \chi$	$(\phi \rightarrow \chi) \wedge (\psi \rightarrow \chi)$
1	1	1	1	1	1	1	1
1	1	0	1	0	0	0	0
1	0	1	1	1	1	1	1
1	0	0	1	0	0	1	0
0	1	1	1	1	1	1	1
0	1	0	1	0	1	0	0
0	0	1	0	1	1	1	1
0	0	0	0	1	1	1	1

ix.

ϕ	ψ	χ	$\psi \to \chi$	$\phi \to (\psi \to \chi)$	$\phi \wedge \psi$	$(\phi \wedge \psi) \to \chi$
1	1	1	1	1	1	1
1	1	0	0	0	1	0
1	0	1	1	1	0	1
1	0	0	1	1	0	1
0	1	1	1	1	0	1
0	1	0	0	1	0	1
0	0	1	1	1	0	1
0	0	0	1	1	0	1

Exercise 7

(a) By exercise 6i $\phi \leftrightarrow \psi$ is equivalent to $(\phi \to \psi) \wedge (\psi \to \phi)$; by exercise 6f $(\phi \to \psi) \wedge (\psi \to \phi)$ is equivalent to $(\psi \to \phi) \wedge (\phi \to \psi)$; and by exercise 6i $(\psi \to \phi) \wedge (\phi \to \psi)$ is equivalent to $\psi \leftrightarrow \phi$.

(b) By exercise 6g $\phi \to \neg\phi$ is equivalent to $\neg\phi \vee \neg\phi$, which is equivalent to $\neg\phi$ by exercise 6a.

(c) Because of associativity of $\wedge$, $\phi \wedge (\psi \wedge \chi)$ is equivalent to $(\phi \wedge \psi) \wedge \chi$, which is equivalent to $(\psi \wedge \phi) \wedge \chi$ because of commutativity of $\wedge$; and $(\psi \wedge \phi) \wedge \chi$ is equivalent to $\chi \wedge (\psi \wedge \phi)$, also because of commutativity of $\wedge$.

(d) By exercise 6o, $\phi \to (\phi \to \psi)$ is equivalent to $(\phi \wedge \phi) \to \psi$, which is equivalent to $\phi \to \psi$ by exercise 6a.

(e) By exercise 6j, $\phi \infty \psi$ is equivalent to $\neg(\phi \leftrightarrow \psi)$, which is equivalent to $\neg(\psi \leftrightarrow \phi)$ by exercise 7a; by exercise 6j $\neg(\psi \leftrightarrow \phi)$ is equivalent to $\neg\psi \leftrightarrow \phi$, which is equivalent to $\phi \leftrightarrow \neg\psi$ by exercise 7a.

(f) $\phi \infty \neg\psi$ is equivalent to $\phi \leftrightarrow \neg\neg\psi$ by exercise 7e. According to the law of double negation, $\phi \leftrightarrow \neg\neg\psi$ is equivalent to $\phi \leftrightarrow \psi$, and $\phi \leftrightarrow \psi$ to $\neg\neg\phi \leftrightarrow \psi$, which is equivalent to $\neg\phi \infty \psi$ by exercise 6j.

Exercise 8 (only the odd parts)

(i)   See figure a.   (v) See figure c.
(iii) See figure b.   (vii) See figure d.

a.

ϕ	$\phi \to \phi$
1	1
0	1

b.

ϕ	ψ	$\phi \vee \psi$	$\phi \to (\phi \vee \psi)$
1	1	1	1
1	0	1	1
0	1	1	1
0	0	0	1

c.

ϕ	$\neg\phi$	$\phi \vee \neg\phi$
1	0	1
0	1	1

d.

ϕ	ψ	$\phi \to \psi$	$\psi \to \phi$	$(\phi \to \psi) \vee (\psi \to \phi)$
1	1	1	1	1
1	0	0	1	1
0	1	1	0	1
0	0	1	1	1

Exercise 9

(i)   See figure i.

i.

p	q	$p \to q$	$q \to p$	$(p \to q) \to (q \to p)$	
1	1	1	1	1	
1	0	0	1	1	
0	1	1	0	0	←
0	0	1	1	1	

So $\not\models (p \to q) \to (q \to p)$. Counterexample: $V(p) = 0$, $V(q) = 1$. For some ϕ and ψ, of course, $(\phi \to \psi) \to (\psi \to \phi)$ is a tautology, e.g., if $\phi = p$, $\psi = p \wedge q$. Therefore this exercise is formulated with p and q.

(ii)   See figure ii.

ii.

p	q	$p \to q$	$p \vee (p \to q)$
1	1	1	1
1	0	0	1
0	1	1	1
0	0	1	1

So $\models p \vee (p \to q)$.

(iii)   See figure iii.

iii.

p	q	$\neg p$	$\neg q$	$\neg p \vee \neg q$	$p \vee q$	$\neg(p \vee q)$	$(\neg p \vee \neg q) \to \neg(p \vee q)$	
1	1	0	0	0	1	0	1	
1	0	0	1	1	1	0	0	←
0	1	1	0	1	1	0	0	←
0	0	1	1	1	0	1	1	

So $\not\models (\neg p \vee \neg q) \to \neg(p \vee q)$. Counterexamples: $V(p) = 1$, $V(q) = 0$ and $V'(p) = 0$, $V'(q) = 1$.

(iv)   See figure iv.

iv.

p	q	p ∨ q	¬p	¬q	¬p → ¬q	(p ∨ q) ∧ (¬p → ¬q)	((p ∨ q) ∧ (¬p → ¬q)) → q
1	1	1	0	0	1	1	1
1	0	1	0	1	1	1	0 ←
0	1	1	1	0	0	0	1
0	0	0	1	1	1	0	1

So ⊭((p ∨ q) ∧ (¬p → ¬q)) → q. Counterexample: V(p) = 1, V(q) = 0.

(v)   See figure v.

v.

p	q	p → q	(p → q) → p	(p → q) → q	((p → q) → p) → ((p → q) → q)
1	1	1	1	1	1
1	0	0	1	1	1
0	1	1	0	1	1
0	0	1	0	0	1

So ⊨((p → q) → p) → ((p → q) → q).

(vi)   See figure vi.

vi.

p	q	r	p → q	(p → q) → r	q → r	p → (q → r)	((p → q) → r) → (p → (q → r))
1	1	1	1	1	1	1	1
1	1	0	1	0	0	0	1
1	0	1	0	1	1	1	1
1	0	0	0	1	1	1	1
0	1	1	1	1	1	1	1
0	1	0	1	0	0	1	1
0	0	1	1	1	1	1	1
0	0	0	1	0	1	1	1

So ⊨((p → q) → r) → (p → (q → r)).

Exercise 10

(1) Contingent, logically equivalent to χ
(2) Tautological
(3) Contradictory
(4) Contingent, logically equivalent to χ

(5) Contradictory
(6) Tautological
(7) Contingent

Exercise 11

(ia) Suppose $\phi \rightarrow \psi$ is a contradiction. Then $V(\phi \rightarrow \psi) = 0$ for each valuation V. From the truth table for $\rightarrow$ it can be read that this means that for each V, $V(\phi) = 1$ and $V(\psi) = 0$. Hence, ϕ is a tautology and ψ a contradiction.

(ib) $\Rightarrow$: Suppose $\phi \wedge \psi$ is a tautology. Then $V(\phi \wedge \psi) = 1$ for each valuation V. From the truth table for $\wedge$ it can be read that this means that for each V, $V(\phi) = 1$ and $V(\psi) = 1$. Hence, ϕ is a tautology and ψ is a tautology.

$\Leftarrow$: Suppose ϕ is a tautology and ψ is a tautology. Then $V(\phi) = V(\psi) = 1$ for each valuation V. From the truth table for $\wedge$ it can be read that this means that for each V, $V(\phi \wedge \psi) = 1$. Hence, $\phi \wedge \psi$ is a tautology.

(ii) A counterexample is given by the formula p $\vee$ ¬p. This formula is a tautology, but neither p nor ¬p is a tautology.

(iii) $\Leftarrow$: This side of the equivalence holds for every ϕ and ψ. If, e.g., ϕ is a tautology, then $V(\phi) = 1$ for each valuation V. By the truth table for $\vee$ it is clear that $V(\phi \vee \psi) = 1$ for each V. Hence, $\phi \vee \psi$ is a tautology. If ψ is a tautology, the reasoning is similar.

$\Rightarrow$: For this direction the extra assumption is needed: assume ϕ and ψ have no propositional letters in common, and $\phi \vee \psi$ is a tautology, i.e., $V(\phi \vee \psi) = 1$ for each V. Assume the conclusion is false, i.e., neither ϕ nor ψ is a tautology. Then there are valuations V_1 and V_2 such that $V_1(\phi) = 0$ and $V_2(\psi) = 0$. Now define $V_3(p) = V_1(p)$ for any propositional letter occurring in ϕ, and $V_3(q) = V_2(q)$ for any propositional letter in ψ. As no propositional letter occurs in both ϕ and ψ, the definition is correct. Moreover, it is clear that $V_3(\phi) = V_1(\phi) = 0$, because V_3 and V_1 are the same on the propositional letters in ϕ, and similarly $V_3(\psi) = V_2(\psi) = 0$. By the truth table for $\vee$ it also follows that $V_3(\phi \vee \psi) = 0$. The latter is impossible by the assumption that $\phi \vee \psi$ is a tautology; so the assumption that the conclusion is false cannot be maintained.

Exercise 12

(1) Five valuations: p/q/r = 1/1/0 or 0/1/1 or 0/1/0 or 0/0/1 or 0/0/0.
(2) Three valuations: 0/1/0 and 0/0/0 no longer qualify.
(3) Two valuations: 0/0/1 no longer qualifies, p/q/r = 1/1/0 and 0/1/1 remain.

Exercise 13

(a) $\neg(\neg p \lor q \lor \neg r) \lor \neg(p \lor \neg q \lor \neg r) \lor \neg(p \lor \neg q \lor r)$.

(b) (i)   By the proof of theorem 5, every formula ϕ is equivalent to a formula $\phi_1 \lor \ldots \lor \phi_n$, where in $\phi_1, \ldots, \phi_n$ only $\land$ and $\neg$ occur. It follows that formula ϕ is equivalent to $\neg(\neg \phi_1 \land \ldots \land \neg \phi_n)$ in which $\land$ and $\neg$ also are the only connectives. So $\land$ and $\neg$ form a functionally complete set.

   (ii)   Suppose that in ϕ only $\lor$ and $\neg$ occur. Then one can replace all subformulas of the form $\psi \lor \chi$ in ϕ successively by $\neg \psi \to \chi$. As $\psi \lor \chi$ is equivalent to $\neg \psi \to \chi$, we obtain in this way a formula containing only $\to$ and $\neg$, which is equivalent to ϕ.

(c) $\neg \phi$ is equivalent to $\phi \,¥\, \phi$, as can be seen from the truth table.

c.	ϕ	$\neg \phi$	$\phi \,¥\, \phi$
	1	0	0
	0	1	1

It is also clear that $\phi \lor \psi$ is equivalent to $\neg(\phi \,¥\, \psi)$ and so to $(\phi \,¥\, \psi) =$ Y $(\phi \,¥\, \psi)$. Because $\lor$ forms together with $\neg$ a functionally complete set of connectives, every formula is equivalent to a formula in which the only connectives are $\lor$ and $\neg$. These can be replaced by occurrences of $=$ Y, as above. So $¥$ itself is a complete set of connectives. The conjunction corresponding to $¥$ is *neither . . . nor*.

Exercise 14

The number is 6, with the following representatives: $p \to p$, p, q, $p \to q$, $q \to p$, $(p \to q) \to q$. (Note that the latter is a purely implicational definition for $p \lor q$.) Further applications of $\to$ will yield no new truth table.

Exercise 15

$p \land q$, $p \land \neg q$, $p \to q$, $\neg p \lor \neg q$.

Exercise 16

$\land(0)$ is the unary truth function giving a constant value 0; $\land(1)$ is the identity function on truth values.

Chapter 3

Exercise 1

a. Njp.   Key: Nxy: x is nicer than y; j: John; p: Peter.

b. Nc ∧ ¬Ne.   Key: Nx: x is nice; c: Charles; e: Elsa.
c. Gpcba   Key: Gxyzw: x went with y on z to w; p: Peter; c: Charles; b: Marion's new bicycle; a: Zandvoort.

d. ¬Hpnc → Hpne   Key: Hxyz: x heard y from z; n: the news; e: Elsa; c: Charles; p: Peter.

e. Bc ∨ Ic   Key: Bx: x is boring; Ix: x is irritating; c: Charles.

f. Hm ∧ Wm   Key: Hx: x is happy; Wx: x is a woman; m: Marion.

g. Bb   Key: Bx: x is a best-selling author; b: Bee.
h. Bce ∨ Nce   Key: Bxy: x and y are brother and sister; Nxy: x and y are nephew and niece; c: Charles; e: Elsa.

i. Cjp   Key: Cxy: x and y are close friends; j: John; p: Peter.

j. Ajj   Key: Axy: x admires y; j: John.
k. Gj → Hjj   Key: Gx: x gambles; Hxy: x will hurt y; j: John.

l. (Hjm ∧ Hmj)   Key: Lxy: x loves y deeply; Uxy: x makes
   ∧ (Ujm ∧ Umj)   y very unhappy; j: John; m: Mary.

Exercise 2

a. ∀xLxm   Key: Lxy: x loves y; m: Marion.
b. ∃x(Px ∧ Hx)   Key: Px: x is a politician; Hx: x is honest.
c. ¬∃x(Px ∧ ¬Ax)   Key: Px: x is a politician; Ax: x is ambitious.
d. ¬∀x(Ax → ¬Hx)   Key: Hx: x is honest; Ax: x is ambitious.
e. ∀x((Ax ∧ Bx) → Cx)   Key: Bx: x is blond; Ax: x is an author; Cx: x is clever.

f. ∃x(Ax ∧ Bx)   Key: Ax: x is a best-selling author; Bx: x is blind.

g. Ap ∧ ∃x(Bx ∧ Sx ∧ Wpx)   Key: Ax: x is an author; Bx: x is a book; Sx: x is best-selling; Wxy: x has written y; p: Peter.

Exercise 3

Kind of formula		Scope for	Free	Sentence
(i)	Existential	∃x: Axy ∧ Bx	y	no
(ii)	Conjunction	∃x: Axy	y	no
			x in Bx	

Kind of formula	Scope for	Free	Sentence
(iii) Implication	∃x: ∃yAxy ∃y: Axy	x in Bx	no
(iv) Existential	∃x: ∃yAxy → Bx ∃y: Axy	none	yes
(v) Implication	∃x: ∃yAxy ∃y: Axy	x in Bx	no
(vi) Universal	∀x: ¬∃yAxy ∃y: Axy	none	yes
(vii) Implication	∀y: ¬Axy ∨ Bx	x y in Cy	no
(viii) Existential	∃x: Axy ∨ By	y	no
(ix) Disjunction	∃x: Axx ∃y: By	none	yes
(x) Existential	∃x: ∃yAxy ∨ By ∃y: Axy	y in By	no
(xi) Universal	∀x: ∀y((Axy ∧ By) → ∃wCxw) ∀y: (Axy ∧ By) → ∃wCxw ∃w: Cxw	none	yes
(xii) Universal	∀x: ∀yAyx → By ∀y: Ayx	y in By	no
(xiii) Implication	∀x: ∀yAyy ∀y: Ayy	x in Bx	no

Exercise 4

The depth d(ϕ) of an arbitrary formula ϕ is given by the following inductive definition:

$d(\phi) = 0$ for atomic formulas ϕ
$d(\neg\phi) = d(\phi)$
$d(\phi \circ \psi) = \text{maximum}(d(\phi), d(\psi))$ for binary connectives $\circ$
$d(Qx\phi) = d(\phi) + 1$ for quantifiers Q.

Exercise 5

(i)　Translation: ∀x(Bx ∨ Sx).
　　Key: Bx: x is bitter; Sx: x is sweet.
　　Domain: edible things.
(ii)　Translation: ∀xBx ∨ ∀xSx.
　　Key: Bx: x is bitter; Sx: x is sweet.
　　Domain: edible things.
(iii)　Translation: ∀x(Wx → Mx).
　　Key: Wx: x is a whale; Mx: x is a mammal.
　　Domain: animals.

(iv)   Translation: Wt.
       Key: Wx: x is a whale; t: Theodore.
       Domain: animals.

(v)   Translation: ∃x(Hmx ∧ Bx ∧ Nx).
       Key: Hxy: x has y; Bx: x is a bike; Nx: x is new; m: Mary Ann.
       Domain: people and means of transportation.

(vi)   Translation: ∃x(Otx ∧ Cx ∧ Bx).
       Key: Oxy: x owns y; Cx: x is a car; Bx: x is big; t: this man.
       Domain: people and means of transportation.

(vii)   Translation: ∀x∃yLxy.
       Key: Lxy: x loves y.
       Domain: people.

(viii)   Translation: ∃x∀yLyx.
       Key: Lxy: x loves y.
       Domain: people.

(ix)   Translation: ¬∃x(Tx ∧ Gexc).
       Key: Tx: x is a thing; Gxyz: x gets y from z; e: Elsie; c: Charles.
       Domain: people and things.

(x)   Translation: ∃x(Px ∧ Glxj) ∧ ¬∃x(Tx ∧ Glxp).
       Key: Px: x is a present; Tx: x is a thing; Gxyz: x gets y from z; l: Lynn; j: John; p: Peter.
       Domain: people and things.

(xi)   Translation: ∃x(Px ∧ (Sxm ∨ Bxm)).
       Key: Px: x is a person; Sxy: x stole y; Bxy: x borrowed y; m: Mary's new bike.
       Domain: people and things.

(xii)   Translation: ∀x(Cxi → Ejx).
       Key: Cxy: x is a cookie of y; Exy: x has eaten y; i: I; j: you.
       Domain: people and edible things.

(xiii)   Translation: ¬∃x¬∃yLyx.
       Key: Lxy: x loves y.
       Domain: people.

(xiv)   Translation: ∀x(Lx → Sx) → Sa.
       Key: Lx: x is a logician; Sx: x is smart; a: Alfred.
       Domain: people.

(xv)   Translation: ∃x(Mx ∧ ¬Ax) ∧ ∃x(Wx ∧ ¬Ax).
       Key: Mx: x is a man; Ax: x is mature; Wx: x is a woman.
       Domain: people.
       Also good is the translation ∃x∃y(Mx ∧ Wy ∧ ¬Ax ∧ ¬Ay), but ∃x(Mx ∧ Wx ∧ ¬Ax) is not good, because then x is supposed to be both a man and a woman.

(xvi)   Translation: ∀x((Dx ∧ Bx) → ¬Ix).
       Key: Dx: x is a dog; Bx: x barks; Ix: x bites.
       Domain: animals.

(xvii) Translation: ∀x((Dx ∧ Ojx) → ¬∃y(Py ∧ Sjxy)).
    Key: Dx: x is a dog; j: John; Oxy: x owns y; Px: x is a person; Sxyz: x
    shows y to z.
    Domain: people and animals.
(xviii) Translation: ∃x(Whx ∧ Bx ∧ Hxh).
    Key: Wxy: x has y as his wife; Bx: x is beautiful; Hxy: x hates y.
    Domain: people.
(xix) Translation: ¬∃x(Lxu ∧ ¬Bxu).
    Key: Lxy: x lives in y; Bxy: x was born in y; u: Urk.
    Domain: people and places.
(xx) Translation: ∃x(Bx ∧ Ojxp ∧ ¬Gjxp).
    Key: Bx: x is a book; Oxyz: x has borrowed y from z; Gxyz: x has
    given y back to z.
    Domain: people and things.
(xxi) Translation: ∃x∃y(Nxy ∧ Byx ∧ Oxy)
    Key: Nxy: x is nice to y; Bxy: x is y's boss; Oxy: x is offended by y.
    Domain: people.
(xxii) Translation: ∀x∀y((Hx ∧ Ay ∧ ∃z(Hz ∧ Pxyz)) → Dxy).
    Key: Hx: x is human; Ax: x is an act; Pxyz: x promises y to z; Dxy: x
    should do y.
    Domain: people and actions.
(xxiii) Translation: ∀x((Px ∧ (Lxa ∨ Bxa)) → ∃y(Cy ∧ Oxy)).
    Key: Px: x is a person; Lxy: x lives in y; Bxy: x lives close by y; Cx: x
    is a car; Oxy: x owns y; a: Amherst.
    Domain: people, cars, and places.
(xxiv) Translation: ∀x(Sjx → ¬∃y(Ly ∧ Gjyx)).
    Key: Sxy: x sees y; Lx: x is a letter; Gxyz: x should give y to z; j: you.
    Domain: people and means of communication.
(xxv) Translation: ∀x((Dx ∧ Opx) → Bpx).
    Key: Dx: x is a donkey; Oxy: x owns y; Bxy: x beats y; p: Pedro.
    Domain: people and animals.
(xxvi) Translation: ∀x((Px ∧ ¬∃y(Cy ∧ Oxy)) → ∃y(My ∧ Oxy)).
    Key: Px: x is a person; Cx: x is a car; Oxy: x owns y; Mx: x is a
    motorbike.
    Domain: people and means of transportation.
(xxvii) Translation: ∀x(¬Mx → Lx) → Li.
    Key: Mx: x can make a move; Lx: x has lost; i: I.
    Domain: people.
(xxviii) Translation: ∃x(Px ∧ ∃y(My ∧ Bxy ∧ Rxy)).
    Key: Px: x is a person; Mx: x is a motorbike; Bxy: x has borrowed y;
    Rxy: x is riding y.
    Domain: people and motorbikes.
(xxix) Translation: ∃x∃y∃z(Px ∧ Py ∧ Mz ∧ Bxzy ∧ ¬Rxzy).

Key: Px: x is a person; Mx: x is a motorbike; Bxyz: x borrows y from z; Rxyz: x returns y to z.
Domain: people and motorbikes.

(xxx)   Translation: $\exists x Nx \rightarrow \forall y Ay$.
Key: Nx: x is noisy; Ax: x is annoyed.
Domain: people.

(xxxi) Translation: $\forall x(Nx \rightarrow \forall y Ayx)$.
Key: Nx: x is noisy; Axy: x is annoyed at y.
Domain: people.

Exercise 6

(i) and (iii) are shallow; (ii) and (iv) are not, but (iv) is equivalent to the shallow formula $\exists x(\forall y Rxy \wedge \forall z Sxz)$.

Exercise 7

(a) $I(a_1) = P_1$, $I(a_2) = P_2$, $I(a_3) = P_3$, $I(A) = \{P_1, P_2\}$
$I(R) = \{\langle P_1, P_2 \rangle, \langle P_1, P_3 \rangle, \langle P_3, P_2 \rangle, \langle P_3, P_3 \rangle\}$

(b)   (i)   This formula says that there is a point from which two arrows lead to two points, one of which is encircled and the other not. This obtains at least for P_1, so the sentence is true. The justification by means of definition 7 proceeds as follows: $V_M(Ra_1a_2) = 1$ and $V_M(Ra_1a_3) = 1$, because $\langle P_1, P_2 \rangle$ and $\langle P_1, P_3 \rangle$ are elements of $I(R)$. $V_M(Aa_2) = 1$, because $P_2 \in I(A)$, whereas $V_M(Aa_3) = 0$, because $P_3 \notin I(A)$. From this together with clause (ii) it follows that $V_M(\neg Aa_3) = 1$. From this and clause (iii) it follows that $V_M(Ra_1a_2 \wedge Aa_2 \wedge Ra_1a_3 \wedge \neg Aa_3) = 1$. From this together with clause (viii), it follows that $V_M(\exists z(Ra_1a_2 \wedge Aa_2 \wedge Ra_1z \wedge \neg Az)) = 1$. Applying (viii) twice again we obtain first $V_M(\exists y \exists z(Ra_1y \wedge Ay \wedge Ra_1z \wedge \neg Az)) = 1$ and then $V_M(\exists x \exists y \exists z(Rxy \wedge Ay \wedge Rxz \wedge \neg Az)) = 1$.

(ii)   This formula says that from every point an arrow leads to itself. This is false. It does not obtain for P_1. Complete justification: it follows directly from $\langle P_1, P_1 \rangle \notin I(R)$ that $V_M(Ra_1a_1) = 0$. From this and clause (vii) it follows immediately that $V_M(\forall x Rxx) = 0$.

(iii) This formula says that an arrow leads from a point to this point itself exactly in case it is not encircled. This true, because it is only from P_3 that an arrow leads to itself, and it is only P_3 that is encircled. Complete justification: $V_M(Ra_1a_1) = 0$ and $V_M(Aa_1) = 1$, so $V_M(\neg Aa_1) = 0$ and $V_M(Ra_1a_1 \leftrightarrow \neg Aa_1) = 1$. $V_M(Ra_2a_2) = 0$ and $V_M(Aa_2) = 1$, so $V_M(\neg Aa_2) = 0$ and $V_M(Ra_2a_2 \leftrightarrow \neg Aa_2) = 1$. Finally, $V_M(Ra_3a_3) = 1$ and $V_M(Aa_3) = 0$, so $V_M(\neg Aa_3) = 1$ and $V_M(Ra_3a_3 \leftrightarrow \neg Aa_3) = 1$. Now clause (vii) can be applied.

(iv) This formula says that there is an arrow between two (not necessarily different) points neither of which is encircled. This is true by the addition *not necessarily different;* from P_3 an arrow leads to itself and P_3 is not encircled. Justification: $V_M(Ra_3a_3) = 1$ and $V_M(Aa_3) = 0$, so $V_M(\neg Aa_3) = 1$. That is, $V_M(Ra_3a_3 \wedge \neg Aa_3 \wedge \neg Aa_3) = 1$, and from this it follows that $V_M(\exists y(Ra_3y \wedge \neg Aa_3 \wedge \neg Ay)) = 1$ and $V_M(\exists x \exists y(Rxy \wedge \neg Ax \wedge \neg Ay)) = 1$ by applying (viii) twice.

(v) This formula says that from every point having an arrow leading to itself there is an arrow leading to a point that is encircled. This is true: P_3 is the only point with an arrow leading to itself, and from P_3 an arrow leads to P_2 which is an encircled point. Justification: $V_M(Ra_1a_1) = 0$, so $V_M(Ra_1a_1 \rightarrow \exists y(Ra_1y \wedge Ay)) = 1(*)$. Also: $V_M(Ra_2a_2) = 0$, so $V_M(Ra_2a_2 \rightarrow \exists y(Ra_2y \wedge Ay)) = 1(**)$. With respect to a_3 the following obtains: $V_M(Ra_3a_2) = 1$ and $V_M(Aa_2) = 1$, so $V_M(Ra_3a_2 \wedge Aa_2) = 1$, and also $V_M(Ra_3a_3 \rightarrow \exists y(Ra_3y \wedge Ay)) = 1$. From this, together with clause (vii) and $(*)$ and $(**)$, it follows that $V_M(\forall x(Rxx \rightarrow \exists y(Rxy \wedge Ay))) = 1$.

(vi) This formula says that from every point that is encircled, an arrow leads to some point. This is not true: P_2 is encircled and there is no arrow leading from P_2 to any points. Justification: $V_M(Ra_2a_1) = 0$ and $V_M(Ra_2a_2) = 0$ and $V_M(Ra_2a_3) = 0$. From this it follows that $V_M(\exists y Ra_2y) = 0$. Likewise $V_M(Aa_2) = 1$, so $V_M(Aa_2 \rightarrow \exists y Ra_2y) = 0$, and finally, $V_M(\forall x(Ax \rightarrow \exists y Rxy)) = 0$.

(vii) This formula says that there are two points connected by just one arrow such that one can reach the second point from the first also indirectly by way of an intermediate point. This is true: from P_1 an arrow leads to P_2, and not the other way around, whereas there is an arrow leading from P_1 to P_3 and from P_3 to P_2. Justification: $V_M(Ra_1a_2) = 1$ and $V_M(Ra_2a_1) = 0$, so $V_M(\neg Ra_2a_2) = 1$. Furthermore, $V_M(Ra_1a_3) = 1$ and $V_M(Ra_3a_2) = 1$, so $V_M(Ra_1a_2 \wedge \neg Ra_2a_1 \wedge \exists z(Ra_1z \wedge Rza_2)) = 1$. By applying (viii) twice we obtain $V_M(\exists x \exists y(Rxy \wedge \neg Ryx \wedge \exists z(Rxz \wedge Rzy))) = 1$.

Exercise 8

(i) The most illuminating way is to choose g such that $g(x) = P_1$, $g(y) = P_2$, and $g(z) = P_3$ (of course, it is irrelevant which g is chosen). On this assignment $\langle g(x), g(y) \rangle \in I(R)$ holds, because $\langle g(x), g(y) \rangle = \langle P_1, P_2 \rangle$, and similarly $\langle g(x), g(z) \rangle \in I(R)$. This means that $V_{M,g}(Rxy) = 1$ and $V_{M,g}(Rxz) = 1$. Also, $g(y) \in I(A)$ holds, so $V_{M,g}(Ay) = 1$, whereas $g(z) \notin I(A)$, so $V_{M,g}(Az) = 0$ and $V_{M,g}(\neg Az) = 1$. Altogether this gives us $V_{M,g}(Rxy \wedge Ay \wedge Rxz \wedge \neg Az) = 1$. Because $g(z)$

$= P_3$, it follows that $g[z/P_3] = g$ and so $V_{M,g[z/P_3]}(Rxy \wedge Ay \wedge Rxz \wedge \neg Az) = 1$ holds good, giving $V_{M,g}(\exists z(Rxy \wedge Ay \wedge Rxz \wedge \neg Az)) = 1$. In the same way, $g[y/P_2] = g$. Thus, $V_{M,g[y/P_2]}(Rxy \wedge Ay \wedge Rxz \wedge \neg Az) = 1$ holds, and so $V_{M,g}(\exists y \exists z(Rxy \wedge Ay \wedge Rxz \wedge \neg Az)) = 1$. Likewise, $g[x/P_1] = g$ holds, so it follows that $V_{M,g[x/P_1]}(Rxy \wedge Ay \wedge Rxz \wedge \neg Az) = 1$. From this it follows that $V_{M,g}(\exists x \exists y \exists z(Rxy \wedge Ay \wedge Rxz \wedge \neg Az)) = 1$. We may write $V_M(\exists x \exists y \exists z(Rxy \wedge Ay \wedge Rxz \wedge \neg Az)) = 1$, because the formula is a sentence.

(iii) Because $\langle P_1, P_1 \rangle \notin I(R)$, $V_{M,g[x/P_1]}(Rxx) = 0$ holds. Now, $P_1 \in I(A)$ holds, so both $V_{M,g[x/P_1]}(Ax) = 1$ and $V_{M,g[x/P_1]}(\neg Ax) = 0$ hold. Consequently, (*) $V_{M,g[x/P_1]}(Rxx \leftrightarrow \neg Ax) = 1$ holds good. (This is all independent of what values are assigned by g.) In exactly the same way one obtains (**) $V_{M,g[x/P_2]}(Rxx \leftrightarrow \neg Ax) = 1$ by replacing P_1 with P_2. Now $\langle P_3, P_3 \rangle \in I(R)$, so $V_{M,g[x/P_3]}(Rxx) = 1$. Because $P_3 \notin I(A)$, $V_{M,g[x/P_3]}(Ax) = 0$, hence $V_{M,g[x/P_3]}(\neg Ax) = 1$. Thus it follows that $V_{M,g[x/P_3]}(Rxx \leftrightarrow \neg Ax) = 1$, and from this, together with (*) and (**), it also follows that $V_{M,g}(\forall x(Rxx \leftrightarrow \neg Ax)) = 1$.

(v) Because $\langle P_1, P_1 \rangle \notin I(R)$, $V_{M,g[x/P_1]}(Rxx) = 0$ holds, and so (*) $V_{M,g[x/P_1]}(Rxx \rightarrow \exists y(Rxy \wedge Ay)) = 1$. In the same way one obtains (**) $V_{M,g[x/P_2]}(Rxx \rightarrow \exists y(Rxy \wedge Ay)) = 1$. Because $\langle P_3, P_2 \rangle \in I(R)$ and $P_2 \in I(A)$ hold, both $V_{M,g[x/P_3][y/P_1]}(Rxy) = 1$ and $V_{M,g[x/P_3][y/P_1]}(Ay) = 1$ hold, and consequently $V_{M,g[x/P_3][y/P_1]}(Rxy \wedge Ay) = 1$. From this we get $V_{M,g[x/P_3]}(\exists y(Rxy \wedge Ay)) = 1$, and so $V_{M,g[x/P_3]}(Rxx \rightarrow \exists y(Rxy \wedge Ay)) = 1$. From this, together with (*) and (**), it follows that $V_{M,g}(\forall x(Rxx \rightarrow \exists y(Rxy \wedge Ay))) = 1$.

Exercise 9

(i) One has to prove that for all **M**, if $V_M(\forall x \phi) = 1$, then also $V_M(\exists x \phi) = 1$. For in that case one has proven that $V_M(\forall x \phi) = 1$ and $V_M(\exists x \phi) = 0$ are impossible, so that for each model **M**, $V_M(\forall x \phi \rightarrow \exists x \phi) = 1$. Suppose now that $V_M(\forall x \phi) = 1$. This means that for every constant c, $V_M([c/x]\phi) = 1$. Because D is nonempty, there is at least one constant c, such that $V_M([c/x]\phi) = 1$, which proves that $V_M(\exists x \phi) = 1$ is the case.

(v) Suppose that $V_M(\exists x(\phi \wedge \psi)) = 1$. From this it follows that there is a constant c such that $V_M([c/x](\phi \wedge \psi)) = 1$. It is to be proven that $V_M(\exists x \phi \wedge \exists x \psi) = 1$. The formula $[c/x](\phi \wedge \psi)$ is $[c/x]\phi \wedge [c/x]\psi$, so $V_M([c/x]\phi \wedge [c/x]\psi) = 1$. From this it follows both that $V_M([c/x]\phi) = 1$ and that $V_M([c/x]\psi) = 1$, and from this that $V_M(\exists x \phi) = 1$ and $V_M(\exists x \psi) = 1$, so that $V_M(\exists x \phi \wedge \exists x \psi) = 1$.

(ii) Suppose $V_{M,g}(\forall x \phi) = 1$. It is to be proven that $V_{M,g}([t/x]\phi) = 1$. That $V_{M,g}(\forall x \phi) = 1$ means that for all $d \in D$, $V_{M,g[x/d]}(\phi) = 1$. In particular, $[\![t]\!]_{M,g}$ is such an element of D. Hence $V_{M,g[x/[\![t]\!]_{M,g}]}(\phi) = 1$. From this it follows that $V_{M,g}([t/x]\phi) = 1$ (strictly, this should be proven with induction on the length of ϕ).

(vii) Suppose $V_{M,g}(\forall xAxx) = 1$. From this it follows that $V_{M,g[x/d]}(Axx) = 1$, for all $d \in D$. This means that for all $d \in D$, $\langle d, d \rangle \in I(A)$. Now $g[x/d][y/d](x) = d$ and $g[x/d][y/d](y) = d$. So for each $d \in D$, $\langle g[x/d][y/d](x), g[x/d][y/d](y) \rangle \in I(A)$ is true, which means that for all $d \in D$, $V_{M,g[x/d][y/d]}(Axy) = 1$ and also that $V_{M,g[x/d]}(\exists yAxy) = 1$. From this it follows immediately that $V_{M,g}(\forall x\exists yAxy) = 1$, which was to be shown.

Exercise 10

There are eight possibilities, which can be ordered according to descending strength as follows:

$$\{\forall x\forall yRxy, \forall y\forall xRxy\}$$
$$\downarrow \qquad\qquad \downarrow$$
$$\{\exists x\forall yRxy\} \qquad \{\exists y\forall xRxy\}$$
$$\downarrow \qquad\qquad \downarrow$$
$$\{\forall y\exists xRxy\} \qquad \{\forall x\exists yRxy\}$$
$$\downarrow \qquad\qquad \downarrow$$
$$\{\exists x\exists yRxy, \exists y\exists xRxy\}$$

Exercise 11

(a) Translation: $\neg\exists x(Mx \wedge Cxx)$.
Domain: people.
Key: Mx: x is a man; Cxy: x is more clever than y.

(b) Translation: $\forall x(Mx \rightarrow \exists y(My \wedge y \neq x \wedge Cyx))$.
Domain: people.
Key: Mx: x is a man; Cxy: x is more clever than y.

(c) Translation: $\exists x(Mx \wedge \forall y(y \neq x \leftrightarrow Cxy))$.
Domain: people.
Key: Mx: x is a man; Cxy: x is more clever than y.

(d) Translation: $\exists x(\forall y(y \neq x \rightarrow Cxy) \wedge x = p)$.
Domain: people.
Key: Cxy: x is more clever than y; p: the prime minister.

(e) Translation: $\exists x\exists y(Qx \wedge Qy \wedge x \neq y)$.
Domain: people.
Key: Qx: x is a queen.

(f) Translation: $\forall x\forall y\forall z((Qx \wedge Qy \wedge Qz) \rightarrow (x = y \vee x = z \vee y = z))$.
Domain: people.
Key: Qx: x is a queen.

(g) Translation: ¬∃x(Qx ∧ x ≠ b) ∧ Qb.
Domain: people.
Key: Qx: x is a queen; b: Beatrix.
Comment: If one takes it that the sentence merely presupposes that Beatrix is a queen but does not say it, then one leaves ∧Qb out.

(h) Translation: ∀x∀y((x ≠ y ∧ Exy) → ((Bx ∧ ¬By) ∨ (¬Bx ∧ By))).
Domain: people.
Key: Exy: x and y make an exchange; Bx: x will be badly off.

(i) Translation: ∀x∃y∃z(y ≠ z ∧ ∀w(Rxw ↔ (w = y ∨ w = z))).
Domain: people.
Key: Rxy: y is a parent of x.

(j) Translation: ∀x(Lmx → Mx).
Domain: people.
Key: m: Mary; Lxy: x likes y; Mx: x is a man.

(k) Translation: ∀x(Lcx ↔ (x = e ∨ x = b)).
Domain: people.
Key: Lxy: x loves y; c: Charles; e: Elsie; b: Betty.

(l) Translation: ∀x(Lcx ↔ Lbx).
Domain: people.
Key: Lxy: x loves y; c: Charles; b: Betty.

(m) Translation: ¬∃x∃y(Uxy ∧ ∀z(Lyz ↔ z = m)).
Domain: people.
Key: Uxy: x understands y; Lxy: x loves y; m: Mary.

(n) Translation: ∀x(Hix → Hxx).
Domain: people.
Key: Hxy: x helps y; i: I.

(o) Translation: ∀x∃y∀z(Lxz ↔ z = y).
Domain: people.
Key: Lxy: x loves y.

(p) Translation: ∀x∃y∀z((Lxz ∧ x ≠ z) ↔ z = y)
Domain: people.
Key: Lxy: x loves y.

(q) Translation: ∀x∀y(x ≠ y → ∃w∃z(w ≠ z ∧ Lxw∧Lyz))
Domain: people.
Key: Lxy: x loves y.

(r) Translation: ∀x∀y(Lxy ↔ x = y)
Domain: people.
Key: Lxy: x loves y.

(s) Translation: ∀x(∀y(Lxy ↔ x ≠ y) → Ax)
Domain: people.
Key: Lxy: x loves y; Ax: x is an altruist.

(t) Translation: ∀x∀y((Ax ∧ Ay ∧ x ≠ y) → (Lxy ∧ Lyx)).
Domain: people.
Key: Lxy: x loves y; Ax: x is an altruist.

(u) Translation: $\forall x \forall y((Lxy \wedge Lyx \wedge x \neq y) \rightarrow (Hx \wedge Hy))$.
Domain: people.
Key: Lxy: x loves y; Hx: x is happy.

Exercise 12

(a) (i) Means: There is a paragraph that depends on itself. False.

(ii) Means: There are two different paragraphs that depend on each other. False.

(iii) Means: There is a paragraph that depends on no other paragraph and on which no paragraph depends. True; §1.2.

(iv) Means: There are exactly two paragraphs on which no paragraphs depend. True; §§1.2 and 1.3.

(v) Means: There is a paragraph on which exactly two paragraphs depend. True; §4.1.

(vi) Means: There are two paragraphs with the same (actually existing) paragraphs depending on them. True; e.g., §§2.3 and 3.2.

(vii) Means: There is a sequence of seven paragraphs such that each paragraph depends on the previous one. False; the longest such sequences (e.g., §§1.3–1.4–2.1–2.2–2.3–3.4) have length 6.

(viii) Means: For no triple of distinct mutually independent paragraphs is there a paragraph depending on all three of them. False; §3.4 is dependent on §§2.3, 3.2, and 3.3.

(ix) Means: There are no two distinct mutually independent paragraphs on which two distinct mutually independent paragraphs depend. False; §§3.2 and 3.3 depend on §§2.2 and 3.1.

(b) (i) Means: Everything on which something lies is a line, and vice versa. True.

(ii) Means: For each pair of lines there is a point lying on both of them. True.

(iii) Means: Through each pair of points there is a line that goes through both of them. False; there is no line that goes through P_1 and P_3.

(iv) Means: There are two lines such that each point occurs on at ' least one of them. True.

(v) Means: There is a line with exactly three points on it. True; e.g., on l_3.

(vi) Means: There are two distinct points and two distinct lines such that both points lie on both lines. False; such a situation is impossible.

(vii) Means: If a point lies between two points in a certain order, then it lies also between them when they are given in the reverse order. True.

(viii) Means: On each line three points can be found, of which one lies between the other two. False; see l_4.

(ix)   Means: Of each three points that lie on a line there is exactly one that lies between the other two. True.

(x)   Means: Each point that lies on two distinct lines lies between two points. False; see P_1 and P_3.

Exercise 13

All the interpretations assigning to R one of the patterns shown in the figure.

$\bullet \underset{\longleftarrow}{\longrightarrow} \bullet \longrightarrow \bullet$ $\bullet \longrightarrow \bullet \underset{\longrightarrow}{\longrightarrow} \bullet$

Exercise 14

(i)   "Apply ∀y to x": a contradiction results, which is true in no model.

(ii)   The only models for this formula have either one object (with I(R) empty and I(P) arbitrary), or they have two objects, one of which has I(P) and one of which lacks it, with the corresponding I(R) as in the figure:

$\overset{P}{\bullet} \underset{\longleftarrow}{\longrightarrow} \overset{\neg P}{\bullet}$

More than one P or ¬P is impossible. Some R-arrow would then have to lie within I(P) or within the interpretation of ¬P (by the first conjunct), which is forbidden by the second conjunct.

(iii) Models for this formula contain at least one infinite ascending chain of objects $d_1 I(R) d_2 I(R) d_3 \ldots$, which alternately are in I(P) and not in I(P).

Exercise 15

Only groups of 'finite loops' qualify, of the forms depicted in the figure:

$\overset{\longrightarrow}{\underset{\longleftarrow}{}}$

$\bullet \rightarrow \bullet \underset{\longleftarrow}{\rightarrow} \bullet$

$\bullet \underset{\longleftarrow}{\rightleftarrows} \bullet \underset{\longleftarrow}{\rightleftarrows} \bullet$

$\bullet \underset{\longleftarrow}{\rightrightarrows} \bullet$

$\bullet \underset{\longleftarrow}{\rightrightarrows} \bullet$
. . .

The argument that these are the only possibilities takes too much room to write out in detail. In any case, one of the advantages of predicate-logical semantics over its propositional counterpart is that it often allows us to think pictorially about what is true or not.

Exercise 16

(i)   is persistent: the 'witness' to I(P) remains one in enlargements.
(ii)   is not persistent: it may be falsified by adding objects lacking the property P.
(iii) is not persistent: someone may love everyone in San Francisco, without the same being true for the northern hemisphere.
(iv)   is persistent: its truth amounts to the existence of some pair of objects not standing in the relation I(R), and such a pair will also refute ∀x∀yRxy in all enlargements. (In general, only those predicate-logical formulas will be persistent which are *existential*, in a technical sense not explained here.)

Exercise 17

	(i)	(ii)	(iii)	(iv)	(v)	(vi)	(vii)	(viii)	(ix)
reflexive	no	no	no	yes	no	no	no	yes	no
irreflexive	yes	yes	yes	no	yes	yes	yes	no	yes
symmetric	no	no	no	yes	no	no	no	no	yes
asymmetric	yes	yes	yes	no	yes	yes	yes	no	no
antisymmetric	yes	yes	yes	no	yes	yes	yes	yes	no
transitive	no	yes	yes	yes	no	yes	yes	yes	no
connected	no	no	no	no	no	no	yes	no	yes

Exercise 18

(i)   If H is reflexive, then evidently −H does not need to be, while Ȟ must be.
(ii)   If H is symmetric, then so is −H: ∀x∀y(Rxy → Ryx) is equivalent to ∀x∀y(¬Ryx → ¬Rxy), this is equivalent to ∀y∀x(¬Ryx → ¬Rxy), and this to ∀x∀y(¬Rxy → ¬Ryx). So if I(R) = H, and H is symmetric, then ⟨x, y⟩ ∈ −H implies ⟨y, x⟩ ∈ −H. Likewise, symmetry of H implies that of Ȟ.
(iii) Transitivity is also preserved under converses: if ⟨x, y⟩ ∈ Ȟ, ⟨y, z⟩ ∈ Ȟ, then ⟨y, x⟩ ∈ H, ⟨z, y⟩ ∈ H; so by the transitivity of H, ⟨z, x⟩ ∈ H, i.e., ⟨x, z⟩ ∈ Ȟ. But, for instance, identity is a transitive relation, whereas nonidentity is not (see exercise 17).

Chapter 4

Exercise 1

(a) See figure i. From that figure it is clear that p ∧ q ⊨ p.
(b) For the rest we mostly give just the answer: p ∧ q ⊨ q.

(c) p ∨ q ⊭ p. Counterexample: V(q) = 1, V(p) = 0.
(d) p, q ⊨ p ∧ q.
(e) p ⊨ p ∨ q.
(f) q ⊨ p ∨ q.
(g) See figure ii. From that figure it is clear that p ⊭ p ∧ q and that V(p) = 1, V(q) = 0 constitutes a counterexample.
(h) See figure iii. From that figure it is clear that p, p → q ⊨ q.

i.

p	q	p ∧ q	/	p
1	1	1	*	1
1	0	0		
0	1	0		
0	0	0		

ii.

p	q	/	**p ∧ q**
1	1	*	1
1	0	*	0 ←
0	1		
0	0		

iii.

p	q	p → q	/	q
1	1	1	*	1
1	0	0		
0	1	1		
0	0	1		

iv.

p	q	q → p	/	q
1	1	1	*	1
1	0	1	*	0 ←
0	1	0		
0	0	1		

v.

p	q	r	p ∨ q	p → r	q → r	/	r
1	1	1	1	1	1	*	1
1	1	0	1	0	0		
1	0	1	1	1	1	*	1
1	0	0	1	0	1		
0	1	1	1	1	1	*	1
0	1	0	1	1	0		
0	0	1	0	1	1		
0	0	0	0	1	1		

(i) See figure iv. From that figure it is clear that p, q → p ⊭ q, and that V(p) = 1, V(q) = 0 constitutes a counterexample.
(j) p, ¬p ⊨ q. (There is no counterexample. Compare this with the interpretation in predicate logic of the universal quantifier in *all A are B*.)

(k) $p \rightarrow (q \wedge \neg q) \vDash \neg p$.

(l) See figure v. From that figure it is clear that $p \vee q$, $p \rightarrow r$, $q \rightarrow r \vDash r$.

(m) See figure vi. From that figure it is clear that $p \vee q$, $(p \wedge q) \rightarrow r \nvDash r$ and that $V_1(p) = 1$, $V_1(q) = 0$, $V_1(r) = 0$ constitutes a counterexample as well as $V_2(p) = 0$, $V_2(q) = 1$, $V_2(r) = 0$.

(n) $p \vee q$, $p \rightarrow q \vDash q$.

(o) $p \vee q$, $p \rightarrow q \nvDash p$. A counterexample is $V(p) = 0$, $V(q) = 1$.

(p) $p \rightarrow q$, $\neg q \vDash \neg p$.

(q) $p \rightarrow q \nvDash \neg p \rightarrow \neg q$. The valuation $V(p) = 0$, $V(q) = 1$ constitutes a counterexample.

vi. p	q	r	p ∨ q	p ∧ q	(p ∧ q) → r	/	r
1	1	1	1	1	1	*	1
1	1	0	1	1	0		
1	0	1	1	0	1	*	1
1	0	0	1	0	1	*	0 ←
0	1	1	1	0	1	*	1
0	1	0	1	0	1	*	0 ←
0	0	1	0	0	1		
0	0	0	0	0	1		

Exercise 2

(a) $D = \{1, 2\}$; $I(A) = \{1\}$; $I(B) = \{2\}$.

An object (1) for which $I(A)$ holds, an object (2) for which $I(B)$ holds, but none for which both hold.

(b) The same model as in the case of (a) does the job. For each object $I(A)$ or $I(B)$ holds, but not for all objects $I(A)$ or for all objects $I(B)$.

(c) $D = \{1, 2\}$; $I(A) = \{1\}$ and $I(B) = \{1\}$.

For the conclusion to be false, $I(A)$ has to hold for some object (1), and because of the first premise, $I(B)$ has to hold for that object too. According to the second premise, there has to be an object (2) for which $I(B)$ does not hold, and according to the first premise, $I(A)$ does not hold for that object either.

(d) $D = \{1, 2\}$; $I(A) = \{1\}$; $I(B) = \{1, 2\}$; $I(C) = \{2\}$.

(e) $D = \{1, 2\}$; $I(A) = \{1\}$; $I(B) = \{2\}$; $I(C) = \emptyset$.

For all objects for which $I(A)$ as well as $I(B)$ hold, $I(C)$ has to hold too. If the conclusion is to be false, then $I(C)$ cannot hold for any object, so neither for any object can $I(A)$ and $I(B)$ both hold at once.

(f) $D = \{1, 2\}$; $I(A) = \{1\}$; $I(B) = \emptyset$ (or else $I(B) = \{1\}$).

For the first premise to be true, there has to be an object (1) for which $I(A)$ holds but $I(B)$ doesn't. Furthermore, $I(A)$ cannot hold for all objects if one wants the conclusion to be false (and neither can $I(B)$, if the second premise is true, but that has already been taken care of).

(g) D = {1}; I(A) = {1}; I(B) = ∅ or I(B) = {1}
To falsify the conclusion we don't have to do anything: ∃x(Bx ∧ ¬Bx) is a contradiction.

(h) D = {1, 2}; I(R) = {⟨1, 2⟩, ⟨2, 1⟩}.
See figure vii. An arrow departs from each point, but there is no point with an arrow to itself.

(i) D = {1, 2}; I(R) = {⟨1, 1⟩, ⟨2, 2⟩}.
See figure viii. If the premise is true, then each point needs an arrow to itself. For the conclusion to be false, it is sufficient for there to be at least one missing arrow. (So either an arrow from 1 to 2 or an arrow from 2 to 1 could have been added.)

(j) D = {1, 2, 3}; I(R) = {⟨1, 1⟩, ⟨1, 2⟩, ⟨1, 3⟩, ⟨2, 2⟩, ⟨3, 3⟩}.
See figure ix. At least one point (1) has arrows to all points. All points have arrows to themselves. And to falsify the conclusion, there are two points not connected by any arrow.

(k) D = {1, 2}; I(R) = {⟨1, 2⟩, ⟨2, 1⟩}; I(A) = ∅.
See figure x. According to the second premise, I(A) holds for exactly the points with arrows to themselves.

(l) D = {1, 2, 3}; I(R) = {⟨1, 1⟩, ⟨2, 2⟩, ⟨3, 3⟩, ⟨1, 2⟩, ⟨2, 3⟩, ⟨3, 1⟩}.
See figure xi. According to the second premise, between each two (not necessarily distinct) points there is at least one arrow; this also applies to a point and itself: each point has an arrow to itself. Thus the first premise is verified too. To falsify the conclusion we must ensure that the relation is not transitive. In the picture this has worked out properly: 1 has an arrow to 2, and 2 has an arrow to 3, but 1 has no arrow to 3.

(m) For this argument schema there is no countermodel with a finite domain. If one tries for that, one will see that there are problems when circles appear; see figure xii. In order to make such a circle transitive, one must make all the points have arrows to themselves. On the other hand, to falsify the conclusion, such 'reflexive' elements are not allowed to occur. An infinite counterexample is the following:
D = {1, 2, 3, . . .}; I(R) = {⟨i, j⟩ ∈ D² | i < j}.
So I(R) holds between two natural numbers if the first is smaller than the second.

(n) D = {1}; I(R) = ∅.
Because the premises are universally quantified implications, they can be made true by introducing no arrows at all. If one does that, the conclusion will be false too.

(o) D = {1, 2}

(p) D = {1, 2}

(q) D = {1, 2, 3, 4}; I(R) = {⟨1, 1⟩, ⟨1, 2⟩, ⟨2, 1⟩, ⟨2, 2⟩, ⟨3, 3⟩, ⟨3, 4⟩, ⟨4, 3⟩, ⟨4, 4⟩}.
See figure xiii. The model consists of two detached transitive parts. The relation I(R) is not connected.

(r) D = {1, 2}; I(R) = {⟨1, 1⟩, ⟨1, 2⟩, ⟨2, 2⟩}; I(A) = {1}.

See figure xiv. According to the first premise, I(A) holds exactly for those points that have an arrow to all points. The second premise states that there is exactly one such point. According to the conclusion, there is at most one reflexive element. Therefore to falsify the conclusion we have to provide at least two reflexive elements.

vii.

viii.

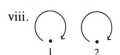

ix.

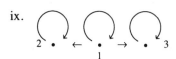

x.

xi.

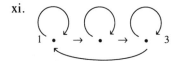

xii.

xiii.

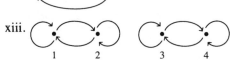

xiv.

Exercise 3

(a) 1. p   assumption
     2. q   assumption
     3. p ∧ q   I∧, 1, 2
(b) 1. p   assumption
     2. q   assumption
     3. r   assumption

    4.   p ∧ r   I∧, 1, 3
    5.   q ∧ (p ∧ r)   I∧, 2, 4

Exercise 4

    1.   p ∧ (q ∧ r)   assumption
    2.   q ∧ r   E∧, 1
    3.   r   E∧, 2
    4.   p   E∧, 1
    5.   r ∧ p   I∧, 3, 4

Exercise 5

(a) 1.   p → (q → r)   assumption
    2.   p   assumption
    3.   q   assumption
    4.   q → r   E→, 1, 2
    5.   r   E→, 4, 3
(b) 1.   p → (q ∧ r)   assumption
    2.   r → s   assumption
    3.   p   assumption
    4.   q ∧ r   E→, 1, 3
    5.   r   E∧, 4
    6.   s   E→, 2, 5

Exercise 6

(a) ┌ 1.   p → (q → r)   assumption
     │┌ 2.   p ∧ q   assumption
     ││ 3.   p   E∧, 2
     ││ 4.   q → r   E→, 1, 3
     ││ 5.   q   E∧, 2
     ││ 6.   r   E→, 4, 5
     │└───
     │ 7.   (p ∧ q) → r   I→
     └──
        8.   (p → (q → r)) → ((p ∧ q) → r)   I→

(b) ┌ 1.   p → (p → q)   assumption
     │┌ 2.   p   assumption
     ││ 3.   p → q   E→, 1, 2
     │└ 4.   q   E→, 3, 2
     │└───
     │ 5.   p → q   I→
     └──
        6.   (p → (p → q)) → (p → q)   I→

Exercise 7

(a) 1. $p \lor (p \land q)$ assumption
     2. p assumption
     3. p Rep, 2
     4. $p \to p$ I$\to$
     5. $p \land q$ assumption
     6. p E$\land$, 5
     7. $(p \land q) \to p$ I$\to$
     8. p E$\lor$, 1, 4, 7

(b) 1. $p \lor q$ assumption
     2. $p \to q$ assumption
     3. q assumption
     4. q Rep, 3
     5. $q \to q$ I$\to$
     6. q E$\lor$, 1, 2, 5
     7. $(p \to q) \to q$ I$\to$
     8. $(p \lor q) \to ((p \to q) \to q)$ I$\to$

(c) 1. $p \lor (q \lor r)$ assumption
     2. p assumption
     3. $p \lor q$ I$\lor$, 2
     4. $(p \lor q) \lor r$ I$\lor$, 3
     5. $p \to ((p \lor q) \lor r)$ I$\to$
     6. $q \lor r$ assumption
     7. q assumption
     8. $p \lor q$ I$\lor$, 7
     9. $(p \lor q) \lor r$ I$\lor$, 8
    10. $q \to ((p \lor q) \lor r)$ I$\to$
    11. r assumption
    12. $(p \lor q) \lor r$ I$\lor$, 11
    13. $r \to ((p \lor q) \lor r)$ I$\to$
    14. $(p \lor q) \lor r$ E$\lor$, 6, 10, 13
    15. $(q \lor r) \to ((p \lor q) \lor r)$ I$\to$
    16. $(p \lor q) \lor r$ E$\lor$, 1, 5, 15

Exercise 8

(a) 1. p assumption
     2. $\neg p$ assumption
     3. $\bot$ E$\neg$, 2, 1
     4. $\neg\neg p$ I$\neg$
     5. $p \to \neg\neg p$ I$\to$

(b)

	1.	p ∧ ¬q	assumption
	2.	p → q	assumption
	3.	p	E∧, 1
	4.	q	E→, 3, 2
	5.	¬q	E∧, 1
	6.	⊥	E¬, 5, 4
	7.	¬(p → q)	I¬
	8.	(p ∧ ¬q) → ¬(p → q)	I→

(c)

	1.	p → q	assumption
	2.	¬q	assumption
	3.	p	assumption
	4.	q	E→, 1, 3
	5.	⊥	E¬, 2, 4
	6.	¬p	I¬
	7.	¬q → ¬p	I→
	8.	(p → q) → (¬q → ¬p)	I→

(d)

	1.	p → ¬q	assumption
	2.	q	assumption
	3.	p	assumption
	4.	¬q	E→, 1, 3
	5.	⊥	E¬, 4, 2
	6.	¬p	I¬
	7.	q → ¬p	I→

Exercise 9

(a)

	1.	(p → q) → p	assumption
	2.	¬p	assumption
	3.	p	assumption
	4.	⊥	E¬, 2, 3
	5.	q	EFSQ, 4
	6.	p → q	I→
	7.	p	E→, 1, 6
	8.	⊥	E¬, 2, 7
	9.	¬¬p	I¬
	10.	p	¬¬, 9
	11.	((p → q) → p) → p	I→

(b)

1.	$\neg(p \wedge q)$	assumption
2.	$\neg(\neg p \vee \neg q)$	assumption
3.	p	assumption
4.	q	assumption
5.	$p \wedge q$	$I\wedge$, 3, 4
6.	$\bot$	$E\neg$, 1, 5
7.	$\neg q$	$I\neg$
8.	$\neg p \vee \neg q$	$I\vee$, 7
9.	$\bot$	$E\neg$, 2, 8
10.	$\neg p$	$I\neg$
11.	$\neg p \vee \neg q$	$I\vee$, 10
12.	$\bot$	$E\neg$, 2, 11
13.	$\neg\neg(\neg p \vee \neg q)$	$I\neg$
14.	$\neg p \vee \neg q$	$\neg\neg$, 13
15.	$\neg(p \wedge q) \rightarrow (\neg p \vee \neg q)$	$I\rightarrow$

(c)

1.	$\neg(p \rightarrow q)$	assumption
2.	$\neg p$	assumption
3.	p	assumption
4.	$\bot$	$E\neg$, 2, 3
5.	q	EFSQ, 4
6.	$p \rightarrow q$	$I\rightarrow$
7.	$\bot$	$E\neg$, 1, 6
8.	$\neg\neg p$	$I\neg$
9.	p	$\neg\neg$, 8
10.	q	assumption
11.	p	assumption
12.	q	Rep, 10
13.	$p \rightarrow q$	$I\rightarrow$
14.	$\bot$	$E\neg$, 1, 13
15.	$\neg q$	$I\neg$
16.	$p \wedge \neg q$	$I\wedge$, 9, 15
17.	$\neg(p \rightarrow q) \rightarrow (p \wedge \neg q)$	$I\rightarrow$

Exercise 10

(a)
1.	$p \land (q \lor r)$	assumption
2.	p	$E\land$, 1
3.	$q \lor r$	$E\land$, 1
4.	q	assumption
5.	$p \land q$	$I\land$, 2, 4
6.	$(p \land q) \lor (p \land r)$	$I\lor$, 5
7.	$q \to ((p \land q) \lor (p \land r))$	$I\to$
8.	r	assumption
9.	$p \land r$	$I\land$, 2, 8
10.	$(p \land q) \lor (p \land r)$	$I\lor$, 9
11.	$r \to ((p \land q) \lor (p \land r))$	$I\to$
12.	$(p \land q) \lor (p \land r)$	$E\lor$, 3, 7, 11

(b)
1. $(p \land q) \lor (p \land r)$	assumption
2. $p \land q$	assumption
3. p	$E\land$, 2
4. q	$E\land$, 2
5. $q \lor r$	$I\lor$, 5
6. $p \land (q \lor r)$	$I\land$, 3, 5
7. $(p \land q) \to (p \land (q \lor r))$	$I\to$
8. $p \land r$	assumption
9. p	$E\land$, 8
10. r	$E\land$, 8
11. $q \lor r$	$I\lor$, 10
12. $p \land (q \lor r)$	$I\land$, 9, 11
13. $(p \land r) \to (p \land (q \lor r))$	$I\to$
14. $p \land (q \lor r)$	$E\lor$, 1, 7, 13

(c)
1.	$p \to (q \to r)$	assumption
2.	$p \to q$	assumption
3.	p	assumption
4.	q	$E\to$, 2, 3
5.	$q \to r$	$E\to$, 1, 3
6.	r	$E\to$, 5, 4
7.	$p \to r$	$I\to$
8.	$(p \to q) \to (p \to r)$	$I\to$
9.	$(p \to (q \to r)) \to$ $((p \to q) \to (p \to r))$	$I\to$

(d)   1. p → q   assumption
        2. r → s   assumption
        3. p ∨ r   assumption
        4. p   assumption
        5. q   E→, 4, 1
        6. q ∨ s   I∨, 5
        7. p →(q ∨s)   I→
        8. r   assumption
        9. s   E→, 2, 8
       10. q ∨ s   I∨, 9
       11. r → (q ∨ s)   I→
       12. q ∨ s   E∨, 3, 7, 11
       13. (p ∨ r) → (q ∨ s) I→

(e)   1.   p → ¬p   assumption
        2.   ¬p → p   assumption
        3.   p   assumption
        4.   ¬p   E¬, 1, 3
        5.   ⊥   E¬, 4, 3
        6.   ¬p   I¬
        7.   p   E→, 2, 6
        8.   ⊥   E¬, 6, 7

Exercise 11

No reasonable meaning can be given to this connective, since introducing it would lead to $\phi \vdash \psi$ for arbitrary ϕ, ψ:

   1. ϕ assumption
   2. $\phi \circ \psi$ I∘, 1
   3. ψ E∘, 2

Exercise 12

   1.   Aa → Bb   assumption
   2.   ∃y(Aa → By)   I∃, 1 (Aa → By)
   3.   ∃x∃y(Ax → By) I∃, 2 (∃y(Ax → By))

Exercise 13

(a) 1.   ∀xAxx   assumption
      2.   Aaa   E∀, 1 (Axx)

(b) 1. ∀x∀yAxy   assumption
    2. ∀yAay   E∀, 1 (∀yAxy)
    3. Aab   E∀, 2 (Aay)
(c) 1. ∀x∀yAxy   assumption
    2. ∀yAay   E∀, 1 (∀yAxy)
    3. Aaa   E∀, 2 (Aay)

Exercise 14

(a) 1. ∀x(Ax ∧ Bx)   assumption
    2. Aa ∧ Ba   E∀, 1
    3. Aa   E∧, 2
    4. ∀xAx   I∀, 3
    5. Ba   E∧, 2
    6. ∀xBx   I∀, 5
    7. ∀xAx ∧ ∀xBx   I∧, 4, 6
(b) 1. ∀xAx ∧ ∀xBx   assumption
    2. ∀xAx   E∧, 1
    3. Aa   E∀, 2
    4. ∀xBx   E∧, 1
    5. Ba   E∀, 4
    6. Aa ∧ Ba   I∧, 3, 5
    7. ∀x(Ax ∧ Bx)   I∀, 6
(c) 1. ∀x∀yAxy   assumption
    2. ∀yAay   E∀, 1
    3. Aab   E∀, 2
    4. ∀yAby   E∀, 1
    5. Aba   E∀, 4
    6. Aab ∧ Aba   I∧, 3, 5
    7. ∀y(Aay ∧ Aya)   I∀, 6
    8. ∀x∀y(Axy ∧ Ayx)   I∀, 7
(d) 1. ∀x(Ax → Bx)   assumption
    2. ∀xAx   assumption
    3. Aa → Ba   E∀, 1
    4. Aa   E∀, 2
    5. Ba   E→, 3, 4
    6. ∀xBx   I∀, 5
(e) 1.   ¬∃xAx   assumption
    ┌ 2.   Aa   assumption
    │ 3.   ∃xAx   I∃, 2
    │ 4.   ⊥   E¬, 1, 3
    └
      5.   ¬Aa   I¬
      6.   ∀x¬Ax   I∀, 5

(f) 1.   ¬∃x¬Ax   assumption
┌ 2.   ¬Aa   assumption
│ 3.   ∃x¬Ax   I∃, 2
└ 4.   ⊥   E¬, 1, 3
    5.   ¬¬Aa   I¬
    6.   Aa   ¬¬, 5
    7.   ∀xAx   I∀, 6

Exercise 15

(a) 1.   ∃x(Ax ∧ Bx)   assumption
┌ 2.   Aa ∧ Ba   assumption
│ 3.   Aa   E∧, 2
│ 4.   ∃xAx   I∃, 3
│ 5.   Ba   E∧, 2
│ 6.   ∃xBx   I∃, 5
└ 7.   ∃xAx ∧ ∃xBx   I∧, 4, 6
    8.   (Aa ∧ Ba) → (∃xAx ∧ ∃xBx) I→
    9.   ∃xAx ∧ ∃xBx   E∃, 1, 8

(b) 1.   ∀x(Ax → Bx)   assumption
    2.   ∃xAx   assumption
┌ 3.   Aa   assumption
│ 4.   Aa → Ba   E∀, 1
│ 5.   Ba   E→, 4, 3
└ 6.   ∃xBx   I∃, 5
    7.   Aa → ∃xBx   I→
    8.   ∃xBx   E→, 2, 7

(c) 1.   ∃x¬Ax   assumption
┌ 2.   ¬Aa   assumption
│┌ 3.   ∀xAx   assumption
││ 4.   Aa   E∀, 3
│└ 5.   ⊥   E¬, 2, 4
└ 6.   ¬∀xAx   I¬
    7.   ¬Aa → ¬∀xAx   I→
    8.   ¬∀xAx   E∃, 1, 7

(d)

1.	∀x¬Ax	assumption
2.	∃xAx	assumption
3.	Aa	assumption
4.	¬Aa	E∀, 1
5.	⊥	E¬, 4, 3
6.	Aa → ⊥	I→
7.	⊥	E∃, 2, 6
8.	¬∃xAx	I¬

(e)

1.	¬∀xAx	assumption
2.	¬∃x¬Ax	assumption
3.	¬Aa	assumption
4.	∃x¬Ax	I∃, 3
5.	⊥	E¬, 2, 4
6.	¬¬Aa	I¬
7.	Aa	¬¬, 6
8.	∀xAx	I∀, 7
9.	⊥	E¬, 1, 8
10.	¬¬∃x¬Ax	I¬
11.	∃x¬Ax	¬¬, 10

(f)

1.	∀x(Ax → Bx)	assumption
2.	∃x¬Bx	assumption
3.	¬Ba	assumption
4.	Aa	assumption
5.	Aa → Ba	E∀, 1
6.	Ba	E→, 5, 4
7.	⊥	E¬, 3, 6
8.	¬Aa	I¬
9.	∃x¬Ax	I∃, 8
10.	¬Ba → ∃x¬Ax	I→
11.	∃x¬Ax	E∃, 2, 10

(g)
	1.	∀x(Ax ∨ Bx)	assumption
	2.	∃x¬Bx	assumption
	3.	¬Ba	assumption
	4.	Aa ∨ Ba	E∀, 1
	5.	Aa	assumption
	6.	∃xAx	I∃, 5
	7.	Aa → ∃xAx	I→
	8.	Ba	assumption
	9.	⊥	E¬, 3, 8
	10.	∃xAx	EFSQ, 9
	11.	Ba → ∃xAx	I→
	12.	∃xAx	E∨, 4, 7, 11
	13.	¬Ba → ∃xAx	I→
	14.	∃xAx	E∃, 2, 13

(h)
	1.	∀x(Ax → Bx)	assumption
	2.	∃x(Ax ∧ Cx)	assumption
	3.	Aa ∧ Ca	assumption
	4.	Aa → Ba	E∀, 1
	5.	Aa	E∧, 3
	6.	Ba	E→, 4, 5
	7.	Ca	E∧, 3
	8.	Ba ∧ Ca	I∧, 6, 7
	9.	∃x(Bx ∧ Cx)	I∃, 8
	10.	(Aa ∧ Ca) → ∃x(Bx ∧ Cx)	I→
	11.	∃x(Bx ∧ Cx)	I∃, 2, 10

Exercise 16

What is to be shown is that ⊢ φ ∧ ψ ⇔ ⊢ φ and ⊢ ψ.

⇒: Assume ⊢ φ ∧ ψ. That means that there is a derivation of the form:

1.   . . .
            . . .
            . . .
            . . .
n.   φ ∧ ψ

This derivation can be extended to

1.	$\ldots$		1.	$\ldots$
	$\ldots$			$\ldots$
	$\ldots$	as well as to		$\ldots$
	$\ldots$			$\ldots$
n.	$\phi \wedge \psi$		n.	$\phi \wedge \psi$
n + 1.	ϕ		n + 1.	ψ

Hence, $\vdash \phi$ and $\vdash \psi$.

$\Leftarrow$: Assume $\vdash \phi$ and $\vdash \psi$. That means that there are two derivations of the form:

1.	$\ldots$		1.	$\ldots$
	$\ldots$			$\ldots$
	$\ldots$	and		$\ldots$
	$\ldots$			$\ldots$
n.	ϕ		m.	ψ

Renumber the second derivation as n + 1, . . . , n + m (including the necessary changes in the numbers occurring after the formulas). Put the two derivations in sequence and follow them with the conclusion $\phi \wedge \psi$ by means of $I\wedge$. The result is the following derivation:

1.	$\ldots$	
	$\ldots$	
	$\ldots$	
	$\ldots$	
n.	ϕ	
n + 1.	$\ldots$	
	$\ldots$	
	$\ldots$	
	$\ldots$	
n + m.	ψ	
n + m + 1.	$\phi \wedge \psi$	$I\wedge$, n, n + m

This derivation shows that $\vdash \phi \wedge \psi$.

Exercise 17

(i)   No. Take X = {p}, Y = {¬p}.

(ii)   Yes. If X is consistent, then it has a model **M.** Either **M** $\models \phi$, and X $\cup \{\phi\}$ is consistent, or **M** $\nvDash \phi$ and X $\cup \{\neg\phi\}$ is consistent.

(iii) Yes. Enumerate X as $\{\psi_1, \ldots , \psi_n\}$. Define Y in stages as follows. $Y_0 = \emptyset$. Since ϕ is not universally valid, $Y_0 \nvDash \phi$. Consider ψ_1. If $Y_0 \cup \{\psi_1\} \nvDash \phi$, then set $Y_1 = Y_0 \cup \{\psi_1\}$; otherwise set $Y_1 = Y_0$. Continuing in this way, we arrive at a largest $Y_i \subseteq X$ not implying ϕ. Such a set Y_i may depend on the particular enumeration chosen and hence need not be unique. E.g., let $X = \{\neg p, p \lor q, \neg q\}$, $\phi = q$: both $\{\neg p, \neg q\}$ and $\{p \lor q, \neg q\}$ are maximal consistent subsets of X not implying q.

Exercise 18

(i)   All of them are. A nonuniversal example would be $\forall x \exists y R x y$ (*succession*) or $\forall x \forall y (R x y \rightarrow \exists z (R x z \land R z y))$ (*density*).

(ii)   If $\phi_1, \ldots, \phi_n, \psi$ are universal, and $\phi_1, \ldots, \phi_n \not\models \psi$, then there is a counterexample where $\phi_1, \ldots, \phi_n$ hold but ψ fails. For the failure of such a universal ψ, it suffices to have a certain finite number of objects (no more are needed than the number of quantifiers starting ψ) standing in some atomic (non-) relations. This failure would still persist if we considered a model consisting of *only* those individuals. Moreover, the universal statements $\phi_1, \ldots, \phi_n$ would remain true under this translation. Thus, it suffices to inspect all models up to a certain finite size for possible counterexamples: if none are found there, none exist at all. And this task is effectively performable in a finite time. (Incidentally, mutual derivability between the earlier relational conditions of §3.3.8 is decidable.)

Bibliographical Notes

These bibliographical notes contain suggestions for further reading without any pretence at being exhaustive. In general, references to literature in the text are not repeated.

Chapter 1

A short introduction to the history of logic can be found in Scholz 1967. Comprehensive studies are Bochenski 1956 and Kneale and Kneale 1962. An interesting logico-historical study centering around a systematic theme is Barth 1974.

An well-known introduction to the history of linguistics is Robins 1967. A collection of various studies is Parret 1976.

Ayer 1959, Flew 1952–53, Feigl and Sellars 1949, and Linsky 1952 are collections of important papers in the fields of analytic philosophy and logical positivism. See also Caton 1963, Rorty 1967, and Davidson and Harman 1972, and the literature mentioned in the text.

Chapters 2, 3, and 4

There are many good introductory texts on standard logic, the older ones mostly with a philosophical or a mathematical slant, and the more recent ones also discussing connections with computer science.

A more linguistic perspective is found in Hodges 1977; Allwood, Andersson, and Dahl 1977; McCawley 1981; as well as Dowty, Wall, and Peters 1981.

A useful introduction to set theory is Van Dalen, Doets, and de Swart 1978.

The calculus of natural deduction is a central feature of Anderson and Johnstone 1962. The related method of 'semantic tableaux' appears in Jeffrey 1967 and Smullyan 1968.

More advanced background material may be found in the four volumes of the *Handbook of Philosophical Logic*, Gabbay and Guenthner, eds., 1983–88, of which the first is a good survey of basic logic.

A good textbook on mathematical logic is Enderton 1972. More extensive in its coverage is Bell and Machover 1977. The standard handbook is Barwise 1977.

Chapters 5 and 6

A survey of nonstandard logical systems from a philosophical point of view is given in Haack 1978. See also Quine 1970.

Frege's views on definite descriptions can be found in Frege 1892, 1893. Russell's theory is given in Russell 1905. For Strawson's criticism of Russell, see Strawson 1950.

A mathematically oriented introduction to higher-order logic can be found in Enderton 1972.

For a survey and an extensive bibliography of many-valued logics, see Rescher 1969. Lukasiewicsz's system is presented in Lukasiewicsz 1920, that of Kleene in Kleene 1952, and Bochvar's in Bochvar 1939. The method of supervaluations is described in Van Fraassen 1969, 1971.

The literature on the subject of presuppositions is abundant and still growing. From Wilson 1975; Kempson 1975; Gazdar 1979a, b; Soames 1979, 1982; Karttunen and Peters 1979; Link 1986; Sperber and Wilson 1986; and Van der Sandt 1988 one may get an overview of relevant viewpoints and arguments. See also the chapter on presuppositions in Levinson 1983.

Quine's paper on the elimination of variables is Quine 1966.

A good textbook on pragmatics is the above-mentioned Levinson 1983.

Grice's theory of implicatures was originally developed in the William James Lectures of 1967. Parts were published in Grice 1975, 1978. See also Grice 1981. Various aspects of Grice's theory are discussed in the literature on presuppositions mentioned above and in Cohen 1971, Walker 1975, Groenendijk and Stokhof 1980. See also the relevant chapter in Levinson 1983.

Chapter 7

Basic facts about formal languages and automata may be learned from Partee, ter Meulen and Wall 1989. The standard textbook is Hopcroft and Ullman 1979.

References

Allwood, J., L. Andersson, and O. Dahl. 1977. *Logic in Linguistics*. Cambridge: Cambridge University Press.

Anderson, J., and H. Johnstone. 1962. *Natural Deduction*. Belmont: Wadsworth.

Austin, J. L. 1956. A Plea for Excuses. *Proceedings from the Aristotelian Society*, n.s. 57. Also in Austin 1962b.

Austin, J. L. 1962a. *How to Do Things with Words*. Oxford: Oxford University Press.

———. 1962b. *Philosophical Papers*. Oxford: Oxford University Press.

Ayer, A. J., ed. 1959. *Logical Positivism*. New York: Free Press.

Bar-Hillel, Y. 1953. Logical Syntax and Semantics. *Language* 29.

Bar-Hillel, Y., ed. 1971. *Pragmatics of Natural Language*. Dordrecht: Reidel.

Barth, E. M. 1974. *The Logic of the Articles in Traditional Philosophy*. Dordrecht: Reidel.

Barwise, J., ed. 1977. *Handbook of Mathematical Logic*. Amsterdam: North-Holland.

Bell, J., and M. Machover. 1977. *A Course in Mathematical Logic*. Amsterdam: North-Holland.

Blackburn, S., ed. 1975. *Meaning, Reference, and Necessity*. Cambridge: Cambridge University Press.

Bochenski, I. M. 1956. *Formale Logik*. Freiburg: Orbis Academicus.

Bochvar, D. A. 1939. Ob odnom trehznachom iscislenii i ego primeneii k analizu paradoksov klassicskogo rassirennogo funkcional "nogo iscislenija." *Matematiciskij sbornik* 4.

Carnap, R. 1931–32. Überwindung der Metaphisik durch logische Analyse der Sprache. *Erkenntnis* 10. English translation in Ayer 1959.

Caton, Ch., ed. 1963. *Philosophy and Ordinary Language*. Urbana: University of Illinois Press.

Chomsky, N. 1954. Logical Syntax and Semantics: Their Linguistic Relevance. *Language* 30.

———. 1957. *Syntactic Structures*. The Hague: Mouton.

Cohen, L. J. 1971. The Logical Particles of Natural Language. In Bar-Hillel 1971.

Cole, P., ed. 1978. *Syntax and Semantics 9: Pragmatics*. New York: Academic Press

———. 1981. *Radical Pragmatics*. New York: Academic Press.

Cole, P., and J. Morgan, eds. 1975. *Syntax and Semantics 3: Speech Acts*. New York: Academic Press.

Davidson, D. 1967. Truth and Meaning. *Synthese* 17.

Davidson, D., and G. Harman, eds. 1972. *Semantics of Natural Language*. Dordrecht: Reidel.

Dowty, D. R., R. E. Wall, and S. Peters. 1981. *Introduction to Montague Semantics.* Dordrecht: Reidel.

Enderton, H. B. 1972. *A Mathematical Introduction to Logic.* New York: Academic Press.

Feigl, H., and W. Sellars, eds. 1949. *Readings in Philosophical Analysis.* New York: Appleton-Century Croft.

Flew, A., ed. 1952–53. *Logic and Language I & II.* Oxford: Blackwell.

Frege, G. 1879. *Begriffsschrift.* Halle: Verlag Louis Nebert.

———. 1892. Uber Sinn und Bedeutung. *Zeitschrift fur Philosophie und philosophische Kritik* 100. Also in Frege 1962. English translation in Geach and Black 1960.

———. 1893. *Grundgesetze der Arithmetik,* vol. 1. Jena: Verlag H. Pohle.

———. 1962. *Funktion, Begriff, Bedeutung: Fünf logische Studien,* ed. G. Patzig. Gottingen: Vanden Hoeck.

Gabbay, D., and F. Guenthner, eds. 1983–88. *Handbook of Philosophical Logic.* Dordrecht: Reidel.

Gazdar, G. 1979a. A Solution to the Projection Problem. In Oh and Dinneen 1979.

———. 1979b. *Pragmatics.* New York: Academic Press.

Gazdar, G., and G. Pullum. 1987. Computationally Relevant Properties of Natural Languages and their Grammars. In W. Savitch et al., eds., *The Formal Complexity of Natural Language.* Dordrecht: Reidel.

Geach, P., and M. Black, eds. 1960. *Translations from the Philosophical Writings of Gottlob Frege.* Oxford: Blackwell.

Gödel, K. 1930. Die Vollstandigkeit der Axiome des logischen Funktionen-Kalkuls. In *Monatshefte fur Mathematik und Physik* 37. English translation in Van Heijenoort 1967.

Gödel, K. 1931. Über formal unentscheidbare Sätze der Principia Mathematica und verwandter Systeme I. *Monatshefte für Mathematik und Physik* 38. English translation in Van Heijenoort 1967.

Grice, H. P. 1975. Logic and Conversation. In Cole and Morgan 1975.

———. 1978. Further Notes on Logic and Conversation. In Cole 1978.

———. 1981. Presupposition and Conversational Implicature. In Cole 1981.

Groenendijk, J., D. de Jongh, and M. Stokhof, eds. 1986. *Foundations of Pragmatics and Lexical Semantics.* Dordrecht: Foris.

Groenendijk, J., and M. Stokhof. 1980. A Pragmatic Analysis of Specificity. In Heny 1980.

Haack, S. 1978. *Philosophy of Logics.* Cambridge: Cambridge University Press.

Heidegger, M. 1929. *Was ist Metaphysik.* Frankfurt: Vittorio Klosterman.

Hempel, C. 1950. Problems and Changes in the Empiricist Criterion of Meaning. *Revue International de Philosophie* 4. Also in Ayer 1959 and in Linsky 1952.

Henkin, L. 1949. The Completeness of the First-Order Functional Calculus. In *Journal of Symbolic Logic* 14.

Heny, F., ed. 1980. *Ambiguities in Intensional Contexts.* Dordrecht: Reidel.

Hilbert, D., and P. Bernays. 1934–39. *Grundlagen der Mathematik.* 2 vols. Berlin.

Hodges, W. 1977. *Logic.* Harmondsworth: Penguin.

Hopcroft, J., and J. Ullman. 1979. *Introduction to Automata Theory, Languages, and Computation.* Reading, Mass.: Addison-Wesley.

Hunter, G. 1971. *Metalogic: An Introduction to the Metatheory of Standard First-Order Logic*. London: Macmillan.

Jeffrey, R. C. 1967. *Formal Logic: Its Scope and Limits*. New York: McGraw-Hill.

Karttunen, L., and S. Peters. 1979. Conventional Implicature. In Oh and Dinneen 1979.

Katz, J. 1966. *The Philosophy of Language*. New York: Harper & Row.

Katz, J., and J. Fodor. 1962. What's Wrong with the Philosophy of Language? *Inquiry* 5.

Katz, J., and P. Postal. 1964. *An Integrated Theory of Linguistic Description*. Cambridge, Mass.: MIT Press.

Kempson, R. M. 1975. *Presupposition and the Delimitation of Semantics*. Cambridge: Cambridge University Press.

Kleene, S. C. 1952. *Introduction to Metamathematics*. Amsterdam: North-Holland.

Kneale, W., and M. Kneale. 1962. *The Development of Logic*. Oxford: Oxford University Press.

Lambert, K., ed. 1969. *The Logical Way of Doing Things*. New Haven: Yale University Press.

Levinson, S. C. 1983. *Pragmatics*. Cambridge: Cambridge University Press.

Link, G. 1986. Prespie in Pragmatic Wonderland, or, the Projection Problem for Presuppositions Revisited. In Groenendijk, de Jongh, and Stokhof 1986.

Linsky, L., ed. 1952. *Semantics and the Philosophy of Language*. Urbana: University of Illinois Press.

Łukasiewicz, J. 1920. O logice trojwartosciowej. *Ruch Filozoficzny* 5. English translation in McCall 1967.

McCall, S., ed. 1967. *Polish Logic: 1920–1939*. Oxford: Oxford University Press.

McCawley, J. D. 1981. *Everything That Linguists Have Always Wanted to Know About Logic*. Chicago: University of Chicago Press.

Montague, R. 1970. Universal Grammar. *Theoria* 36. Also in Montague 1974.

Montague, R. 1974. *Formal Philosophy: Selected Papers of Richard Montague*, edited and with an introduction by Richmond H. Thomason. New Haven: Yale University Press.

Moortgat, M. 1988. *Categorial Investigations: Logical and Linguistic Aspects of the Lambek-Calculus*. Dordrecht: Foris.

Oh, C., and D. Dinneen, eds. 1979. *Syntax and Semantics 11: Presupposition*. New York: Academic Press.

Parret, H., ed. 1976. *History of Linguistic Thought and Contemporary Linguistics*. Berlin: de Gruyter.

Partee, B., A. ter Meulen, and R. Wall. 1989. *Mathematical Methods in Linguistics*. Dordrecht: Reidel.

Pereira, F., and S. Shieber. 1987. *Prolog and Natural Language Analysis*. Chicago: University of Chicago Press.

Prawitz, D. 1965. *Natural Deduction*. Stockholm: Almqvist & Wicksell.

Quine, W. V. O. 1951. *Mathematical Logic*. Cambridge, Mass.: Harvard University Press.

———. 1966. Variables explained away. In *Selected Logic Papers*. New York: Random House.

———. 1970. *Philosophy of Logic*. Englewood Cliffs: Prentice-Hall.

Reichenbach, H. 1947. *Elements of Symbolic Logic*. New York: Macmillan.

Rescher, N. 1969. *Many-Valued·Logic*. New York: McGraw-Hill.

———. 1976. *Plausible Reasoning*. Assen: van Gorcum.

Robins, R. H. 1967. *A Short History of Linguistics*. London: Longmans.

Rorty, R., ed. 1967. *The Linguistic Turn*. Chicago: University of Chicago Press.

Russell, B. 1905. On Denoting. *Mind* 14. Also in Feigl and Sellars 1949.

Ryle, G. 1931. Systematically Misleading Expressions. In *Proceedings from the Aristotelian Society*, n.s. 32. Also in Flew 1952–53.

Savitch, W., E. Bach, W. Marsh, and G. Safran-Naveh, eds. 1987. *The Formal Complexity of Natural Language*. Dordrecht: Reidel.

Scholz, H. 1967. *Abriss der Geschichte der Logik*. Freiburg: Karl Alber.

Searle, J. R. 1969. *Speech Acts*. Cambridge: Cambridge University Press.

Smullyan, R. 1968. *First-Order Logic*. Berlin: Springer.

Soames, S. 1979. A Projection Problem for Speaker Presuppositions. *Linguistic Inquiry* 10.

———. 1982. How Presuppositions Are Inherited: A Solution to the Projection Problem. *Linguistic Inquiry* 13.

Sperber, D., and D. Wilson. 1986. *Relevance, Communication, and Cognition*. Oxford: Blackwell.

Strawson, P. F. 1950. On Referring. *Mind* 59. Also in Strawson 1971.

———. 1971. *Logico-Linguistic Papers*. London: Methuen.

Tarski, A. 1933, Der Wahrheitsbegriff in den formalisierten Sprachen. *Studia Philosophia* 1. English translation in Tarski 1956.

———. 1939. *Introduction to Logic and to the Methodology of Deductive Sciences*. Oxford: Oxford University Press.

———. 1956. *Logic, Semantics, Metamathematics*. Oxford: Oxford University Press.

Van Benthem, J. 1986. *Essays in Logical Semantics*. Studies in Linguistics and Philosophy vol. 29. Dordrecht: Reidel.

———. 1987. Logical Syntax. *Theoretical Linguistics* 14.

Van Dalen, D., H. C. Doets, and H. de Swart. 1978. *Sets: Naive, Axiomatic, and Applied*. Oxford: Pergamon Press.

Van der Sandt, R. A. 1988. *Context and Presupposition*. London: Croom Helm.

Van Fraassen, B. C. 1969. Presuppositions, Supervaluations, and Free Logic. In Lambert 1969.

———. 1971. *Formal Semantics and Logic*. New York: Macmillan.

Van Heijenoort, J., ed. 1967. *From Frege to Gödell: A Source Book in Mathematical Logic 1879–1931*. Cambridge, Mass.: Harvard University Press.

Vendler, Z. 1967. *Linguistics in Philosophy*. Ithaca: Cornell University Press.

Walker, R. 1975. Conversational Implicatures. In Blackburn 1975.

Wilson, D. M. 1975. *Presupposition and Non-Truth-Conditional Semantics*. New York: Academic Press.

Wittgenstein, L. 1921. *Tractatus Logico-Philosophicus/Logisch-philosophische Abhandlung*. In *Annalen der Naturphilosophie*. English translation by D. F. Pears and B. F. McGuinness (1961). London: Routledge & Kegan Paul.

———. 1953. *Philosophische Untersuchungen*. Oxford: Blackwell.

Index

Made in the USA
San Bernardino, CA
06 January 2015